The Nationalities Factor
in Soviet Politics and Society

The John M. Olin Critical Issues Series

Published in cooperation with the
Harvard University Russian Research Center

The Nationalities Factor in Soviet Politics and Society, edited by Lubomyr Hajda and Mark Beissinger

The Soviet Union in the Third World, edited by Carol R. Saivetz

Soviet Social Problems, edited by T. Anthony Jones, Walter D. Connor, and David E. Powell

The Nationalities Factor
in Soviet Politics and Society

EDITED BY

Lubomyr Hajda
HARVARD UNIVERSITY

Mark Beissinger
UNIVERSITY OF WISCONSIN–MADISON

Westview Press
BOULDER, SAN FRANCISCO, & OXFORD

The John M. Olin Critical Issues Series

Copyright © 1990 by the Harvard University Russian Research Center

Published in 1990 in the United States of America by Westview Press, Inc., 5500 Central Avenue, Boulder, Colorado 80301, and in the United Kingdom by Westview Press, Inc., 36 Lonsdale Road, Summertown, Oxford OX2 7EW

Library of Congress Cataloging-in-Publication Data
The Nationalities factor in Soviet politics and society/edited by
    Lubomyr Hajda and Mark Beissinger.
       p.   cm.—(The John M. Olin critical issues series)
    ISBN 0-8133-7689-0. ISBN 0-8133-1067-9 (pbk.).
    1. Soviet Union—Ethnic relations. 2. Nationalism—Soviet Union.
3. Soviet Union—Politics and government—1985–   . 4. Minorities—
Soviet Union. I. Hajda, Lubomyr. II. Beissinger, Mark R.
III. Series.
DK33.N294 1990
305.8′00947—dc20
                                                                                    89-70469
                                                                                    CIP

Printed and bound in the United States of America

The paper used in this publication meets the requirements
of the American National Standard for Permanence of Paper
for Printed Library Materials Z39.48-1984.

10   9   8   7   6   5   4   3   2

Contents

Acknowledgments

The editors express their gratitude to the John M. Olin Foundation for its financial assistance and to the Harvard University Russian Research Center for the facilities and staff support that made this project possible. We wish to thank those who contributed their invaluable scholarly advice, including Vernon Aspaturian, Abram Bergson, Steven Blank, Walker Connor, Robert Conquest, Murray Feshbach, Erich Goldhagen, Richard Pipes, and Marc Raeff. We gratefully acknowledge the assistance of Barbara A. Anderson and Brian D. Silver with Soviet demographic data used throughout the volume. Susan Zayer and Karen Taylor-Brovkin provided able administrative help. For skillful technical assistance with the manuscript we are indebted to Jane Prokop, Elizabeth Taylor, and Alison Koff. Catherine Reed, Susan Gardos-Bleich, Christine Porto, and Alex Sich helped generously in diverse ways. Finally, the editors profited at every stage from the congenial working atmosphere and the encouragement of colleagues at the Russian Research Center too numerous to mention. To all of them goes our deep appreciation.

Lubomyr Hajda
Mark Beissinger

CHAPTER 1

The Imperial Legacy and the Soviet Nationalities Problem

Roman Szporluk

What is meant when one speaks about the legacy of Imperial Russia in the nationalities problem of the contemporary Soviet Union?[1]

The most visible legacy of Imperial Russia is the territorial configuration and ethnic composition of the USSR. The resemblance becomes even more striking when one compares the world map of 1913 with that for 1990 and notes the absence from the latter of the colonial empires of Britain, France, Germany, Belgium, the Netherlands, and Portugal, with their vast possessions in Asia and Africa. The contours of Russia then and the USSR now, in the meantime, have hardly changed. Admittedly, neither Helsinki nor Warsaw lies within the USSR, but their loss has been compensated by gains of areas that in 1913 had been known as Galicia, Bukovina, and the Ruthenian counties of Hungary. Then they belonged to the Austro-Hungarian Empire— of which no trace remains today.

That the Soviet Union is a multinational state, territorially largely coterminous with the former Russian Empire, does not in itself prove the existence of an "imperial legacy" in Soviet *politics*, however. More important is the question whether the Soviet Union is just "another name" for the Russian Empire or a fundamentally new kind of polity. To attempt an answer to this question it is essential to identify the specifically *political* points of similarity and contrast between the two states.

The first and perhaps most important issue concerns the relationship between state and society in the pre- and post-1917 eras. It is the contention of this essay that the nationalities problem is defined by the nature of this fundamental relationship. Thus we need to examine the structure of state-society relations under the Tsars and compare it with that in the Soviet period.

The nature of this relationship between state and civil society will emerge more fully in the course of our discussion. At this point suffice it to say that the autocratic Tsarist state, which in its origins was based on a religious and dynastic legitimization, failed to adjust to the modern political principle of constitutionalism, let alone that of sovereignty of the nation. It also took the state in Russia much longer than elsewhere in Europe to accept the

1

2 ROMAN SZPORLUK

principle of private property and the related distinction between the Tsar's authority as sovereign and as owner of property. In Tsarist ideology and practice the Tsar was the owner and master of his realm, not merely a ruler in the public sphere. Nonetheless, a civil society had emerged in Russia by the early twentieth century. In the Bolshevik revolution, however, not only the state, which had been a legacy of Tsarism, but that very civil society was destroyed, and the new rulers, the Bolsheviks, proclaimed an entirely new concept of social organization.[2]

The second question, in a sense the obverse of the first, concerns the status of Russians in the Tsarist and the Soviet state. How does the Soviet Marxist-Leninist state relate to the Russians as a nation? And, vice versa, how do the Russians, in terms of their national aspirations, relate to the state? The Tsarist Empire ultimately did not succeed in establishing a modus vivendi with the Russian nation as it was represented by the emerging civil society and failed to gain acceptance as a Russian national state. We shall try to determine whether the Soviet state is accepted as "Russian" in a sense in which its imperial predecessor was not.

At this stage, by way of establishing an agenda for discussion, it should be noted that the empire never became a Russian nation-state. Instead, in the words of Ladis K. D. Kristof, it promoted "Rossification," which meant "the development of an unswerving loyalty and direct attachment to the person of the tsar, by God's will the sole power-holder (*samoderzhets*) and head of *the* Church." The essence of "Rossification" lay in Orthodoxy, not in Russianism. "The Orthodox idea, not the Russian tongue or civilization, was the *spiritus movens* of the Tsardom. Russia was first of all Holy, not Russian."[3] This explains, for example, why the Tsarist authorities approved the publication of Orthodox texts in Tatar to promote the "Rossification" of the Muslims. In this respect "Rossification" resembles the postrevolutionary policy of Sovietization, with its principle of "national in form, socialist in content."

"Russification," on the other hand, aimed at making the non-Russian subjects of the state Russian in language and identity. This was the goal of Russian nationalists, whatever their other differences. Although, in its last decades especially, Tsarism also promoted "Russification" policies, one may agree with Kristof's notion of a discrepancy or conflict between the "state idea" of the imperial regime and the "national idea" of the Russians. Kristof recognizes that in reality "the difference between the state and national idea is rather subtle, a matter of shades," but he believes that in Russia it became more acute than elsewhere and found reflection in the "dichotomy between *narod* and *gosudarstvo*—the aims and ideals of 'the people' and 'the state'." Even the language recognized "the distinction between *russkii* and *rossiiskii*, between what pertains to the (Great) Russian people and what to All-the-'Russias'." The German, French and Spanish nations had "their" empires, Kristof continues, but the Tsarist Empire was not officially "Russian." Its formal name was *Rossiiskaia Imperiia*, not *Russkaia Imperiia*, and the Tsar likewise was not *russkii*, but *vserossiiskii imperator*.

Admittedly, certain Russian statesmen supported the *russkaia* (i.e., the national) idea, while others preferred the *rossiiskaia* (i.e., the state or, rather, imperial) idea; "still others tried to fuse the two."[4]

Thus, we may conclude that before the Revolution, the Russians themselves were not of one mind about what kind of country they wished Russia to be. Their search involved not only a political debate, but also an important debate about the geographical shape of Russia, for it was understood that geography, culture, and politics were intertwined. Kristof distinguishes at least four different ideas or models of "Russia" in Russian political thought: "Kievan," "Muscovite," "St. Petersburg," and "Eurasian."[5] (We shall return to the topic of models of "Russia" when we discuss the "Russian problem" in the USSR.)

The Russian problem, albeit unique in kind, was only one of the nationality problems in the empire. The empire encompassed many other ethnic and national groups, and their treatment by the state, and by Russians of different persuasions, depended on a variety of factors. Among these were religion (the Jews were the worst treated), and attitudes toward Russian rule (the Poles were the least willing to accept Russian domination and suffered severe repressions, but as a nation with a long tradition of independent statehood, they also enjoyed certain privileges that others lacked). The Ukrainian problem posed a special challenge to the state and to Russian nationalists. For historic reasons—including religious, as the Russians interpreted them—the Ukrainians were viewed as a branch of the Russian nation. Precisely because they were thought to be closer to the Russians than any other group (save the Belorussians), expression of Ukrainian distinctness was especially subject to persecution. Still another category of ethnic groups was represented by the so-called diaspora peoples, including, besides the Jews, the Germans and Armenians. Only Finland was actually recognized as a political nation; but as Russian nationalism gained ascendancy at the imperial court, the Tsarist government began curtailing Finland's autonomy, despite that nation's loyalty to the throne.

In the end, Russian nationalism failed to transform the Tsarist Empire into a liberal, democratic Russian nation-state. Nor did the nationalists among the non-Russian nationalities, with several exceptions, succeed in establishing their own states by secession from Russia. (These important exceptions— Finland, Poland, and, for about twenty years, Latvia, Lithuania, and Estonia— need, however, to be kept in mind.) Those who won the Russian civil war advanced a program that claimed to transcend the nationalist way of thinking altogether. Since it is their ideological and political heirs who rule the Soviet Union today, it may be useful to cite Lenin's assessment of the nationalities problem prior to World War I.

> Throughout the world, the period of the final victory of capitalism over feudalism has been linked up with national movements. For the complete victory of commodity production, the bourgeoisie must capture the home market, and there must be politically united territories whose population speak a single language, with all obstacles to the development of that language and

to its consolidation in literature eliminated. Therein is the economic foundation of national movements. Language is the most important means of human intercourse. Unity and unimpeded development of language are the most important conditions for genuinely free and extensive commerce on a scale commensurate with modern capitalism, for a free and broad grouping of the population in all its various classes and, lastly, for the establishment of a close connection between the market and each and every proprietor, big or little, and between seller and buyer.

Especially important for our purpose is his conclusion:

Therefore, the tendency of every national movement is towards the formation of *national states*, under which these requirements of modern capitalism are best satisfied. The most profound economic factors drive towards this goal, and, therefore, for the whole of Western Europe, nay, for the entire civilised world, the national state is *typical* and normal for the capitalist period.[6]

Lenin's assessment of the nature of nationality under the conditions of capitalism—no matter how one judges his analysis of capitalism—can serve us as a point of reference today. It prompts the question whether under Soviet-style socialism, especially now, in the period of *perestroika*, the introduction of elements of market economy will tend to intensify ethnic identities. Is "the tendency of every national movement . . . towards the formation of *national states*" also operative under "socialism" of the Soviet kind? This critical question in the "state-nationalities" area at the present time is attended by a host of others. What will the non-Russians do now as they search for their own options, and as they consider, in this search, the behavior of the Russians? Will they view the Russians' national aspirations today as a legacy of the Tsarist, imperial era? Will they define their own aims in a manner Lenin had considered in 1914 as normal, legitimate, and consistent with the historical process itself?

One final point that requires consideration is the Tsarist Empire's—and the Soviet Union's—standing in the world. As we shall argue later, the legitimacy of the Tsarist regime within the state, whether among Russians or non-Russians, was determined among other factors by the state's performance abroad as a Great Power. Will the same apply to the Soviet Union, and will its peoples' perception of the Communist party and the Soviet state's legitimacy be influenced by how they judge the Soviet Union's status in the world at large?

By way of introducing all these questions as they arise today, let us consider the current Soviet political agenda, and then see where on this agenda the "nationality question" fits in.

Gorbachev's Revolution

According to Mikhail Gorbachev, there is a revolution under way in the USSR today. "We are talking about restructuring and related processes of the thoroughgoing democratization of society, having in mind truly revolutionary and comprehensive transformations in our society." Gorbachev acknowledges that "this fundamental change of direction" is necessary because the Soviets "simply have no other way."[7]

On more than one occasion Gorbachev has admitted that unless the Soviet Union carries out the necessary revolutionary changes in its economy, political system, and culture, its standing as a great world power will be in danger as it slips further behind the advanced countries of the capitalist world. (There is no more talk of catching up with and surpassing "the West.") How serious is the condition of the Soviet Union was evident from the general secretary's 28 June 1988 address to the Nineteenth Party Conference. The greatest accomplishment of the new course over the past three years, said Gorbachev, consists in that "through the efforts of the party and the working people, we managed to halt the country's slide toward a crisis in the economic, social, and spiritual spheres."[8] But Gorbachev warned his audience and the Soviet public at large that much more remains to be done, because "the revolutionary transformations" have not yet become irreversible.[9]

Gorbachev and his supporters now admit that the economic improvement necessary for keeping up with the West is impossible without deep political and social, as well as cultural and intellectual, changes in the Soviet Union. This is the major difference between the present approach and the Soviet reform efforts of the 1950s and 1960s, which were limited to the economy. This recognition of the centrality of *political* reform was restated by Gorbachev at the Party Conference: The "crucial" question is that of reforming the political system.[10]

Thus, Gorbachev identifies the source of the Soviet Union's problems in the model of state-society relations established after the Revolution, although he prefers to speak about Lenin's death as the time when things took a wrong turn. That model is not effective and, indeed, it is now admitted, has never suited the Soviet Union. Gorbachev thus virtually repudiates the whole Soviet historical experience, albeit claiming to reject only its Stalinist distortions. The political system established in the USSR under Stalin and surviving to this day is now generally characterized as a "command-administrative" system. It is openly admitted that under Stalin—and under his successors before Gorbachev—there had taken place a virtual absorption of society within the all-powerful party-state. That absorption is now considered to have been a negative development, a development contradicting the "real meaning" of Leninism and Marxism.

For decades, however, the merger of society within the state, and consequently the abolition of the tension between the two, was represented as socialism's great achievement, socialism's special claim to superiority over capitalism. Although Stalin is being condemned now by Communists, he long expressed their view with exceptional clarity. Stalin quite openly and proudly used to define the "system of the dictatorship of the proletariat" as a "mechanism" or structure in which the party constitutes "the main guiding force." All the remaining organizations—the soviets, trade unions, women's and youth groups, etc.—were, according to Stalin, instruments to "link" the party with "the masses."[11] In essence, Stalin proclaimed the absorption of society by the state and the destruction of all intermediate associations between the state and the masses: "The Soviet state apparatus, in the profound meaning of the term," he wrote, "consists of the Soviets, plus all the diverse non-Party and Party organizations, which embrace millions, which unite the Soviets with the 'rank and file.'" They "merge the state apparatus with the vast masses and, step by step, destroy everything that serves as a barrier between the state apparatus and the people."[12]

Thus, Gorbachev's policy of *glasnost'* and *perestroika* constitutes a genuine revolution not only against Stalinist theory and practice—that is, in effect, against most of Soviet history—but also against the classic Marxist tradition, including the "statist" tradition of the Second International (1889–1914). It does not matter whether Gorbachev himself understands or accepts the implications of his course; his argument reintroduces into the political agenda concepts that Marxism, and not only Stalinism, has long regarded as out of place under the rule of the proletariat.[13]

In his struggle for reform Gorbachev is also dealing with a legacy of Imperial Russia—an issue the Tsarist state never resolved. This was Tsarism's stubborn refusal to accept the autonomy of society, and its insistence that the state is the sole creative force. Society, in this view, was merely an instrument, if not mindless material, at the state's disposal. Even though the Tsarist regime was forced after 1905 to accept constitutional limitations on its powers, it never fully reconciled itself to a Western, liberal system for Russia.

State and Society

Intentionally or not, Gorbachev has unleashed, as we are witnessing today, the demand, indeed a movement, for the establishment of a civil society in the Soviet Union. Gorbachev has implicitly admitted—and the public, insofar as it is able to speak, heartily agrees with him—that the Soviet state controlled by the Communist party has failed in its self-appointed historic mission. Sooner or later the party will have to decide how its role as "the leading force" in every aspect of public life can be reconciled with autonomous expressions of opinion and autonomous actions necessary, as he admits, for the success of the economic and scientific transformation.

According to Ernest Barker, the distinguished British scholar and political theorist,

> a nation is simultaneously, and co-extensively, two things in one. It is a social substance, or Society, constituted of and by a sum of voluntary associations, which have mainly grown of themselves—in the sense that they have been formed by voluntary and spontaneous combination—and which desire to act and to realize their purposes as far as possible by themselves. That is one side of the nation. The other side (which we may call either the reverse or the obverse, according to our preference) is that it is a political, or, as it is

perhaps better called, a legal substance; a single compulsory association including all, and competent, in all cases where it sees fit, to make and enforce rules for all.[14]

Barker's use of the term "nation" may seem to be singularly inappropriate in a Russian or Soviet context, where "nation" has a different meaning from that in which Barker employed it: the term "polity" would be more appropriate here. But despite this terminological infelicity, Barker's ideas can certainly be "retranslated" and applied in a discussion of the Russian and Soviet cases. According to Barker, "this double nature of the nation—this simultaneity and coextension of its social and its legal aspect—raises a threefold problem." Since they are applicable to our subject, we may quote Barker's questions verbatim, while remembering that his understanding of "nation" is not ours:

1) What are the things which belong to the nation in its legal aspect, as an organized State?
2) What are the things which belong to the nation in its social aspect, as a sum of voluntary associations?
3) What control should the nation, as organized in a State (and therefore competent to deal with all persons and judge in all cases *in the legal sphere*), exercise over itself as organized in a society of voluntary associations acting *in the social sphere*?[15]

While it would be very premature to say that Barker's language describes the Soviet reality, it certainly describes the issues currently being debated and fought in the USSR. It is quite evident that Gorbachev's declarations and actions have resulted in the formation of a public opinion that demands the legalization of independent groups and the establishment of an independent press. In other words, calls are being heard for legal steps that would make "society" a meaningful concept in the Soviet polity and give it a place in the system.[16]

What does all this mean for specific Soviet nationalities? How will it affect the "nationalities problem" as a whole? It raises, first of all, the question regarding the meaning and tenability of the concept of the "Soviet people." That concept, as we shall see, is intrinsically related to the Soviet theory and practice of socialism, and specifically to the idea of the state. What does the rejection of the latter imply for the future of the "Soviet people"?

The "Soviet People"

If one took Stalin's point to its logical conclusion, the Soviet state apparatus—"in the profound meaning of the term"—encompassed the entire population of the Soviet Union. Although Stalin never admitted this explicitly, his view implied depriving individual Soviet nationalities of any autonomy, in the same manner as all associations and organizations were deprived of theirs.

8   ROMAN SZPORLUK

One spoke of "peoples of the USSR" (*narody SSSR*), of course, of their self-determination and even "sovereignty," but these were meaningless phrases if the party controlled everything. Gradually, a new term, the "Soviet people" (*sovetskii narod*), was introduced to designate all citizens of the Soviet Union in order to emphasize their unity above differences of nationality. According to the official view, the peoples of the USSR formed an integrated whole, a single entity, in that they all shared an allegiance to Marxism-Leninism as their world view and to the party and state that represented and realized that outlook in practice. In this sense, the "Soviet people" was another name for "the state apparatus" as defined by Stalin.

It was also argued that the shared historical experience of building socialism and communism forged the unity of the "Soviet people." (Their common historical experience also included the defense of "socialist achievements" against external enemies, notably Nazi Germany in World War II.) The promoters of the concept of a "Soviet people" thus tried to support an ideologically legitimized Soviet system with an historical argument that stressed the people's shared experience and hence a community of outlook and character.

In the early 1920s the leaders of the new Soviet state proclaimed the principle of national equality and self-determination, which meant the equality of the non-Russian peoples with the Russians. In the "Union of Soviet Socialist Republics," "Russia" was one of several, constitutionally equal constituent parts. This constitutional arrangement recognized the power of nationalism among the non-Russians and, in the opinion of Lenin, was the only way to legitimate the linking of the Russians and the non-Russians in one political structure in the age of nationalist revolutions.[17] In a way, it was also a measure that "downgraded" the Russians from their former superior position in Tsarist Russia, though most Russians did not seem to take this implication too seriously. As Richard Pipes has noted, the Soviet Union was "a compromise between doctrine and reality: an attempt to reconcile the Bolshevik strivings for absolute unity and centralization of all power in the hands of the party, with the recognition of the empirical fact that nationalism did survive the collapse of the old order." The Bolsheviks viewed it as "a temporary solution only, as a transitional stage to a completely centralized and supra-national world-wide Soviet state."[18]

Although the new Soviet state was unitary, centralized, and totalitarian, Pipes noted that "by granting the minorities extensive linguistic autonomy and by placing the national-territorial principle at the base of the state's political administration, the Communists gave constitutional recognition to the multinational structure of the Soviet population." And since language and territory are very important in the development of national consciousness—particularly for people who, like the non-Russian peoples, had had some experience of autonomy during the Revolution—"this purely formal feature of the Soviet Constitution may well prove to have been historically one of the most consequential aspects of the formation of the Soviet Union."[19]

The Great Contest Lost

As was suggested earlier, the concept of the "Soviet people" was meant to deprive the ethnic factor of any capacity to challenge the unitary Stalinist system. To have built socialism was an experience and a bond far superior to any ethnic ties or allegiances. To proceed further and build communism would complete the union and fusion of all Soviet peoples. Khrushchev certainly thought so when he announced, in 1961, that by 1980 the Soviet Union would become the first society to have built "communism."

There is no reason to assume a priori that the policy of creating a "Soviet people" by an ideological bond was doomed to fail. As Eric J. Hobsbawm has noted, "even where the common criteria of belonging to a state are constructed on entirely non-traditional lines (and even when they may actually be deliberately ecumenical in their ideological content), the very fact of their being the possession of one state among several others, is likely to infuse them with a 'national' or 'nationalist' element."[20] Hobsbawm illustrates his point by noting that "Americanism," ("whatever its present political connotation"), had been originally "a universal programme . . . an invitation to all men to become Americans if they so chose, as well as an ideal description of those who already were. This has not prevented it from turning into a strongly nationalist slogan."[21]

One might apply this argument to the Soviet case and say that "Sovietism" also originally had been a universal formula that subsequently might have become a "nationalist slogan." Has it indeed become one? Is there a "Soviet people" analogous to the "American people"? And if not—why not? Perhaps what was needed for the "Soviet people" to become a reality was for the "Soviet dream" to become a reality—at least to the extent that the "American dream" has. There was a time when even those who did not necessarily share Khrushchev's millennnarian moods—"a millennium in twenty years"— had been prepared to recognize the Soviet achievement as an unprecedented feat. Foreign observers, whether Marxist or non-Marxist, were ready to recognize that whatever else they may have failed to do, the Bolsheviks had found a way previously unknown to raise Russia out of its historic backwardness. It had been generally recognized that the division of the globe into the advanced and the underdeveloped countries was "the most profound and the most lasting" of the consequences of the French Revolution and the Industrial Revolution. The Bolsheviks' main claim to recognition, therefore, was that in the 1930s they "developed means of leaping this chasm between the 'backward' and the 'advanced.'"[22]

This Soviet achievement would have matched the American achievement— were it true. But it is now being denied by no less a person than the current Soviet leader: contradicting Hobsbawm (and many other writers), Gorbachev now says that the Russians have *not* found a new way to overcome backwardness. What *did* happen in the 1930s, according to him, has made it even more difficult for the Soviet Union to advance. It is the legacy of the 1930s that the Soviets are now trying to overcome. In the process they are acknowledging that in relation to the West they continue to remain "backward" in science, technology, standard of living, and so forth. The most fundamental claim of the Revolution's historical legitimacy—the transformation of the Soviet Union into a modern society and the creation of a civilization that was to be an alternative to the West and free of its drawbacks—is thus denied. The Soviets now admit that they have not found a socialist way out of backwardness and toward modernity—one that would prove superior to what the West has produced. Indeed, the recently launched revolution is necessary to stop the USSR from falling further behind "the West."

To make matters worse, what Hobsbawm thinks the (*communist*) Russians achieved in the 1930s has been, in fact, accomplished by the (*capitalist*) *Japanese*. This appeared as a shocking discovery to the Soviet people in the 1980s. Some members of the younger generation have been inspired by this discovery to ask awkward questions—for example, whether socialism is capable of competing with capitalism. *Komsomol'skaia pravda*, the main youth daily, reported in the spring of 1988 that at a student discussion on the topic, "Socialism: Collapse or Rise?," a question was raised whether it would have not been better for Russia to follow the capitalist way instead of the course adopted in 1917. When asked how they imagined their future, some young people replied: a well-paid job, comfortable living conditions, wonderful technology—"like in Japan."[23] Japan is clearly on many Soviet minds. Olzhas Suleimenov, the Kazakh writer, in a recent interview said among other things: "And now our country is in the twenty-fourth place in computerization. When I asked a Japanese specialist when we would be able to catch up with you, the response was: never, for we shall not stand still, either . . ."[24]

We may better understand what "Japan" evokes in Soviet thinking when we consult a Western historian, a specialist in the history of science and technology in Russia, who draws apt parallels between the present situation and Russia's imperial past. The late Kendall E. Bailes wrote in 1986, when *perestroika* was only beginning:

> More rapid economic growth is essential if the Soviet leadership is to meet its goals of catching up with the West economically. In fact, one of the real dangers for the Soviet Union is that Japan . . . will catch up with and surpass the Soviet Union in the next few years. If this happens, it would be a major humiliation for the Soviet Union, nearly as important, I think, as the defeat of Russia by Japan in 1905—a military defeat that sent shock waves through the Russian Empire. An economic defeat of the Soviet Union by Japan would probably send similar shock waves through the Soviet leadership . . . if not through the population as a whole . . . Since both nations began their emergence from a traditional economic and social system at approximately the same time—in the 1860s—a rapidly growing Japan that may surpass an increasingly sluggish Soviet Union in the near future would dramatize the failures of the Soviet system, much as the defeats at Port Arthur, Mukden, and Tsushima in 1904–1905 dramatized the failures of tsarist Russia.[25]

Mention of the Russo-Japanese War of 1904–5 also recalls Stalin's famous 1945 speech in which he expressly treated the Soviet victory over Japan in World War II as *Russia's* revenge for the defeat it had sustained in the earlier war. To suffer a defeat by Japan in economic development forty years after that military revenge must bring to many Soviet minds truly ominous, if not apocalyptic, images.

The relationship between economic performance and political legitimacy and identity is well worth pondering as one analyzes the Soviet situation. It would seem that the cumulative effect of the revelations of Stalin's crimes *and* the admission that all those inhuman sufferings and exertions had failed in the economic sphere as well would have an impact on the popular perception of the Soviet system's legitimacy, and even on the viability of the "Soviet people" as an integrated political entity.

Legitimacy and Identity

The Russian Revolution of 1905, as is well-known, was directly inspired by Tsarism's defeat in the Japanese war. Tsarist Russia might not be democratic or liberal—so the argument in its favor ran—but at least it was a Great Power. To have lost a war with Japan, therefore, meant that Tsarism was compromised and deprived of legitimacy in a critical area. The revolution, as Hugh Seton-Watson has noted, was not only a revolution of workers, peasants, and radical intellectuals against autocracy, but "a revolution of non-Russians against Russification." Seton-Watson further noted: "The two revolts were, of course, connected: the social revolution was in fact most bitter in non-Russian regions, with Polish workers, Latvian peasants, and Georgian peasants as protagonists."[26]

Now that Marxism-Leninism is no longer a guide to the future, and the state is forced to allow a measure of autonomous opinion and action, what will become of the "Soviet people"? What will hold all the peoples of the USSR together—other than the Soviet state and the Communist party, whose historical legitimacy and record are now openly proclaimed wanting? Will a lost economic competition with Japan—and with capitalism as a whole— accelerate the Gorbachev revolution of the late 1980s, just as a lost war contributed to the revolt of 1905? Will the revolution in process be primarily political and social, or ethnic and nationalist, or a combination of both, just as the revolution of 1905 was?

Turning to the first question, the very reality of a "Soviet people" is being openly questioned today, though important officials have spoken in its defense. One of them is Yulian Bromlei, Brezhnev's chief specialist in matters of nationality and long-time head of the Institute of Ethnography at the Academy of Sciences of the USSR (replaced only in April 1989 by Valerii Tishkov). According to Bromlei, the "Soviet people" is a real community that is held together by common socialist features. It is a "meta-ethnic community."[27]

Another defense of the concept of the "Soviet people" comes from Genrikh Borovik, the prominent publicist-commentator and head of the

Soviet Peace Committee. In his speech at the Nineteenth Party Conference, Borovik disagreed with those who claim that the "Soviet people" is an "invention" or "fiction" (*vydumka*). "But the Soviet people is not a fiction. It is, fortunately, a reality." Borovik continued: "We are talking about the rise of national self-consciousness. This is wonderful. But not at the expense of the Soviet national [*sic*] self-consciousness. [Or at the expense] of the self-consciousness of citizens of the Soviet Union and of Soviet patriotism."[28]

The fact that these two prominent defenders of the concept of the "Soviet people" understand quite different things by the term is additional proof of the present ideological confusion, if not crisis. Bromlei calls it a *meta-ethnic* entity, Borovik calls it *national*. This lack of clarity about what should be a basic concept supports the argument of another prominent figure, the historian Yurii Afanasiev, who speaks about an ideological "identity vacuum" in the USSR. According to Afanasiev, historical memory is the most important, indeed, a constitutive or formative element of social identity. However, a "systematic destruction of collective memory" was being carried out under Stalin and under Brezhnev, and this destruction has resulted in a "crisis of identity of our contemporary society." This in turn has created an ideological "identity vacuum" that made possible the rise of "such chauvinist, anti-Semitic groups like the extremists from *Pamiat'*, who by flirting with irrational, easily excitable elements are capable of putting forward their own variant of identity: an antihistorical, mythical, racist one—anything you want . . ."[29]

Afanasiev's reference to *Pamiat'*, the extremist Russian nationalist organization, warrants a closer look at the situation prevailing in "Russia proper," among the Russians themselves. One of the strongest currents in the post-Brezhnev Soviet Union is Russian national assertiveness, Russian nationalism. Let us examine this phenomenon, bearing in mind the larger issue that underlies this essay—the legacy of Imperial Russia in current Soviet politics. In what ways does contemporary Russian nationalism reopen the unsolved agenda of Tsarist Russia? Are the Russians as a nation suing for divorce, as it were, from the Soviet state?

De-Sovietization of Russia

It is common knowledge that Stalin and his successors—Khrushchev, Brezhnev, Andropov, and Chernenko—manipulated the symbols of Russian nationhood and promoted Russification of the non-Russians. But it is also well-known that at the same time the Soviet leaders did not allow the Russian nation to express itself—indeed, to exist—independently of the party and the state: the Russian nation itself was dissolved in the Stalinist state. Official propaganda glorified the "great Russian people" and "Russia" in ways that were insulting to non-Russians and embarrassing to many Russians, but the Russian nation, culture, and history were manipulated in order to achieve specific political goals. The Soviet scholar, Gavriil Popov, has recently pointed out that the Russian nation's historical experiences and memories were selectively manipulated by Stalin in order to make the Russians a pliable instrument in his rule over the Soviet Union.[30] (This meant obliterating from collective memory libertarian traditions and ideas.) In other words—Stalin (and his successors) sought to create an image of a "Russia" that would serve the system.

It is understandable that the Russians should be the first to express themselves as a nation under Gorbachev's *perestroika*. Even though Russian identity had been managed by the party, the Russians have always had at their disposal the necessary infrastructure—the journals, research institutes, theaters, publishing houses, etc.—to express themselves more easily in the cultural sphere than, say, the Ukrainians or Georgians. Precisely because of this rich infrastructure, and because they always enjoyed special privileges as the "leading nation," and the "elder brother," it proved easier for the Russians to emancipate themselves from "Sovietism." The fusion of state and civil society sought by Stalin had never been complete in the cultural sphere—and it is natural that artists, writers, and playwrights would be the first to assert their autonomy. If one were to describe their achievement in a single phrase, the most accurate would be "de-Sovietization of Russian culture." But since culture is a defining marker of a nation, the issue of "de-Sovietization of Russia" has become an important item on the political agenda as well.

Recent developments in Russian culture are well-known. A number of major writers whose total oeuvre or most important works had been banned— for example, Anna Akhmatova, Mikhail Bulgakov, Evgenii Zamiatin, Boris Pasternak, and Vladimir Nabokov—have become available to a wide reading public for the first time. The same is true for many of Russia's pre-Soviet or non-Soviet historians, philosophers, and social thinkers, including Nikolai Karamzin, Petr Chaadaev, Sergei Soloviev, and Vasilii Kliuchevsky. Cumulatively, all these moves are leading to a gradual but comprehensive devaluation of the specifically Soviet cultural figures and their alleged accomplishments. (This tendency is reflected in attempts to "debunk" Gorky and Mayakovsky, for example.) Of the great men and women who wrote in the post-1917 era, those who were victims of the Soviet regime seem to be the most highly regarded now. It is in this sense that Russian culture is becoming "de-Sovietized."

Another element in the emerging de-Sovietized model of "Russia" has been the new treatment of the Russian Orthodox Church, highlighted during the celebrations of the Millennium of the introduction of Christianity in Kievan Rus'. The Orthodox Church is the only Russian institution in the USSR that represents a pre-Soviet Russia, one without the Communist party and without Lenin. "The Orthodox Church," says Edward L. Keenan, "is slowly recapturing a role in which it has often been cast by both well-wishers and enemies—that of the only authentically Russian national institution."[31]

The emergence of that complex phenomenon, Russian nationalism, has understandably attracted scholarly attention abroad, as the writings of

Alexander Yanov, John B. Dunlop, and Dina Rome Spechler attest. It has also given rise to certain political hopes that seem at best premature. Thus, David A. Moro, who views "the emergence of a new national consciousness among ethnic Russians" as the most important of "internal Soviet developments in recent decades," expects that "Russianization" of the Soviet Union might prompt "Russia" to abandon its Communist global goals. This, in turn, should shape a new American strategy, which "would be to induce the Soviet state to move from its present ideocratic, totalitarian structure toward a more traditional nation-state with a nationalist rather than a Communist orientation. This evolution, if it could be brought about, would remove the root causes of Soviet aggressiveness."[32]

Indeed, Moro continues, "Russians are in no meaningful sense a favored nationality under Soviet rule—since 1917 their people and culture have endured persecutions far greater than those inflicted on minority nationalities." Russian dominance is a "myth" that "is easy to feed, given Russia's imperial past and the Soviet state's outward physiognomy (a multinational empire controlled from the Russian capital, with Russian as the official language)." But Moro dismisses this "myth": in his view, "by giving Russian imperialist overtones to its domination of other peoples, the regime deflects the resentment of other nationalities from the Communist state entity onto the Russian national entity."[33]

Moro does not ask what the reaction of the non-Russian peoples would be if the Soviet Union became an openly Russian "nation-state," a prospect he would clearly welcome. It is far from self-evident that the adoption of "Russianism" as the state's official ideology would make the non-Russian nationalities less resentful of the Russians than they are now, when, purportedly, that resentment is misplaced and should be addressed instead to the non-national regime.

Moro's view of the Soviet Union as Russia is hardly unique among Western writers. Mark Frankland, the author of *The Sixth Continent: Russia and Mikhail Gorbachev,* as one of his reviewers, Alastair McAuley, has noted, "could be mistaken for a Russian nationalist." He "has produced a marvelous evocation of Russia, rather than the Soviet Union as a whole." Frankland conveys the Russians' "almost mystical pride in the Russian language and its literature, their identification with the villages, fields and woods of the Russian countryside. He gives the impression that he shares in this pride." But, McAuley points out, Frankland "fails to convey any sense of the tensions that come from the fact that the Soviet Union is a multiethnic state and that the Russians about whom he writes so lovingly make up little more than half the population."[34]

The Non-Russians

The other half of the Soviet population has responded to the revival of Russia by asking questions like that posed by the Ukrainian writer, Pavlo Zahrebel'nyi: "There is much talk these days about Russian patriotism

. . . But has anyone ever said anything about Ukrainian patriotism? And now, when the histories written by Kliuchevsky, Soloviev, and Karamzin are being republished, perhaps we should raise the question of republishing *The History of Ukraine-Rus'* by Hrushevs'kyi, on whose pages the issues of Ukrainian patriotism are elucidated . . ."[35]

Thus, as the non-Russians witness the restoration of non-Communist figures and institutions as part of the *Russian* ethnic and national heritage, they cannot help but notice that this heritage is not *theirs*. They have responded to the de-Sovietization of Russia by raising analogous demands for the rehabilitation of *their* respective cultural figures from both their Soviet and pre-Soviet histories who had been suppressed under Stalin. This movement has been stimulated, and certainly legitimized, by the developments in ethnic Russia, which are being carefully studied in the non-Russian republics. The phrase, "as our Russian brothers are showing us, it is necessary to love one's language, study one's history, rehabilitate suppressed historical figures, etc.," is frequently met in non-Russian cultural periodicals and at cultural gatherings.

With specific reference to religion, it is obvious that an open incorporation of Orthodoxy into the Russian national identity not only further de-Sovietizes Russia but also further separates the Russians from other Soviet peoples. This is bound to complicate, especially, Russian-Ukrainian and Russian-Belorussian relations—for two reasons. First, the Soviet state, in full accord with the Russian Church, had banned separate Belorussian and Ukrainian Orthodox Churches, while the Russian Orthodox Church continues to treat these two East Slavic peoples as part of a "Russian" nation. Second, the state, in a dramatic demonstration of its direct engagement in religious matters, had also banned the Uniate Church. In the Soviet context, the rehabilitation of Russian Orthodoxy revives an old imperial legacy: the Tsarist policy of denying the Ukrainians and Belorussians a distinct identity, including a separate identity in religious matters.[36]

While the Russian-Ukrainian and Russian-Belorussian relationship concerns peoples with a long common cultural and religious past, the Soviet nationality problem is much broader and more complex. This complexity, too, in all its aspects, is an inheritance, a legacy taken over from Imperial Russia. There are the Baltic peoples, with their Protestant and Catholic religious background, their German, Polish, and Swedish historical ties, and living memories of independent statehood between 1918 and 1940. Then there are the peoples whom John A. Armstrong calls "mobilized diasporas"— Jews, Armenians, Germans. These peoples had played "key roles as innovators and managers" in the past, and the question now is whether the dominant nation will allow them to resume those roles as the Soviet Union tries to modernize itself again.[37]

The Armenians are, of course, not only a "diaspora" people, but also— like the neighboring Georgians—a nation with its own territorial homeland and republic. The recent upheavals in the Nagorno-Karabakh region have been largely viewed as an Azerbaidzhani-Armenian territorial dispute. While this is correct, the ramifications are much broader, as Armstrong helps us to see in his essay. Armstrong analyzes Muslim-Christian relations in Yugoslavia and the Soviet Union and reminds us of some significant history:

> The three great empires—Austro-Hungarian, Ottoman, and Tsarist Russian—which divided East Europe and its borderlands prior to World War I all arose during the struggle between Islam and Christianity. Since recent evidence indicates the strong, indeed almost incredible persistence of a distinctive Islamic culture, one may expect East Europe to present in the future, too, not *one* system of nations but *two* distinctive types: a "Christian" and an "Islamic."[38]

The latter, Armstrong explains, includes not only the Middle East but also "numerous nations" of Muslim background in Yugoslavia and the USSR. Speaking of these, Armstrong presents a broad historical assessment:

> In crucial respects these nations are linked more closely to the Middle Eastern northern tier (Afghanistan, Iran, Turkey) than to the historic Orthodox Christian centers (Moscow, Belgrade) which dominate their present state institutions. Today, of course, both these centers are formally Leninist . . .
>
> Persistent variation between nations of the Moslem type and those of Christian background reflect incompatible ways of life and historic symbols more than overt religious cleavage, although religious revival draws strength from distinctive traditions. Incompatibility of ways of life is indicated by objective social characteristics (notably demographic patterns) as well as by in-group attitudes . . . Given the enduring force of these incompatibilities, any polity composed of nations of Islamic as well as of Christian background is likely to become fragile.[39]

One can only speculate on the likely impact of the "de-Sovietization of Russia"—or of Moscow's becoming *less* Leninist in order to maintain its Great Power standing—on the Muslim peoples of the Soviet Union. One would like to know, for instance, what natives of Tashkent, Samarkand, and Dushanbe—or, for that matter, people in Novosibirsk and Vladivostok—think of Mikhail Gorbachev's idea of the Soviet Union as belonging to a "Europe from the Atlantic to the Urals."[40] When Gorbachev calls Europe "our common home,"[41] do they not ask themselves if they are "at home" in that Europe too?

On the other hand, one may well imagine such "European" talk evoking very positive feelings in Riga, Vilnius, Lviv, and Kiev. The idea of a European unity is also likely to be received with understanding and support by *some* people in Moscow, and even more so in the city formerly known as St. Petersburg.

But the emphasis should be on *some*: for not all Russians necessarily agree that Russia's "home" is in Europe—or only, or mainly, in Europe. Just as they had before 1917, the Russians are still debating the question of their country's identity.

Conclusions

Historical evidence suggests that the unity of multiethnic polities depends largely on the willingness of the dominant element *not* to think of itself as an *ethnic* category. It is not enough for the state to seek to assimilate its diverse groups; the dominant element in the state has to dissolve itself within or identify itself with a broader territorial, political, and/or ideological concept as well. And so we have Americans, not "WASPS"; Ottomans, not Turks; British, not English; Spaniards, not Castilians.

The likelihood of the rise of a new, more authentically common Soviet political identity, therefore, will largely depend on the willingness of the Russians to submerge or dissolve themselves in a broader entity encompassing all the peoples of the state. The viability of the "Soviet people" remains problematic for reasons indicated earlier: how can there be a "Soviet people" as long as there is no "Soviet power" in the Soviet Union, as long as political power belongs to the party, and not to the (popularly and freely elected) *soviets* (councils)?

There were moments in Imperial Russia's history when one could be a Russian in the political or, more precisely, dynastic sense (a *rossiianin*), without being an ethnic Russian (*russkii*). Today, as Russians seek to reconstitute their national memories and build a *Russian* national identity, they are in effect telling all others in the USSR what they think about the "Soviet people" (*sovetskii narod*): they show not the slightest inclination to call their country anything but "Russia," or themselves anything but "Russians." They are *russkie*, not *sovetskie*—Russian, not Soviet, people.

This does not mean that all Russians know what parts of the Soviet Union they understand "Russia" to include, or whom they consider to be Russian and whom not. Many conflicting answers to these questions are being currently offered.[42] Thus, some Russians seem prepared to accept the "RSFSR" (the Russian Soviet Federated Socialist Republic) as their narrower homeland within the USSR. Others think of the entire USSR as Russia— although not all of them necessarily accept all Soviet citizens as their compatriots in that "Russia."

There is another current of Russian thought—or better, model or image of "Russia"—that finds adherents in the Soviet Union today. This is "Eurasianism," of which Kristof provides a succinct summary:

> . . . the Eurasian image of Russia identifies Russia with that vast stretch of continental land from the Carpathians to the Pacific, which was for centuries controlled by the nomads who roamed the grassy plains between Mongolia and the Pripet marshes. The Eurasiatic steppe, it is said, was the cradle of an imperial state-idea, and the Russians rule an empire which preceded them. There was a "Russia" (or, rather, a *Rossiia*) prior to the Russian Russia. The Russians have inherited a cultural-political domain and with it a certain teleological impetus conditioned by history and geography. They are the non-nomadic heirs to the nomads; they have rebuilt the Mongol empire from its Western end. In other words, the concept of Russia as Eurasia unites two

distinct historical realities and epochs, and it is both logically and historically a two-way street: before there was a European Asia there was an Asiatic Europe.[43]

In the Eurasianist point of view, the peoples of the old empire possessed a common past that preceded both Tsarism and Soviet communism. Those ties were forged during the Middle Ages, in the period of the so-called "Mongol Yoke." Russia, therefore, was an Asian as much as a European power—in brief, it was special, "Eurasian."

Although it was first formally developed over sixty years ago, Eurasianism has relevance to the present national debate. It has become clear, in the late 1980s, that what Pipes once called a "purely formal feature of the Soviet Constitution," has acquired—or recovered—a life of its own. Some Russians grasped as early as the 1920s the fundamental importance of this revolutionary transformation of the position of the non-Russian nations and therefore also of the Russian nation. Among them was Prince Nikolai Trubetskoi, one of the main proponents of Eurasianism. His interesting attempt to reconcile the doctrines of Eurasianism with the consequences of the Russian Revolution in the area of nationality affairs deserves attention today. Writing in 1927, Trubetskoi argued that the Russian nation had saved the unity of the state, which otherwise would have disintegrated into a number of independent units, by sacrificing its "previous status of the only master of the state." Thus, the non-Russian peoples acquired a position in the state they had never enjoyed before, and the Russians ceased to be the ruling nation. The Russian nation "is no longer the master of the household, but only the first among equals." The rights the non-Russians had won "cannot any more be taken away from them."[44]

Clearly, Eurasianism is a doctrine that supports with broad historical and cultural arguments the unity of the present USSR, a unity otherwise threatened by the failure of Marxism-Leninism. (It would let the Balts secede, however, which should win it mass support in Riga, Tallinn, and Vilnius.) One might also argue that Eurasianism represents an early attempt to forestall or preempt the rise of an anti-Russian Muslim separatism of whose potential Armstrong speaks. Whether Eurasianism is an influential political current in the USSR today is not clear. But it does have vocal intellectual spokesmen. Lev Gumilev is the chief proponent for the view that the USSR is neither a Russian nor a Slavic state, but one that is both Slavic *and* Turkic, European *and* Asian, Christian *and* Muslim. For understandable reasons the party does not encourage "Eurasianism," although the view finds its way into print.[45] Nor is this model of Russia likely to generate much enthusiasm among the Leningrad and Moscow intelligentsia, whose mental map of the world clearly includes Paris, New York, and Munich, but seldom Ulan-Ude and Karaganda.

The politically dominant trend in the Soviet Union today is "statism" or "imperial nationalism," although these names are not used except by its critics. This trend may be said to represent a Communist version of the "Official Nationality" concept of the Russian nation from Tsarist times, except that it inserts Marxism-Leninism in place of Orthodoxy, and party rule in place of autocracy. Although it is ostensibly a non-national ideology, Marxism-Leninism became in Stalin's time a "neo-Tsarist Marxism," or "imperial Bolshevism," as Robert C. Tucker has termed it.[46] Tucker also calls Stalinism "a nationalistically and imperialistically wayward form of Bolshevism, a Bolshevism of the radical right."[47] However, just as the apologists of Tsarism were not altogether clear what they understood by "nationality," so the Soviet ideologues, as we have seen, are having trouble with defining the nature of the "Soviet people." Statist or imperial nationalism does not believe that political freedom is a desirable goal for the Russians— especially not if it should threaten the territorial integrity of the state.

There are Russians who oppose the idea of an empire in principle, such as Alexander Zinoviev (although he is rather vague on details). In an interview several years ago, Zinoviev stated that his "sole concern is the future of the Russian people." Since he wanted "the Russian people to be educated, cultured, and self-confident so that they can share the treasures of world culture and contribute to them," and thus "lift the Russians out of centuries-old backwardness and subjection," he understood that it "is impossible to attain any of these things within the Soviet empire."[48]

It is impossible to tell how numerous or influential are those Russians who share Zinoviev's view of the empire. Recently, however, the Soviet press has published criticisms of the outlook termed "imperial consciousness" (*imperskoe soznanie*). Thus, the Leningrad historian Evgenii Anisimov attributed the present sharpening (*obostrenie*) of national relations in Soviet society to various and serious shortcomings in the treatment of the history of Soviet nationalities, especially the "relapses into imperial consciousness" (*retsidivy imperskogo soznaniia*). Anisimov cites examples of "imperial" thinking on such topics as the conquest of the Caucasus and the "Shamil problem," and observes that "about the partitions of Poland, the suppression of Polish uprisings, or of the Hungarian uprising of 1849, one does not talk at all"— and if one does, it is in "Aesopian language."[49]

These practices denounced by Anisimov can only mean that the Soviet Union is indeed perceived as an heir of the Tsarist Empire—or, rather, that the empire is viewed as a "Soviet Union before the name." Interestingly, the Communist authorities in Poland had also treated criticism of Tsarist Russia as attacks on the Soviet Union, thus assuming the continuity if not identity between the two states. Polish censors in Gierek's time (1970–80) openly stated that the party treats any criticism of Tsarism as a camouflaged criticism of the Soviet Union. Accordingly, certain works of Adam Mickiewicz (1798–1855) were not published for decades, and scholars were not allowed to write on such topics as the Tsarist Russification of Poland or the Tsarist deportations of Poles to Siberia.[50]

It is not surprising, therefore, that "imperial consciousness" or "imperial outlook," that legacy of Tsarist Russia, is especially evident in the current Ukrainian-Russian relationship. An essay about the Tsarist state's (and Russian "society's") treatment of the "Ukrainian Question," written before 1917 by Volodymyr [*Russ.* Vladimir] Vernadsky, the famous scientist, sounds quite topical and relevant today, and may be treated as a critique of the present Soviet treatment of Ukraine.[51]

The current leader of the Soviet Union is committed to a policy that, if it is to succeed, requires the restoration of civil society. But civil society under Soviet conditions means something quite different from what Ernest Barker envisaged when he differentiated between the State, or the legal sphere, and Society, the social sphere. In the Soviet Union, the restoration of the social sphere immediately produces a number of entities that want to perform the functions of the state, to exercise the prerogatives of sovereign nations. The conflict between Armenia and Azerbaidzhan is the first and most dramatic illustration of what is likely to happen when the party really abdicates its authority or simply chooses on occasion not to exercise it.

What will be the response of Moscow if the non-Russians again go "too far"? What will happen if the Russians press on with their nationalist goal to transform the Soviet Union into a Russian nation-state free of Marxism-Leninism and the party?

Paul Goble, an American analyst of Soviet nationality problems, says: ". . . Gorbachev may now be learning what many students of that part of the world have long suspected: that a liberalized Russia might be possible but that a significantly liberalized Soviet Union is probably a contradiction in terms."[52] A very similar view was stated by a Czech historian twenty years earlier. In 1969, shortly after the suppression of the Prague Spring, Milan Švankmajer published an article on Tsar Nicholas I and his struggles against the revolutionary movements in Europe in 1848–49. According to Švankmajer, the Russian Empire was "constantly exposed to the danger of disintegration, which can be prevented only by a strong central government." The very existence of multinational empires is threatened by "civil rights," and Russia intervened in 1849 because civil rights and national self-determination "threatened the very foundations of Russian autocracy."[53]

Will the reformer Gorbachev one day have to face the problem that the reactionary Nicholas I faced? If he does, will he respond differently? Paul Goble, as we see, doubts it. Should Goble prove wrong, should the Soviet Union become a liberal polity while remaining multinational, more than "imperial consciousness"—that attitude some contemporary Soviet historians now discern in the USSR's treatment of the non-Russians within its borders and in its dealings with such foreign countries as Poland—will need to be overcome. A way will have to be found to satisfy the national aspirations of the Soviet peoples, including the Russian people, to their own political autonomy and cultural self-expression, and at the same time it will be necessary to convince them of the benefits of maintaining a larger, supranational framework in which no one nation dominates the others. In the meantime, an "imperial consciousness" is alive in the USSR seventy years after the death of the empire. This means either that this consciousness is a "false consciousness"—or that the empire is not dead after all and that therefore those conditions of equality are still lacking.

Notes

1. While it is superfluous in an essay of this kind to cite the standard literature, it may be helpful to identify some of those works the author found particularly important. For the treatment of the nationality question as an essential aspect of Russian history, see especially Hugh Seton-Watson, *The Decline of Imperial Russia, 1855–1914* (New York: Praeger, 1961), and idem, *The Russian Empire, 1801–1917* (Oxford: Oxford University Press, Clarendon Press, 1967). The "Russian problem" in all its ramifications, including historical continuities and discontinuities, is treated by many scholars in two collective volumes: Robert Conquest, ed., *The Last Empire: Nationality and the Soviet Future* (Stanford: Hoover Institution Press, 1986), and Edward Allworth, ed., *Ethnic Russia in the USSR: The Dilemma of Dominance* (New York: Pergamon, 1980). For a thorough account of how the Bolsheviks dealt with nationalism, see Richard Pipes, *The Formation of the Soviet Union: Communism and Nationalism, 1917–1923*, rev. ed. (New York: Atheneum, 1968). The current Soviet agenda is presented in James Cracraft, ed., *The Soviet Union Today: An Interpretive Guide*, 2d ed. (Chicago: University of Chicago Press, 1988).

2. For a more detailed discussion by the author, see Roman Szporluk, "The Ukraine and Russia," in Conquest, *The Last Empire*, pp. 151–82, where references to the relevant literature may also be found, and *Communism and Nationalism: Karl Marx versus Friedrich List* (New York: Oxford University Press, 1988). Richard Pipes, *Russia under the Old Regime* (New York: Charles Scribner's Sons, 1974) presents a full-scale treatment of the Russian state as "the Patrimonial State" and its ideology of "Patrimonialism."

3. Ladis K. D. Kristof, "The Russian Image of Russia: An Applied Study in Geopolitical Methodology," in Charles A. Fisher, ed., *Essays in Political Geography* (London: Methuen, 1968), p. 350.

4. Ibid., pp. 349–50.

5. Ibid., pp. 356–64. Those who saw in Kievan Rus' the real core of Russia denied by definition that Ukrainians were a nation distinct from the Russians. This conclusion was not implicit in the "Muscovite" or "St. Petersburg" models of Russia, although their proponents, with few exceptions, also held that position.

6. "The Right of Nations to Self-Determination" (1914), in V. I. Lenin, *Collected Works*, vol. 20 (Moscow: Progress, 1964), pp. 396–97; see also A. W. Orridge, "Uneven Development and Nationalism: II," *Political Studies*, vol. 29, no. 2 (June 1981), pp. 185–86.

7. Mikhail Gorbachev's report to the CPSU Central Committee, 27 January 1987, *Pravda*, 28 January 1987, as translated in *Current Digest of the Soviet Press* (henceforth *CDSP*), vol. 39, no. 4 (25 February 1987), p. 6.

8. "On Progress in the Implementation of the Decisions of the 27th Party Congress and the Tasks of Deepening Perestroika," Report by Mikhail Gorbachev, General Secretary of the CPSU Central Committee, at the 19th All-Union CPSU Conference, 28 June 1988, *Pravda*, 29 June 1988, translated in *CDSP*, vol. 40, no. 26 (27 July 1988), p. 7.

9. Ibid.

10. Ibid., p. 7 and pp. 11–22.

11. J. V. Stalin, *Works*, vol. 8 (Moscow: Foreign Languages Publishing House, 1954), pp. 37–38; see also Szporluk, *Communism and Nationalism*, p. 221.

12. Stalin, *Works*, vol. 7 (1954), p. 164.

13. For an informative and stimulating guide to the current socialist attempts to free socialism from its historic attachment to statism and to establish the validity of

the state versus civil society dualism in socialism, see John Keane, *Democracy and Civil Society: On the Predicaments of European Socialism, the Prospects for Democracy, and the Problem of Controlling Social and Political Power* (London: Verso, 1988), and idem, ed., *Civil Society and the State: New European Perspectives* (London: Verso, 1988).

14. Ernest Barker, *Principles of Social and Political Theory* (Oxford: Oxford University Press, Clarendon Press, 1956), p. 4.

15. Ibid.

16. Before any of these desiderata are realized, however, it will be more realistic to look for elements of an *independent society*, the term preferred by H. Gordon Skilling to describe those departures from Stalinism emerging in Eastern Europe and, more recently, in the Soviet Union. Skilling recognizes that an "independent society" is a significant phenomenon, a major modification of the old model, but he warns against viewing it as a development that can be described in terms of the "civil society vs. the state" dichotomy. He points out, for example, that an "independent society" does not enjoy a legally recognized autonomy—and that the state is not a *Rechtsstaat*. (See H. Gordon Skilling, *Samizdat and an Independent Society in Central and Eastern Europe* [Basingstoke: Macmillan, 1988]. I am grateful to Professor Skilling for his comments on an earlier version of this paper.)

17. Pipes, *The Formation of the Soviet Union*, is the standard account and analysis of the events of 1917–23. For briefer, capsule histories of the major Soviet nationalities, see Zev Katz, Rosemarie Rogers, and Frederic Harned, eds., *Handbook of Major Soviet Nationalities* (New York: The Free Press, 1975). For a detailed development of my view of this problem in a broader context of interaction between Marxism-Leninism and nationalism, see Szporluk, *Communism and Nationalism*, pp. 229–33.

18. Pipes, *The Formation of the Soviet Union*, p. 296.

19. Ibid, pp. 296–97.

20. Eric J. Hobsbawm, "Some Reflections on Nationalism," in T. J. Nossiter, A. H. Hanson, and Stein Rokkan, eds., *Imagination and Precision in the Social Sciences: Essays in Memory of Peter Nettl* (London: Faber & Faber, 1972), p. 395.

21. Ibid.

22. Eric J. Hobsbawm, *The Age of Revolution, 1789–1848* (New York: New American Library, 1962), p. 217, quoted (and discussed) in Szporluk, *Communism and Nationalism*, p. 148.

23. *Komsomol'skaia pravda*, 27 March 1988.

24. *Komsomol'skaia pravda*, 3 June 1988.

25. Kendall E. Bailes, "Science and Technology in the Soviet Union: Historical Background and Contemporary Problems," in Alexander Dallin and Condoleezza Rice, eds., *The Gorbachev Era* (Stanford: Stanford Alumni Association, 1986), pp. 69–70.

26. Hugh Seton-Watson, *Nations and States* (Boulder, CO: Westview, 1977), p. 87, quoted by Benedict Anderson, *Imagined Communities: Reflections on the Origin and Spread of Nationalism* (London: Verso, 1983), p. 83.

27. Iulian Bromlei, "Byt' tsementiruiushchei siloi," *Sovetskaia kul'tura*, 25 June 1988.

28. Genrikh Borovik, speech at the Nineteenth Party Conference, *Pravda*, 2 July 1988.

29. Iurii Afanas'ev, "Perestroika i istoricheskoe znanie," *Literaturnaia Rossiia*, 17 June 1988, pp. 2–3 and 8–9; reference to "identity crisis" is on p. 9.

30. G. Kh. Popov and Nikita Adzhubei, "Pamiat' i *Pamiat'*," *Znamia*, 1988, no. 1, pp. 192–93.

31. Edward L. Keenan, "The Millennium of the Baptism of Rus' and Russian Self-Awareness," *The Harriman Institute Forum*, vol. 1, no. 7 (July 1988), p. 3.

32. David A. Moro, "The National Rebirth of Russia: A U.S. Strategy for Lifting the Soviet Siege," *Policy Review*, no. 43 (Winter 1988), p. 2.

33. Ibid., p. 5.

34. Alastair McAuley, "Ready for Action," *The Times Literary Supplement* (London), 14 August 1987, p. 883.

35. "Spravi perebudovy—tvorchu initsiatyvu," *Literaturna Ukraina*, 28 July 1988. Consciously or not, Zahrebel'nyi was paraphrasing the famous question asked by Mykola Khvyl'ovyi in the 1920s: "Is Russia independent? It is? Well, then Ukraine is independent too."

36. See Szporluk, "Ukraine and Russia," in Conquest, *The Last Empire*, pp. 162–63 and p. 177, n. 27.

37. John A. Armstrong, "Toward a Framework for Considering Nationalism in East Europe," *Eastern European Politics and Societies*, vol. 2, no. 2 (Spring 1988), pp. 280–305, esp. pp. 296–97, 300–301, and 304. Also see idem, "Mobilized and Proletarian Diasporas," *American Political Science Review*, vol. 70, no. 2 (June 1976), especially pp. 403–4.

38. Armstrong, "Toward a Framework," p. 301.

39. Ibid., p. 302.

40. Gorbachev's speech in Prague (1987), quoted in Karen Dawisha, *Eastern Europe, Gorbachev and Reform: The Great Challenge* (Cambridge: Cambridge University Press, 1988), p. 192.

41. Ibid.

42. For a more detailed discussion of this problem, see Roman Szporluk, "Dilemmas of Russian Nationalism," *Problems of Communism*, vol. 38, no. 4 (July–August 1989), pp. 15–35.

43. Kristof, "Russian Image," in Fisher, *Essays in Political Geography*, p. 363.

44. N. S. Trubetskoi, "Obshcheevraziiskii natsionalizm," *Evraziiskaia khronika* (Paris), 1927, no. 9, pp. 24–25.

45. See Iu. Afanas'ev, "Proshloe i my," *Kommunist*, 1985, no. 14, p. 110, for a scornful reference to "Evraziistvo."

46. Robert C. Tucker, *Political Culture and Leadership in Soviet Russia: From Lenin to Gorbachev* (New York: Norton, 1987), pp. 67 and 97.

47. Ibid., p. 70.

48. George Urban, "Portrait of a Dissenter as a Soviet Man: A Conversation with Alexander Zinoviev," *Encounter*, vol. 62, no. 4 (April 1984), p. 23.

49. E. V. Anisimov, "U zhurnala dolzhna byt' svoia pozitsiia," in the symposium titled "'Kruglyi stol': Istoricheskaia nauka v usloviiakh perestroiki," *Voprosy istorii*, 1988, no. 3, p. 17.

50. See the report titled "'Belye piatna': Ot emotsii k faktam," in *Literaturnaia gazeta*, 11 May 1988.

51. V. I. Vernads'kyi, "Ukrains'ke pytannia i rosiis'ka hromads'kist'," *Moloda hvardiia* (Kiev), 12 March 1988; translated in *Soviet Ukrainian Affairs* (London), vol. 2, no. 2 (Summer 1988), pp. 22–26. The main Ukrainian literary journal *Vitchyzna* (Kiev) published the whole Vernadsky text in the June 1988 issue.

52. Paul Goble, "Gorbachev and the Soviet Nationality Problem," in Maurice Friedberg and Heyward Isham, eds., *Soviet Society under Gorbachev* (Armonk, NY: M. E. Sharpe, 1987), p. 99.

53. Milan Švankmajer, "The Gendarme of Europe," *Dějiny a současnost* (Prague), vol. 11, no. 4 (April 1969), quoted by Antonin J. Liehm, "East Central Europe and the Soviet Model," *Problems of Communism*, vol. 30, no. 5 (September–October 1981), p. 52.

CHAPTER 2

Nationality Elites and Political Change in the Soviet Union

Steven L. Burg

It has long been noted that Soviet officials whose careers have been associated with specific economic functions or activities tend, in the course of policy debates, to advance those economic interests. Similarly, long career association with a particular territory often produces cadres sympathetic to the interests of that territory, or "localism." Both these arguments may be usefully applied to the ethnonational dimension of Soviet politics as well. For cadres drawn from the indigenous nationalities, the coinciding ethnic, economic, and administrative-territorial cleavages that divide the minority nationality territories in the periphery from the Russian political center of the USSR are likely to lend both additional strength and an ethnic dimension to the representation of local interests.

Under emerging conditions, the participation of such representatives of ethnic interests in central policy-making processes should have profound consequences for the development of the Soviet political order, for their presence introduces greater complexity into the decision-making process by increasing the representation of divergent interests. The emphasis on openness in policy debate under Gorbachev makes it likely that the representation of divergent interests will give rise to conflicts, and the ethnic implications of such conflicts are almost certain to increase the difficulty of resolving them to the satisfaction of all the participants. If prolonged, such conflicts might very well lead cadres who are dissatisfied with the outcome—whether minority or Russian—to question established rules for decision making.

Questioning of the "rules of the game" introduces an element of instability into any political system. Under present Soviet conditions such questioning provides yet another powerful impetus to the redistribution of power in the Soviet political order. Precisely for this reason, then, the Russians, who constitute the senior political leadership in Moscow, can be expected carefully to limit the role of minority elites in the Soviet policy-making process.

Multinationality and Political Change

Claude Ake has defined political stability as "the regularity of the flow of political exchanges." He argues that "there is political stability to the extent

24

that members of society restrict themselves to the behavior patterns that fall within the limits imposed by political role expectations." Political behavior is "irregular" when it violates established patterns or expectations.[1] Following this definition, stability in the elite decision-making process may be defined as adherence to the sometimes explicit, but usually implicit, rules for decision making. Elite behavior is "irregular" when it violates established patterns or expectations, i.e., when it violates the rules for decision making.

Elite expectations define the limits of acceptable, or regular, political behavior. Behavior that is at first irregular but which becomes acceptable with time leads to change that might be characterized as reform. Sustained irregular behavior that is not accepted, however, may become the basis for a challenge to the legitimacy of existing rules for decision making and thereby lead to systemic change.

One of the most important sources of irregular elite behavior is structural— the conflicting political demands placed upon those who occupy elite roles. In the Soviet case, for example, members of the central decision-making elite are expected to function both as agents of central power, who use their local authority to enforce central policy, and as representatives of local interests, who use their elite positions to secure resources and other advantages for their "constituencies." In some cases, and particularly in instances of ethnic self-assertion, these roles come into conflict.

Declining performance on the part of decision-making bodies is another important impetus to irregular elite behavior. The ability of any group to make decisions is affected by its composition. Heterogeneous groups are less efficient decision-making organs than homogeneous ones.[2] Ethnicity is only one of many potentially salient bases of heterogeneity in the Soviet leadership. But, given the coincidence between ethnic and other divisions in the USSR, even declining performance arising from other differences in the leadership is likely to affect different ethnic elites differently.

Except at the extremes, it is difficult to know whether irregular behavior is even taking place, let alone whether it will result in reform or systemic change, or whether it will simply be suppressed. Open, publicly expressed intraelite disputes and policy deadlocks are usually indications that such behavior is occurring. Attempts to politicize ethnic identity and to mobilize popular support through public demonstrations are almost certain evidence of such behavior. But in the absence of such evidence, this is usually an ex post facto judgment.

Minority Elites in the Soviet Leadership

In the post-Stalin period, and especially during Brezhnev's tenure as general secretary, increasing numbers of minority elite cadres achieved membership in key leadership groups in the USSR's ethnonational territories and, to a lesser extent, in central decision-making organs. At the center of Soviet power, as many as six first secretaries of non-Russian republican party organizations were included in the Brezhnev Politburo at one time, although the majority of these held only candidate status.[3] In the Central Committee, only Ukrainians and, less extensively, Kazakhs were granted more than a token presence under Brezhnev. Beyond these two groups, most non-Russians in the Central Committee seem to have been there ex officio, as chairmen of republican Councils of Ministers or Supreme Soviet presidiums.[4]

Yet, even this limited participation appears to have contributed to the decisional malaise under Brezhnev. Despite the enormous importance of the proposal to divert the flow of Siberian rivers to Central Asia, for example, the Brezhnev leadership was unable to overcome the obvious interregional conflict over this issue and settle on a consistent policy. There can be little doubt that the presence of Central Asian party secretaries in the Politburo contributed to the apparent inability of that body to decide the matter. Indeed, it was resolved only after their participation had been reduced, and then the decision went "against" them. That there were substantial objective reasons for such a negative decision, entirely apart from the nationality dimension of the issue, only lends additional support to the argument that membership in the Politburo can, by itself, provide minority elites with policy leverage otherwise unavailable to them.

Mikhail Gorbachev made no effort at the outset of his tenure as general secretary to define a nationalities policy per se. But he appeared less sensitive to nationality concerns than his predecessors, and inclined to reverse the "nativization" of local elite structures, the expansion of local autonomy for native elites in the national territories, and the growing participation by non-Russians at the center that had taken place under Brezhnev. Indeed, in a major ideological address in December 1984, shortly before he became general secretary, Gorbachev suggested in a brief remark that he intended to reevaluate the role of nationality in the "selection and placement of cadres in Moscow and in the republics alike,"[5] thereby calling into question minority elites' claim to *both* participation at the center *and* priority in the appointment of local officials.

In his address to the Twenty-seventh Party Congress in February 1986, Gorbachev made it clear that nationality issues would be secondary to economic considerations in the formulation of policy. He emphasized the need to "accelerate the country's social and economic development" by switching from the long-standing Stalinist strategy of extensive economic growth to a strategy of intensive growth. This would require, he argued, a "restructuring of the economy" through "radical reform." Such reform would aim at "enhancing the effectiveness of the centralized management of the economy and strengthening the role of the center in realizing the basic goals of the party's economic strategy and in determining the rates and proportions of the development of the national economy and its balance." Emphasizing control from the center, Gorbachev further spoke of "ensuring the unconditional priority of countrywide interests over the interests of branches and regions" as an "urgent task," and called for the subordination of the republican economies ". . . to the development of the single national economic complex . . ."[6]

The implications of these views for nationalities policy were made explicit by Yegor Ligachev, secretary of the Central Committee in charge of party ideology and personnel, in his speech before the Congress. He cautioned that the "clear" need for cadres from the minority nationalities did not legitimize "parochial, localistic sentiments." Such attitudes "impeded the promotion to leadership posts of representatives of all nationalities, and they have impeded exchanges of cadres among regions and exchanges of experienced officials between republics and the center and among the country's districts and cities." In other words, they interfered with the free assignment of Russian or other Slavic cadres from the center or from other regions to leading posts in the minority territories, and thereby reduced the center's control. Ligachev reiterated Gorbachev's demand that no organization or territory remain outside the influence of the center. By presenting an undifferentiated list of major cities, republics, and RSFSR oblasts as examples of territories that should be subject to central control, he implied that the non-Russian republics no longer enjoyed any special status in the party hierarchy.[7]

This emphasis on central control, and the consequent downgrading of the status of national territories, was reflected in elite personnel appointments. The pattern of dismissals and promotions in the years following Brezhnev's death, at the center and in the regions, made it clear that the policy of according circumscribed participation at the center to minority elites, characteristic of the late 1970s and early 1980s, had ended. The new Belorussian, Georgian, Azerbaidzhani, and Uzbek party leaders were not granted the candidate memberships in the Politburo held by their predecessors. Even the first secretary of the Ukrainian party, always a full member of the Politburo and a powerful figure in Soviet politics, came under pressure from the center and was replaced.

As a result of these changes, the central leadership under Gorbachev has undergone a process of "Russianization." The key positions from which the decision-making process is controlled are now occupied entirely by Russians or by non-Russians with centrally based, rather than regionally based, careers. For example, Nikolai Sliunkov, a Belorussian who was promoted to secretary of the Central Committee, had long been a central Gosplan official before his short tenure as first secretary of the Belorussian party organization. Among ethnic minority elites at the center with substantial regional career experience, only Geidar Aliev and Eduard Shevardnadze benefitted from post-Brezhnev turnovers, but the former was soon removed, while the latter, it can be argued, was moved to a position (minister of foreign affairs) from which he was *less* likely to influence the domestic policy-making process.

The sharp reversal in policy implied by these changes was reflected in an article by a leading Soviet expert on nationalities policy, Yulian Bromlei, in *Kommunist* in mid-1986.[8] Bromlei argued that ethnic identity should not be the basis of either privilege or discrimination in the selection and appointment of leading cadres. In particular, he stressed the need to pay greater attention to ensuring the representation of non-native groups in elite positions in the republics. In effect, he was calling for an end to the policy of "affirmative action" for non-Russians that had characterized the Brezhnev years.

Bromlei was not indifferent to the potential consequences of such a policy shift, however. He noted that increasing levels of education among the non-Russians were producing a revolution of rising expectations, especially with respect to career opportunities. Frustrations arising from unfulfilled expectations, he warned, could be a major stimulus to nationalism.

Ethnosociology and the Revolution of Rising Expectations

Bromlei's warning was undoubtedly based on the findings produced by empirical research into interethnic relations carried out by the ethnosociologists in the Academy of Sciences' Institute of Ethnography, of which he was the head, and by the many researchers associated with the Scientific Council for the Nationality Problem of the Social Sciences Section of the Presidium of the USSR Academy of Sciences, of which he is the chairman. Throughout the 1970s and 1980s, these scholars conducted a series of empirical research projects exploring the nature of social development among the nationalities and the impact of general social factors on the nature of internationality relations. Major scholarly investigations were conducted in the Tatar ASSR, Estonia, Moldavia, several regions of the RSFSR, and Uzbekistan, as were numerous other smaller or more specialized studies in these and other areas of the Soviet Union.[9] A systematized summary of their findings is presented in an important volume, *Sotsial'no-kul'turnyi oblik sovetskikh natsii*, edited by Bromlei and Yurii Arutiunian, but written collaboratively by several of the scholars directing this research.[10]

The researchers report a positive association between socioeconomic status and favorable attitudes toward internationality relations; that is, the higher a respondent's education, and the higher the professional level of his employment, the more likely he is to report favorable attitudes toward interaction with other nationalities. "Education is a powerful factor . . . shown to be positively associated with a favorable orientation toward internationality relations everywhere and among all groups. [It is] also positively associated with knowledge of Russian, itself powerfully associated with a favorable orientation."[11] The professional level of employment of a respondent, however, seemed to be associated with internationality relations only indirectly.

The Soviet researchers point out that these findings were obtained at a time of substantial upward social mobility, which ". . . could not but prompt in people a sense of satisfaction of national interests, which facilitated the formation of friendly interethnic orientations."[12] Among those "overeducated" for their current employment status, and those not satisfied with either opportunities for expressing initiative on the job or the job itself, attitudes toward internationality relations were not as positive.[13] And, where the demand for employment exceeded the supply of positions, "this situation created in people a certain sense of competition in the labor sphere, which in a multinational context was to some degree projected onto national relations."[14] These findings suggest it was the experience of upward mobility rather than the social status of the current occupations of respondents that was the source of favorable attitudes.

But upward mobility ". . . is not always accompanied by adequate improvement in the internationality orientation of people, since it is accompanied by [increased] expectations . . ."[15] Indeed, Soviet researchers found that the achievement by nationality groups of "significant representation" in desirable positions ". . . created on the one hand a sense of satisfaction, but on the other—in accord with the law of rising expectations—gave birth to really high demands, especially among the intelligentsia."[16]

The process of socioeconomic and cultural development that made accelerated rates of upward social mobility possible was also found to have "stimulated the development of national self-awareness . . ."[17] Thus, paradoxically, it is the very success of Soviet developmental efforts that contributes to the rise of national self-awareness among the peripheral nationalities, and it is the main beneficiaries of Soviet-sponsored social and economic development, the rising native elites, who are likely to experience the strongest increase in such self-awareness.

Ethnosociologists note an overall trend in educational enrollments toward the preparation of a surplus of indigenous specialist personnel.[18] This trend is reinforced by widespread aspirations among the indigenous populations for high-status employment for their children, aspirations that are most widespread among those who themselves enjoy such status.[19] And it is a trend unlikely to be counterbalanced by the migration of surplus indigenous cadres to other, cadres-deficient regions of the USSR. Soviet research reveals that indigenous specialist personnel have not migrated out of their native republics even when faced with a shortage of opportunities for appropriate employment.[20] This suggests that, if the increased national self-awareness that comes with continuing development of these republics is not to become the basis of disaffection, the Soviet leadership will have to create an ever increasing number of professional positions in the ethnic peripheries and reserve an increasing proportion of them for indigenous personnel.

Among the republics and regions surveyed by Soviet ethnosociologists, this connection between socioeconomic conditions and ethnic relations proved strongest in Uzbekistan, selected for study as representative of a group of "eastern" republics that also included Kirghizia, Tadzhikistan, and Turkmenia.[21] ". . . [T]he more eastern and southern the national regions," they concluded, "the more powerful the influence of traditional ethnic peculiarities of the social life of nations on their everyday behavior."[22] Among nations of the western or European "type," "such social indicators . . . as education, socio-professional composition, increase in qualifications, social activity, [and] intensity of cultural life were practically independent of national characteristics."[23] In effect, Estonians, Russians, and "to a certain degree" Georgians and Moldavians were characterized by ". . . a certain autonomy of purely ethnic relations."[24]

Thus, the impact of ethnicity on behavior, and especially attitudes toward internationality relations, might be susceptible to management through social and economic policies among the so-called "eastern" nationalities. But they might also be affected unintentionally by policies seemingly unrelated, at least in the minds of the leadership, to nationality.

Bromlei proved prescient when precisely the kind of displacement of frustration against which he warned and an attempt by native elites to mobilize ethnic identity followed the removal of Dinmukhamed Kunaev, a Kazakh, as first secretary of the Kazakh party organization in December 1986. Kunaev was replaced by Gennadii Kolbin, a Russian. Two days of violent street demonstrations took place in Alma-Ata immediately following the public announcement of his appointment. The demonstrations were organized and carried out, with the apparent support of local Kazakh officials, by Kazakh university students and faculty members resentful of the appointment of a Russian as first secretary and fearful of an attempt to reduce the number of elite positions in the local party and state bureaucracies available to them. Kolbin called in the military to suppress the demonstrations and restore order, and moved to have the organizers and participants arrested or expelled from the university.[25]

In the aftermath of these events, a new "council for work with cadres" was created within the Kazakhstan Central Committee apparatus, with the new Russian first secretary as its chairman. The announced tasks of this council included ensuring ethnic proportionality in the local elite, ending the reservation of certain positions for cadres of a particular nationality, and even training native cadres for promotion to central organs.[26] Gorbachev reinforced this assertion of a proportionality rule in the assignment of cadres by declaring a month later, at the January 1987 CPSU Central Committee plenum, that "it is necessary to follow firmly the line of all nations and ethnic groups of the country being represented in party, state and economic bodies, *including at all-union level* [emphasis added], so that the composition of the leading cadres most fully reflect the country's national structure."[27]

The demonstrations in Alma-Ata were followed by organized mass demonstrations by Estonians, Latvians, and Lithuanians marking their loss of independence and calling for increased local autonomy, by Crimean Tatars seeking restoration of their homeland, and by Armenians seeking to reestablish Armenian sovereignty over their co-nationals in the Nagorno-Karabakh region of the neighboring Azerbaidzhani republic.

These events seem to have sensitized Gorbachev to the ethnic dimension of Soviet politics. Only a month after the Alma-Ata events, in a report to the January 1987 plenum of the Central Committee, he conceded that national feelings deserve "respect," and that policies affecting nationality relations required "special tact and care."[28] In his report to the June 1987 plenum he included ethnic group interests among those he identified as interests that would have to be taken into account in the policy-making process.[29] And in his report to the February 1988 plenum, he elevated the national question to an issue of "vital" importance.[30] Thus, as ethnic minorities have become more assertive, Gorbachev's views appear to have progressed from outright indifference to the ethnic dimension of Soviet politics to open concern to respond to ethnic sensitivities. Indeed, as the ethnic conflict between Armenians and Azerbaidzhanis intensified, Gorbachev even allowed himself to become personally involved by meeting with Armenian activists and by making vague promises to redress their grievances.[31]

But this sensitivity was tempered by an obvious commitment to maintaining the system of power. Two weeks after the Alma-Ata events, *Pravda* published a reaffirmation of the center's commitment to transfer cadres from region to region as it saw fit,[32] a position reiterated in January 1987 by the Central Committee.[33] Gorbachev attempted to deflect the mobilization of nationalist sentiment in the Baltic by granting limited authority to so-called popular front organizations. And he refused to permit any redrawing of republican boundaries in the Caucasus. Instead, Gorbachev resorted to the threat of force in an attempt to suppress mass discontent.[34]

Despite his rhetorical support for minority participation at the center, Gorbachev has made no effort to bring non-Russian elites into the central political leadership. Instead, he has dismissed native party leaders in Estonia, Uzbekistan, Armenia and Azerbaidzhan, and replaced them with other native cadres who were expected to pay closer attention to central priorities than to local ones by virtue of their prior isolation from local political influences as the result of service in central bureaucracies or even outside the country, in the diplomatic corps.

Multinationality and Policy Conflict

The promotion of minority elites to positions in the central leadership could be expected to complicate an already difficult task. With the slowdown in the Soviet economy, the task of Soviet decision makers has moved quite definitively away from the *distribution* of resources and toward their *redistribution*. Following William Zimmerman,[35] it may be argued that distribution decisions are accompanied by a politics based on implicit rules of exchange and carried out by solitary actors and function-based groups that form around issues, operate on the basis of fluid alliances, and are committed to operating within the "rules of the game." Such politics are premised on the availability of sufficient resources to ensure an equitable distribution of the burdens and benefits of policy decisions. And they are characterized by relatively low levels of intraelite conflict. In the Soviet Union, resources were not sufficiently abundant to permit an equal distribution of burdens and benefits. Instead, a stable coalition of institutional groups enforced, over time, a set of rules for decision making that resulted in an asymmetrical distribution of resources to their own benefit.

Now, however, the Soviet commitment to a "restructuring" of the economy requires central decision makers to *redistribute* rather than distribute resources.

Their decisions—if experience elsewhere is any guide—are likely to take on the characteristics of a "politics of scarcity" or, to use Seweryn Bialer's term, a "politics of stringency."[36] Redistribution approximates a "zero-sum game," in which the availability and divisibility of resources are low, and the distribution of the burdens and benefits of policy decisions is unequal. Even more importantly, as Zimmerman points out, it tends to be accompanied by the rise of political actors based on social or solidarity groups, including both class and ethnicity. Such group formation occurs either spontaneously, as the result of perceived deprivation, or as the result of mobilization by elites attempting to increase their political resources in the policy-making process.[37]

The multinational condition of the USSR impinges on all policy issues and decisions. As Paul Goble has suggested, "all Soviet institutions exist in a multinational milieu, and all policies are affected by this environment. Conversely, all Soviet policies have ethnic consequences."[38] But multinationality appears particularly salient for questions of regional economic development. Differences in the patterns of economic development, if not outright inequalities, reinforce rather than cut across ethnonational boundaries in the Soviet Union.[39] The potential for national unrest in such a situation is obvious. Michael Hechter has argued, for example, that "where economic disadvantages are superimposed upon objective cultural differences"—that is, where a pattern of "internal colonialism" exists—"political demands are most likely to be made on a status-group basis."[40]

Western analysts of the regional economy of the Soviet Union suggest the existence of a relationship between Central Asia and the USSR that closely parallels Hechter's model of "internal colonialism." The development of Central Asia has taken place in an essentially dependent mode. The region still has "by far the least manufacturing per capita, with the relative level actually declining in every republic . . . ," and its "resources . . . are shipped overwhelmingly to the European USSR and for export in virtually unprocessed form."[41] These are two of the key structural characteristics of internal colonialism. Nancy Lubin carefully documents the ethnic stratification of the Uzbek economy,[42] and in so doing provides powerful evidence for the existence of a third characteristic of internal colonialism, what Hechter calls a "cultural division of labor."[43]

The "fit" to Hechter's model is not precise. The measurement of regional living standards and particularly per capita income, another key variable in Hechter's model, for example, remains uncertain. However, even Lubin, who argues strongly against the probability of national unrest in the region, suggests the existence of a set of attitudes and behaviors among the native population of Uzbekistan that correspond very closely to those hypothesized by Hechter.[44] Indeed, Soviet ethnosociologists report that "when nationalities in contact with one another are represented unequally in [visible positions of privilege] . . . these professional privileges are in everyday consciousness associated with nationality." And they concede that such inequality is evident on a daily basis "as a result of the varying proportions of the nationalities in the urban population."[45] Thus, current conditions point to the increasing salience of nationality at both the elite and mass levels in Uzbekistan and other "eastern type" republics. And a similar argument could be made for other national territories in the USSR.

Redistributive policies aimed at economic sectors might be expected to give rise to something more akin to class-based rather than ethnic politics. But even sectoral issues have important regional or republican dimensions in the Soviet Union. Given the extensive overlap among economic regions, republics, and nationalities, it is difficult for the leadership to exclude any of these dimensions from consideration in the decision-making process, or even to keep them separate. This would become even more difficult if elite "representatives" of the minority nationality territories were to participate in these decisions.

Analyses by Howard Biddulph and George Breslauer suggest that, when given the opportunity to do so, cadres responsible for the administration of territorial "constituencies" function as the advocates of local interests.[46] Even in the open contexts of party congresses, Central Committee meetings, and contributions to the controlled media, republican and oblast first secretaries alike attempt to increase the resources available for the development of their territories by altering the priority assigned to issues on the policy agenda or even by altering the agenda itself. Some of the resentment of officials in the ethnic territories surfaced at the Nineteenth Party Conference in June 1988, as when Vladimir Melnikov, first secretary of the Komi ASSR, complained bitterly about the exploitation of his constituency's natural resources and the failure of the center to provide capital resources in return.[47]

It is important to note that attempts to secure an increased share of available resources not only pit regional cadres against the established priorities of the center, but against each other as well. Thus, increased participation by minority elites in central decision making need not necessarily result in the emergence of a bloc of non-Russian leaders united in opposition to Moscow, but it would certainly introduce greater complexity and conflict in decision making, arising out of increased competition for resources. Biddulph suggests, in fact, that competition among regional elites has increased as resources have become more scarce[48]—a relationship widely noted in the more general literature on multiethnic politics.[49]

Minority elite participation in central decision making need not result in increased support for decentralization and reform either. Some regions of the USSR have clearly benefited from the power of the central authorities to transfer resources from region to region according to political, rather than strictly economic, criteria. If the participation of cadres from such regions were to increase at the center, and these cadres were, at the same time, to continue to function as the advocates of local economic interests, they might become strong supporters of continued central control and its use to transfer resources from region to region, irrespective of the impact of such transfers on economic efficiency.

At least until the early 1960s, the central leadership remained committed to "both massive transfer payments from the more developed regions to the less developed ones and an affirmative action system designed to place non-Russians in at least the most visible if not the most powerful positions at the republic and local level."[50] These policies were aimed at securing the political integration of the peripheral territories, as well as increasing their contributions to the economic development of the country as a whole. They were legitimized by the incompatibility of vast interregional inequalities with an essentially egalitarian ideology. However, as these inequalities were reduced or, at least, as the level of development of the peripheries improved, the commitment to these policies weakened. That commitment seems to have disappeared almost entirely as concern for the economy as a whole has increased.

Moreover, there is also an ethnic dimension to this declining commitment. Paul Goble has suggested that

> as the inequalities were reduced and in certain areas even reversed, many Russians came to the conclusion that what had appeared to be reasonable affirmative action for the non-Russians was in fact unreasonable reverse discrimination against themselves. Their anger, which surfaced increasingly often in the 1960s, 70s, and 80s, was only increased by the decline of their own region, their direct experience in non-Russian regions, the attitude of many non-Russians that this form of affirmative action was theirs by right, and the findings of many economists that past investment in the periphery had combined with inefficient, even corrupt republic-level management to slow down the country's rate of economic growth. As a result, many Russian officials have been seeking to reduce the importance of nationality in the system both for instrumental reasons and as a way of enhancing their own clout.[51]

Given the overwhelming size of the RSFSR and the numerical preponderance of Russians in the USSR, the pattern of dependent development of the peripheries, and the "Russianization" of the central leadership in the post-Brezhnev period, reducing the importance of nationality in the system, or, as Gorbachev stated at the Twenty-seventh Party Congress, stressing the "unconditional priority of countrywide interests" will inevitably, if not intentionally, produce a tendency to equate Russian interests with "countrywide" interests.

The reintroduction of minority cadres into the central elite, however, might make such a tendency more controversial. Experience elsewhere has demonstrated that where elite participants in the policy-making process represent ethnonational "constituencies" with divergent economic interests, it becomes very difficult for them to support policies ostensibly adopted for the "common good" when these have significantly asymmetrical consequences. Minority elite participants in central decision making, therefore, might soon make it difficult for the Russians, who now dominate the decision-making process, to preserve one of the fundamental "rules" of decision making in the post-Brezhnev era: that decisions—and especially economic decisions—be made on the basis of the "common interest." Such disputes over what the "common good" actually is quickly turn into disputes over how to determine it. In other words, they turn into intraelite disputes over the "rules of the game"—which are, even in the absence of mass unrest, profoundly destabilizing.

Minority elite cadres who participate in central decision-making processes need not necessarily question the emerging "rules of the game," however. The recent examples of Ukrainian party first secretaries in the Politburo are instructive in this respect. On the one hand, there is the case of Petr Shelest, who presided over a nativization of the Ukrainian party, sought to limit central interference in republican cadres policies, advocated and defended regional economic interests against the center, supported (if not encouraged) the development of Ukrainian culture, and may even have given some support to Ukrainian intellectual and cultural dissent.[52] On the other hand, Shelest's successor, Vladimir Shcherbitsky, oversaw the restoration of central control over the assignment of cadres and the further Russification of the republic, and supported the subordination of Ukrainian regional economic interests to centrally determined, "all-union" priorities.[53]

Yet very little in the position of Ukraine in the Soviet economy or in central economic priorities had changed to prompt this shift in behavior. Part of the explanation of these differences in their behavior surely lies in these individuals' differing relationships to power politics among central leaders: Shelest had been the protégé of Podgorny, while Shcherbitsky had been a protégé of Brezhnev. As long as Podgorny remained a key figure in the leadership and that leadership remained divided, Shelest could exercise his authority relatively independently. But as Podgorny's power faded and Brezhnev's increased, Shelest's room for maneuver disappeared and, eventually, Brezhnev replaced him with his own supporter, Shcherbitsky. Shcherbitsky, however, inherited a position significantly more constrained by Brezhnev's emergence as leader and his consolidation and extension of central power. The existence of a cohesive "core leadership," coupled with dependence on one or more members of that core for elite status, imposes powerful constraints on the behavior of any territorial elite—minority or otherwise—elevated to the central decision-making organs. In the post-Brezhnev era, with the emergence of a new leadership at the center and with a new set of policy priorities and role expectations for other members of the Soviet elite, Shcherbitsky (and others) became subject to new pressures and constraints.

In the case of Central Asia, those elevated to the Politburo have approximated the "Shcherbitsky model" more closely than the "Shelest model." The Kazakh first secretary, Dinmukhamed Kunaev, earned promotion to full Politburo status through his career associations with Brezhnev and, like Shcherbitsky, was constrained by a combination of the cohesion of the central leadership and his dependency on Brezhnev. Former Uzbek first secretary, Nuratdin Mukhitdinov, had become a candidate and later full member of the Politburo, and then secretary of the Central Committee, under the personal sponsorship of Khrushchev at a time when the latter was engaged in a struggle for power within the leadership, but soon lost those positions. The only lasting impact of his tenure was to pave the way for the promotion of Sharaf Rashidov, his successor as first secretary of the Uzbek party organization, to candidate membership in the Politburo upon his own ouster.[54]

If long tenure is any indication, then Rashidov appears to have behaved in accordance with the expectations of at least some of his status superiors in the Politburo. It is worth noting that these expectations apparently allowed for a considerable amount of "interest articulation," as suggested, for example, by Rashidov's advocacy of local claims with respect to the diversion of Siberian rivers. Moreover, as Donald Carlisle has suggested,[55] Rashidov was able to direct resources to his own *local* preferences. But his actions, which had been possible because of the extensive autonomy granted to him and other republican first secretaries, are being posthumously attacked as "corruption" by the leadership that has assumed power in Moscow since 1985.

The leadership that emerged under Gorbachev initially sponsored a campaign against local autonomy, not only in Central Asia, but throughout the Soviet Union. In 1985–86 they replaced native party leaders in Kazakhstan, Tadzhikistan, Turkmenia, and Kirghizia, accusing them, through charges of "corruption," of misusing their authority. In 1988 they removed Rashidov's successor as Uzbek first secretary, Inamzhon Usmankhodzhaev, and subjected him to charges of corruption as well. Careful not to repeat the mistake committed in Kazakhstan, where a Russian was brought in to assert central control, the leadership in Moscow appointed an Uzbek as his successor. But they selected an individual who spent fifteen of the previous eighteen years abroad as a Soviet diplomat and, therefore, was expected to have fewer connections to local influence networks.[56] In Transcaucasia, the Armenian first secretary, who had already been the target of criticism for failing to end "corruption" in that republic, was removed in May 1988 in response to the outbreak of ethnic conflict there. At the same time, the Azerbaidzhani party leader was removed. Ethnically native cadres were appointed to both the Armenian and the Azerbaidzhani leadership posts. But in the case of Azerbaidzhan, Moscow again selected a diplomat with few immediate connections to local politics. In a similar move a month later, an Estonian who had served abroad as a Soviet diplomat was appointed first secretary of the Estonian party. The first secretaries of Latvia and Lithuania were replaced in October 1988, and those of Ukraine and Moldavia in the fall of 1989, completing the change in political leadership in the increasingly volatile national republics.

Minority nationality cadres appear unlikely to attain elite status in the future, and are almost certain not to retain such status for very long, unless they adhere closely to the role definitions being advanced by the central leadership. However, as long as such cadres remain subject to pressure from below in the form of popular nationalism, or in the form of local material demands that conflict with central policies, minority elite cadres will continue to experience the kind of role conflict that gives rise to irregular behavior. The removal of Usmankhodzhaev in Uzbekistan for engaging in precisely the kind of corruption he was appointed to clean up, the tolerance and even support of expressions of nationalist sentiment and of demands for local autonomy shown by Baltic leaders,[57] the attempt by the Russian first secretary of the Kazakh party to learn the Kazakh language and speak it at Kazakh party meetings,[58] and the inability of both the Armenian and Azerbaidzhani party leaders to quell popular unrest are only the most vivid evidence of such pressures and the resulting role conflict.

Under what conditions, then, are minority elites, and especially those elevated to participation in central decision-making bodies such as the Politburo, likely to manifest "irregular" behavior? Albert Hirschman has suggested that the articulation of policy grievances intended to effect change—what he calls "voice"—is possible when four conditions are present: first, when there is a perceived deterioration in the performance of the regime; second, when an individual has sufficient influence and bargaining power to create the prospect of success; third, when success promises worthwhile benefits; and fourth, when "exit," or withdrawal, is a possibility, but not "too easy or too attractive."[59]

The first and last of these conditions appear already to be present in the Soviet case. Deterioration of the economic performance of the system as a whole is now widely acknowledged by the Soviet leadership itself, and motivates the changes now underway. For many of the peripheral minority territories, the shift toward redistribution of resources toward sectors of the economy concentrated in the European and Siberian territories promises to increase economic stringencies. Since secession does not yet appear to be a realistic alternative, we may conceive of the subversion of central priorities, or corruption, as a substitute for "withdrawal." But, as the removals of local elites in Uzbekistan, Tadzhikistan, Kirghizia, Turkmenia, and Kazakhstan suggest, this is not going to be "too easy or too attractive."

If we consider mass demonstrations as a manifestation of "voice," then it is clear that—at least for broad segments of the native elite or near-elite in Kazakhstan, and for both cultural elites and the mass populations in Armenia and the Baltic republics—the second and third conditions are present as well. Gorbachev's emphasis on *glasnost'* appears to have increased hopes among Armenians, Estonians, Latvians, and Lithuanians of achieving changes they obviously value very highly.

In Uzbekistan, the pattern of internal colonialism noted earlier creates fertile ground for mass political action. Indeed, Lubin testifies to the presence of widespread popular discontent among Uzbeks based precisely on their perceptions of a deterioration in economic performance and linked to an awareness of the material consequences of the cultural division of labor in that republic. Moreover, successive demonstrations in Kazakhstan, the Baltic republics, Transcaucasia, and Moldavia suggest that mass unrest engenders substantially fewer costs than in the past and has thus become a more probable instrument of local leverage against the center. Indeed, the direct involvement of Gorbachev in the Armenian-Azerbaidzhani conflict, the material concessions made by Moscow to local Armenian interests in the hope of quieting the unrest, the responsiveness of local Armenian and Azerbaidzhani politicians to popular pressures, and coverage of these events in the central media have provided a clear demonstration to ethnic elites, intellectuals, and political entrepreneurs throughout the Soviet Union of the power available to them by politicizing and mobilizing ethnic identity.

Thus, it would seem that the "only" conditions not yet present for the emergence of intraelite conflict over the "rules of the game" in Soviet politics are the participation in central decision-making bodies of minority elites who have enough influence and bargaining power to suggest the prospect of at least some success in altering the pattern of decisions, and a decision by them that the benefits of doing so are worth the effort.

Prospects

Economic "restructuring" has introduced serious new social problems into Soviet politics. It is already producing unemployment, inflation, and recession.[60] It will inevitably produce a redistribution of resources and increased levels of material inequality among individual workers and between branches of the economy. Indeed, the leadership has sanctioned the rise of such inequalities as a necessary incentive to worker productivity. But, as a result of regional economic specialization and differential rates of employment of ethnic groups in various branches of the economy even within regions, inequalities between ethnic groups and regions are also likely to increase. At the same time, "democratization" of the political system has the effect of subjecting local political elites all over the Soviet Union to increased pressure to respond to local interests. This has created significant incentives for even those ethnic elites who remain loyal to the Soviet system to politicize and mobilize ethnic identities as a means of solidifying their local support and increasing their leverage in the political struggle for resources. Under these conditions, interregional and interethnic conflict over the allocation of resources in the Soviet system is almost certain to increase.

The mobilization of ethnic identity to gain political leverage will not be restricted to the minority nationalities. Russian nationalism and activity by Russian nationalist groups are on the rise. In the short run, the political threat posed by this development may be ameliorated by the fact that change will tend to benefit Russian economic elites and Russian territories. But, as the level of conflict over resources increases, Soviet politics is likely to take on the characteristics of a "zero-sum game" in which any gain by the minority nationalities is seen by Russians as their own loss.

This is especially true for the many Russians in elite positions in the economies of the non-Russian territories. They are coming under increased pressure from natives intent on extending their control to the economic sector now dominated by Russians and other Slavs. For all Russians in the minority territories, the affirmation of native languages and cultures that accompanies any resurgence of nationalist sentiments threatens their claim to equal status in these republics, and perhaps even their sense of personal security. Russians in the non-Russian territories, therefore, represent a potentially powerful base of support for conservative opposition to any changes that might enhance the local autonomy of native elites.

Of course, not all Russians will take conservative positions favoring centralized economic control and political power. Some might favor an outcome that frees the Russian republic—with its vast economic infrastructure, its highly developed intellectual resources, and its enormous energy and other natural resources in Siberia—to pursue a more autonomous developmental strategy. Conversely, non-Russians in regions that have benefited from the investment of Soviet resources might support the continuation of a highly centralized economy and a powerful central authority, as long as it remains committed to regional development. Thus, the ethnic political forces that will come into play as the changes initiated by Gorbachev are implemented are highly unpredictable. The unpredictability of such forces alone argues against permitting them to become a part of the decision-making process.

Even if minority elites do participate in central decision making in the near term, they may not be able to affect the distribution of resources. If brought into the Politburo, they will probably be limited to candidate membership with decidedly subordinate rank. And their "constituencies," with the important exception of Ukraine, simply may not be "important" enough to give them sufficient "bargaining power" to win many concessions to local interests. The "Shelest model," after all, is based on the first secretary of a nationality territory that is *extremely* important to the center on *many* dimensions, not the least of which is the economic. While it is difficult to pinpoint what is and is not, in fact, "important" to the leadership, it is clear that Ukraine is *far* more important than any of the Central Asian, Transcaucasian, or Baltic republics with respect to all but a very few of the policy issues confronting the central leadership, and that the Ukrainian first secretary, therefore, enjoys substantially greater "bargaining power" under any conditions.

Future conflicts between Russians and minority elites over resources, power, and policies may be more susceptible to long-term solution than either the Armenian-Azerbaidzhani conflict over Nagorno-Karabakh, or the conflict between the Baltic peoples and Moscow over local economic and political autonomy. Power and resources, after all, are divisible, while sovereignty is not. But the resolution of such conflicts requires the investment of material and political resources that the Russian leadership of the USSR may deem too valuable to be used for this purpose. Moreover, permitting regional, and especially ethnic, interests to play a role in policy deliberations makes the already difficult task of drafting and implementing plans for reform even more difficult.

The Russians who comprise the senior leadership in Moscow, therefore, may make it personally very costly for any minority elites who engage in "irregular behavior" in the decision-making process. They would like to ensure that these elites decide for themselves that the effort involved in exercising "voice" is not "worth it." Yet, herein lies the danger of the present moment for the Soviet leadership. To the extent that elite politics in the Soviet Union is not merely a struggle over personal power and, therefore, the substance of policy actually "counts" to those who participate in it, minority elites promoted to regional leadership positions or to the center are likely to become increasingly frustrated with their inability to represent the economic and other interests of their regions effectively. Soviet research has already identified a tendency to displace frustrations in other areas onto ethnic relations. The burgeoning Western literature on nationalism in developed societies suggests very clearly that the frustration of such upwardly mobile ethnic elites in the competition for resources often leads them to abandon their attempts to "play" the existing political "game" at all. It leads them instead to turn their attention from "voice" to "exit."

Notes

1. Claude Ake, "A Definition of Political Stability," *Comparative Politics*, vol. 7, no. 2 (January 1975), p. 273.

2. Marvin E. Shaw, *Group Dynamics: The Psychology of Small Group Behavior* (New York: McGraw-Hill, 1981), pp. 249–51.

3. John H. Kress, "Representation of Positions on the CPSU Politburo," *Slavic Review*, vol. 39, no. 2 (June 1980), tables 2 and 3 (pp. 223, 226) and p. 228.

4. Data drawn from the database developed for Joshua B. Spero, "The Soviet Political Elite: Trends in the Composition of the CPSU Central Committee, 1971–1981" (Senior Thesis, Department of Politics, Brandeis University, 1985).

5. M. S. Gorbachev, *Zhivoe tvorchestvo naroda* (Moscow: Izdatel'stvo politicheskoi literatury, 1984), p. 31.

6. *Pravda*, 26 February 1986, as translated in The Current Digest of the Soviet Press, *Current Soviet Policies IX* (Columbus, OH: Current Digest of the Soviet Press, 1986), pp. 10–46.

7. *Pravda*, 28 February 1986, in *Current Soviet Policies IX*, pp. 74–76.

8. *Kommunist*, 1986, no. 8, pp. 78–86.

9. For a description of these studies and a bibliography of the publications they have generated, see Iu. V. Arutiunian et al., *Etnosotsiologiia: Tseli, metody i nekotorye rezul'taty* (Moscow: Nauka, 1984).

10. Iu. V. Arutiunian and Iu. V. Bromlei, eds., *Sotsial'no-kul'turnyi oblik sovetskikh natsii: Po rezul'tatam etnosotsiologicheskogo issledovaniia* (Moscow: Nauka, 1986).

11. Ibid., p. 380.

12. Ibid., p. 359.

13. Ibid., pp. 365–66.

14. Ibid., p. 364.

15. Ibid., p. 378.

16. Ibid., p. 366.

17. Ibid., p. 362.

18. Ibid., pp. 91–92.

19. Ibid., p. 78.

20. Ibid., p. 82.

21. Arutiunian, *Etnosotsiologiia*, p. 112.

22. Arutiunian and Bromlei, *Sotsial'no-kul'turnyi oblik*, p. 430.

23. Ibid., p. 421.

24. Ibid., p. 422.

25. U.S. Department of State, Bureau of Intelligence and Research, *Soviet Nationalities Survey*, no. 13 (n.d.), pp. 1–6.

26. *Kazakhstanskaia pravda*, 18 January 1987, as translated in U.S. Foreign Broadcast Information Service, *Daily Report: Soviet Union* (henceforth FBIS, *Daily Report*), 27 January 1987, pp. R1–R4.

27. TASS report (in English), 27 January 1987, in FBIS, *Daily Report*, 28 January 1987, p. R28.

28. Ibid.

29. *Pravda*, 26 June 1987, in FBIS, *Daily Report*, 26 June 1987, p. R5.

30. *Pravda*, 19 February 1988, in FBIS, *Daily Report*, 19 February 1988, p. 49.

31. *New York Times*, 28 February and 11 March 1988.

32. *Pravda*, 30 December 1986, as cited in *Soviet Nationalities Survey*, no. 13, p. 15.

33. *Pravda*, 29 January 1987, in FBIS, *Daily Report*, 30 January 1987, p. R6.

34. *New York Times*, 20 and 26 July 1988.

35. William Zimmerman, *Open Borders, Nonalignment, and the Political Evolution of Yugoslavia* (Princeton: Princeton University Press, 1987), pp. 52–55. Cf. James Q. Wilson, *American Government* (Lexington, MA: D.C. Heath, 1980), pp. 410ff.

36. Seweryn Bialer, "The Politics of Stringency," *Problems of Communism*, vol. 29, no. 3 (May–June 1980), pp. 19–33.

37. On the role of elites in the mobilization of ethnic identity, see Robert Melson and Howard Wolpe, "Modernization and the Politics of Communalism: A Theoretical Perspective," *American Political Science Review*, vol. 64, no. 4 (December 1970), pp. 1112–30; and Ronald Rogowski, "Causes and Varieties of Nationalism: A Rationalist Account," and "Conclusion," in Edward A. Tiryakian and Ronald Rogowski, eds., *New Nationalisms of the Developed West* (Boston: Allen & Unwin, 1985), pp. 87–108 and 374–87.

38. Paul A. Goble, "Managing the Multinational USSR," *Problems of Communism*, vol. 34, no. 4 (July–August 1985), p. 83.

39. Descriptions of the regional economies can be found in I. S. Koropeckyj and Gertrude E. Schroeder, eds., *Economics of Soviet Regions* (New York: Praeger, 1981). Cf. James W. Gillula, "The Economic Interdependence of Soviet Republics," in U.S. Congress, Joint Economic Committee, *Soviet Economy in a Time of Change* (Washington: U.S. Government Printing Office, 1979), pp. 618–55, esp. pp. 649–52.

40. Michael Hechter, *Internal Colonialism* (Berkeley: University of California Press, 1975), p. 333; cf. pp. 344–46.

41. Leslie Dienes, "Regional Economic Development," in Abram Bergson and Herbert Levine, eds., *The Soviet Economy toward the Year 2000* (London: Allen & Unwin, 1983), pp. 240–41.

42. Nancy Lubin, *Labour and Nationality in Soviet Central Asia: An Uneasy Compromise* (Princeton: Princeton University Press, 1984), pp. 83ff.

43. Hechter, *Internal Colonialism*, pp. 38, 314–16.

44. Lubin, *Labour and Nationality*, pp. 228–35.

45. Arutiunian and Bromlei, *Sotsial'no-kul'turnyi oblik*, p. 379.

46. Howard L. Biddulph, "Local Interest Articulation at CPSU Congresses," *World Politics*, vol. 36, no. 1 (October 1983), pp. 28–52; and George W. Breslauer, "Is There a Generation Gap in the Soviet Political Establishment?: Demand Articulation by RSFSR Provincial Party First Secretaries," *Soviet Studies*, vol. 36, no. 1 (January 1984), pp. 1–25.

47. *Pravda*, 1 July 1988, in FBIS, *Daily Report*, 5 July 1988, pp. 31–32.

48. Biddulph, "Local Interest Articulation," pp. 39ff.

49. See, for example, Martin O. Heisler and B. Guy Peters, *The Implications of Scarcity for the Management of Conflict in Multicultural Societies* (Glasgow: University of Strathclyde, 1978).

50. Paul A. Goble, "Gorbachev and the Soviet Nationality Problem," in Maurice Friedberg and Heyward Isham, eds., *Soviet Society under Gorbachev* (Armonk, NY: M. E. Sharpe, 1987), p. 79. Daniel Bond suggests that these transfers continued through at least 1975; see his "Multiregional Economic Development in the Soviet Union: 1960–1975" (Ph.D. diss., University of North Carolina at Chapel Hill, 1979). Cf. Gillula, "Economic Interdependence."

51. Goble, "Gorbachev and the Soviet Nationality Problem," p. 80.

52. Yaroslav Bilinsky, "Mykola Skrypnyk and Petro Shelest: An Essay on the Persistence and Limits of Ukrainian National Communism," in Jeremy R. Azrael, ed., *Soviet Nationality Policies and Practices* (New York: Praeger, 1978), pp. 119ff.

53. Ibid., and idem, "Shcherbytskyi, Ukraine, and Kremlin Politics," *Problems of Communism*, vol. 32, no. 4 (July–August 1983), pp. 1–20.

54. Donald S. Carlisle, "The Uzbek Power Elite: Politburo and Secretariat (1938–83)," *Central Asian Survey*, vol. 5, no. 3–4 (1986), pp. 91–132, esp. pp. 106–11.

55. Ibid.

56. TASS report (in English), 12 January 1988, in FBIS, *Daily Report*, 12 January 1988, p. 49.

57. *New York Times*, 21 July 1988.

58. TASS report (in English), 3 July 1988, in FBIS, *Daily Report*, 6 July 1988, p. 28.

59. Albert O. Hirschman, *Exit, Voice, and Loyalty* (Cambridge, MA: Harvard University Press, 1970), pp. 4, 37–40, 70–71.

60. U.S. Congress, Joint Economic Committee, Subcommittee on National Security Economics, "Gorbachev's Economic Program: Problems Emerge." A report by the Central Intelligence Agency and the Defense Intelligence Agency, 13 April 1988 (mimeo).

CHAPTER 3

Nationalities and
the Soviet Economy

Gertrude E. Schroeder

The multinational character of the Soviet state, especially the concentration of particular nationalities in historically defined geographic areas, has greatly complicated the formulation of economic policy, planning, and administration in the USSR from the beginning to the present. There are two main reasons for this. First, the central government has had to formulate a set of policies to deal with the fact that initially the constituent republics, each dominated by a distinct ethnic group, differed greatly in levels of economic development, as they did in other ways. Second, the government had to devise a system of economic administration that both took account of the political sensitivities of major nationalities and simultaneously ensured the fulfillment of centrally dictated priorities.

Lenin's much-touted "nationalities policy" has provided the ideological framework for coping with the large economic and cultural disparities among ethnic groups. In Soviet political rhetoric, this policy aimed to promote both the "flourishing" (rastsvet) of all national groups and their "convergence" (sblizhenie) in a variety of respects. In the economic area, the first aspect of policy—"flourishing"—has been defined to mean that each nationality both contributes to and benefits from the drive for rapid industrialization and modernization that has been a priority goal of the Soviet state from the beginning. The latter facet of policy—"convergence"—came to signify the objective of "equalization" (vyravnivanie) of the levels of economic development among the republics and the standards of living among ethnic groups. Initially, such a policy required resource transfers from the richer to the poorer republics, in order to upgrade the education and skills of the work force and to launch the development process in relatively backward regions. The gradual equalization of levels of development among national groups was a stated objective in the directives for the successive five-year plans, including that for 1971–75. After Leonid Brezhnev, in his speech of December 1972 commemorating the fiftieth anniversary of the USSR, declared that "the problem of the equalization of development of the national republics has been resolved, on the whole,"[1] the word "equalization" disappeared from published plan documents. The directives for the Twelfth Five-Year

Plan, for example, state merely that "the harmonious economic and social development of all republics is to be assured. . . . Their contribution to the consolidation of the country's unified national economic complex and to the solution of social tasks is to be increased."[2]

Since its formation, the Soviet Union has been organized administratively on the basis of union republics, each being the designated homeland of a particular indigenous nationality. Lower ranked administrative units— autonomous republics, oblasts, and districts—have been established within several union republics for other, usually smaller, ethnic groups. Like everything else, the economy is administered through this structure, which is thus largely organized on the basis of nationalities and national territories, some of which had formed independent states at one time or another. This momentous fact of political life has seriously complicated the task of economic planning and administration. Not only have the central planners had to take local preferences into account, but they also had to make sure that local interests did not subvert the purposes and priorities of the all-union, Russian-dominated political leadership. In addition, the central authorities have had to strive for a tolerable degree of efficiency in the economic-administrative process. These imperatives have posed a perennial dilemma: how to decentralize decision making without losing economic and/or political control.[3]

Dealing with the nationality factor in economic policy making and management—never an easy task—has become more difficult in recent years. The rate of economic growth has fallen dramatically in the past quarter century, making resource allocation decisions more difficult, particularly in view of the urgent need for a major breakthrough in economic efficiency if the growth slide is to be halted or reversed. Moreover, widely differing demographic trends among regions, while producing little growth in the labor force overall in the 1980s, have resulted in stagnation or decline in some republics and rapid expansion in others, notably in the Muslim republics of Central Asia and Azerbaidzhan. The large size and complexity of the present Soviet economy in itself immensely complicates the task of the central planners, irrespective of the nationality factor. Substantial economic and administrative decentralization would appear imperative, but the political dilemmas posed by decentralization, with their troublesome ethnic dimension, remain a major impediment.

Trends and Relative Levels of Economic Development

The Data

Assessing the economic fortunes of ethnic groups in the USSR is complicated by the fact that the available data pertain not to nationalities but to administrative units—the union republics and their political subdivisions. Because the populations of all republics consist of diverse nationalities, the propriety of using data for the republics as a proxy for the absent data on

TABLE 1. Selected Population Characteristics of Republics and Their Titular Nationalities

Republic	Titular Nationality as Percent of Total Population of Republic		Percentage Concentration of Nationality in Titular Republic		Percent Urban		Educational Attainment [a]	
					Titular Nationality	Republic	Titular Nationality	Republic
	1959	1989	1959	1989	1970	1970	1970	1970
RSFSR	83.3	81.3	85.8	82.6	65.6	62.3	242	238
Ukraine	76.8	72.6	86.3	84.7	45.8	54.5	224	258
Belorussia	81.1	77.8	82.5	78.7	37.1	43.4	186	224
Moldavia	65.4	64.4	85.2	83.2	17.2	31.7	109	170
Lithuania	79.3	79.6	92.5	95.3	45.9	50.2	167	185
Latvia	62.0	52.0	92.7	95.1	51.7	62.5	240	271
Estonia	74.6	61.5	90.3	93.8	54.7	65.0	241	265
Georgia	64.3	70.2	96.6	95.1	42.7	47.8	405	371
Armenia	88.0	93.3	55.7	66.6	62.7	59.5	321	315
Azerbaidzhan	67.5	82.6	84.9	85.4	41.3	50.1	237	262
Kazakhstan	30.0	39.7	77.2	80.3	26.3	50.3	201	221
Kirghizia	40.5	52.3	86.4	88.0	14.5	37.4	196	222
Turkmenia	60.9	71.9	92.2	92.9	31.7	47.9	177	213
Uzbekistan	62.1	71.3	83.8	84.6	23.0	36.6	206	237
Tadzhikistan	53.1	62.3	75.2	75.1	25.5	37.1	162	193

Sources: All calculations based on 1959, 1970, and 1989 census data. Itogi Vsesoiuznoi perepisi naseleniia 1959 goda, 16 vols. (Moscow: Gosstatizdat, 1962). Itogi Vsesoiuznoi perepisi naseleniia 1970 goda (Moscow: Statistika, 1974), vols. 1, 3, and 4. Data for 1989 are from preliminary unpublished results of the 1989 census, and are subject to correction.

[a] Number of persons aged 10 or over with completed secondary education per 1,000 population.

nationality groups requires close examination. To what extent do economic progress and relative levels of economic development shown by the data for republics reflect the experience of their titular nationalities? The information assembled in Table 1 provides a reasonably satisfactory basis for making such judgments.

One primary indicator is the proportion of the titular nationality in the total population of each republic. According to the 1989 census, the titular nationality comprised approximately four-fifths or more of the total population in five republics, between roughly two-thirds and three-fourths of the total in five republics, and between one-half and two-thirds in four others. Only in Kazakhstan did the titular nationality comprise less than half of the population—39.7%. Central Asian nationalities not residing in their own republics tend to live in contiguous republics of Central Asia. With a few exceptions, these proportions did not change greatly between the censuses of 1959 and 1989. In general, the preponderance of the titular nationality has increased in the republics of Central Asia and Transcaucasia and decreased in Latvia and Estonia. On this criterion, the use of republican data to examine the fortunes of their titular nationalities would seem reasonable for all groups except the Kazakhs and possibly the Kirghiz and Latvians. This conclusion is reinforced by the strong proclivity of all nationalities to reside in their own republics; over three-fourths of the members of each group, except the Armenians, did so, according to the 1989 census. For the most part, these ethnic concentration ratios remained stable or increased between 1959 and 1989.

Other information derived from data for the republics helps clarify the experience of their titular nationalities, especially with regard to living standards. According to the 1979 census data, there is a strong tendency for the titular nationalities to reside in rural areas; except for the Russians and Armenians, the titular nationalities were substantially less urbanized than their republics' total population. The margins ranged from 4 percentage points for Lithuanians and Georgians to 23 percentage points for the Kazakhs.[4] Also important for estimating relative levels of income is the fact that titular nationalities tend to be less well educated than other residents of their republics, a condition that correlates with their more rural character. In class composition, moreover, the proportion of collective farmers among the titular nationalities tends to be higher than in the total population of their republics;[5] educational levels tend to be relatively low among the *kolkhozniki*. In 1970, the latest year for which a direct comparison can be made, the number of secondary school graduates per 1,000 persons aged 10 or over was markedly lower for the titular nationalities than for their republics as a whole; the only exceptions were Russians in the RSFSR, Georgians in Georgia, and Armenians in Armenia. Thus, relative to the rest of the population in each republic, titular nationalities are likely to be more concentrated in low wage sectors, such as agriculture, the light and food-processing industries, and the trade and services branches.

Economic Development

Having concluded that, for the most part, the data for the republics reflect reasonably well the overall experience of their respective titular nationalities (with the provisos noted), the evidence depicting trends and relative levels of economic development can now be examined. As statistical indicators, it is necessary, unfortunately, to use the official indexes of national income and industrial production published by the Soviet government. Western scholarship has found that these data seriously overstate real growth for the USSR as a whole.[6] Only one study has attempted to assess this issue for a republic.[7] The study, which developed a Western-type industrial production index for Ukraine, found that the degree of overstatement of industrial growth in the official index was the same as—or possibly a little greater than—that shown by similar studies for the USSR as a whole. Nonetheless, the long-term trends revealed by official and Western-type indexes are similar. Since identical definitions and statistical procedures are supposed to be employed union-wide, one might expect the degree of upward bias to be similar among the republics, if one could allow for the differing sectoral and branch composition of output.

As Table 2 shows, all republics experienced rapid growth during the past quarter century. Growth rates of national income ranged from 4.2% in Turkmenia to 7.8% in Armenia, compared with 5.5% for the USSR as a

TABLE 2.   Average Annual Growth of National Income and Industrial Production
by Republic, 1960-1985

	National Income					Industrial Production				
	1961-1970	1971-1980	1981-1985	1961-1985 Total	Per Capita	1961-1970	1971-1980	1981-1985	1961-1985 Total	Per Capita
USSR	7.1	4.9	3.5	5.5	4.4	8.5	5.9	3.7	6.5	5.4
RSFSR	6.9	5.0	3.5	5.5	4.7	8.0	5.7	3.4	6.2	5.4
Ukraine	6.9	3.9	3.6	5.0	4.2	8.6	5.6	3.4	6.4	5.6
Belorussia	8.2	6.7	5.6	7.1	6.3	11.4	8.8	5.4	9.2	8.4
Moldavia	8.4	4.9	3.3	6.0	4.8	10.8	7.4	4.9	8.3	7.1
Lithuania	9.1	3.8	4.8	6.1	5.0	11.7	6.5	4.6	8.2	7.1
Latvia	7.4	4.9	3.8	5.7	4.9	9.5	5.1	3.3	6.5	5.7
Estonia	7.5	4.9	3.3	5.6	4.7	9.2	5.7	2.7	6.5	5.6
Georgia	6.9	6.7	4.9	6.4	5.4	8.0	6.9	5.4	7.0	6.0
Armenia	8.9	7.6	5.8	7.8	5.2	10.4	7.8	5.9	8.5	5.9
Azerbaidzhan	5.1	7.2	4.9	5.9	3.6	6.9	8.2	5.4	7.1	4.8
Kazakhstan	7.9	4.2	1.3	5.1	3.1	9.8	5.3	3.5	6.7	4.7
Kirghizia	8.2	4.1	4.3	5.8	3.2	11.9	6.7	4.6	8.4	5.8
Turkmenia	5.2	4.0	2.6	4.2	1.4	7.2	5.6	2.6	5.6	2.8
Uzbekistan	7.0	6.1	3.4	5.9	2.8	7.3	6.7	4.7	6.5	3.4
Tadzhikistan	7.8	5.0	2.9	5.7	2.4	8.7	6.1	4.8	6.9	3.6

Source: Growth rates were calculated from indexes given in Narodnoe khoziaistvo SSSR
(henceforth Narkhoz) 1970, pp. 140, 534; Narkhoz 1980, pp. 130-31, 379; and
Narodnoe khoziaistvo SSSR za 70 let, pp. 123, 134.

whole. By way of perspective, Western measures of GNP show an average annual growth of 3.4% for the USSR during 1961–85.[8] Since population growth rates differed markedly among the republics, the increase in national income per capita averaged less than 3% annually in Azerbaidzhan, Kazakhstan, and Central Asia, taken together; per capita growth was 4.4% for the USSR as a whole. As official Soviet indexes show, industrial growth also was rapid everywhere during 1961–85, with growth rates ranging from 5.6% in Turkmenia to 9.2% in Belorussia, compared to 6.5% for the entire country. A Western measure shows a growth rate of 4.6% for the USSR during this period. Except for Azerbaidzhan, all republics experienced the marked slowdown in the growth of national income and industrial production characteristic of the Soviet economy during the past fifteen years. Even so, the patterns were quite diverse among the republics, probably reflecting their differing agricultural performance and industrial structures. Agricultural production increased in all republics, with average annual rates of growth ranging from 1.7% in the RSFSR to 4.7% in Azerbaidzhan and averaging 2.1% for the USSR as a whole. The highest rates were achieved in the Transcaucasian and Central Asian republics and in Moldavia.

Additional evidence for relative rates of development is provided by data on the extent of urbanization and the shares of the agricultural and industrial sectors in total employment (Table 3). Although the proportion of urban dwellers in the total population increased everywhere, the rates of growth differed widely.[9] The urban share doubled between 1959 and 1985 in Belorussia and Moldavia, where industrial growth was very rapid. The

48   GERTRUDE E. SCHROEDER

TABLE 3.   Urbanization Rates and Distribution of Employment by Republic, 1959-1985

| | Level of Urbanization | | | | Percent of Total Employment in | | | | | |
| | | | | | Industry | | | Agriculture | | |
	1959	1970	1979	1985	1960	1970	1985	1960	1970	1985
USSR	47.9	56.3	62.3	65.2	23.8	26.6	27.1	38.0	29.4	22.3
RSFSR	52.4	62.3	69.3	72.6	28.5	30.7	30.2	31.3	23.6	17.5
Ukraine	45.7	54.5	61.3	65.4	20.5	24.7	28.1	45.6	35.5	24.8
Belorussia	30.9	43.4	55.1	62.0	14.5	21.0	25.9	57.1	43.6	28.6
Moldavia	22.3	31.7	39.3	44.7	10.1	15.3	20.5	59.8	45.6	34.4
Lithuania	38.6	50.2	60.7	66.7	14.4	22.2	25.3	56.8	41.0	29.3
Latvia	56.1	62.5	68.5	70.5	24.9	29.4	28.4	39.0	28.6	23.1
Estonia	56.5	65.7	69.7	71.4	25.1	30.5	29.9	32.4	23.4	20.1
Georgia	42.4	47.8	51.9	53.8	16.1	17.8	18.0	44.1	36.4	29.1
Armenia	48.3	59.5	63.8	67.6	21.1	26.7	29.1	38.4	25.3	17.6
Azerbaidzhan	47.8	50.1	53.1	53.7	15.1	17.3	16.2	46.3	36.1	32.2
Kazakhstan	43.8	50.3	53.9	58.4	15.6	19.1	18.8	41.6	33.4	28.5
Kirghizia	33.7	37.4	37.0	39.6	14.9	18.4	18.7	45.7	36.9	33.0
Turkmenia	46.2	47.9	48.0	47.4	11.8	11.4	10.1	43.2	39.1	35.7
Uzbekistan	33.6	36.6	41.2	41.9	12.9	14.0	14.7	53.3	42.9	35.1
Tadzhikistan	32.6	37.1	34.9	34.2	10.0	13.0	13.8	55.7	44.5	37.7

Sources: Urban shares of the population were calculated from census data for the years 1959, 1970, and 1979 (15 or 17 January), and for 1 January 1985 from data given in Narkhoz 1984, pp. 8-9. Shares of industry and agriculture in total employment were calculated from my estimates of total employment, including private plot employment in agriculture. Industrial employment in 1985 had to be estimated mainly on the basis of the change in employment between 1970 and 1985 implied by indexes of production and labor productivity published in Narkhoz 1985, pp. 102-3, 113. The results are subject to small margins of error. Agricultural employment estimates are my calculations of employment in purely agricultural activities. A description of the methodology is given in Ann Goodman, Margaret Hughes, and Gertrude Schroeder, "Raising the Efficiency of Soviet Farm Labor: Problems and Prospects," in U.S. Congress, Joint Economic Committee, Gorbachev's Economic Plans (Washington: U.S. Government Printing Office, 1987), vol. 2, p. 118. Virtually all of the rest of employment is in the construction, trade, and service branches of the economy.

Central Asian republics and Azerbaidzhan experienced the slowest rates of change; indeed, in Tadzhikistan and Turkmenia, the level of urbanization declined slightly between 1970 and 1985. In the latter year, the urban population was still less than half of the total in all of Central Asia and Moldavia. The rates at which labor was transferred from the agricultural sector also differed greatly among the republics. The data for 1961–85 (Table 3) depict this diversity. (I have attempted to measure employment in agricultural activity alone by removing estimated employment in nonagricultural activity on state and collective farms and by developing estimates of average annual employment on private plots by republic.) The fastest rates of labor transfer occurred in Belorussia and Lithuania, where the agricultural share fell by nearly half. In 1985, over 30% of the labor force was still engaged in agriculture in Central Asia, Azerbaidzhan, and Moldavia, and in only two republics was the share below one-fifth. For the USSR as a whole, nearly five million workers were released from agriculture during this twenty-five-year period, and the total number engaged in that sector fell in many republics. Agricultural employment rose substantially, however, in Central Asia, Kazakhstan, and Azerbaidzhan.

Although the share of the industrial sector in total employment rose significantly in most republics during this period, there was considerable diversity in the extent of industrial employment among republics. In 1985, industry's share was less than one-fifth in seven republics, and in Turkmenia it was only 10%. Data giving the distribution of industrial employment by branch have been largely unavailable since 1975. Data for earlier years show a tendency for republican specialization rather than substantial diversification, with the southern republics tending to specialize in the light and food industries, and the machinery and chemicals industries remaining largely the province of the RSFSR and Ukraine.[10] But Belorussia is an exception. Its fast-paced development in the postwar years has been accompanied by considerable diversification; in 1980, for example, the shares of the machinery and (most probably) the chemicals industries in total industrial employment exceeded those for the USSR as a whole, whereas they had been well below that level in 1960.[11]

In addition to the pace of economic growth in the republics, it would be important to establish the relative levels of development achieved. Although the data for this, reported in accordance with Soviet definitions, are not ideal, they probably are not grossly misleading for what they purport to measure—national income (net material product) per capita and industrial production (gross value of output) per capita, extrapolated with official "constant price" indexes from current price values available for 1970.[12] They very likely are the kind of data that Soviet officials and planners use to judge such matters. National income per capita in 1985 ranged from less than half the all-union average in Tadzhikistan to more than one-third above that average in Latvia and Estonia, with Belorussia and the RSFSR next. These latter four republics, along with Lithuania, also ranked highest with regard to industrial output per capita, while the four Central Asian republics were lowest on both measures. Although differentials clearly have widened during the past twenty-five years, the relative ranking of the republics has hardly changed. The exceptions are Belorussia, with a greatly improved position, and Turkmenia, with a much lower ranking. If Brezhnev had looked at such measures when he declared in 1972 that equalization of levels of economic development had been achieved "on the whole," he evidently did not consider the rather sizable interrepublican differences to be a matter of concern. Disparities on these measures were greater in 1985 than in 1970.

Living Standards

Turning from the production side of the development process to the consumption side, it is necessary to consider trends and relative living standards among the republics. Again, data for republics must suffice, since none are available for nationalities per se. To assess progress in raising living standards, the Soviet government employs a measure termed "real per capita incomes of the population." This concept is supposed to measure the value of material goods and the material component of all services provided to the population, deflated by an index of prices of goods and services.[13] The price index has not been published; nor has the methodology for constructing it been described in any detail. Although the relative levels of real incomes per capita were not reported for the republics, republican statistical yearbooks regularly include temporal indexes. Since this measure has well-known conceptual flaws, and because the price index is believed to have a serious downward bias, I have attempted to develop an alternative measure for the republics, patterned as closely as possible after the measure of real per capita consumption that is a part of the Western effort to construct Gross National Product measures for the USSR in current and constant values.[14] The methodology for measuring real per capita consumption in the republics relies in part on the meticulous work of Alastair McAuley[15] and has been described elsewhere.[16] In essence, the procedure is to estimate per capita consumption (by Western definition) in current prices for the selected years (1960, 1970, 1980, 1985) for each republic and then to deflate these values by a uniform price index that is implicit in Western measures of nominal and real consumption for the USSR as a whole. Although this methodology is far from ideal and involves some assumptions whose validity cannot be determined for lack of data,[17] I believe that the results are plausible, providing a far better basis for assessing trends and relative living standards among the republics than do the official statistics on national income or retail sales per capita that are often used. The results, moreover, are largely consistent with a variety of relevant data that cannot be aggregated. For example, the ranking of republics with respect to per capita consumption in 1985 was quite similar to their ranking with respect to per capita retail sales; the rankings were the same for eight republics on both measures.

The measures of growth rates and relative levels of per capita consumption in the republics are shown in Table 4. Living standards, by this gauge, improved markedly in all republics during the past twenty-five years, but the pace of improvement varied considerably—from growth at an average rate of 2% annually in Tadzhikistan to almost double that rate in Moldavia. Rates of improvement in the Central Asian republics were consistently lower than the all-union average annual rate of 2.7%. Well above average gains were registered in Belorussia and Moldavia—republics that had also exhibited the most rapid rates of urbanization. All republics experienced markedly lower growth in real per capita consumption during 1971–85 than in the 1960s, a pattern that is more uniform than that derived from growth rates of production among the republics. In the first half of the 1980s, only two republics registered average annual growth rates in real per capita consumption as high as 2%, and by my measure per capita consumption actually fell in three republics. In this period, at least, the central government clearly did not try to stem a relative deterioration in living standards in Central Asia that resulted largely from rapid population growth.

TABLE 4.   Growth Rates and Relative Levels of Consumption Per Capita by Republic, 1960-1985

	Average Annual Rate of Growth				Relative Levels			
	1961-1970	1971-1980	1981-1985	1960-1985	1960	1970	1980	1985
USSR	3.8	2.5	0.8	2.7	100.0	100.0	100.0	100.0
RSFSR	3.8	2.7	0.9	2.8	106.1	107.1	109.2	110.0
Ukraine	4.0	2.0	1.2	2.7	94.3	96.6	92.3	94.4
Belorussia	5.0	3.0	1.2	3.4	84.4	95.0	99.5	101.4
Moldavia	6.1	3.2	1.0	3.9	72.5	90.8	97.2	98.5
Lithuania	4.6	2.3	-0.1	2.7	109.9	118.4	116.2	111.5
Latvia	3.7	1.6	0.1	2.1	127.3	126.3	115.3	111.3
Estonia	4.0	2.4	0.3	2.6	130.2	132.9	131.2	128.2
Georgia	3.0	3.1	2.3	2.9	95.4	88.9	94.0	101.2
Armenia	3.6	2.4	0.4	2.5	87.0	85.9	85.1	83.6
Azerbaidzhan	3.0	2.3	1.4	2.4	74.4	69.4	67.9	70.2
Kazakhstan	3.3	2.3	0.5	2.3	95.6	91.2	89.6	88.3
Kirghizia	4.0	2.0	0.9	2.6	74.7	76.1	72.7	73.2
Turkmenia	3.7	2.0	-0.9	2.2	82.4	82.2	78.1	74.4
Uzbekistan	3.4	2.4	-0.6	2.3	80.4	78.1	77.6	74.1
Tadzhikistan	3.2	1.8	0.1	2.0	70.5	66.7	62.2	59.8

Sources: Figures for 1960 and 1970 are taken from my article, "Regional Living Standards," in I. S. Koropeckyj and Gertrude E. Schroeder, eds., Economics of Soviet Regions (New York: Praeger, 1981), p. 129. The sources and methodology are described there. Figures for 1980 and 1985 were obtained using similar sources and methods.

Sizable differences in the relative levels of per capita consumption in the republics are apparent throughout the period. In 1985, per capita consumption in the Baltic republics exceeded the all-union average by 12% to 28%, whereas it was below the all-union average in Tadzhikistan by more than 40%. Differences widened over the twenty-five year period; the coefficient of variation rose from .10 in 1960 to .14 in 1985, the major increase apparently having occurred in the first half of the 1970s. Again, however, republican rankings have been remarkably stable, with the Baltic republics occupying the top position by sizable margins throughout the period and the Central Asian republics and Azerbaidzhan bringing up the rear. The relative position of the latter group has tended to deteriorate, while that of Moldavia and Belorussia (the republics urbanizing at the fastest rates) improved substantially. While these regional differentials in living standards are not especially large by international comparison (they are much narrower than in Yugoslavia, for instance), they are substantial nonetheless, and the differences certainly are not being reduced.[18]

While it has not proved possible to disaggregate consumption into its major components for the republics, as has been done for the USSR as a whole, a wide variety of officially published data indicate that all republics have made substantial progress in all major areas—food, soft goods and durables, housing, services, health care, and education.[19] The gains in these categories have been far from uniform among the republics, but the differences display a pattern that is quite similar to that revealed by overall measures of per capita consumption. The Baltic republics have relatively more of everything, and the Central Asians have less. Also, the quality of the goods and services provided no doubt differs among republics, probably being poorer in the rural regions.

It may be of interest to inquire how living standards in the various republics compare with those in nearby countries. Sweeping under a very large rug the many methodological and conceptual problems involved, one can venture such an assessment using studies of relative levels of GNP and purchasing power parities for a number of Western and some Communist countries in 1975, together with a reasonably comparable set of data on consumption in the USSR and the United States in 1976.[20] The above estimates of relative levels of per capita consumption for the republics allow for such an international perspective. Tenuous though it may be, the general picture that this comparison provides is not grossly misleading. It suggests that living standards in Central Asia and Azerbaidzhan in 1985 were roughly the same as those in Syria and Iran in 1975, that living standards in the Baltic republics were nearest those in Hungary, Poland, and Ireland, and that living standards in the USSR as a whole and in all its constituent republics are far below those prevailing in most of the rest of Europe, Japan, and the United States.

Finally, it remains to examine the extent to which the measures of relative living standards among republics reflect the situation of their titular nationalities. We know from the data in Table 1 that titular nationalities tend overwhelmingly to reside in their own republics and that they comprise more than half the population in all republics but Kazakhstan. We know as well that the titular nationalities tend to reside in rural areas in their republics and that rural living standards, while improving relatively, are still well below those in urban areas—perhaps two-thirds to three-fourths of the urban level. We also know that the titular nationalities tend to be less well' educated than the average for their republics and are therefore more likely to be found in relatively low wage sectors and occupations. It seems reasonable, then, to conclude that the living standards of the titular nationalities probably are appreciably below those measured here for their republics, although the precise data needed to substantiate this are not available.[21] Russians in the RSFSR, Armenians in Armenia, and Estonians in Estonia might prove to be the exceptions. Titular nationalities in the other republics, however, may have experienced a more rapid improvement in incomes than the aggregate populations of their respective republics, because rural living standards in the USSR and, apparently, in all republics have been rising faster than urban living standards.

Investment Allocation and Productivity

If the central government had been determined to equalize levels of development among nationality groups, this policy presumably would have

TABLE 5. Republican Shares of Total Investment and Levels of Investment Per Capita, 1961-1985

	Shares of Total Gross Fixed Investment					Levels of Gross Fixed Investment Per Capita				
	1961-1965	1966-1970	1971-1975	1976-1980	1981-1985	1961-1965	1966-1970	1971-1975	1976-1980	1981-1985
USSR	100.0	100.0	100.0	100.0	100.0	100.0	100.0	100.0	100.0	100.0
RSFSR	60.3	59.0	60.4	62.0	62.2	108.8	109.5	113.0	117.6	119.7
Ukraine	17.2	16.6	15.9	14.8	13.9	87.1	84.8	82.3	77.8	74.8
Belorussia	2.2	3.1	3.3	3.3	3.4	58.9	83.0	87.9	90.5	92.9
Moldavia	1.0	1.1	1.2	1.2	1.1	68.9	76.2	80.9	78.5	74.8
Lithuania	1.1	1.3	1.4	1.3	1.3	85.3	103.4	104.3	98.3	101.0
Latvia	1.0	1.1	1.1	1.0	1.0	104.6	108.7	110.8	101.7	104.5
Estonia	0.7	0.7	0.7	0.6	0.6	122.7	127.8	115.4	108.9	106.4
Georgia	1.3	1.4	1.2	1.3	1.5	66.0	70.8	62.5	66.9	77.3
Armenia	0.9	1.0	0.9	0.8	0.9	93.7	101.5	82.5	73.1	72.6
Azerbaidzhan	1.5	1.5	1.3	1.4	1.7	78.4	69.3	60.5	63.2	72.3
Kazakhstan	7.2	6.7	6.3	6.0	5.9	139.7	124.2	112.9	106.4	102.8
Kirghizia	0.8	0.9	0.8	0.7	0.7	73.0	72.1	64.7	55.4	52.6
Turkmenia	0.8	1.0	1.0	0.9	1.0	106.8	111.9	107.9	90.0	88.8
Uzbekistan	3.2	3.8	3.7	3.9	4.1	74.1	81.6	71.5	68.7	65.2
Tadzhikistan	0.8	0.8	0.8	0.8	0.7	77.3	69.2	60.3	53.0	45.2

Sources: Shares and per capita levels are based on values of total gross fixed investment in comparable prices and population data published in annual statistical handbooks for the USSR (e.g., Narkhoz 1985, pp. 8, 369).

been most apparent in the allocation of investment. Even if this were not the only objective, its systematic implementation, given the large development gaps already existing, would have required an extensive and persistent favoring of the less developed regions, especially if equalizing the levels of development were to be achieved on a per capita basis. Table 5 provides data on the allocation of total gross fixed investment by republic during the years 1961–85. Investment in the USSR as a whole tripled during this period and increased substantially in each successive five-year plan in all republics, although at differing rates. The most notable trends are the fairly steady rise in the share of investment allocated to the RSFSR and Belorussia and the fall in the shares of Ukraine and Kazakhstan. The relative priority of the RSFSR is associated with the decision to develop natural resources and energy in the eastern regions, and that of Belorussia with the rapid industrial development promoted there. The share given to Central Asia rose by nearly one percentage point during this period, and that of Transcaucasia also increased slightly, while the shares of the Baltic republics and Moldavia remained essentially stable. When relative rates of population growth are taken into account, we again observe a marked improvement in the relative positions of the RSFSR and Belorussia and a substantial deterioration in the relative positions of Ukraine and Kazakhstan over this period. The position of Central Asia also dropped markedly; per capita investment in those republics in 1981–85 was less than two-thirds of the all-union level, compared to about three-fourths in 1961–65. The positions of the Trans-caucasian republics fluctuated considerably during the period, possibly reflecting political factors, but per capita investment remained well below the union-wide average. Patterns of gross fixed investment per capita in the Baltic republics and Moldavia have been quite diverse, though the consistent erosion of the position of Estonia should be noted. Although the trends remain similar, the differences among republics are reduced considerably when investment is expressed per worker rather than per capita. For example, in the period 1981–85, investment per worker ranged from 70% of the all-union average in Kirghizia to 119% of that average in Turkmenia. The relative positions of the Central Asian republics and Azerbaidzhan—republics with especially fast rates of population growth—appear to be significantly higher on this measure.

The distribution of investment among republics during this period does not reveal any systematic effort to use investment as a means of reducing development gaps, particularly when allowance is made for differential population growth. Rather, it seems that the central government, while providing an increment in investment to ensure some development in all republics, based its allocation decisions on a variety of other factors, such as resource development in Siberia (with its attendant high costs), consideration of relative rates of return on investment, and geo-political considerations. This general observation accords with the conclusions reached by other investigators who have analyzed Soviet regional development and investment policy.[22] Detailed investigations for individual republics might offer further insights—for example, the changing fortunes of Georgia and Azerbaidzhan in the past decade might have an important political dimension. In any event, in explaining shifts in investment allocations among republics over the past three five-year plans, the primacy of all-union considerations over considerations of equalization is quite evident—an outcome appropriate for a government that viewed equalization as "basically" achieved.[23]

Rapid growth in investment has produced rapid increases in the capital stock and in capital/labor ratios in all republics. According to calculations made by Gillula, capital stocks in the material sectors of production increased during 1961–75 at average annual rates ranging from 6.3% in Azerbaidzhan to 11.7% in Moldavia and Uzbekistan, with an average of 8.9% for the USSR as a whole.[24] During the same period, fixed capital per worker increased at average annual rates ranging from 4.1% in Azerbaidzhan to 8.7% in Moldavia, and averaging 7.0% for the USSR. While these measures cannot be extended to 1985 with available data, it is nonetheless evident that growth in total capital stock and capital per worker continued in all republics, though at slower rates. Increased capital/labor ratios, in turn, have contributed to increased productivity in all republics. Using official data, Ivan Koropeckyj has estimated that factor productivity (national income per unit of combined capital and labor) increased at widely varying average annual rates among republics during 1961–75—from a mere 0.1% in Turkmenia to 4.1% in Belorussia, with an all-union average of 2.7%.[25] Levels of productivity also differ greatly among republics. According to a Soviet source, the productivity of social labor (national income per worker in

TABLE 6.   Indicators of Growth and Relative Levels of Labor Productivity by Republic, 1960-1985

	Industry					Agriculture				
	Average Annual Rate of Growth			Relative Level		Average Annual Rate of Growth				Relative Level
	1961-1970	1971-1980	1981-1985	1961-1985	1980	1961-1970	1971-1980	1981-1985	1961-1985	1980
USSR	5.2	4.5	3.1	4.5	100	3.6	2.2	1.9	2.7	100
RSFSR	5.3	4.7	3.1	4.6	99	3.9	1.5	2.4	2.6	105
Ukraine	4.9	3.8	2.7	4.0	93	3.5	2.9	3.4	3.3	98
Belorussia	5.7	6.0	4.0	5.5	123	3.2	3.4	5.9	3.9	93
Moldavia	3.4	4.1	3.3	3.7	114	4.5	2.7	2.5	3.4	96
Lithuania	5.0	4.6	3.3	4.5	118	4.8	1.6	5.9	3.7	97
Latvia	5.8	4.5	3.2	4.8	118	2.9	2.0	3.5	2.7	123
Estonia	5.9	4.9	2.6	4.8	109	3.5	2.7	0.2	2.5	182
Georgia	4.9	5.2	3.6	4.8	105	4.0	3.4	1.7	3.3	69
Armenia	4.2	4.3	3.2	4.0	99	3.4	2.5	3.2	3.0	77
Azerbaidzhan	3.6	5.6	3.9	4.5	135	3.6	5.7	0.8	3.6	81
Kazakhstan	4.7	3.3	2.1	3.6	93	2.6	1.3	1.3	1.3	119
Kirghizia	5.4	3.6	3.5	4.3	90	2.8	1.4	-1.8	1.3	86
Turkmenia	4.4	3.1	1.0	3.2	131	3.2	1.7	-1.0	1.2	91
Uzbekistan	3.0	3.3	1.5	2.8	111	2.7	2.9	-2.3	1.8	87
Tadzhikistan	2.9	2.6	1.2	2.4	101	5.1	2.3	-1.5	2.7	75

Sources: Growth rates of industrial labor productivity were calculated from indexes given in Narkhoz 1970, p. 163, and Narkhoz 1985, p. 113. Levels of industrial labor productivity in 1980 are based on the gross value of output in 1966 from input/output tables, extended to 1980 with indexes of gross output in constant prices published in Narkhoz. I am indebted to Blaine McCants for providing these data. Employment data are my estimates obtained as explained in the source note for Table 3.   Rates of growth of agricultural labor productivity were calculated from indexes of gross value of output regularly published in Narkhoz and my estimates of total "pure" agricultural employment (including the private sector).   Levels of agricultural labor productivity are based on gross value of output by republic in 1973 prices given in Narkhoz 1980, p. 206, and my estimates of employment.

material production) ranged in 1970 from 72% of the union-wide average in Moldavia to 120% in Estonia.[26] Martin Spechler estimated the relative levels in 1978 to range from 65% in Kirghizia to 124% in Estonia, and concluded that the differentials widened between 1970 and 1978.[27]

When central planners appraise relative trends and levels of efficiency in resource use among the republics, they focus on labor productivity, often citing Lenin's dictum that its growth is "the main thing, the most important thing for the victory of socialism." Table 6 assembles some data that planners might look at when evaluating labor productivity for the period of the five most recent five-year plans (1961–85). The official data for the industrial sector show that all republics participated in the marked slowdown in the growth of labor productivity characteristic of the USSR as a whole over this period. This suggests that the causes usually identified to explain the pronounced general slowdown were probably present in each republic.[28] In the two most recent plan periods, the lowest rates of growth in labor productivity are to be found in Central Asia and Kazakhstan. The reasons for the relatively favorable performance by the Transcaucasian republics are not readily apparent; a detailed investigation of the kind that has been made for Belorussia would seem desirable.[29] The data giving relative levels of industrial labor productivity represent gross value of output (in 1966 prices) per worker in 1980; they appear consistent with similar calculations for 1971 based on a Soviet source and published growth rates for labor productivity.[30] By definition, the relative levels reflect the product mix produced in each republic and the relative prices set for those products by the government. If the central planners use such data, they might conclude that the Central Asian republics are not as much a drag on overall productivity as one might think, even though their rate of improvement is slower. For agriculture, however, both rates of growth and relative levels of labor productivity tend to be low there. In any event, the planners evidently have not allocated investment funds to their most productive uses, as is revealed by data such as these. Even if they had done so, the choices hardly could have been optimal, given the well-known deficiencies of Soviet prices.

Ethnic Dimensions of the Manpower Problem

The USSR is in the midst of a manpower management problem of un-precedented scope, complicated by its ethnic dimension. The situation has been created by declining birth rates overall and by the large differences in birth rates among nationalities. Table 7 presents data on the increments to the working-age population by republic for the period 1976–2000. During the Eleventh Five-Year Plan (1981–85), the total addition to the working-age population in the USSR was only 3.6 million, compared with 11.8 million in 1976–80. All of the increment in 1981–85 came from the non-Russian republics, principally Central Asia, Kazakhstan, and Azerbaidzhan. In the period of the Twelfth Five-Year Plan, the total increment will be a mere 2.3 million, and will rise to only 2.9 million in the following five-year period. During the decade 1986-95, the working-age population will increase by 4.7 million in Central Asia and decline by 1.7 million in the RSFSR. Even in the last quinquennium of this century the estimated addition to the population of working age in Central Asia (3.3 million) will be double that in the RSFSR.

The labor problems confronting the USSR in the last two decades of the century are the subject of a sizable literature.[31] Essentially, the government's options for dealing with the problems are: (1) to encourage or compel migration from labor-surplus regions (mainly the southern republics) to areas of labor deficit (mainly the RSFSR); (2) to reallocate investment and the location of new facilities toward labor-surplus areas; or (3) to adopt some combination of these two approaches. From experience in 1981–85 and from the published targets for the Twelfth Five-Year Plan, we can observe the approach that the government has elected to take—one of "muddling through" with a wide variety of policies intended to make the situation reasonably tolerable. Although Western scholars have debated the probability of sub-stantial out-migration from Central Asia,[32] whose peoples have shown great reluctance to relocate, Soviet policy makers are not opting for such a solution.

TABLE 7. Increments in the Population of Working Age by Republic, 1976-2000
(Thousands of Persons)

	1976-80	1981-85	1986-90	1991-95	1996-2000
USSR	11,788	3,649	2,341	2,932	7,240
RSFSR	4,956	-248	-1,081	-645	1,632
Ukraine	1,393	-39	-13	-262	184
Belorussia	451	134	25	22	224
Moldavia	193	87	83	100	147
Lithuania	135	53	30	11	35
Latvia	38	-14	-19	-30	-23
Estonia	22	-3	-3	-9	-2
Georgia	278	135	67	78	156
Armenia	287	167	110	121	200
Azerbaidzhan	596	499	341	314	518
Kazakhstan	1,148	772	670	674	891
Kirghizia	293	238	249	287	380
Turkmenia	247	231	235	274	345
Uzbekistan	1,416	1,296	1,316	1,594	2,045
Tadzhikistan	335	342	329	413	508

Source: Increments are calculated from population data as of 1 January
given in U.S. Bureau of the Census, Foreign Demographic Analysis
Division, Population Projections by Age and Sex for the Republics
and Major Economic Regions of the USSR, 1970 to 2000, International
Population Reports, Series P-91, No. 26 (1979), p. 128. The
"medium" series was used here for projections.

Note: Working age in the USSR is 16-59 for men, 16-54 for women.

Figures may not add to total due to rounding.

The government has not announced substantial new incentives to foster migration, other than touting examples of brigades of Central Asians that have gone to work on showcase projects in Siberia and elsewhere in the RSFSR. Indeed, there is evidence that such migrants have soon returned, and that many were, in fact, local Russians rather than members of indigenous Central Asian nationalities. One writer states: "Let us look at the example of population movement from the so-called labor-surplus areas to labor-deficit areas, from Uzbekistan to Ivanovo oblast, in particular. Who came here? Not Uzbeks, but mainly Russians, and even the latter usually left the area soon afterwards."[33]

Any projected large-scale program to redistribute population from the labor-surplus regions of the south to the labor-deficit regions of the north would be extremely costly. Moreover, it would encounter strong resistance, from both the sending regions and those that would have to absorb large numbers of new migrants with radically different ethnic and cultural characteristics. The government wisely has chosen, at least for the time being, not to take this approach. Although the evidence is fragmentary, it is clear that no significant population redistribution from the south to the north is taking place. Data on employment and productivity by republic in 1981–

85 suggest that instead the rapidly growing working-age population in Central Asia is being absorbed mainly by continuing rising employment in agriculture and probably also in the private sector—leading to even greater underemployment of manpower, with an adverse effect on productivity.[34] In the relatively labor-short areas of the north, the government has actively promoted a variety of policies to force managers to cope with fewer workers, and these policies have had some success. During the 1981–85 period, increased labor productivity accounted for 91% of the growth of industrial production in the RSFSR compared with 79% in 1976–80; in agriculture, employment declined by 4% in 1981–85 while output rose by 8%, a marked improvement over the preceding five years. The Twelfth Five-Year Plan indicates that these trends are expected to continue.

The government could balance the regional disproportions in labor force growth through systematic efforts to expand industry and economic infrastructures in the regions of fastest population growth, especially Central Asia, but also southern Kazakhstan and Transcaucasia. The regional distribution of investment indicates that the government in fact has elected to pursue that option, but not with much vigor and with considerable differentiation among the republics. Transcaucasia's share of total investment increased from 3.5% in 1976–80 to 4.1% in 1981–85, a shift sufficient to improve its relative position on a per capita basis. By contrast, Central Asia's relative standing on a per capita basis deteriorated markedly, even though the region's share of total investment rose from 6.2% to 6.5% during this period. Regions with fast-growing populations, of course, require more investment—not only to provide new industrial jobs, but also to build more schools, hospitals, and other service facilities. They also need additional budget allocations to finance current operations of public services. Although budget data do not fully reflect the relative appropriations, these, together with investment allocations, have been sufficient to permit real per capita consumption to grow faster in Transcaucasia than in the RSFSR in the 1981–85 period. In Kazakhstan and Central Asia, however, improvements in living standards were less substantial than in the RSFSR; by our measures there was a decline in Uzbekistan and Turkmenia.

The directives for the Twelfth Five-Year Plan indicate that this policy of temporizing and hoping for the best was to continue over the 1986–90 period. The plan called for new facilities to be sited to make fuller use of the labor and natural resources in Central Asia, southern Kazakhstan, and Transcaucasia, while the European regions were to be developed primarily through retooling and reconstructing existing enterprises, with a reduction in the number of persons employed in material production.[35] The plan envisioned above-average growth in industrial production in most of the republics with a rapidly increasing population. Data on planned investment allocations for 1986–90 in all republics can be culled from the press, mainly from the speeches by republican leaders at the Twenty-seventh Party Congress. From this information we can conclude that past regional allocation policies were planned to continue. According to these data, Central Asia's share in total investment in 1986-90 would rise slightly from 1981–85, Kazakhstan's share was to drop slightly, and Transcaucasia's to remain about the same. Ukraine's investment share would continue to drop, and the RSFSR's share to rise, perhaps to as much as 64%. But the population of Central Asia will have increased by about 14% during 1986-90, and that of Kazakhstan and Transcaucasia by about 8%, compared with less than 2% in the RSFSR and 4% in the USSR as a whole. On a per capita basis, then, the relative position of the RSFSR would rise and that of most other republics, particularly in Central Asia, would fall. This was essentially the pattern that prevailed in 1986–87.[36]

The Nationalities Factor in Economic Administration

From Stalin to Gorbachev

From the advent of central planning, the Soviet economy has been administered largely on the basis of the union republics, each the "homeland" of a distinct nationality that constitutes in most cases the majority population, with many of the symbolic trappings and constitutionally sanctioned, though unrealized, prerogatives characteristic of a nation-state. The nationalities factor, therefore, inescapably politicizes all decision making at the central government level with regard to economic planning and administration, and lends the process a definite—and potentially divisive—ethnic dimension. Any scheme for the decentralization of decision-making authority aimed at improving economic management has had to be appraised with that dimension in mind. Initially, Stalin resolved the issue by establishing a highly centralized form of economic administration, with ever more numerous central ministries organized along sectoral lines and with planning authority centered in Moscow in the USSR Gosplan. The union republican Councils of Ministers and the republican Gosplans played a minor role in this scheme. For reasons both political and economic, Nikita Khrushchev in 1957 jettisoned virtually all of the sectoral administrative structures in favor of a system based on regional (republican) authority. His stated objectives were to eliminate the "departmentalism," inefficient and duplicative supply arrangements, inattention to regional planning, and excessive bureaucratism and red tape stemming from the overburdening of higher echelons in Moscow. Under the new scheme, the chain of authority went from the USSR Gosplan to the Councils of Ministers of the union republics and their Gosplans, then to 105 regional economic councils (*sovnarkhozy*), largely coterminous with oblasts, and finally to production enterprises. This drastic restructuring of the economic administrative machinery was bitterly controversial, with the nationalities element looming large.[37]

Such a radical devolution of administrative responsibility to the republics and their subunits created difficulties even more serious than those the new system was designed to eliminate. Since the decentralization was administrative and not economic in nature, problems of coordination of supply and demand for materials among the regional units became endemic. Tendencies toward "localism" and regional autarky were much in evidence in the behavior of the new *sovnarkhozy*. Complaints were made about imbalances in and inattention to the development of particular industrial branches. To cope with the growing mess, the central government drastically reduced the number of *sovnarkhozy*, established one coordinating body after another in a growing pyramid, gave ever more power to the USSR Gosplan, and reestablished the former ministries in the guise of state committees. Accusations of localism and regional autarky, as well as perennial disputes over investment and budgetary allocations, often acquired a nationalist coloration. Several major shakeups of republican leaderships occurred during this period.[38]

Khrushchev's successors moved quickly to end the experiment in regional economic administration, which surely was regarded as one of the deposed leader's "hare-brained schemes." The former system of economic management through all-union, union-republican and republican ministries was restored in 1965, and consequently the authority of the union republics sharply curtailed. Nonetheless, the question of how much decision-making authority to vest in the union republics and their subordinate units remained on the agenda. Apparently in an effort to assuage the feelings of republican leaders, the central leadership had intimated when the ministerial system was restored that additional authority in economic affairs would be accorded the republics.[39] In his report to the Central Committee Plenum in September 1965, Premier Kosygin stated that the republican Gosplans were to prepare draft plans for developing their regions, including the activities of enterprises under all-union ministries.[40] This procedure was codified in a Methodological Instruction issued by the USSR Gosplan in 1969.[41] Presumably, the republican leaderships could lobby for resources to carry out those plans, which otherwise did not seem to be binding on anyone.

The new Soviet constitution, adopted in 1977, neither ended the federal system, as some centralizers had recommended, nor expanded the powers of the republics and their local soviets, as regional leaders had urged. However, a planning reform decree of July 1979 directed the ministries to coordinate their annual and five-year plans with the relevant republican Councils of Ministers, which then would draw up and supervise the implementation of specific plans for "production of local building materials and consumer goods" and for "construction of housing and municipal and cultural services."[42] A decree issued in 1981 aimed to expand the role of local soviets by (1) requiring enterprises to obtain concurrence by the local soviet for all plans relating to "land use, environmental protection, construction, labor utilization, and social-cultural services"; (2) recommending that enterprises producing primarily for local consumption be put under the local soviets; and (3) assigning, "as an experiment," to republican Councils of Ministers all funds designated for investment in housing and services.[43] The latter provision sought to end the perennial tug of war between local authorities and the branch ministries, which control a substantial part of the funds for construction of housing and many service facilities.

These attempts to shift more control over economic affairs to regional levels evidently had little impact on economic administration, which had become highly complex. In Donetsk oblast of the Ukrainian SSR, for example, there were 404 enterprises subordinate to 26 all-union ministries; 2,787 enterprises under 55 union-republican ministries; and 2,339 enterprises under 21 different republican, local, and other jurisdictions.[44] This situation created severe problems for republican Gosplans, which, as the penchant for "improving planning" through "complex programs" grew, had to undertake very difficult tasks.[45] From time to time, the suggestion had surfaced that the economy should be administered through the nineteen large regions delineated for long-range planning purposes. Under this scheme, the Baltic, Transcaucasia, and Central Asia are treated as single suprarepublican regions; Kazakhstan, Belorussia, and Moldavia each constitute a single region; Ukraine is divided into three regions and the RSFSR into ten. Possibly referring to such suggestions, the 1961 Party Program had mentioned the possible establishment of "interrepublican economic organs," arousing fears among the nationalities that the republics might be weakened. The 1986 Party Program contains no such reference. But in the pre-congress discussion of that program, Pravda again published an article proposing that the present economic regions serve as administrative units.[46] Another would-be reformer recommended that the country be divided into "territorial-production complexes" and administered regionally on that basis, but with the retention of the branch ministerial structure.[47]

Not only did the nationality factor constrain decisions about how best to organize the administration of the economy, but it also politicized and sharpened the inevitable conflicts over budget allocations for social services and investment.[48] When Ukrainian leaders argued for development of Donbas coal, they could be seen as trying to promote Ukrainian interests at the expense of other republics and the country as a whole. For years, a Central Asian "lobby" had sought funding for a mammoth project to divert water from Siberian rivers to the south in order to promote more diversified agricultural development there. Having failed in their attempt, the native Central Asians can allege discrimination and neglect of their vital interests by the central—easily construed as Russian—government.

Gorbachev's Initiative

Frustration over ethnically divisive issues such as these was evident in Gorbachev's speech to the Twenty-seventh Party Congress, in which he talked about "contradictions," inveighed against "parochialism" and "attitudes of living at the expense of others," and even suggested that "thought should be given about how to link more closely the volume of resources allocated for social needs with the efficiency of the regional economy." He spoke even more sharply:

Strengthening of the territorial principle of management requires a rise in the level of economic management in every republic, oblast, city and district. Frequently proposals come in from local bodies that have not been studied properly, are dictated not by national-economic interests, but rather by parasitical or even selfish interests, and that involve the economy in capital-intensive and inefficient projects.[49]

Such sentiments, repeated in subsequent major speeches, found expression in those parts of Gorbachev's program of economic reform that impinge on the relations between the central government and the republics. In July 1986 the CPSU, the Supreme Soviet, and the USSR Council of Ministers adopted a decree that considerably broadened the responsibility and authority of the republican governments, especially their subordinate local soviets.[50] This decree, in its focus on the consumer sector, reiterated and expanded many of the provisions of the earlier 1981 decree, which evidently had had little effect. As part of the package of measures promulgated to implement the overall economic reforms adopted by the CPSU in late June 1987,[51] a decree dated 17 July 1987 extended the authority of the republican governments even further.[52] Although it contains much ambiguity, the decree apparently does the following: (1) vests the republican Councils of Ministers with near total authority to plan economic and social development and to allocate investment, although coordination with all-union ministries is mandatory; (2) requires republican organs to ensure that the allocation of funds for social development in their territories depends on economic performance there; (3) expands the budgetary authority of local soviets and prescribes additional sources of revenues; (4) makes all regional bodies assume responsibility for coordinating and monitoring the activities of all enterprises on their territory in matters affecting the welfare of the local populations; (5) requires regional bodies to reduce staffs and simplify organizational structures, but also specifies that new planning-economic departments are to be established in the local soviets; and (6) stipulates that heavy industry, for the most part, be managed through all-union ministries, while the consumer sector is to be managed largely by the republics. In the implementation of this last provision, seven union-republic ministries were converted to all-union status in 1987 and 1988.[53]

In the discussions that preceded the Nineteenth Party Conference in June 1988, there surfaced the idea of introducing economic accountability (*khozraschet*) for an entire republic. This is analogous to the principle of self-financing on which the operation of all Soviet enterprises will be based beginning in 1989—an arrangement under which they are required to finance all their activities from internally generated funds and are accorded wide latitude in making decisions about production, inputs and the use of profits. Delegates from a few republics supported the idea, while others urged greater regional autonomy in general. The Conference resolution on the nationalities issue stated that the "idea of republics and regions going over to *khozraschet* is worth considering, with a clear definition of what they are expected to contribute to Union-wide programmes."[54] Subsequently, the idea became a rallying cry for the newly formed "Popular Front" groups in the Baltic republics. Apparently with the tacit approval of Gorbachev, representatives of the government and academic communities in the three republics drafted a document specifying the basic features of the proposed new system of autonomy. With an obviously ethnic cast, they are quite radical: republican ownership of all productive property except defense installations; abolition of the subordination of local enterprises and organizations to all-union organs; republican control of all economic activity on its territory, including issuance of currency and conduct of foreign trade; payment of a tax to the all-union budget to finance defense and foreign policy expenditures; conduct of economic relations with other republics on the basis of voluntary contracts, reflecting "mutually equivalent terms of exchange."[55]

Perhaps in an effort to steal a march on the more radical reformers, the USSR Council of Ministers at about the same time sanctioned an experiment with regional *khozraschet* to begin in 1989 in the three Baltic republics, Belorussia, Sverdlovsk oblast, the Tatar ASSR, and Moscow. In connection with the presentation of the 1989 plan and budget to the Supreme Soviet at the end of October 1988, both the chairman of the USSR Gosplan and the minister of finance referred to a document still in preparation to establish a new mechanism for the management of regional economies.[56] This document, which was published in March 1989 in the form of a draft law, is far less radical than that put forth by representatives of the Baltic republics.[57] Essentially, the document spells out in some detail the provisions for enhanced republican authority for managing their economies and new budgetary arrangements with Moscow as laid out in the overall program for economic reform. In September the Supreme Soviet remanded the draft to the Council of Ministers with instructions to bring it into conformity with other proposed new laws on property, land, and related matters. In the interim, the Baltic republics and Belorussia have been authorized to experiment with various models of economic autonomy, beginning on 1 January 1990. Along with all this, a divisive discussion has surfaced over the question of resource transfers among the republics—the question of "Who feeds whom?". The arbitrary nature of Soviet prices and budgetary policies precludes a definitive resolution of that issue, which would require a price reform that reveals the actual costs and values of products and resources.

Finally, Gorbachev has continued to insist on the primacy of state interests in the management of the periphery. In his speech to the Nineteenth Party Conference, for example, he warned that "those who believe that decentralization is opening up the floodgates for parochialism or national egoism will be making a grave mistake," and that "any obsession with national isolation can only lead to economic and cultural impoverishment."[58] This theme was emphasized once more in his address at the Central Committee Plenum on nationalities policy held in September 1989.[59] The new party platform that was adopted at this plenum stressed the need to retain a large role for the central government in managing the economy and setting economic policy, while simultaneously according the republics wide latitude for decision making within that framework.[60] Such has been the thrust of economic *perestroika* from the outset. The current slogan is: "strong center, strong republics."

Conclusions

Over the past two decades, the official rhetoric on the economic aspects of the nationalities problem has changed dramatically. Before Brezhnev's speech in 1972 on the fiftieth anniversary of the formation of the USSR, economic plans and party statements had routinely declared the goal of equalizing the levels of economic development and living standards among national groups. Since then, this objective has disappeared from official documents, replaced by an ever more forceful stress on developing the USSR as a "unified national-economic complex." The CPSU resolution adopted in early 1982 to commemorate the sixtieth anniversary of the establishment of the USSR stressed this theme, declaring the intent to "decide economic and social questions primarily from a general state approach," while resolutely combatting all manifestations of "parochialism" and "nationalism."[61] In the past three five-year plans, the goal of equalizing development rates has been replaced by a stated intent to ensure economic development in all republics. According to some Soviet scholars, the very success of past policies in equalizing development rates and educational and cultural levels among national groups now makes it possible, indeed imperative, for all peoples to contribute to economic progress in the country as a whole.[62] This theme was emphasized in Gorbachev's speech to the Twenty-seventh Party Congress: "It is especially important to see to it that the contribution of all the republics to the development of the single national-economic complex corresponds to their increased economic and spiritual potential."[63]

The change in policy, or at least rhetoric, is revealed clearly in a comparison of statements in the new Party Program adopted in 1986 with those in its predecessor approved in 1961.[64] The 1961 Program enunciated a policy of ensuring "actual equality of all nations with full consideration for their interests and devoting special attention to those areas of the country that are in need of more rapid development." The 1986 Program declares that the "nationalities question inherited from the past has been successfully solved" and stresses the primacy of all-union interests and the promotion of division of labor among the republics. The new Program also states the intent to "struggle consistently against any manifestations of parochialism and national narrow-mindedness" while "showing constant concern for further increasing the role of the republics, autonomous oblasts and autonomous districts in carrying out countrywide tasks."

Another theme stressed in recent policy pronouncements is the critical importance of full integration of the republican economies into the all-union economy. Gorbachev stated in February 1986 that "the development of cooperative production arrangements, cooperation and mutual assistance among the republics is in the highest interests of our multinational state and of each republic."[65] Past Soviet regional development policies already have produced an intricate web of mutual economic dependencies among the republics. As revealed by regional input/output data, each republic is now both a major exporter and importer of goods to and from other republics. As would be expected, the small republics are much more trade-dependent than the larger ones: according to Gillula's estimates for 1966, the ratios of exports to total output were 23% to 29% in the Transcaucasian republics, Moldavia, Kirghizia, Tadzhikistan, Estonia, and Latvia, compared to 6% for the RSFSR. Import ratios were of similar magnitude.[66] Gillula also concluded that Soviet development policies have tended to foster regional specialization rather than diversification, notably in Kazakhstan and Central Asia, partly to develop their natural resources as rapidly as possible, and partly to increase their dependence on the rest of the country.[67] As Grey Hodnett has shown with regard to Central Asia, this strategy has been the subject of controversy for decades.[68]

Nonetheless, republican specialization has continued, and republican interdependence has increased. According to the Soviet economist Aleksandr G. Granberg, interrepublican trade rose faster than production during the 1970s.[69] In an unspecified year (possibly 1977), exports as a percent of production exceeded 30% in six of the eleven republics for which data were cited; the ratio of imports to total republican consumption exceeded 30% in nine of them. From input/output tables for the republics, he concludes that, in its relationship with the rest of the country, the RSFSR is basically an exporter of capital goods and an importer of consumer goods. Since production of the latter is more labor-intensive, the RSFSR indirectly imports labor and exports capital. Granberg sees this pattern as an indication of rational specialization and exchange—a trend which, in view of the differential rates of labor force growth between the RSFSR and the other republics, should be strongly promoted. Indeed, a principal theme of recent policy statements is the need to deepen interrepublican—and thus internationality—interdependence. The leadership, no doubt, regards the success achieved thus far as a great political benefit.

Despite repeated assertions that equalization in levels of development among the nationalities has been essentially achieved, a mass of evidence indicates the persistence of substantial development gaps and disparities in living standards among national groups, as we have seen. Even if the leadership had the will to do so, narrowing these gaps, or even keeping them from widening, will prove exceedingly difficult in the near term. Rates of economic growth have decreased markedly, particularly since 1975. Since labor force growth will necessarily be slow because of demographic trends, and since growth of the capital stock will continue to decelerate as a consequence of reduced growth of investment in the past, increasing the rate of economic growth will require a radical breakthrough in productivity. The sources of such a breakthrough are hard to discern. Although the Gorbachev leadership hopes to accelerate rates of growth of national income in each of the three five-year plans during 1986–2000, the Western consensus is that this goal is unrealistic and that the large-scale industrial modernization program envisioned in these plans is likely to require faster investment growth than scheduled. If this assessment is correct, the outlook for consumers is not good. In a period of such stringency, the conflicts over allocation of investment and budgetary resources are bound to be severe. This is already the implication of the current stress on renovating old plants rather than building new ones—a policy that favors the European USSR in the allocation of investment. The Russian-dominated government will be hard pressed to provide enough funds even to ensure some economic progress in all the republics; to support per capita growth in output sufficient to raise the relative position of the poorer republics with fast population growth would be even more difficult. In such an environment of austerity, resource allocation choices will take on even more of an ethnic coloration than usual.

Besides constraining resource allocation choices, the nationalities factor will inhibit the substantial decentralization and devolution of authority to regional and local bodies that constitute a key part of Gorbachev's economic reforms. Indeed, Gorbachev's self-styled "radical" economic reforms pose serious dilemmas. On the one hand, local initiative must be unleashed if productivity is to be raised and the local populations better served. But, as under the *sovnarkhoz* reforms, regional authorities can be expected to promote regional interests; charges of "localism" and counter-measures by the center could be the consequence. Moreover, real decentralization requires large reductions in the regional bureaucracies, where increasingly well-educated local elites have found suitable employment. Such cutbacks, coupled with those mandated for enterprises, will heighten the competition for white-collar jobs. This situation will create much potential for ethnic conflict, which also will be exacerbated by the widened regional income differentials inherent in the economic reforms and the stated investment policies. Republican populations may respond quite differently to newly provided opportunities to form cooperatives and engage in private economic activity. Enterprise autonomy and self-finance may work better in some republics than in others, thus generating more revenues for local budgets and higher worker incomes there. The declared intent to allocate investment and budgetary funds in accordance with a region's "contribution" to the total economy is likely to be seriously divisive, given the present price structure; certainly it would be detrimental to regions with fast-growing populations, whose relative positions have been deteriorating for some time. These regions will have to find jobs for growing numbers of young people. Should the central government decide to provide subsidies to the "have-nots" nonetheless, the "haves" can cry foul, arguing that such a policy inhibits their own development and violates the spirit of the reforms, which aim to achieve an efficient allocation of resources. Slow economic progress will add to these sources of potential ethnic tension.

Gorbachev's economic reforms put the wager on the efficacy of economic stimuli to induce workers to work harder and managers to manage their firms better and more innovatively in order to bring about the dramatic upsurge in productivity that is so urgently needed. That approach may elicit quite different responses among and within the republics as a consequence of differing preferences, values, and cultures. Finally, the declared intent to manage overall economic development, the direction of scientific-technical progress, and heavy industry from the center, and at the same time to vest the republics with broad authority in planning and managing their own development and to hold them responsible for the results is a contradiction in terms. Bitter wrangles, unavoidably with an ethnic coloration, will surely be the result of such inconsistency.

How all these potential consequences of Gorbachev's economic initiatives will play out in the peripheries remains to be seen. Persistent ethnic tensions could threaten his ability to carry out his policies, and ethnic factors could limit their effectiveness. Both relative economic deprivation and frustration of perceived potential for economic gains also could exacerbate ethnic tensions that arise from non-economic sources. Both the economic and the political reforms foster centrifugal forces. The policy of openness (*glasnost'*) and democratization at all levels provides the nationalities with forums in which to lobby for their perceived interests. Mikhail Gorbachev is gambling on his ability to prevent those forces from undermining his program to revitalize the Soviet economy. Thus, the nationalities dimension compounds that already gargantuan task.

Notes

1. *Pravda*, 22 December 1972.

2. *Pravda*, 9 March 1986.

3. Gregory Grossman has described this dilemma in terms of the planners having to face a "triangle of hazards"—localism, overcentralization, and loss of control. Gregory Grossman, "The Structure and Organization of the Soviet Economy," *Slavic Review*, vol. 21, no. 2 (June 1962), p. 219.

4. Iu. V. Arutiunian and Iu. V. Bromlei, eds., *Sotsial'no-kul'turnyi oblik sovetskikh natsii: Po rezul'tatam etnosotsiologicheskogo issledovaniia* (Moscow: Nauka, 1986), p. 38.

5. On this point, compare data for 1970 and 1979 given in *Narodnoe khoziaistvo SSSR 1922–1982* (Moscow: Finansy i statistika, 1982), pp. 32–33, and in Iu. V. Arutiunian, "Korennye izmeneniia v sotsial'nom sostave sovetskikh natsii," *Sotsiologicheskie issledovaniia*, 1982, no. 4, p. 23.

6. Abram Bergson, *The Real National Income of Soviet Russia since 1928* (Cambridge, MA: Harvard University Press, 1961); and Rush V. Greenslade, "Industrial Production Statistics in the USSR," in Vladimir G. Treml and John P. Hardt, eds., *Soviet Economic Statistics* (Durham, NC: Duke University Press, 1972), pp. 155–94.

7. Roman Senkiw, "The Growth of Industrial Production in Ukraine 1945–1971" (Ph.D. diss., University of Virginia, 1974).

8. As Western measures of growth of GNP and its components, I employ indexes calculated by the Central Intelligence Agency. These are described in detail in U.S. Congress, Joint Economic Committee, *USSR: Measures of Economic Growth and Development 1950–80* (Washington: U.S. Government Printing Office, 1982); and in Laurie Kurzweg, "Trends in Soviet Gross National Product," in U.S. Congress, Joint Economic Committee, *Gorbachev's Economic Plans* (Washington: U.S. Government Printing Office, 1987), vol. 1, pp. 126–65.

9. Although our data on urbanization pertain to republics, the rates of change for the titular nationality groups, regardless of residence, in the period 1959–79 were similar. For a detailed assessment of the urbanization process among individual ethnic groups, see Robert A. Lewis, Richard H. Rowland, and Ralph S. Clem, *Nationality and Population Change in Russia and the USSR: An Evaluation of Census Data, 1897–1970* (New York: Praeger, 1976), pp. 129–91.

10. This conclusion is based on employment data given in Stephen Rapawy, "Regional Employment Trends in the USSR: 1950 to 1975," in U.S. Congress, Joint Economic Committee, *Soviet Economy in a Time of Change* (Washington: U.S. Government Printing Office, 1979), vol. 1, pp. 608–11.

11. Matthew J. Sagers, "The Soviet Periphery: Economic Development of Belorussia," *Soviet Economy*, vol. 1, no. 3 (July–September 1985), p. 273.

12. Ruble values of national income for the republics are published in *Narodnoe khoziaistvo Latviiskoi SSSR v 1971 godu* (Riga: Latviiskoe otdelenie izdatel'stva "Statistika," 1972), p. 56. Ruble values of industrial production for the republics are available from their input/output tables for 1966. I am indebted to Blaine McCants for providing these data. Indexes of national income and industrial production, along with population data, are regularly published in *Narodnoe khoziaistvo SSSR*.

13. For a description and evaluation of this official measure, see Gertrude E. Schroeder, "Soviet Wage and Income Statistics," in Treml and Hardt, *Soviet Economic Statistics*, pp. 303–12.

14. The derivation of consumption values in current and constant prices is described in *USSR: Measures of Economic Growth*, pp. 317–401.

15. Alastair McAuley, *Economic Welfare in the Soviet Union: Poverty, Living Standards, and Inequality* (Madison: University of Wisconsin Press, 1979).

16. Gertrude E. Schroeder, "Regional Living Standards," in I. S. Koropeckyj and Gertrude E. Schroeder, eds., *Economics of Soviet Regions* (New York: Praeger, 1981), pp. 149–53.

17. The principal assumptions are that the official indexes of real per capita incomes are of essentially uniform quality among the republics and that uniform price trends prevail. Although neither may be correct, I believe that any disparities are not large enough seriously to distort the general picture.

18. These conclusions accord with those reached by McAuley, using a somewhat different approach. Alastair McAuley, *Economic Welfare*, pp. 99–173.

19. A variety of such data are included in Schroeder, "Regional Living Standards," pp. 131–43.

20. Irving B. Kravis, Alan Heston, and Robert Summers, *World Product and Income: International Comparisons of Real Gross Product*, United Nations International Comparison Project, Phase III (Baltimore: The Johns Hopkins University Press, 1982); and Gertrude E. Schroeder and Imogene Edwards, *Consumption in the USSR: An International Comparison*, U.S. Congress, Joint Economic Committee (Washington: U.S. Government Printing Office, 1981).

21. In a study of living standards in the six Muslim republics in 1975, McAuley concludes that personal per capita incomes of their Muslim populations were no more than 570–600 rubles per year, but that their "living standards were perhaps twice those of Muslims elsewhere in the region." Alastair McAuley, "The Soviet Muslim Population: Trends in Living Standards, 1960–75," in Yaacov Ro'i, ed., *The USSR and the Muslim World: Issues in Domestic and Foreign Policy* (London: George Allen & Unwin, 1984), pp. 95–114.

22. For example, I. S. Koropeckyj, "Growth and Productivity," in Koropeckyj and Schroeder, *Economics of Soviet Regions*, pp. 96–106.

23. There is a large and contentious literature assessing Soviet policies and achievements with regard to the equalization of levels of development among the nationalities. For a survey of this literature, see Donna Bahry and Carol Nechemias, "Half Full or Half Empty?: The Debate over Soviet Regional Equality," *Slavic Review*, vol. 40, no. 3 (Fall 1981), pp. 366–83.

24. James W. Gillula, "The Growth and Structure of Fixed Capital," in Koropeckyj and Schroeder, *Economics of Soviet Regions*, p. 167.

25. I. S. Koropeckyj, "Growth and Productivity," p. 109.

26. T. V. Checheleva and N. S. Kozlova, "Vyravnivanie urovnia ekonomicheskogo razvitiia soiuznykh respublik SSSR," in *Problemy ekonomiki razvitogo sotsializma v SSSR* (Alma-Ata: Nauka, 1974), p. 147.

27. Martin C. Spechler, "Regional Developments in the USSR, 1958–78," in *Soviet Economy in a Time of Change*, vol. 1, p. 151.

28. Gertrude E. Schroeder, "The Slowdown in Soviet Industry, 1976–82," *Soviet Economy*, vol. 1, no. 1 (January–March 1985), pp. 42–74.

29. Matthew J. Sagers, "The Soviet Periphery: Economic Development of Belorussia," *Soviet Economy*, vol. 1, no. 3 (July–September 1985), pp. 261–84.

30. Checheleva and Kozlova, "Vyravnivanie," p. 137.

31. For example, Ann Goodman and Geoffrey Schleifer, "The Soviet Labor Market in the 1980s," in U.S. Congress, Joint Economic Committee, *Soviet Economy in the 1980s: Problems and Prospects* (Washington: U.S. Government Printing Office, 1981), vol. 2, pp. 323–48; and Gertrude E. Schroeder, "Managing Labour Shortages in the Soviet Union," in Jan Adam, ed., *Employment Policies in the Soviet Union and Eastern Europe* (London: Macmillan, 1982), pp. 3–35.

32. Murray Feshbach, "Prospects for Outmigration from Central Asia and Kazakhstan in the Next Decade," in *Soviet Economy in a Time of Change*, vol. 1, pp. 656–709; Robert A. Lewis and Richard H. Rowland, *Population Redistribution in the USSR: Its Impact on Society, 1897–1977* (New York: Praeger, 1979), pp. 404–27; and Michael Rywkin, *Moscow's Muslim Challenge: Soviet Central Asia* (Armonk, NY: M. E. Sharpe, 1982), pp. 58–82.

33. Iu. V. Arutiunian, "Natsional'nye osobennosti sotsial'nogo razvitiia," *Sotsiologicheskie issledovaniia*, 1985, no. 3, p. 29.

34. For an excellent analysis of manpower problems in Central Asia, see Nancy Lubin, *Labour and Nationality in Soviet Central Asia: An Uneasy Compromise* (Princeton: Princeton University Press, 1984).

35. *Pravda*, 9 March 1986.

36. *Narodnoe khoziaistvo SSSR v 1987 g.* (Moscow: Finansy i statistika, 1988), p. 297.

37. For an account of this period, see Harry Schwartz, *The Soviet Economy since Stalin* (Philadelphia: J. B. Lippincott, 1965), pp. 87–89; S. A. Billon, "Centralization of Authority and Regional Management," in V. N. Bandera and Z. L. Melnyk, eds., *The Soviet Economy in Regional Perspective* (New York: Praeger, 1973), pp. 221–28; and Herbert S. Levine, "Recent Developments in Soviet Planning," in U.S. Congress, Joint Economic Committee, *Dimensions of Soviet Economic Power* (Washington: U.S. Government Printing Office, 1962), pp. 49–65.

38. Grey Hodnett, "The Debate over Soviet Federalism," *Soviet Studies*, vol. 18, no. 4 (April 1967), pp. 458–59.

39. See Robert Conquest, *Soviet Nationalities Policy in Practice* (New York: Praeger, 1967), p. 128.

40. *Pravda*, 28 September 1965.

70   GERTRUDE E. SCHROEDER

41. Gosplan SSSR, *Metodicheskie ukazaniia k sostavleniiu gosudarstvennogo plana razvitiia narodnogo khoziaistva SSSR* (Moscow: Ekonomika, 1969), pp. 672–83.

42. *Pravda*, 29 July 1979.

43. *Izvestiia*, 29 March 1981.

44. V. M. Birenberg, "Sovershenstvovanie upravleniia promyshlennym proizvodstvom," in N. G. Chumachenko et al., *Intensifikatsiia promyshlennogo proizvodstva* (Kiev: Naukova dumka, 1985), p. 94.

45. See, for example, V. M. Borodiuk et al., *Kompleksnye tselevye programmy v soiuznoi respublike* (Kiev: Naukova dumka, 1984), pp. 6, 43.

46. *Pravda*, 18 January 1986.

47. G. Kh. Popov, *Effektivnoe upravlenie* (Moscow: Ekonomika, 1985), pp. 235–41.

48. For an excellent analysis of the regional politics of budgetary allocations, see Donna Bahry, *Outside Moscow: Power Politics and Budgetary Policy in the Soviet Republics* (New York: New York University Press, 1987).

49. *Pravda*, 26 February 1986, translated in *Current Digest of the Soviet Press* (henceforth *CDSP*), vol. 38, no. 8 (26 March 1986), p. 17.

50. *Pravda*, 30 July 1986.

51. *Pravda*, 27 June 1987. The document is entitled "Basic Provisions for Radically Restructuring Economic Management."

52. *O korennoi perestroike upravleniia ekonomikoi: Sbornik dokumentov* (Moscow: Gospolitizdat, 1988), pp. 208–35.

53. In 1985–86, the share of industrial output managed by all-union ministries ranged from 29% to 40% in the seven republics for which data were available in their statistical handbooks.

54. *19th All-Union Conference of the CPSU: Documents and Materials* (Moscow: Novosti Press Agency Publishing House, 1988), p. 48.

55. *Sovetskaia Estoniia*, 27 September 1988, translated in U.S. Foreign Broadcast Information Service, *Daily Report: Soviet Union*, 27 October 1988, pp. 56–57.

56. *Pravda*, 28 October 1988.

57. *Pravda*, 14 March 1989.

58. *19th All-Union Conference of the CPSU*, pp. 60, 64.

59. *Pravda*, 20 September 1989.

60. *Pravda*, 24 September 1989.

61. *Pravda*, 21 February 1982.

62. For example, M. P. Osad'ko, "Vyravnovanie urovnei ekonomicheskogo razvitiia soiuznykh respublik," in V. N. Cherkovets, ed., *Teoreticheskie problemy formirovaniia i razvitiia edinogo narodnokhoziaistvennogo kompleksa* (Moscow: Izdatel'stvo Moskovskogo universiteta, 1985), pp. 36–49.

63. *Pravda*, 26 February 1986, in *CDSP*, vol. 38, no. 8 (26 March 1986), p. 23.

64. The full text of the 1961 Party Program was published in *Pravda*, 2 November 1961, and in English translation as: *Programme of the Communist Party of the Soviet Union* (Moscow: Foreign Languages Publishing House, 1961), the section on national relations on pp. 93–97. The new Program was published in *Pravda*, 7 March 1986, and in translation: *The Programme of the Communist Party of the Soviet Union: A New Edition* (Moscow: Novosti Press Agency Publishing House, 1986), the section on national relations on pp. 61–63.

65. *Pravda*, 26 February 1986, in *CDSP*, vol. 38, no. 8 (26 March 1986), p. 23.

66. James W. Gillula, "The Economic Interdependence of Soviet Republics," in *Soviet Economy in a Time of Change*, vol. 1, p. 640.

67. Ibid., pp. 646–52.

68. Grey Hodnett, "Technology and Social Change in Soviet Central Asia: The Politics of Cotton Growing," in Henry W. Morton and Rudolph L. Tőkés, eds., *Soviet Politics and Society in the 1970s* (New York: The Free Press, 1974), pp. 60–117.

69. A. G. Granberg, "Ekonomicheskoe vzaimodeistvie sovetskikh respublik," *Ekonomika i organizatsiia promyshlennogo proizvodstva*, 1982, no. 12, pp. 3–37.

CHAPTER 4

Nationalities and the Soviet Military

Teresa Rakowska-Harmstone

The Soviet Armed Forces are multiethnic in composition and a model "Soviet" institution. The military service in the USSR is promoted as the "School of the (Soviet) Nation" where young men of diverse ethnic origins and cultures are molded into model soldiers—and prototypes of the new "Soviet man." But the USSR's military and national heritage has produced a model soldier who is unabashedly Russian. The language, culture, training, and tradition of military service in the Soviet Union closely follow the models that had been developed by the Imperial Russian Army, and political military training efforts as well as the management of the ethnic factor in the distribution of military manpower have always been subordinated to the primary aims of military effectiveness—namely, the national integration and military cohesion of the forces and their maximum combat readiness.[1]

The ethnic heterogeneity of the forces reflects the national diversity of the Soviet population, though not in the same proportions, given the shifting ethnic balance within discrete age cohorts.[2] Through the late 1980s the Russians accounted for just over one-half of the Soviet population. The other half comprised representatives of more than one hundred nations and nationalities, among whom the other Slavs (Ukrainians and Belorussians) and the rapidly expanding Muslim groups are the most numerous. The growth, level of development, and differences in culture and attitudes of the Soviet nationalities have made the ethnic factor an important variable in military policy since the Red Army's birth. Indeed, its importance has grown in the four decades since the end of World War II—the "Great Patriotic War."

The separatist potential of national minorities was well understood by Lenin, and he used it to excellent advantage in facilitating the breakup of Imperial Russia. His recognition of the right to national self-determination, however, did not extend to the minorities once the power of the new Soviet state was established and consolidated. In military matters in particular, Lenin never deviated from the conviction that central control was essential, especially after the experience in 1918–19 with the Soviet military formations in the western borderlands (Ukrainian, Belorussian-Lithuanian, Latvian, and

Estonian)—which were willing to cooperate with the Workers'-Peasants' Red Army, but from the position of national autonomy—and after similar problems with autonomous Caucasian and Muslim military units. By the end of the Civil War all autonomous military formations were integrated into the Red Army or abolished.

The issues of ethnic autonomy and national rights, including the minorities' right to territorial military formations, came to a head at the Twelfth Congress of the Russian Communist Party (bolsheviks) in 1923, when the Ukrainian Communists openly accused the Red Army of being an instrument of Russification. In military matters a compromise was reached, which allowed for the coexistence of national formations with a cadre army but did not affect the principle of centralized command and control. A 1924–25 military reorganization resulted in three types of national formations. The first, larger "national military divisions," and second, smaller "ethnic units," were parts of regular formations of the standing army. The third type consisted of reserves organized in territorial divisions of the militia.

The importance of national formations was deemphasized in the late 1920s and early 1930s, and they were abolished in the military reform of 7 March 1938, which introduced a new principle of individual conscription. National military formations were briefly reinstated in World War II, largely because the military manpower that remained available after the Nazi blitzkrieg cut off the western borderlands was ethnically largely Turkic and Caucasian. The units' ethnic character served to enhance morale, facilitate command and socialization tasks (in the local languages), and mobilize the support of the soldiers' home communities. But the units' particular ethnic character was gradually diluted through high losses and their multiethnic replacements. By the end of the war it was in most cases retained in name only. National formations were gradually phased out after 1945.

Since the war's end the Soviet Armed Forces have been constituted as a single, integrated army. In a return to the principles of the 1938 reform, all male citizens are subject to universal military service based on individual recruitment and serve in ethnically mixed units. The language of the forces is exclusively Russian, and ethnic Russians predominate in the professional cadre. Unlike the Red Army of the 1920s, the manpower of which was 80% Slavic, the ethnic composition of annual draft cohorts of the Soviet Armed Forces reflects that of the population, but the recruits' postings in the service follow unofficial rules that favor Russians or Russified elements for special and elite combat services. As in the old Imperial Army, the Soviet Armed Forces have been the focus of Russian patriotism, and the traditions of the Imperial Army survive in the approach to military doctrine and application of military tactics, and in the in-service training methods, with their emphasis on drill, discipline, and habit-forming exercises. In the training and perceptions of officers the Imperial traditions not only survive, but seem to have been deliberately revived.[3]

The primary mission of the Soviet Armed Forces is the defense of the country. But the mission has been defined officially as the "defense of socialism," and as such transcends the Soviet boundaries. Since 1945 this has included the defense of the "socialist community" (the Warsaw Treaty Organization/Council for Mutual Economic Assistance regional state system), both on the "internal" front, against counterrevolution, and on the "external" front, against NATO. Since the 1970s it has been applied to the interests of "socialism" worldwide. Proclaimed by Leonid Brezhnev in 1971, the global aspect of the military's mission appears to have been muted in the reappraisal of Soviet foreign policy under Mikhail Gorbachev.

The "internationalist" aspect of the military's mission is in accord with their multinational composition. It would thus seem natural for it to strike a responsive chord in the soldiers' hearts, especially because Marxist-Leninist dialectics profess to have succeeded in reconciling the conflict between national and internationalist loyalties. But in practice the appeals to "Mother Russia" have tended to obscure (or to merge with) the appeals to the "Socialist Motherland," national loyalty has inspired greater enthusiasm than internationalist duty, and nationalist symbols and images have generated an emotional response more readily than internationalist ones.

In most respects the Russian characteristics of the Soviet Armed Forces appear to contribute to the strength and effectiveness of the military. But, in view of the growing importance and self-assertion of the national minorities, these may prove to be a source of weakness. Cynthia Enloe's perceptive concept of an "ethnic security map" fits well the history of Soviet ethnic relations, in the armed forces in particular.[4] The need to maintain such a map links the Imperial past with the Soviet present, because the Revolution changed neither the Russians' hegemonial role nor their quantitative and qualitative weight in the society. Soviet "internationalism" notwithstanding, the Russians' special position in the political, bureaucratic, and military elites was safeguarded by their having officially acquired the status of the "leading nation" in the "Soviet family of nations," a role that has been described colloquially as that of an "elder brother." Most Russians distrust and denigrate the minorities, the more so as these increase in numbers and become more assertive in their behavior and demands; the fear that their leading status was being threatened stimulated a revival of Russian nationalism in the 1970s and 1980s. They are cognizant of the necessity to maintain, safeguard, and perpetuate their hegemonial status, a perception that has been reflected in the unofficial ethnic key that has governed the distribution of military manpower among others.

The national attitudes of soldiers and officers may well prove to be the variable which ultimately determines—and differentiates—their behavior on the battlefield. It has been characteristic of Russian history, as noted by one perceptive observer, that a gap seems to exist between the Russian/ Soviet armed forces' economic and military potential (as measured by a whole range of objective indicators), and the actual field performance under fire[5]—a gap that an analyst would do well to keep in mind.

Military socialization in the Soviet Armed Forces aims to achieve two levels of integration of servicemen. The first level is the essential minimum of functional integration in terms of linguistic and behavioral conformity—or, in short, obedience to orders. The second and optimal level is an attitudinal (cognitive) integration, which implies the internalization of the regime's value system and the assimilation of its political message into the soldiers' personal weltanschauung, including their enthusiastic acceptance of the notion of self-sacrifice for the Socialist Motherland. The latter aim finds its expression in a phrase that is rarely absent from political officers' lips: the commitment to educate the troops in the "spirit of high idealism, diligence, and selfless devotion." The political education must prevail over ethno-cultural and political perceptions of the serviceman's original social milieu and the attitudes held there, if these are in conflict with the official message. The task is of particular importance in the case of conscripts and reservists as they begin (or resume) their military service. The professional cadres are less affected because their perceptions and attitudes have already been shaped by the military environment they had chosen as a life career, but the impact of the broader setting and of national attitudes should not be discounted here either, particularly in the lower ranks. It is the professional cadre who provides the leadership and sets the tone in the forces. But it is the conscript and the reservist whose actions on the battlefield make for victory or defeat in conventional warfare.

Soviet Nationalities and the Military Service

Not all Soviet nationalities produce recruits who are equally desirable from the point of view of military service, either in terms of preferred attitudes or the necessary educational and technical skills. Moreover, the least desirable of them happen also to be most numerous.

Knowledge of the Russian language, obviously, has been the minimal requirement. Yet, as language statistics from the 1979 census demonstrate, over 35% of the non-Russians—in absolute figures, almost 45 million people—did not speak Russian at all.[6] This group accounted for an approximate 18% (almost one-fifth) of the Soviet population. The share of non-speakers of Russian rises dramatically in the case of major nationalities in the borderlands. For the Central Asians and Transcaucasians it accounted for 50% to 70% of their totals; 71% of the Estonians did not speak Russian; even among the Ukrainians, the second largest national group in the country and the Russians' junior partners, there were many non-speakers of Russian. On the other hand, large national groups located within the Russian republic (such as the Tatars, Bashkirs, Mordvinians, and Chuvash) and the dispersed groups (Jews, Germans, and Poles), as well as most ethnic groups numbering under one million people, were much more proficient in the country's language of "internationality communication." (See Table 1.)

The general language statistics provide the best available indicators to measure levels of attitudinal and functional integration as defined here for purposes of military service. Linguistic assimilation into the Russian language in most cases indicates assimilation into the Russian culture and value

TABLE 1. Major Nationalities: Attitudinal and Functional Integration, 1979, Measured by Linguistic Russification and Bilingualism (in thousands and percent of total)

National Group	Total	Attitudinally Integrated (Russian Native Language)		Functionally Integrated (Bilingual in Russian)		Non-Integrated (Do Not Speak Russian)	
		Total	Percent	Total	Percent	Total	Percent
Ukrainians	42,347	7,214	17.1	21,089	49.8	14,017	33.1
Belorussians	9,463	2,404	25.4	5,394	57.0	1,665	17.6
Moldavians	2,968	178	6.0	1,407	47.4	1,383	46.6
Lithuanians	2,851	48	1.7	1,485	52.1	1,317	46.2
Latvians	1,419	68	4.8	805	56.7	546	38.5
Estonians	1,020	46	4.5	247	24.2	727	71.3
Georgians	3,571	61	1.7	953	26.7	2,557	71.6
Armenians	4,151	349	8.4	1,602	38.6	2,200	53.0
Azerbaidzhanis	5,477	99	1.8	1,616	29.5	3,763	68.7
Uzbeks	12,456	75	0.6	6,141	49.3	6,240	50.1
Kazakhs	6,556	131	2.0	3,429	52.3	2,996	45.7
Tadzhiks	2,898	23	0.8	858	29.6	2,017	69.6
Turkmen	2,028	20	1.0	515	25.4	1,493	73.6
Kirghiz	1,906	10	0.5	560	29.4	1,336	70.1
Tatars	6,317	834	13.2	4,352	68.9	1,131	17.9
Chuvash	1,751	317	18.1	1,135	64.8	229	17.1
Bashkirs	1,371	97	7.1	890	64.9	384	28.0
Mordvinians	1,192	327	27.4	782	65.6	83	7.0
Germans	1,936	825	42.6	1,001	51.7	110	5.7
Jews	1,811	1,509	83.3	248	13.7	54	3.0
Poles	1,151	302	26.2	514	44.7	335	29.1
Total Major Non-Russians	114,640	14,964	13.0	55,023	48.0	44,653	39.0
Total Other Non-Russians	10,028	3,008 est.	30.0 est.	6,518 est.	65.0 est.	501 est.	5.0 est.
Total Non-Russians	124,668	17,972	14.4 est.	61,541	49.4	45,154	36.2
Russians	137,397	137,260	99.9	--	--	--	--
USSR Total	262,065	155,232	59.2	61,541	23.5	45,154	17.2

Source: Calculated from 1979 census data, Chislennost' i sostav naseleniia SSSR: Po dannym Vsesoiuznoi perepisi naseleniia 1979 goda (Moscow: Finansy i statistika, 1984), pp. 71-73.

system, and this, in the military environment, has meant attitudinal integration. Bilingualism in Russian signifies capability to function effectively in a Russian-speaking environment and a willingness to adapt outwardly to prevalent requirements and to obey orders—hence, functional integration. Total ignorance of the dominant language, on the other hand, indicates nonintegration in terms both of alienation and inability to function. In the case of non-integrated Soviet national groups the alienation has been a result either of backwardness combined with the strength of traditional cultures (Central Asians and Transcaucasians), or conscious political self-assertion (Estonians), or both.

The integration criteria so defined allow for an assessment of the incoming recruits from the point of view of their desirability for military service, starting with the "best" and ending with the "least desirable." Accordingly, they can be divided into four groups: (1) group A—those integrated in attitudinal as well as functional terms; (2) group B—those integrated functionally; (3) group C—the non-integrated; and (4) group D—dissident elements.

The preferred group A includes the Russians and Russified elements from among all other Soviet national groups. Many Ukrainians and Belorussians are to be found in the latter category, especially the expatriates living outside their national republics and urban dwellers in the eastern and central portions of their republics, where interaction with the Russians has been most intense. Large segments of the three major dispersed groups (Jews, Germans, and Poles) are also Russified, as are the majorities of practically all the nationalities of less than union republic status, as well as individuals of all ethnic backgrounds who, for whatever reason, have opted to assimilate. In terms of the 1979 population census, group A numbered roughly 155 million people, or close to 60% of the Soviet population, including the approximately 18 million assimilated non-Russians in addition to the ethnic Russians.

Group B includes those non-Russians who, because of their bilingualism in Russian, can function within the "socialist" sector of society and are willing to conform to the official norms, but do not integrate in attitudinal terms because of a commitment to their own national identity and culture. Outwardly a conformist element, this group has retained, nevertheless, a latent hostility towards Russians; its members tend to cluster socially in national enclaves and to support each other in work-related situations. Included in this group are the bilinguals among Ukrainians and Belorussians, as well as Armenians and Georgians, the Balts, and all others, including the Muslims, who have mastered the needed language and technical skills. In rough numerical terms this group approximates the more than 60 million bilingual non-Russians enumerated in the 1979 census (23% of the Soviet population). A willingness to enter the public arena and to conform is an identifying mark of functional integration. This category appears to include one-half of all the non-Russians in the country, but may in fact be smaller, because in some cases bilingualism statistics are known to have been inflated.

Group C comprises the remaining 36% of the non-Russians, those who have not integrated. Persisting in traditional life-styles and unresponsive to integration appeals, they have either not mastered the Russian language or have not acquired the technical attributes that would enable them to participate in the Russian-dominated "socialist" sector, or both. As they acquire functional attributes, many from this group are likely to move to the B category. The C group includes the still overwhelmingly rural non-Russian population that accounted for over 64 million people (ca. 27% of the Soviet population) in 1970, the last year for which such data are currently available. The great majority of Muslims are to be found in this category, as well as the still surprisingly large proportions of other unilingual non-Russians: Georgians and Armenians, Moldavians, even Ukrainians (one-third) and Belorussians (almost one-fifth), among others. (See Table 1.) Most belong to this group by virtue of their still traditional way of life; some—because of a deliberate decision to reject the Russian model. Thus there is an overlap here with the next and last category.

Group D comprises the "dissident" elements. It includes national groups which are seen by the Communist party leadership as politically unreliable: Western Ukrainians and Belorussians, Balts, Jews, and Crimean Tatars. Obviously not all nationals of these groups are dissenters, and some may be among the best integrated, but the label has applied. Another element of the unreliables are individual dissenters, such as national, religious, and civil rights advocates and conscientious objectors. Many are drawn from the "disloyal" groups above, but dissidents come from all ethnic backgrounds, and qualify for inclusion in the group because of personal attitudes and behavior. There are Russians among them. No estimates can be given for the size of this group, but it is not large. It may increase, however, in view of the ethnic turmoil of the late 1980s.

Obviously the A group has been the preferred group for military recruitment, especially in the case of the professional cadres. Group B conscripts have been found acceptable for most types of military service, but group C recruits could be used successfully only for the most basic of military tasks. The proportion of these groups in the draft-age cohorts met the needs of Soviet military deployment adequately until the 1960s, but the situation changed in the 1970s and 1980s when the quality of manpower available was adversely affected by a number of factors.

First, the natural rates of growth of group A have been declining steeply, and those of group B have also been reduced since the 1950s. The minorities in group C, on the other hand, have experienced a veritable population explosion. Thus, the supply of Russian youth—the traditional backbone of the military forces—has shrunk, while the non-integrated minorities began to grow as a proportion of the draft-age cohorts. The changing ratio also meant a deterioration in the technical skills among recruits, many of whom came from rural areas and did not speak Russian, this at a time when the technical complexity of new weapons systems put a special premium on the technical competence of the soldiers.

Secondly, and largely because of a catastrophic increase in alcoholism, health standards in the USSR deteriorated and mortality rates doubled among young men of military age. Moreover, the young men of the A group seemed more affected by these problems than other youths. Finally, the emergence of ethnic nationalism among major nationality groups and a corresponding resurgence of Russian nationalism raised the threshold of ethnic conflict in the society at large. The conflict became increasingly visible also within the armed forces, especially because the Muslims—who, in the eyes of the professional cadres, were clearly substandard and potentially disloyal—accounted for a large proportion of conscripts. Their growing presence was perceived as a long-term threat to the Russian character of the Soviet Armed Forces and caused widespread mutterings about an alleged "yellowing" of the military.[7]

A confidential report that is said to have been prepared for the USSR Ministry of Defense is purported to have stated bluntly that, because of the population explosion in the southeastern republics, the Soviet Armed Forces were facing two major and interrelated problems: the language problem and the patriotism problem. The first was reflected in "an alarming number of new draftees [who] had a poor knowledge of oral and written Russian," the second—in "manifestations of chauvinism and nationalism" that were replacing "the spirit of Soviet patriotism and socialist internationalism" in relations between nationalities in the Army and the Navy.[8] Whether or not the report was genuine, the problems it raised undoubtedly were.

Western estimates of the proportional shift between Slavic and Muslim recruits agree that the share of draft-age Russians will drop, by the end of the century, from one-half of the total military manpower in the 1970s to somewhat over 40%, while that of the Muslims will grow from 13% to approximately one-fourth of the total in the same period. (See Table 2.) Nonetheless, the proportion of Slavs was projected to remain at about 60% until the end of the century, if the current rates of assimilation of the non-Russians into the Russian culture continued. But the prospect that by the year 2000 close to one-third of the draft-age cohorts will be drawn from among the poorly integrated or non-integrated non-Russians has created a need to reassess their deployment pattern in the forces as well as to devise new ways to speed up their integration. It seems that such a reassessment has already commenced.[9]

Military needs have been in the background of an accelerated campaign, which began in the late 1950s, to make Russian "the common language of internationality communication and cooperation of all the peoples of the USSR."[10] The quest for bilingualism has so far undergone two phases: the first, initiated by Khrushchev's education laws of 1958–59, and the second, under Brezhnev in the 1960s and 1970s, that featured a series of conferences on teaching Russian to non-Russians. A conference held in Riga (21–30 June 1982) concentrated on the special relevance of the language and patriotism questions for the upbringing of a Soviet soldier.

But the results have not been impressive. By the early 1980s Soviet sources explicitly admitted that more than half of the population of the southeastern republics could not speak Russian and that, indeed, fewer

TABLE 2.   Ethnic Composition of Cohort Reaching Draft Age (in percent)

National Group	1940-49	1973-77	1977	1988	1997
Russians	57.0	52.6	47.9	42.6	44.3
Ukrainians and Belorussians	22.6	17.5	18.7	18.2	16.1
Total East Slavs	79.6	70.1	66.6	60.8	60.4
Muslims	5.6	12.7	13.1	20.0	22.3
Armenians	1.2	1.7	2.1	1.8	2.0
Georgians	1.3	1.3	1.1	1.4	1.3
Moldavians	1.0	1.2	1.5	1.6	1.4
Balts	2.0	1.6	1.7	2.0	1.5
Others	9.3	11.4	13.9	12.2	11.0

Source: Adapted from Robert Martin, "Ethnic Minorities in the Soviet
Military: Noncombat Units as an Ethnic 'Sponge'" (Paper
delivered at the Joint Conference of the Section on Military
Studies of the International Studies Association and the
Strategic Studies Institute, Carlisle, PA, 20-22 October 1982)

young people there knew Russian than their fathers did[11]—an unacknow-
ledged testimony to the degree of autonomy the republics had gained since
the death of Stalin. The complaints were directed particularly at the language
problem in the military service where, it was reported, numerous members
of military personnel knew Russian poorly or not at all.

Most complaints concerned the Muslim republics, and remedial policies
were largely directed there. There was a renewed emphasis on improving
instruction in the Russian language, specifically including military vocabulary.
A campaign was launched to encourage Muslims to volunteer for officer
schools, one aspect of which was to build up a military ethos based on
Muslim participation in the Great Patriotic War. There even was an effort
to show greater evenhandedness in the promotion of bilingualism as Russian
settlers were encouraged to learn the language of the republic in which
they lived.

Both the language and patriotism campaigns continued under Brezhnev's
successors and were accelerated on Gorbachev's accession. Repeated efforts
were made in all the Muslim republics to improve the "patriotic political"
education of the future soldiers, to motivate young Muslims to learn Russian,
and to convince the most promising among them to volunteer for officer
schools. But, judging by information available, young Muslims remain as
uninterested in military service as they have been in joining the mainstream
of Soviet urban and industrial life or in learning the Russian language,
especially because the treatment of Muslim soldiers in the Soviet forces has
done little to make the prospects of a life-long military career attractive to

them. So far, self-segregation and alienation from Soviet models have been the dominant theme of the USSR's Muslim community.

In the Brezhnev period there undoubtedly were strong elements among the Muslim republican elites favoring functional integration and greater participation in state-sponsored activities. But the changes in Moscow and repeated purges of Central Asians in the name of "corruption," as well as a revival of Russian nationalism in the centers of power, combined to intensify and accelerate Russification policies while reinforcing the Muslim community's negative attitudes. Under *glasnost'* these attitudes found new and vociferous expression in the local media, serving to aggravate ethnic conflict further. Thus, no modifications were to be expected in the prevalent ethnic attitudes, nor any real changes in the relations between soldiers of different nationalities in the ranks.

The "Ethnic Security Map" in the Soviet Armed Forces

In 1989 the Soviet Armed Forces numbered 4,258,000 men—a figure that excluded some 490,000 construction troops as well as paramilitary formations of the KGB (Internal Security) and MVD (Internal Affairs) special troops, which numbered 570,000 men. The Soviet Armed Forces comprised five basic services: Strategic Rocket Forces, Ground Forces (Army), Air Defense Forces, the Air Force, and the Navy. The construction troops (along with most other non-combat personnel) were a part of the Ground Forces total. If they, as well as the KGB forces (Border Troops, Signals, Kremlin Guards, and Special Guards) and the MVD troops, were counted, the Soviet Union had approximately 5.8 million men under arms.[12]

The period of obligatory military service was two years (it was three years prior to 1968), with the three-year term retained only for the Navy and the naval units of the KGB. The age of call-up was eighteen (reduced from nineteen in 1968). The call-up took place twice a year, in the spring and in the fall, and was administered by local military commissariats (*voenkomaty*) according to specifications established by the Soviet Armed Forces General Staff. Every young man of seventeen had to register for the draft with his local military commissariat (at the district/town level), where he was interviewed and underwent a medical examination, and where his dossier was subsequently compiled on the basis of information obtained from his school, workplace, local police, and youth, sports, and other relevant organizations. Émigré reports indicate that the young men were then graded on a scale of "0" (top) to "5" (bottom), according to their perceived "worth" for military purposes. Official expectations were that after conscription their actual service assignments would both conform to the policy directives and accommodate the needs of particular services, provided the necessary manpower mix was available.

But in practice the officials of the *voenkomaty* appeared to enjoy considerable freedom in making the assignments, and it is known that many of them readily succumbed to pressures from local notables or allowed themselves to be bribed by interested recruiters and anguished parents. The evidence of émigrés in this case has been confirmed by the Soviet military press in the years since the advent of *glasnost'*. Western estimates indicate that approximately one-fifth of every draft cohort was excused from the draft in the 1970s; thus, the children of the elite generally escaped either via educational deferments or by joining the foreign service or the KGB. But pressing shortages of manpower that began to be felt by the late 1970s caused a drastic reduction, in 1982, of educational deferments, releasing approximately half a million young men annually for military service. Most of them were members of the choice A group of urban Russian or Russified elements. A 1984 report estimated that some 50,000 to 60,000 of those who failed to qualify for a deferment opted instead for going to an officer school.[13] The deferments were reinstated, however, in early 1989.

By all accounts, induction is a traumatic experience for a Soviet conscript, especially a unilingual non-Russian who is thus immersed into a Russian-speaking environment. The conscripts undergo an initial four to six weeks of orientation, drill, and training which, on the evidence of former Soviet officers, is a "very hard month in a soldier's life." Conditions may improve somewhat once he takes the oath of allegiance and is sent to his assigned unit. But the first year of the service anywhere is very difficult because of the informal system in the Soviet military of merciless hazing of "younger" (first-year) draftees by "older" (second-year) men. This, referred to informally as the master-slave system, customarily leads to excesses of brutality, sometimes even the loss of life.[14] The phenomenon was widely discussed in the military press in 1989, and is now known as "dedovshchina" or "non-regulation behavior." Ethnic antagonisms may further exacerbate the hazing. *Samizdat* sources indicate also that the harshness of treatment intensifies in the case of conscientious objectors and Jewish "refuseniks."

Information available indicates that there clearly is an "ethnic security map" in the Soviet Armed Forces, i.e., a pattern of distribution of ethnic manpower, which conforms to the perceptions of the dominant national group of how best to preserve its power. In the minds of the Soviet military high command this is synonymous with the need to maintain the military's traditional Russian character. The resulting ethnic pattern maximizes the presence of the Russian element in combat and elite formations as well as in the professional cadres, and consigns the most obvious *natsmeny* (a contraction for "national minorities," with a pejorative connotation) and other "untrustworthy" elements to less exposed or non-combatant branches of the service. The maintenance of the ethnic key is considered essential for the security of the regime, a perception that has sharpened considerably in the 1970s and 1980s because of the rise both in non-Russian and Russian nationalisms. These perceptions appear to have been shared by the political leaders, in the Brezhnev era as well as under his successors, including Gorbachev. There are additional, objective reasons that contribute to the maintenance of the ethnic key in the distribution of military manpower.

Differentials in relative economic and social development of non-Russian conscripts have to be recognized in assignments to the more demanding and technically complex services, as must also be their proficiency, or lack thereof, in the Russian language.

Some Western analysts believe that the visible pattern of ethnic distribution in the Soviet military is based solely on educational and technical considerations.[15] It should be kept in mind, however, that educational and technical requirements on the one hand and ethnic security requirements on the other have largely coincided in the case of the two most numerous subgroups: the Russians and Russified elements (group A) are also superior in terms of education and technical skills; the Muslims and other non-integrated nationalities (group C) are also technically and socially the least advanced. The end result has been the ethnic key in the military distribution of manpower, which has served to satisfy both the technical requirements of a modernizing army and the security perceptions of the dominant group. But in cases when the technical and the security requirements do not coincide—the three Baltic nationalities, for example, are at the top of the Soviet development and educational scale but are also the least trusted—the deployment of the particular group in the forces has conformed to security considerations.

There is no official blueprint for the ethnic security map as it has been applied in the Soviet Armed Forces, but two fundamental rules which form the basis for ethnic distribution of military manpower are clearly stated. The first is that each military unit and subunit must be ethnically mixed. The second is that no soldier should be stationed in his home area.[16] The first rule has been modified in practice whenever there is a need to maximize the Russian component in a given unit, but non-Russians have always been included, if in small numbers, in order to maintain the "internationalist" image. In fact, the multiethnic "internationalist" composition of Soviet military units has been a point of great official pride, and the Soviet military press tirelessly describes numerous fraternal "military collectives" in which representatives of the various Soviet nations and nationalities happily soldier together.

The second general rule, that of stationing draftees away from their national areas, seems to be generally followed, although it might have been breached occasionally at the insistence of powerful local leaders, as was apparently the case when Kazakh soldiers were allowed to serve in Kazakhstan to please Politburo member and Brezhnev's friend, the first secretary of Kazakhstan, Dinmukhamed Kunaev.[17] Petitions by Lithuanian conscripts who asked to serve in Lithuania are known to have been rejected.[18] Émigrés who have served in the Soviet military firmly believe that the rule is there to enhance the troops' capacity to suppress local disturbances. Certainly soldiers of military garrisons located in minority territories are kept in isolation from the local population. The isolation is less strict in the Russian areas, and is less strict for the officers than for the men.

Wartime mobilization provides the one general exception to the two rules above, because the call-up of local reservists makes for units of overwhelmingly local ethnic character. The experience of World War II is instructive in this regard, as is the initial composition of Soviet formations which invaded Afghanistan in December 1979 from their staging area in the Central Asian Military District.

The ethnic profile of the Soviet forces reveals a correlation between the ethnic composition of a given military unit and its combat role. The larger the percentage of Russians and other Slavs in a given unit, the more important are the unit's combat and security functions. Ex-servicemen interviewed in the West expressed firm convictions that the *voenkomaty* have standing instructions governing the ethnic distribution of military manpower, and these require that combat and security formations be built around a strong Russian/Slavic core and include only a small percentage of less reliable nationalities.

Information available for the 1960s and 1970s confirms the correlation between the size of the Russian "core" and the security/combat role of a given branch of the service. The KGB Border Troops are said to be staffed almost exclusively by Slavs, with Russians predominating in the formations stationed on the western borders, and Ukrainians and Belorussians—in the formations deployed in the east and in the southeast. Russians also constitute an overwhelming majority in the Soviet formations stationed in Eastern Europe. The Strategic Rocket Forces, the Air Force, and the Navy are reported to be composed mostly of Slavs, with the non-Slavs—who account for approximately 10% of their total manpower—being utilized mostly in support roles. The airborne units are also predominantly Russian. There was no agreement among émigré ex-servicemen, however, which of the elite formations had the first call on scarce priority manpower. Some felt it was the KGB, others—the Navy and the paratroops.

The share of non-Russians was said to be higher in the Ground Forces; they constituted an estimated 20% of the Army's combat formations such as armor, artillery, and infantry. These were recruited mostly from among the B group, i.e., the non-Russians who were functionally integrated. Even so, non-Russians were deployed mostly in support services. The bulk of the non-Slavs, and particularly the non-integrated or poorly integrated members of the C group, were deployed in non-combat formations, particularly in construction and railroad troop units. They were also well represented in the MVD internal security forces.[19] This pattern of ethnic distribution was confirmed by Western analysts. The "national security force," i.e., the five combat services plus the KGB Border Troops, were roughly 80% Slavic and 20% non-Slavic in composition. More than two-thirds of the soldiers in railroad and construction units, on the other hand, and approximately one-half of the MVD internal security forces, were Muslims. These formations may be seen as an "ethnic sponge" soaking up Muslim surpluses in Soviet military manpower, but there is doubt of their capacity to do so in the future, in view of the ever-growing share of Muslim recruits.[20]

The construction battalions (*stroibaty*) are used for civilian as well as military construction projects, a practice that helps to alleviate labor shortages.

In addition to Muslims, they include Slavs (an approximate 20% of the total, mostly dissidents and men with criminal records), with the balance composed of Caucasians, Balts, Jews, and other non-Slavs of doubtful reliability. The soldiers in the *stroibaty* spend their time in service with picks and shovels rather than with rifles, and the service is rated at the bottom of the military scale. But there are advantages to serving in non-combatant units: the environment is in fact multicultural, the discipline is less stringent, and soldiers working on civilian projects are actually paid civilian wages. The heavy presence of Muslims in construction battalions is openly acknowledged. A high-ranking political officer of the Turkestan Military District actually singled out the practice for praise, boasting that

> the representatives from the Central Asian republics take an active part in carrying out the comprehensive program for the development of the Non-Black-Earth Zone, and are working on the major construction projects of our century—the development of oil and gas reserves of Tyumen and the construction of the BAM [Baykal-Amur Mainline].[21]

Not coincidentally, all the projects noted are in the regions of Siberia where Central Asians refuse to go voluntarily.

The heavy Muslim coloration of the MVD troops is not surprising, given the degree of alienation between the Soviet Muslim and European nationalities. Ex-prisoners as well as defectors report that the Muslims' poor knowledge of the Russian language makes it difficult to communicate with them, and, moreover, that they are tough and cruel and have no sympathy for the European dissidents whom they guard—all qualities that make them reliable guardians of Soviet prisons.

The non-commissioned officer cadre has been a weak link in the Soviet forces. It has not been possible to attract sufficient numbers of volunteers in competition with the civilian economy to form an adequate permanent non-commissioned officer corps. Thus, a greater proportion of non-commissioned officers are recruited from the conscript pool and serve for two years only, and few of them reenlist. Military folklore has it that Ukrainians and Tatars make the best NCOs, but the conscripts are chosen for NCO training by the *voenkomaty* at the time of the call-up, the selected candidates being sent for special six months' NCO training. While the candidates should be chosen from a relatively broad ethnic spectrum (after all, there is a need for trained NCOs in the reserves in all areas of the Soviet Union, including minority areas), the selection is limited to those who, at a minimum, can communicate in Russian. In the ranks the prestige of conscript NCOs is overshadowed by that of the "old soldiers" (*stariki*). Thus, and in contrast with the West where professional NCOs form the backbone of an army, in the Soviet Armed Forces many of the traditional NCO duties are performed by junior officers.

Émigré evidence suggests that, in ethnic terms, the draft NCOs are mostly Slavs, and the career NCOs and warrant officers (the latter rank was established in 1971 to make the career more attractive) are overwhelmingly

Slavs. Ukrainians are said to constitute an overwhelming majority of the NCOs, while there are almost no Muslims among them. The predominance of Slavs is due both to the selection criteria and to their relatively high reenlistment rates, because for them a life on military and naval bases is preferable to an existence in remote kolkhozes or provincial towns, and, on retirement, they are eligible for jobs in the militia or in the KGB. Although the same opportunities are available to non-Slavs, the advantages for them are outweighed by the need to Russify, which is an inescapable corollary of a professional military career.

Members of the officer corps are volunteers. Admission to officer schools requires educational and technical skills as well as fluency in the Russian language. Not only do the conditions of entry favor urban and economically more developed elements, but they also limit the intake to the candidates who feel sufficiently at home in the Russian cultural environment of the forces to choose a military career. All of these factors serve to make the professional cadre a preserve of the Slavs. In the post-World War II period there emerged, in fact, an officer caste in the Soviet Armed Forces, with sons following fathers in the service in the old Imperial tradition.

The non-Slavs do have a representation among the Soviet officers, but it has been minimal. Recent efforts, begun in the late Brezhnev period, to attract non-Russians into the officer corps and to introduce an element of multiculturalism there, even if successful, promise to do little to change the basic elements that make the Soviet army into a Russian army, and thus an instrument of Russification. The relatively high level of assimilation among the Belorussians and Ukrainians is due in part to their traditional willingness to follow a military career. This has been true also in the case of the smaller nationalities located in the Russian republic.

Stiff entry examinations into officer schools test not only the candidates' educational and technical skills but also their proficiency in the Russian language and their knowledge of Russian history and culture. They must be recommended by their Komsomol and party organizations and have a clean bill of health from the security police. In addition, there are the less tangible psychological and cultural attributes and behavior patterns "appropriate" for an officer that are a direct throwback to the Imperial traditions. All of these requirements and perceptions tend to discourage, if not to exclude, the non-Russians.

No hard information is ever given on the ethnic composition of the Soviet officer corps, except for occasional historical tidbits, but all Western estimates, based on analysis of ethnic origins of the officers' names, agree that Slavs dominate the ranks, and that approximately 90% of general officers are Slavs.[22] It should be noted that the share of the Slavs (and the Russians) seems to have gone up in the last twenty years in comparison with the immediate post-World War II period, when there was a sprinkling of minorities among the top brass. Their appearance in the top command echelon has shrunk to a virtual zero by the mid-1970s.

A comprehensive survey of a sample of 10,292 names of officers, collected for the period 1976–78, confirms the picture of the Russian/Slav character of the Soviet officer corps. (See Table 3.) It also confirms the assumption that the share of Slavic officers was higher in the elite services than in the Ground Forces, and higher among flag and general officers than in the junior ranks. (See Table 4.) At the same time the survey shows that all major non-Slav nations were represented in the officer corps, but mostly among junior officers, and that their total share was 7.5% of the total as compared to their 25% weight in the Soviet population. Disaggregated by nationalities, the data show that Jews and Armenians were, in fact, over-represented in comparison with their share in the population, while Muslims, with 3% of the total in the officer sample, were grossly underrepresented in comparison with their 17% of the population (in 1979) and more than 30% of the annual call-up cohorts.[23] The campaign to recruit Muslims into the officer corps must have had some success, but it is unlikely that their numbers among the military cadre will grow in the foreseeable future, if for no other reason than because of the polarization of ethnic antagonisms that has developed within the framework of *glasnost'*, and as a result of a repressive "anti-corruption" campaign that Gorbachev has followed in the four Central Asian republics and Kazakhstan, as well as his failure to settle the Nagorno-Karabakh dispute between Armenia and Azerbaidzhan to the satisfaction of either of the protagonists.

Ethnic Attitudes in the Ranks

Ethnic attitudes in the ranks are an accurate reflection of ethnic attitudes at large in the USSR, but the conditions of isolation, close proximity, and confinement that characterize the military environment, and the hothouse atmosphere, tend to sharpen perceptions and intensify antagonisms.

A 1978 study based on interviews with émigrés concluded that harsh living conditions, rigid social stratification, the hazing, ethnic conflict, and, for some—the Muslims, for example—problems with the diet were major depressants of morale. It confirmed the high incidence of desertions and suicide, and the high levels of conflict and physical violence, including assaults by enlisted men on NCOs and officers.[24] Soviet forces have long complained of the existence in the ranks of "microgroups." On close examination these are revealed to be based primarily on ethnic grounds and cut across the two other in-service cleavages, those based on seniority and privilege, and are formed largely as mutual protection groups as each soldier seeks support and succor of his co-nationals and co-religionists. Such groups, based in cultural and/or regional affinity, are both traditional and ubiquitous in the ranks, and also serve to express ethnic antagonisms stimulated by such features of military service as ethnically stereotyped treatment of the "juniors" by the "seniors" and NCOs. Ethnic cleavages exist even in the predominantly Slavic units because of the presence there of highly assimilated but nonetheless nationally conscious soldiers (such as Ukrainians and Tatars).

On the evidence of émigrés and, since *glasnost'*, also of the Soviet military press, the non-Russians are never allowed to forget who they are and that

88

TABLE 3. Total Soviet Officer Personnel and Officer Personnel by Force Components in Sample, by Nationality of Surname, 1976–78, Compared with National Composition of Population, 1979 (in percent)

Nationality of Surname*	Armed Forces Overall**	Ground Forces	Navy	Air and Air Defense Forces	Total Population
Russian	61.37	59.23	66.90	63.53	52.42
Ukrainian	26.25	26.81	23.49	26.08	16.16
Belorussian***	5.06	5.48	4.27	4.53	3.61
Other Slavic	0.07	0.07	0.10	0.05	0.59
Total Slavic	92.75	91.59	94.76	94.19	72.78
Muslim	3.06	3.46	2.28	2.57	16.50
Jewish	2.02	2.43	1.45	1.46	0.69
Armenian	0.76	0.83	0.63	0.65	1.58
Georgian	0.38	0.60	0.04	0.09	1.36
Lithuanian	0.22	0.30	0.09	0.11	1.09
Latvian	0.13	0.16	0.11	0.08	0.55
Estonian	0.08	0.11	0.06	0.03	0.39
Moldavian	0.07	0.04	0.05	0.22	1.13
Other Non-Slavic	0.54	0.48	0.55	0.63	3.93
Total Non-Slavic	7.46	8.41	5.26	5.84	27.22

Source: Allen Hetmanek, Bruce Thompson, and Richard Trout, _Ethnic Composition of the Soviet Officer Corps_, prepared for the Soviet/Warsaw Pact Division, Directorate for Intelligence Research, U.S. Defense Intelligence Agency, September 1979, p. 2, Table 1; Soviet census of 1979.

*The concept of nationality utilized in the population census differs from that underlying the surname data in that the latter reflects more the ethnic origin of an individual than his actual national identity. Also some smaller minority nationalities utilize, to a greater or lesser extent, surnames adopted from the Russians or other Slavs.

**Officers in the Strategic Rockets Forces were excluded since an adequate sample was lacking.

***Some surnames in the sample could be either Russian or Belorussian. The decision as to which name category was used for officers with these names was based on the linguistic origin of the name, a judgment as to its relative frequency among one of these groups as compared to the other, and other factors.

TABLE 4. Proportion of Slavic-Surname Officers among Total Officers in Sample, by Force Component and Level, 1976-78 (in percent)

	Armed Forces Overall	Ground Forces	Navy	Air and Air Defense Forces
Slavic-Surname Officers	92.75	91.59	94.76	94.19
Flag and General Level		93.75	96.86	97.00
Senior Level		90.29	94.42	94.69
Junior Level		92.43	94.72	93.35
Russian-Surname Officers	61.37	59.23	66.90	63.53
Flag and General Level		65.97	70.68	72.00
Senior Level		56.33	65.23	64.45
Junior Level		60.79	67.80	61.55
Ukrainian-Surname Officers	26.25	26.81	23.49	26.08
Flag and General Level		24.65	20.42	21.27
Senior Level		27.68	23.44	24.55
Junior Level		26.37	23.96	28.06
Belorussian-Surname Officers	5.06	5.48	4.27	4.53
Flag and General Level		3.13	5.76	3.73
Senior Level		6.18	5.55	5.69
Junior Level		5.21	2.86	3.65
Others	0.07	0.07	0.10	0.05

Source: Allen Hetmanek, Bruce Thompson, and Richard Trout, Ethnic Composition of the Soviet Officer Corps, prepared for the Soviet/Warsaw Pact Division, Directorate for Intelligence Research, U.S. Defense Intelligence Agency, September 1979 (unclassified, p. 2, Table 3).

they are inferior to the Russians (although tables may be turned if non-Russians happen to be prominent among the "seniors"). Each group is credited with a set of special characteristics. Ukrainians are "nationalistic"; Georgians and Armenians are "insular"; Balts are "fascist" and are respected but disliked. Because of their cultural alienation and different physical appearance Muslims are generally ostracized and regarded as inferior, a perception reflected in the universally applied epithets *chernozhopy* ("black asses") and *churka* (literally, "wood chip," used in the sense of "blockhead"), as well as their discriminatory treatment in assignments.

Antagonism between Muslims and Europeans is one of the two basic ethnic cleavages in the ranks; the other is between Russians and non-Russians. The non-Russians are also divided by conflicts of their own, such as the one between Armenians and Azerbaidzhanis, and some intra-Central Asian feuds. Even groups with limited national consciousness "wake up" to their national identity under the impact of the service, and the greater functional integration that is undoubtedly achieved in the service is often accompanied by an enhanced ethnic militancy after the soldier returns to civilian life.

Ethnic problems in the forces are further exacerbated by the emergence, in the 1970s and 1980s, of the issue of conscientious objectors, the roots of which can be traced to religious and national convictions, and are also reflective of growing pacifism. The prominence given to the issue in the Soviet press indicates that the number of religious objectors must be quite substantial. Because of their refusal to bear arms, they are treated by the Soviet Armed Forces as criminals. *Samizdat* sources report cases of murder of such soldiers because they refuse to abandon their beliefs. In confessional terms they are generally members of Protestant sects such as the Baptists, Seventh-Day Adventists, Pentecostalists, and Jehovah's Witnesses, but include also Roman Catholics and Jewish refuseniks. In ethno-cultural terms most belong to the Western nationalities (Ukrainians and Balts).

Because of the rule that no soldier should serve in his national area, ethnic antagonisms spill over onto relations between the soldiers and the local population. There have been reports of Russian hostility to non-Russian (especially Muslim) troops stationed in Russian areas, and antagonism against Russian troops stationed in nationality areas, particularly in the western borderlands.

In line with their attitude towards hazing, officers tend to turn a blind eye to ethnic infighting in the ranks unless matters get totally out of hand, because the problem is seen both as traditional and intractable, and any interference can only damage the officer's career. But, because of the escalation in ethnic antagonisms, the level of official concern, as expressed in the military press, has substantially increased, although no solutions have been proposed beyond the usual reliance on more effective political education and proposed concessions to ethnic cultural needs, such as providing non-Russian reading materials in military reading rooms and libraries.

The professional officer cadre is very much the bearer of the "Russian message," in composition as well as in attitudes. Thus, there are no open ethnic group cleavages among the officers as there are among soldiers, although such antagonisms are undoubtedly present among junior officers. But officers' attitudes in general, especially in the senior ranks, are openly centralist and Russian nationalist, which means that there is little sympathy for autonomist demands by the non-Russians and no enthusiasm for either compromising the Russian character of the forces or opening up professional ranks to non-integrated ethnics, Muslims especially.

An extraordinary (at the time) condemnation of discrimination in the armed forces on national grounds appeared in the military newspaper *Krasnaia zvezda* in 1980, clearly a warning against the Russifying zeal of the cadres seen as inappropriate in the face of the demographic facts of life:

> In a socialist state there is no place for even the smallest expressions of discrimination against any nation or nationality. In the evaluations of the activities and merits of any of them, what counts is not the national origin of an officer, but his ideological-political and moral maturity, the level of his military preparedness and his organizational capabilities. This or that national identity of a military person cannot become a precondition for assigning him

to whatever service duties. This applies also to soldiers fulfilling their obligations.[25]

Since the mid-1980s the ethnic conflict in the Soviet Armed Forces not only has intensified but has become increasingly visible, due to several factors. First, the demographic trends favoring Muslims and the less integrated nationalities at the expense of the Slavs accelerated instead of slowing down as expected. As a result, in 1988 the conscripts from Central Asia and the Caucasus accounted for 37% of the draft intake, as compared to 28% in 1980[26] and an approximate 17% in the 1970s[27]—a disaster from the point of view of the military's cohesion, surpassing even the most pessimistic earlier scenarios. Secondly, the Afghan conflict has done much to exacerbate and expose ethnic antagonisms within the ranks. The gap between Muslim soldiers—seen as unreliable and used primarily for non-combat tasks—and the Europeans grew even wider, and ethnic violence became commonplace.[28] Thirdly, the magnitude of the problem, combined with *glasnost'*, has brought the ethnic conflict within the military into the open, initiating a remarkably frank and revealing discussion in the military and non-military press.

Conclusion

The ethnic security map in the Soviet Armed Forces has been easy to maintain as long as an appropriate ethnic mix was available in successive call-ups. The problem, in the 1970s and even more acutely in the 1980s, has been that the ethnic mix has been changing in favor of the nationalities that are technically least developed and culturally and politically most alienated. Demographic trends unfavorable to the maintenance of the present pattern are projected to extend well into the next century, and thus place Soviet leaders and military planners before a difficult dilemma. Initiatives introduced in the late Brezhnev era—an invitation to non-Russians to enter professional military service, combined with a new campaign to make non-Russians learn Russian and an intensification of political education efforts—brought few results, largely because they were resisted by the interested parties. The professional military cadres resent any attempt to dilute the military's Russian character. On the other hand, the Muslims and other affected non-Russians show even less inclination than before either to learn Russian or to become professional warriors. Neither side is much impressed by renewed ideological exhortations. As Gorbachev has consolidated political power and replaced practically the entire military command of the Brezhnev era with his own appointees, first steps have been taken in 1988 towards a new military policy, promising a new approach to the old dilemma.

A long-term approach that has emerged from the ongoing discussion so far is the decision to study the sociology of ethnic relations in the military—a welcome shift in emphasis away from the usual exhortations to shape up the political education system. While marginally helpful, this will do little to improve the current situation, however. The true state of affairs in 1990 is that an influx of Muslim recruits can no longer be contained in non-combat roles, or, in other words, that *stroibaty* are no longer able to perform their role as an ethnic sponge. At the same time the Muslims' alienation and their hatred of the Russians have increased, as has the level of alienation and nationalism of other non-Russians.

Yet all the signs indicate that the maintenance of the "ethnic security map" in the armed forces may be even more important to Gorbachev than it had been to his predecessors. In the five years since his accession he has restored unequivocal Russian predominance in the centers of power in the Soviet Union.[29] Although his military policy is still in the process of development, Gorbachev's prescription for dealing with the current situation seems to be a reduction in the numerical strength of the armed forces, a move that has the additional advantage of promoting "peace and disarmament" in foreign policy and reducing economic costs at home. As announced in Gorbachev's "Christmas present" speech to the United Nations in December 1988 in New York, there will be a reduction of half a million in the strength of the Soviet Armed Forces, and much of this reduction will actually come (according to commentaries available), from the officer corps.

The move has apparently been resisted by some senior commanders, but it has several obvious advantages from the point of view of military cohesion and effectiveness. It will make the Soviet Armed Forces "leaner and meaner"—the "leanness" allowing for the preservation, for the time being, of the Russian majority in the professional cadre and in combat and elite formations. Further cuts in the size of the military are not excluded—even with the cuts announced, the Soviet Armed Forces will still number over four million soldiers—which may result in a return to some kind of a core regular army, as in the days of Imperial Russia, that would rely on the Slavic manpower. One might even hazard the speculation that Gorbachev eventually may want to establish a volunteer army, although such a move would constitute a clear break with tradition, Soviet as well as Imperial Russian.

Ethnic conflict in the Soviet Armed Forces intensified in 1989, as has the resistance of young men to the draft. The resistance has been exceptionally pronounced in the national republics, accompanied by popular agitation over the alleged hazing of ethnic recruits. Official demands were made by the Baltic republics and Georgia to allow conscripts to carry out their military service in their national territories. These demands have been coupled with proposals, emanating from the various popular fronts, to reinstitute national military territorial formations. All such demands, as well as any suggestions for a volunteer army, were strongly condemned by military spokesmen.[30] Not since the early 1920s has there been such an open challenge to the traditional Russian military heritage, the challenge that faces Soviet political and military leaders as they plan the future characteristics, composition, and organization of the Soviet Armed Forces.

Notes

1. This article draws extensively on the author's longer study, "USSR," in Teresa Rakowska-Harmstone, Christopher D. Jones, John Jaworsky, Ivan Sylvain, Zoltan

Barany, *Warsaw Pact: The Question of Cohesion*, Phase II, vol. 3, *Union of Soviet Socialist Republics; Bulgaria, Czechoslovakia and Hungary; Bibliography*, ORAE Extra-Mural Paper No. 39 (Ottawa, Canada: Department of National Defence, March 1986), pp. 1–290.

2. See Lubomyr Hajda, "Nationality and Age in Soviet Population Change," *Soviet Studies*, vol. 32, no. 4 (October 1980), pp. 475–99.

3. Chris Bellamy, "Similarities between the Soviet Army and its Tsarist Antecedent," *RUSI Journal for Defence Studies*, vol. 124 (September 1979); Norman Stone, "The Historical Background of the Red Army," in John Erickson and E. J. Feuchtwanger, eds., *Soviet Military Power and Performance* (London: Macmillan, 1979).

4. Cynthia H. Enloe, *Ethnic Soldiers: State Security in Divided Societies* (Harmondsworth, England: Penguin Books, 1980), p. 15.

5. Stone, "Historical Background," p. 4.

6. The preliminary figures on language affiliation from the 1989 census so far available (as published in the Estonian newspaper, *Rahva Hääl*, 19 September 1989) are inadequate for our purposes: they are limited to nationalities of union-republic status and lack sufficient detail on bilingualism. Nevertheless, the overall patterns described here do not appear to be significantly altered.

7. Jeremy A. Azrael, *Emergent Nationality Problems in the USSR*, R-2172-AF (Santa Monica, CA: Rand Corporation, September 1977), p. 16; and S. Enders Wimbush and Dimitry Ponomareff, *Alternatives for Mobilizing Soviet Central Asian Labor: Outmigration and Regional Development*, R-2476-AF (Santa Monica, CA: Rand Corporation, November 1979), p. 5.

8. "Soviet Population Problem," *Intelligence Digest: Weekly Review* (London), 17 November 1982.

9. Information from the 1989 census that is beginning to become available indicates that the Muslims' share in the young annual cohorts have actually been higher than expected, and consequently the estimates will probably have to be revised upwards. See Ann Sheehy, "Russian Share of Soviet Population Down to 50.8 Percent," Radio Liberty, *Report on the USSR*, vol. 1, no. 42 (20 October 1989), pp. 1–5.

10. The wording is that used in the 1961 Party Program. See *Programme of the Communist Party of the Soviet Union (Draft)* (Moscow: Foreign Languages Publishing House, 1961), p. 96.

11. Iu. V. Bromlei, "O nekotorykh aktual'nykh zadachakh etnograficheskogo izucheniia sovremennosti," *Sovetskaia etnografiia*, 1983, no. 6, p. 14.

12. For details, see *The Military Balance 1989–90* (London: International Institute for Strategic Studies, Autumn 1989), pp. 32–42.

13. Air Commodore E. S. Williams, "Morale, Motivation and Leadership in the Soviet Armed Forces," *RUSI Journal of Defence Studies*, vol. 129 (September 1984), pp. 3–7.

14. See Richard A. Gabriel, *The New Red Legions: An Attitudinal Portrait of the Soviet Soldier* (Westport, CT: Greenwood Press, 1980); Viktor Suvorov, *Inside the Soviet Army* (London: Hamish Hamilton, 1982); and others. The hazing practice is now also openly admitted in the official Soviet military press, such as *Krasnaia zvezda*.

15. Ellen Jones, "Minorities in the Soviet Armed Forces," *Comparative Strategy*, vol. 3, no. 4 (1982), pp. 285–318.

16. A. Skryl'nik, "XXVI s"ezd KPSS i internatsional'noe vospitanie voinov," *Voenno-istoricheskii zhurnal*, 1981, no. 11, p. 7.

17. Azrael, *Emergent Nationality Problems*, p. 21.

18. Kestutis K. Girnius, "Continuing Crackdown on Lithuanian Dissidents: Terleckas and Sasnauskas Sentenced," *Radio Liberty Research Bulletin*, RL 351/80 (29 September 1980), p. 4.

19. This and the preceding paragraphs are based on the results of interviews with former Soviet servicemen in Azrael, *Emergent Nationality Problems*; Gabriel, *New Red Legions*; S. Enders Wimbush and Alex Alexiev, *The Ethnic Factor in the Soviet Armed Forces*, R-2787/1 (Santa Monica, CA: Rand Corporation, March 1982); Robert Bathurst, Michael Burger, and Ellen Wolffe, *The Soviet Sailor: Combat Readiness and Morale*, KFR 383-82 (Arlington, VA: Ketron, Inc., 30 June 1982); and Suvorov, *Inside the Soviet Army*.

20. Robert Martin, "Ethnic Minorities in the Soviet Military: Noncombat Units as an Ethnic 'Sponge'" (Paper delivered at the Joint Conference of the Section on Military Studies of the International Studies Association and the Strategic Studies Institute, Carlisle, PA, 20–22 October 1982).

21. Maj. Gen. E. Aunapu, first deputy chief of the Political Administration of the Turkestan Military District, "V dukhe patriotizma i internatsionalizma," *Kommunist vooruzhennykh sil*, 1982, no. 19, p. 36.

22. See Timothy J. Colton, *Commissars, Commanders, and Civilian Authority: The Structure of Soviet Military Politics* (Cambridge, MA: Harvard University Press, 1979), Table 13, p. 261; and Teresa Rakowska-Harmstone, "The Soviet Army as an Instrument of National Integration," in Erickson and Feuchtwanger, *Soviet Military Power*, pp. 143–44.

23. Allen Hetmanek, Bruce Thompson, and Richard Trout, *Ethnic Composition of the Soviet Officer Corps*, prepared for the Soviet/Warsaw Pact Division, Directorate for Intelligence Research, U.S. Defense Intelligence Agency, September 1979 (unclassified).

24. Richard A. Gabriel, "The Morale of the Soviet Army: Some Implications for Combat Effectiveness," *Military Review*, October 1978, pp. 27–39. See also Suvorov, *Inside the Red Army*.

25. N. Shumikhin, "Armiia mnogonatsional'nogo sovetskogo gosudarstva," *Krasnaia zvezda*, 9 October 1980.

26. Ann Sheehy, "Interethnic Relations in the Soviet Armed Forces," *Radio Liberty Research Bulletin*, RL 421/88 (15 September 1988), p. 1, citing Soviet sources.

27. Martin, "Ethnic Minorities," p. 24.

28. Alexander Alexiev, *Inside the Soviet Army in Afghanistan*, R-3627-A (Santa Monica, CA: Rand Corporation, May 1988).

29. See Teresa Rakowska-Harmstone, "Gorbachev's Nationality Policy" (Paper delivered at the Twentieth National Convention of the American Association for the Advancement of Slavic Studies, Honolulu, HI, 18–21 November 1988).

30. See, for example, the statement by Minister of Defense Dmitrii Yazov, *Krasnaia zvezda*, 9 November 1989.

CHAPTER 5

Some Factors in the Linguistic and Ethnic Russification of Soviet Nationalities: Is Everyone Becoming Russian?

Barbara A. Anderson and Brian D. Silver

Language and ethnic affiliation are the most important determinants of the non-Russian peoples' identity in the USSR. Given the country's multiplicity of nationalities, and the political ramifications of this diversity, changes in language behavior and ethnic attachments have significant long-term implications for the Soviet state and society.

Changes in language behavior and ethnic identity of a population seldom take place quickly. When they do occur, it is often an intergenerational process. The levels and rates of assimilation among the Soviet nationalities are influenced by a variety of factors. Regime policies are one, but even sudden shifts in policy often produce an effect only gradually. They are, in any case, not necessarily determinative, for the varying levels of development and the specific experiences of particular groups also play an important role. There is, as well, the impact of critical historical events that may precipitate a process of unforeseen change that becomes fully apparent only after the passage of considerable time.[1]

Our study examines the linguistic and ethnic assimilation of the non-Russian nationalities in the Soviet Union in this light, focusing on a few elements of the process that are important but not well understood.[2]

The Extent of Linguistic Russification

The Soviet censuses of 1959, 1970, 1979, and 1989 each asked every respondent's native language (*rodnoi iazyk*), with parents answering for young

Acknowledgments: Support for the research on which this study is based was provided by the National Science Foundation (grant nos. SES8015074 and SES8015075), the John Simon Guggenheim Foundation, the Russian Research Center of Harvard University, the National Council for Soviet and East European Research (contract nos. 625-9a and 625-9b), and the National Institutes of Health (grant nos. RO1 HD-19915 and P30 HD-10003).

children. This question was supposed to elicit the language that the respondent knew best, not necessarily that which he or she had learned first, and did not have to match his or her self-identified nationality.[3]

The 1970, 1979, and 1989 censuses (but not that of 1959) also asked whether a person could "freely command another language of the peoples of the USSR." The term "freely command" was generally understood to mean "freely converse," but no test of actual language ability was administered. Moreover, only one such other language could be listed in the official census totals, and only from among languages of the "peoples of the USSR"—for example, Russian, Estonian, or Tatar (since Russians, Estonians, and Tatars are considered indigenous "peoples of the USSR"), but not German or Korean (since Germans and Koreans are considered non-indigenous). German, Korean, English or any other language could be reported as native language, however.

Table 1 shows the distribution of all non-Russians by native and second language. At all dates the vast majority of non-Russians claimed the language of their nationality as native language—84% as late as 1989. Those who did not, most frequently cited Russian as their native language—15% of all non-Russians in 1989.

Russian is likewise the most commonly mentioned *second* language, with almost half (48.1%) of all non-Russians claiming it as such in 1989. Less than 3% of all non-Russians declared a language other than Russian or the language of their own group as a second language in 1970, 1979, or 1989. Thus, for most non-Russians, any discussion of linguistic change must focus on the shift between the traditional language of the group and Russian.[4]

Use of Russian both as the native and as a second language has increased in recent years. But the extent of adoption of Russian as native language increased very little between 1959 and 1989, while the extent of its adoption as a second language increased enormously between 1970 and 1979 but then decreased slightly between 1979 and 1989.

As shown in panel C of Table 1, 9.9% of the non-Russians in 1989 had adopted Russian as their native language *and* failed to claim the language of their own nationality as a second language. But 47.5% reported that they freely commanded Russian while claiming their own national language as native; and another 4.7% reported Russian as their native language while retaining that of their own nationality as a second language. Of course, the pattern varies greatly among different groups.

Three factors can explain most of the variation among the nationalities in the adoption of Russian as native language: urbanization, interethnic group contact, and traditional religion.[5] The most linguistically Russified are those that were converted to Russian Orthodoxy in the centuries prior to Soviet rule and those that have experienced extensive intermingling with Russians. Least linguistically Russified are the traditionally Muslim peoples. In short, unless non-Russians have had extensive contact with Russians, or are Orthodox by tradition, or both, they are very unlikely to claim Russian as their native tongue.

TABLE 1. Percentage Distribution of All Non-Russians According to Reported Language Identification in 1959, 1970, 1979, and 1989

A. Reported Native Language

	1959	1970	1979	1989
1. Language of Own Nationality	87.6	87.0	85.6	84.1
2. Russian	10.8	11.5	13.0	14.6
3. Language of Another Nationality	1.6	1.4	1.4	1.3
Total	100.0	99.9	100.0	100.0

B. Reported Second Language

	1959	1970	1979	1989
1. Language of Own Nationality	NA	3.4	3.9	5.4
2. Russian	NA	37.1	49.1	48.1
3. Language of Another Nationality	NA	2.2	2.2	2.2
4. No Second Language	NA	57.3	44.8	44.3
Total	NA	100.0	100.0	100.0

C. Distribution on Scale of Linguistic Russification

	Native Language	Second Language	1970	1979	1989
1. Parochials	Own Nationality	None or Non-Russian	50.6	37.2	36.6
2. Unassimilated Bilinguals	Own Nationality	Russian	36.4	48.4	47.5
3. Assimilated Bilinguals	Russian	Own Nationality	2.7	3.2	4.7
4. Linguistically Assimilated	Russian	None or Own Nationality	8.8	9.8	9.9
5.	Neither Russian nor of Own Nationality		1.4	1.4	1.3
Total			99.9	100.0	100.0

Source: Derived from the Soviet censuses of 1959, 1970, and 1979. Itogi Vsesoiuznoi perepisi naseleniia 1959 goda: SSSR (Moscow: Gosstatizdat, 1962). Itogi Vsesoiuznoi perepisi naseleniia 1970 goda, vol. 4 (Moscow: Statistika, 1974). Chislennost i sostav naseleniia SSSR: Po dannym Vsesoiuznoi perepisi naseleniia 1979 goda (Moscow: Finansy i statistika, 1984). The figures for 1989 are approximations based on unpublished preliminary data from the 1989 Soviet census. Figures in Panel C are derived by the method described in: Brian D. Silver, "Methods of Deriving Data on Bilingualism from the 1970 Soviet Census," Soviet Studies, vol. 27, no. 4 (October 1975), pp. 574-97.

Adoption of Russian as a *second* language, however, correlates only slightly with traditional religion. Thus, Muslim nationalities do not show a special reluctance to learn Russian as a second language. Instead, the most important single factor in the acquisition of Russian as a second language is the level of interethnic group contact. Another important factor is the extent to which native-language schooling is provided. Together, these two factors account for more than 75% of the variation in the extent to which non-Russians claim free command of Russian.[6]

The Pattern of Native-Language Schooling

Probably the most important regime policy with respect to the use of non-Russian languages is the provision of native-language schooling. Whether such schooling is provided through the tenth or seventh or fourth grade, or not at all, registers the degree of the regime's commitment to the maintenance of a particular language. Official pronouncements and publications do not provide the actual decision rules employed in establishing native-language schooling for the non-Russian nationalities. From writings by Soviet scholars, however, three principles appear to be important in determining the actual provision of such schooling: equality, efficiency, and politics.

The dominant theme in Soviet doctrine concerning the non-Russian languages is the equality principle—that each nationality is free to use its mother tongue. Article 121 of the 1936 constitution guaranteed citizens the right to school instruction in their own language. Article 36 of the 1977 constitution assures citizens "the opportunity to use the mother tongue and languages of other peoples of the USSR," and article 45 assures them "the opportunity for school instruction in their native language."

Strictly interpreted, the equality principle has certainly not been followed, since Russian holds the preeminent position among languages in the USSR. It has been designated the "language of internationality discourse" (*iazyk mezhnatsional'nogo obshcheniia*) of the peoples of the USSR, and since 1938 has been a mandatory subject of study in all non-Russian schools. This does not mean, however, that egalitarian considerations were ignored in Soviet language planning. Instead of applying a standard of absolute equality, we may test the equality principle along two *dimensions*: (1) the greater the number of nationalities provided with some form of native-language instruction, the more egalitarian is school-language policy; and (2) the greater the number of school years (i.e., the higher the grade level) in which the non-Russian languages are either the primary medium of instruction or a separate subject of study, the more egalitarian is the policy.

A second principle that might influence the provision of non-Russian-language schooling is the principle of economic efficiency. This has two aspects. From the perspective of the pupil or his parents, it may be an inefficient investment of personal resources to study in a language with limited utility in the job market or a restricted range of cultural opportunities.

From the perspective of the state, it may be inefficient to expend substantial resources to develop teaching capacity in languages that are spoken by only small numbers of people and thus of limited potential use in the modern economy, in science and technology, and in disseminating the cultural achievements of the society as a whole.

Soviet scholars frequently offer arguments consistent with the efficiency principle to explain why Russian is the preferred lingua franca of Soviet nationalities and why the smaller groups often have limited opportunities for native-language schooling. For example, after noting that in the early 1930s instruction was offered in the languages of many small ethnic groups— e.g., the Abaza, Assyrians, Jewish Tats, Nivkhi, etc.—Kuchkar Khanazarov states:

> Subsequent development of school affairs made plain to the smaller peoples, nationalities and ethnic groups that the splintering of schools and instructional classes by language of instruction was inexpedient and, in practical terms, unwarranted. Parents became convinced by practical experience that instruction of their children through the medium of languages that are not widely used is disadvantageous and inconvenient. Such languages have extremely small numbers of speakers, and this greatly lowers the efficacy of the education received.[7]

Others claim that there is no contradiction between the principles of equality and efficiency. Thus, Ivan Tsamerian writes:

> In our country all languages enjoy equal rights and develop freely. This is well known to everyone. But could one on this basis assert that all languages of the peoples of the USSR (including even language-dialects spoken by only a few thousand or hundred people) have the same potentialities or fulfill the same functions in the development of culture in general, and of art and literature in particular? . . . When speaking of the equal rights of languages, one also ought not forget about the objective functional potentialities of each language.[8]

Even the 1938 law making Russian an obligatory subject of study in non-Russian schools is said to be the result of popular demand, a "universal desire to study the Russian language."[9] Soviet educators, language planners, and writers on nationality issues constantly assert that differences in the availability of native-language instruction among the non-Russian nationalities reflect the parents' exercise of their free choice and hence that the differentiation does not contradict the notion of equal opportunity for non-Russians to use their native languages.

A third possible explanation for the differential treatment of the non-Russian languages is the political principle. In its broadest application, this principle would determine opportunities for native-language schooling according to the roles assigned to particular nationalities by the country's political leadership. John Armstrong, for example, has constructed a model of Soviet nationalities policy that assigns specific roles to ethnic groups based on their potential utility in realizing the goals of the Communist party.[10]

The experience of the nationalities deported from their homelands during World War II for alleged collaboration with the Nazis provides a clear-cut illustration of the political principle.[11] All of them lost native-language schooling from the date of their deportation in 1943–44, and most had it restored after their rehabilitation in the late 1950s. The Jews provide another example. They had extensive Yiddish-language cultural facilities in the Soviet Union in the 1920s, and there were Jewish schools until the late 1930s. Jews have not been provided native-language schooling since World War II. There have been proposals to institute such schools in some republics in the last two years, however.

A more systematic and stable political factor could also affect the treatment of the non-Russian languages. The establishment of the USSR as a federal state may be viewed as a pragmatic concession by the Bolshevik party to the nationalities as part of an effort to consolidate control in the non-Russian regions. It may also reflect a real commitment to the long-term maintenance of ethnic distinctions. Accordingly, one might expect that the higher a nationality's status in the federal hierarchy, the greater would be the degree of support for its language.

Determining the Status of Non-Russian Schools

Although Soviet sources sometimes report data on which languages are used in schools in particular regions—including, on occasion, enrollment figures by language of instruction—they seldom report such data by grade level, and only rarely provide figures on the enrollment of children by nationality in schools with particular languages of instruction. There are, however, two other sources of systematic information about native-language schooling: (1) curricula (educational plans), and (2) information on school textbook publication.

The published curricula reveal that, at least in recent years, there have been three main types of general education schools at the primary and secondary levels in the non-Russian republics and provinces. The first includes schools where Russian is the primary medium of instruction and the local languages are not studied. We call these *type 1 Russian schools*. The second includes schools where Russian is the medium of instruction but the language of a non-Russian nationality is studied as a subject. We call these *type 2 Russian schools*. The third type comprises schools where a non-Russian language serves as the medium of instruction for almost all subjects (except Russian and foreign languages) while Russian language and literature are studied only as subjects. In accordance with standard Soviet usage, we call these *national schools*.

The existence of type 2 Russian schools has received scant mention in the Western scholarly literature on Soviet language policy. These schools represent an intermediate alternative to a choice by parents and children between a type 1 Russian school and a national school. Their importance lies in that they provide more support for the maintenance of non-Russian languages than do type 1 Russian schools. In type 2 Russian schools, children have the opportunity to become *literate* in their nationality's traditional language, and its inclusion in the curriculum encourages them to view the study and maintenance of their language as legitimate.

This form of school apparently developed as a consequence of the provision in the 1959 law that gave parents the formal right to choose the language of instruction for their children, as well as to decide whether their children in Russian-language schools would study the local language as a subject.[12] In practice, the real choice offered to parents appears to be not "In what language should your child study?" but rather "What type of school should your child attend?" Since it may not be practical to offer all possible options in each region, however, type 2 Russian-language schooling may not actually be available even as an option in some areas, particularly above a certain grade level. Moreover, as a leading Soviet critic of some of the established policies and practices in language planning has noted, educators often present the "choice" to parents incorrectly—by not acknowledging that there is sometimes an intermediate choice between immersion in a Russian-language school and attendance at a national school:

> Instead of asking about the desired language of instruction, [educators] usually ask: "Do you want your children to know Russian?" Having received a positive reply—and in the overwhelming majority of cases it naturally would be positive—the questioner concludes the conversation: "This means that you want your children to attend a Russian school." But in fact this conclusion, from the standpoint of elementary logic, cannot withstand criticism. It would be correct only were it known in advance that the children already had a satisfactory command of Russian before entering school.[13]

Information on textbook publication by language has allowed us to examine the status of different languages in schools over time. *Knizhnaia letopis'* and *Ezhegodnik knigi* report information on virtually all books published in the Soviet Union by year. The first year for which there are data available on the language in which books were published is 1934. Thus, we may examine which languages were used in textbooks and on this basis investigate the status of native-language schooling opportunities for the years 1934 to 1985, inclusive.

The printing of textbooks in math or science in a given non-Russian language would appear to be a good indicator that the language was used as the primary medium of instruction in at least some schools. If math or science were taught in a given language, it is likely that most other subjects were also taught in that language. Accordingly, for each year between 1934 and 1985, we note for each non-Russian language the highest grade level for which any textbook in math or natural science was reported published. If only one or two subjects were taught in a non-Russian language, likely included would be the national language or literature. Thus, the printing of language or literature textbooks in a given language should indicate that this language was at least a subject of study in at least some schools. Therefore, for the years 1934 to 1985 we also note for each non-Russian language the highest grade level for which any textbook in language or literature was reported published.

These data have some limitations. It is not possible to determine how many hours in the curriculum are devoted to study in the respective languages, or whether these languages are used primarily in the national schools (where they serve as the primary medium of instruction) or in the intermediate type 2 Russian schools (where they are studied as a subject).[14] But the information about textbooks does allow us to assess changes in the maximum grade levels in the school curriculum at which the various languages are employed.

When a non-Russian language continues to figure as a subject of study but no longer as the primary medium of instruction, the national school has been eliminated in favor of the type 2 Russian school. Occasionally we found that textbooks in math or science in a given language were available for a higher grade level than those in language or literature. In such cases we use the higher of the reported figures (math-science or language-literature) as our operational measure of the highest grade level at which a language figured at least as a subject of study.

The Equality Principle

The Soviet Union has provided at least some native-language schooling to the vast majority of nationalities. Eighty-three of the one hundred one groups examined have had schooling where their own language was at least a subject of study at the level of grade one or beyond during at least one year between 1934 and 1985.[15] Thirteen of the eighteen nationalities without any native-language schooling during this period were reported in the 1926 census as lacking a literary language. All of them have small populations and reside in either the Far North or the Caucasus.

Twenty-one nationalities that in 1926 still officially lacked a literary language received some native-language schooling between 1934 and 1985. However, five nationalities with a literary language as of 1926 did not: Albanians, Romanians, Slovaks, Khalkha-Mongols, and Karaim, of whom only the Karaim are indigenous to the USSR. Native-language schooling, however, has been provided during some years for such non-indigenous nationalities as the Poles, Uighurs, Hungarians, Czechs, Kurds, Assyrians, Chinese, and Koreans. Each of these may have played a special role in Soviet foreign policy, and furthermore, each has distinct areas of residential concentration that made it feasible to organize at least some schools in their traditional language. For the past twenty-five years, the Poles, Hungarians, and Uighurs have each had some ten-year schools with their own language as the primary medium of instruction.

The remainder of our discussion of bilingual schooling focuses on groups that are indigenous to the USSR (in the official Soviet parlance, as reflected in recent census reports). These number eighty-one. According to our

TABLE 2.   Number of Indigenous Non-Russian Nationalities with Native-Language
Schooling, 1934-1985, by Type of Schooling

	Number with Language of Own Nationality Used to Teach Math-Science	Number with Language of Own Nationality Used to Teach Language-Literature	Number with Language of Own Nationality Used for either Math-Science or Language-Literature
1934-1940	64	65	65
1941-1945	49	44	51
1946-1950	50	51	52
1951-1955	50	49	51
1956-1960	52	55	55
1961-1965	47	52	52
1966-1970	39	49	49
1971-1975	36	53	53
1976-1980	35	53	53
1981-1985	32	52	52
Ever in 1934-1985	67	67	67

Note: Estonians, Latvians, Lithuanians, and Tuvinians included at all dates
even though their basic territories were annexed to the USSR in 1940.

information on the publication of math-science or language-literature textbooks, of these eighty-one nationalities, sixty-seven (83%) have had schooling
with their national language at least as a subject of study through at least
the first grade for at least one year between 1934 and 1985 (see the Appendix
for the list of languages). Judging by our data on math or science textbooks
alone, sixty-seven nationalities have also at some time had schooling with
their traditional language as the primary medium of instruction.

Although this record is impressive, it is also important to know how the
availability of native-language schooling has changed over time. To determine
this, we broke the 52-year time series into ten intervals: 1934–40, 1941–
45, 1946–50, 1951–55, 1956–60, 1961–65, 1966–70, 1971–75, 1976–80, and
1981–85. For each of these intervals, and also for the entire 1934–85 period,
we have calculated the number of indigenous nationalities that had schools
using math or science textbooks published in their own language. We have
also calculated the number of nationalities with schools using language or
literature textbooks in their own language. The results of these calculations
are given in Table 2.[16]

The figures in Table 2 show that non-Russian schools flourished before
World War II. During the 1934–40 period, sixty-four nationalities had schools
in which math-science was taught in the national language, and sixty-five
had schools where language-literature was so taught. The number of nationalities with schools employing their national language to teach math-
science has declined substantially since 1934. After a plateau of about fifty
between 1946 and 1965, this number dropped in each succeeding period
to a low of thirty-two in 1981–85, half of the prewar number. The pattern
of use of the non-Russian languages as a subject of study is very different,

however. Since 1945, in every subperiod about forty-two nationalities had schools where their national language was studied at least as a subject—four-fifths of the prewar number.

Table 2 indicates the dying out of the national schools—those where the national language serves as the primary medium of instruction—for most non-Russian languages. Increasingly over time, the national schools have been replaced by type 2 Russian schools. This suggests that the status of the non-Russian languages in education is being increasingly reduced to the level of a subject of study in Russian-language schools. But there is substantial intergroup variation in the extent to which this is taking place. Obviously, the equality principle cannot explain this differential treatment.

The Efficiency Principle

One indicator of the efficiency of providing native-language schooling to a given nationality is the nationality's population size. The larger the population, the more economic sense it makes to provide schooling in the group's language. In addition, the more concentrated the settlement of a nationality, the more efficient it is to maintain schools in the national language.

Before World War II, efficiency considerations appear to have been very important in the provision of native-language schooling. Although many very small nationalities were provided native-language schooling at least in the early primary school classes, the larger the group the higher was the average grade level at which such schooling was provided. After World War II, the highest grade level at which the non-Russian language served as the primary medium of instruction seemed to be determined largely by factors other than efficiency.

The Political Principle

The essence of the political principle is that the differential provision of cultural opportunities among nationalities is determined by the extent to which groups are viewed favorably by the central political authorities. The deported nationalities, for instance, suffered the loss of all native-language cultural facilities during their period of exile. But the political principle is also in evidence in the correlation between provision of native-language schooling and a nationality's formal status in the federal hierarchy.

Tables 3 and 4 show for each period the average highest school year in which textbooks in the national language were published—in math-science or language-literature (Table 3), and in math-science alone (Table 4)—for nationalities grouped by their formal political status. The graphs in Figures 1 and 2 plot the data in Tables 3 and 4, respectively. The classification of all the indigenous nationalities accords with the current status of their official territories: (1) union republic (SSR) nationalities; (2) autonomous republic (ASSR) nationalities; (3) autonomous oblast (AO) nationalities; (4) autonomous district (*avtonomnyi okrug*—here abbreviated AD) nationalities; and (5) other indigenous nationalities (here abbreviated as IND).

TABLE 3. Average Highest Grade with the Non-Russian Language as a Subject of Study in Schools, by Status of Titular Areas in the Federal System of the USSR, 1934-1985

	1934-1940	1941-1945	1946-1950	1951-1955	1956-1960	1961-1965	1966-1970	1971-1975	1976-1980	1981-1985
All	4.9	3.8	4.6	4.5	5.1	5.3	5.2	5.7	5.7	5.5
(N)	(77)	(77)	(81)	(81)	(81)	(81)	(81)	(81)	(81)	(81)
SSR	9.8	9.1	10.0	10.0	10.0	10.0	10.0	10.0	10.0	10.0
(N)	(11)	(11)	(14)	(14)	(14)	(14)	(14)	(14)	(14)	(14)
ASSR	6.7	5.8	6.5	6.5	7.9	8.2	8.3	9.3	9.5	8.9
(N)	(25)	(25)	(26)	(26)	(26)	(26)	(26)	(26)	(26)	(26)
AO	6.5	4.5	5.2	5.5	6.9	6.7	6.7	7.9	8.1	7.4
(N)	(6)	(6)	(6)	(6)	(6)	(6)	(6)	(6)	(6)	(6)
AD	2.8	1.2	2.0	2.0	1.9	1.9	1.2	2.0	2.0	1.9
(N)	(8)	(8)	(8)	(8)	(8)	(8)	(8)	(8)	(8)	(8)
IND	1.4	0.5	0.5	0.4	0.5	0.6	0.4	0.5	0.5	0.4
(N)	(27)	(27)	(27)	(27)	(27)	(27)	(27)	(27)	(27)	(27)

TABLE 4. Average Highest Grade with the Non-Russian Language as the Primary Medium of Instruction, by Status of Titular Areas in the Federal System of the USSR, 1934-1985

	1934-1940	1941-1945	1946-1950	1951-1955	1956-1960	1961-1965	1966-1970	1971-1975	1976-1980	1981-1985
All	4.5	3.4	3.9	4.1	3.8	3.5	3.0	2.8	2.7	2.6
SSR	9.8	8.7	10.0	10.0	10.0	10.0	10.0	10.0	10.0	10.0
ASSR	6.2	5.0	5.2	5.7	5.1	4.7	3.6	3.2	2.8	2.5
AO	5.6	4.1	3.9	4.0	3.7	3.0	1.3	1.0	0.7	1.2
AD	2.3	1.0	1.4	1.3	0.8	0.2	0.1	0.1	0	0
IND	1.2	0.2	0.3	0.3	0.2	0.2	0*	0*	0	0

*The value is less than 0.05 but not actually zero.

Figures 1 and 2 both show that the availability of schooling in a national language is related to the group's formal political status. The status groupings always remain in the expected rank order. The highest school year in which the traditional language is used is always lower on average for the ASSR nationalities than for the SSR nationalities. The corresponding figures for the AO nationalities are lower on average than those of the ASSR groups during each period. And the figures for the AD nationalities are lower on average than those of the AO groups, but higher than those for the groups with no official territory (IND).

106

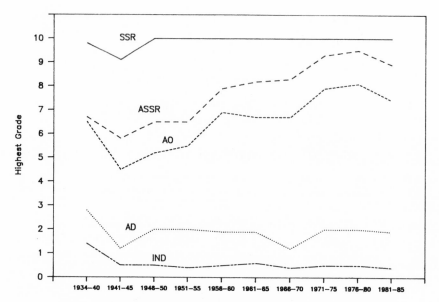

Figure 1. Average Highest Grade in Which Nationality's Language is a Subject
of Study, by Political Status of Nationality

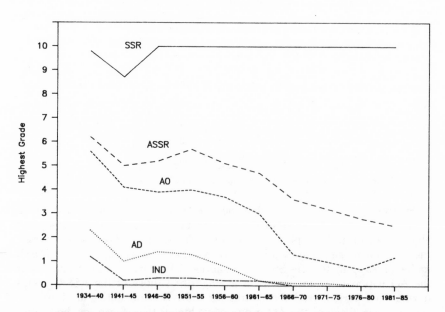

Figure 2. Average Highest Grade in Which Nationality's Language is the
Primary Medium of Instruction, by Political Status of Nationality

Figure 1 depicts the average highest grade levels at which the non-Russian languages were at least studied in school as a *separate subject.* It demonstrates the steady increase since World War II in the grade levels at which the languages of all groupings of AO status and higher were part of the school curriculum. After lagging behind the SSR nationalities by an average of over three grade levels in the 1934–40 period, the ASSR nationalities improved their position to such an extent that it has nearly matched that of the SSR nationalities since the 1970s. The AO nationalities have followed a similar upward trajectory over time, but lag behind the ASSR nationalities. In contrast, after a decline in the status of their languages between 1934–40 and 1941–45, both the AD and IND groups have experienced little change.

The trends in the use of the non-Russian languages as a *medium of instruction* are very different, however. Figure 2 shows that all groupings except the SSR nationalities have experienced steady reductions over time in the highest school year in which their languages were used as the primary medium of instruction. The validity of this generalization is not contradicted by the brief recovery following World War II for the non-SSR groupings.

By each of the two indicators of native-language schooling, the political status groupings divide along two patterns. While the ASSR and AO nationalities have experienced steady increases in the grade levels at which their languages are at least studied as a subject, they have experienced steady decreases in the grade levels at which their languages are used as the primary medium of instruction. This implies that native-language education for the ASSR and AO nationalities is increasingly taking place not in the national schools but in the type 2 Russian schools. For the AD and IND nationalities, in contrast, schooling in their traditional languages is disappearing completely, with children increasingly attending only type 1 Russian schools.

Thus, no single pattern of change applies to all Soviet ethnic groups. Our results show how complex and varied the changes in native-language schooling policies have been. The upward trends in Figure 1 run counter to the common supposition in the West that the non-Russian languages are disappearing from use in the educational system. The downward trends in Figure 2, however, indicate increasing Russianization of the bulk of the school curriculum for members of non-SSR nationalities.

A nationality's formal political status is related to the extent to which it has been provided schooling in its own language. But differential availability of native-language schools is also consistent with the efficiency principle, since groups with a higher status in the political hierarchy tend to have larger populations. However, we have found that, on balance, before World War II population size was more important than political status in the determination of availability of native-language schooling, while after World War II political status tended to become more important. Even after the war, however, efficiency considerations continued to play a role in determining whether a particular language was used as the medium of instruction; groups below the SSR level were able to maintain their language as the primary medium of instruction only if they resided in large numbers in the nationality's titular unit.

Periodization in the Evolution of Policy Toward Non-Russian Languages

Our analysis of information on school textbooks allows us to identify three main periods in the evolution of Soviet policy toward the use of non-Russian languages in schools: (1) 1917–38; (2) 1938–59; (3) 1959–85. This division does not fit a conventional Western periodization of Soviet history based on major changes in the country's political leadership; it does correspond closely to the periodization of language policy by the Soviet scholar Iunus D. Desheriev.[17]

The first period begins with the October Revolution and ends with the 1938 decree that made Russian a mandatory subject of study in school. The second period begins with this decree and ends with the adoption of the 1959 education law. The third period runs from 1959 to 1985. This periodization is linked to important changes in the legal framework for language use in schools. The actual consequences of these legal changes were sometimes delayed by half a decade or more. For example, World War II interrupted the full implementation of the 1938 decree, and the 1959 reforms were introduced only gradually in the 1960s.[18]

The first period, between 1917 and 1938, may be characterized as *egalitarian*. It saw enormous efforts to construct new alphabets, open non-Russian schools, and limit the role of the Russian language in the non-Russian areas. The model "national school" was one in which all subjects were taught in the national (native) language of the non-Russian pupils. In this period of "nativization" (*korenizatsiia*) the Russian language may have been studied as a subject, but was not usually mandatory. Nonetheless, there was an important measure of pragmatism in the development of native-language schools even in this "egalitarian" period, reflected in the strong relationship between a nationality's population size and how far in the curriculum children could obtain schooling with their national language as the primary medium of instruction.

The second period was one of *differentiated bilingual education*. During this time Russian became a mandatory subject of study in the non-Russian schools, but the model "national school" remained one in which the non-Russian language served as the primary medium of instruction. It became acceptable for non-Russians to attend Russian-language schools. As educational attainment increased, and greater numbers of non-Russians attended secondary schools, the earlier differentiation of native-language schooling opportunities was more or less frozen into established policy. About fifty languages of indigenous non-Russian nationalities were used as a medium of instruction. In this second period, the highest grade for which a given non-Russian language could serve as the primary medium of instruction remained quite stable, but was tied less to the nationality's population size than to its formal status in the federal system. If they were to complete their secondary education, most children belonging to non-SSR nationalities had to attend schools with Russian as the language of instruction.

The third period was one of *highly differentiated bilingual education*. It dates from the 1959 education law, which nominally changed the study of the Russian language by non-Russians from an obligatory to a voluntary act and gave parents the right to choose the language of instruction for their children. In this period, the model non-Russian school diverged into two main types: (1) the traditional "national school," with a non-Russian language as the primary medium of instruction and Russian only as a subject of study; and (2) the school with Russian as the main language of instruction and the non-Russian language as a subject. There was a sharp decrease in the 1960s and 1970s in the number of languages used as the primary medium of instruction, as well as in the highest grade level at which the non-Russian languages might serve in that capacity. To preserve their national languages as the medium of instruction, groups below the SSR level had to have a large population and be concentrated geographically. The use of the non-Russian languages for purposes of instruction became more closely linked to formal status in the federal system.

It is not accidental that the rank ordering we have found in the opportunities to use the non-Russian languages in schools closely parallels the formal status of nationalities in the federal hierarchy. During the third period, the established Soviet scholarly classification of languages spoken in the USSR even defined the social functions of languages by explicit reference to the territorial status of the corresponding nationalities. For example, using a formula shared by others who are associated with Desheriev, Magomet I. Isaev classified Soviet languages into five groups: (1) Russian, the "language of internationality discourse of the peoples of the Soviet Union"; (2) the "national literary languages of the union republics"; (3) the "literary languages of the autonomous republics and oblasts"; (4) the "written languages" fulfilling highly limited functions in the national (autonomous) districts and among some of the small ethnic groups in Siberia and elsewhere; and (5) the "unwritten languages." Isaev writes: "In this grouping of languages, the preferred indicator for classification is the form of statehood or autonomy."[19]

What do the patterns of native-language schooling for the nationalities imply for the maintenance of the non-Russian languages? Analysis of the relationship between language policy and language behavior of non-Russians shows that if the Russian language serves as the primary medium of instruction, then students will tend to claim Russian at least as a second language. But the further in the school curriculum that non-Russians can study their national language at least as a separate subject, the less likely they are to abandon it and to adopt Russian as their native language. Therefore, the general Soviet policy of maintaining non-Russian languages as a subject of study, though severely limiting their use as the medium of instruction, contributes to the retention of the national language as native language while promoting the acquisition of Russian as a second language.

TABLE 5. Number of Males per 1,000 Females Alive in 1959, by Year of Birth, for Several Groupings of Nationalities

Nationality Grouping	Year of Birth: Age in 1943:	1909- 1913 30-34	1914- 1918 25-29	1919- 1923 20-24	1924- 1928 15-19	1929- 1933 10-14	1934- 1938 5-9
Balts		698	702	720	781	948	928
Russians		589	606	605	807	955	973
Ukrainians		629	611	645	797	933	982
Belorussians		647	650	678	792	976	965
Moldavians		852	803	853	892	914	850
Armenians-Georgians		803	703	747	996	996	891
Non-Muslim ASSR		565	558	572	811	927	915
Tatars-Bashkirs		544	577	618	844	971	944
Muslim SSR		873	755	784	1093	1022	943
Daghestanis		760	632	745	1064	988	926
Deported		982	799	779	1034	1052	864

Source: Derived from 1959 Soviet census.

The Role of World War II
in Precipitating Linguistic and Ethnic Russification

The direct effects of World War II on the Soviet population are well known. In the course of the war, over twenty million people are reported to have died. More than twenty-five million people found their territories annexed to the USSR in the period just preceding, during, or immediately after the war. At least ten million children were not born who otherwise would have been. Three million people emigrated or remained permanently displaced from Soviet territory after the war. More than a million non-Russians were uprooted from their homelands and deported to Siberia and Central Asia.

The war, we believe, also accelerated the linguistic and ethnic Russification of many nationalities. This occurred as an indirect consequence of population losses and migration. The normal balance between the number of males and females became so skewed for some nationalities that many women, if they were to find husbands at all, had to marry men of other nationalities. The sex imbalance caused by the war worked through ethnic intermarriage and other intervening social mechanisms to increase linguistic and ethnic Russification.[20]

The relative losses by nationality attributable to World War II can be gauged by examining age-specific sex ratios (the number of males per 1,000 females in an age group). The sex ratios are presented in Table 5 for the indigenous non-Russian nationalities (collapsed into ten groupings) and for the Russians.[21]

It is often noted that the Russians, Ukrainians, and Belorussians suffered severely in World War II. This is reflected in large male deficits (low sex ratios) for these Slavic nationalities among those born in 1909–33 (aged 10–34 in 1943). In the cohort of Russians aged 20–24 in 1943, for example, there were only 605 males for every 1,000 females alive in 1959. In the same cohort of Ukrainians there were 645 males, and among Belorussians 678 males per 1,000 females.

It is surprising that in the same cohort the male deficit for the Tatar-Bashkir grouping is even greater than for the Ukrainians and Belorussians, and that the deficit for the traditionally non-Muslim ASSR nationalities in the Russian republic exceeds that of any of the three Slavic nationalities. For every 1,000 females in the cohort aged 20–24 in 1943 among the Tatars-Bashkirs, 618 males were still alive in 1959, and among the non-Muslim ASSR nationalities, 572 males. In the next older cohort (aged 25–29 in 1943), both the Tatars-Bashkirs and the non-Muslim ASSR nationalities had a larger male deficit in 1959 than any of the three Slavic nationalities. Our evidence suggests that even though most of the ASSRs lay beyond the front, an extremely high proportion of their males were drafted and died during the war. Viktor I. Kozlov attributes this deficit to the fact that these groups were predominantly rural, and hence few men would have been deferred from military service because they held strategic civilian jobs.[22]

A high proportion of SSR-level Muslims also were rural. Their male war losses, however, were apparently less severe than those suffered by the nationalities from the European parts of the USSR, perhaps because conscripts from the more distant Muslim SSRs generally served in less hazardous locations.

Another concomitant of the war is a change in patterns of language preference. For example, census data show that among successive cohorts of Ukrainians, Belorussians, and Moldavians born before the 1917 Revolution, growing proportions of the population were shifting to Russian as their native language. This trend was reversed immediately after the Revolution. The first few cohorts of Ukrainians, Belorussians, and Moldavians born after the Revolution showed successively smaller proportions who claimed Russian as their native language; this decline in linguistic Russification may be related to the establishment of native-language schools. For Ukrainian, Belorussian, and Moldavian children reaching school age during World War II (the cohort aged 5–9 in 1943), there was a slight increase in the proportion claiming Russian as native language in 1959. Among the postwar cohorts this was followed by somewhat lower levels of linguistic Russification. For these nationalities, the upward shift toward Russian as the native language associated with World War II was short-term, affecting only those of primary school age at the height of the war.

A similar pattern of changing proportions claiming Russian as native language in the cohorts reaching school age before the 1917 Revolution can be found among many ASSR nationalities of the RSFSR. But for these—in contrast to the Ukrainians, Belorussians, and Moldavians—the increased linguistic Russification of the cohort aged 5–9 in 1943 marked the beginning of a sharp and sustained upturn in linguistic Russification for successive cohorts.

Figures 3 and 4 illustrate these trends in linguistic Russification. They show, for Ukrainians and Chuvash respectively, the number per thousand population (by age, sex, and rural-urban residence) claiming Russian as native language in 1959. The Chuvash case is representative of the experiences of other non-Muslim ASSR nationalities in the RSFSR.

The postwar trends are clearly different for the Ukrainians and the Chuvash. In our view, World War II precipitated a long-term change in linguistic and ethnic identification among the Chuvash that did not occur among the Ukrainians. Although both groups experienced the loss of many men during the war, the loss appears proportionately greater for the Chuvash. Also, while Ukrainians tend to live in areas of primarily Ukrainian settlement, the Chuvash live in the Russian republic, surrounded by Russians. The severe male deficit, coupled with a relatively small population size and a geographic location in the midst of long-term Russian settlement, made the Chuvash especially susceptible to linguistic and ethnic Russification.

The most obvious way in which the sex imbalance could have promoted Russification is through ethnic intermarriage. Linguistic Russification would be more common among children of interethnic marriages than among children whose parents were both of the same non-Russian nationality. In marriages between Russians and non-Russians, children typically become bilingual. The children of non-Russian women who marry Russian men would more likely come to claim Russian as their native language than would the women themselves. Ethnic intermarriage thus sets the stage for the linguistic and ethnic Russification of the next generation.

The unbalanced sex ratio also affected linguistic and ethnic Russification in another way. In those ASSRs that experienced a severe male deficit, an increasing proportion of jobs for specialists with secondary or higher education came to be held by Russians. This created a situation in which role models for occupational success were Russians, and this could have further increased the attractiveness of Russian self-identification.

Increased facility in Russian, whether resulting from a high incidence of ethnic intermarriage or from emulation of Russian role models, is likely to lead to a decrease in the availability of schooling in the non-Russian languages. In the postwar years, provision (reduction) of native-language schooling for a given nationality has reportedly been based in part on the prevailing degree of bilingualism among children.[23] Any decrease in native-language schooling in turn could lead to further loss of facility in the non-Russian languages and to accelerated ethnic Russification.

Ethnic intermarriage could be especially important in the process of assimilation in the USSR because of the workings of the internal passport system. Children of parents of the same nationality are legally required to declare that nationality as their own on their internal passport; those whose parents are of different nationalities can legally claim the nationality of

Figure 3: Number of Ukrainians per Thousand with Russian as Native Language in 1959 by Age, Sex, and Urban-Rural Residence.

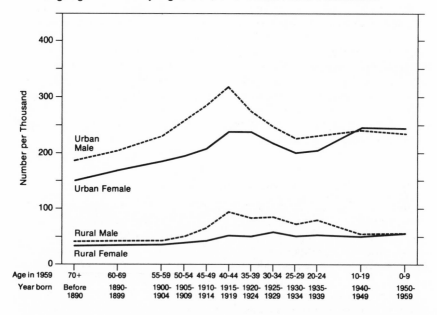

Figure 4: Number of Chuvash per Thousand with Russian as Native Language in 1959 by Age, Sex, and Urban-Rural Residence.

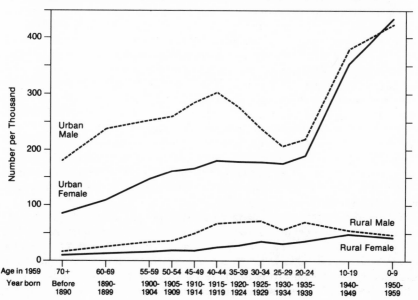

either.[24] This legal control on ethnic affiliations also could regulate the shift of subjective identifications. Even the supposedly completely free reporting of nationality to the census taker may be strongly affected by the "official" nationality listed on the passport (and other official documents). The leading Soviet ethnic demographer, Viktor I. Kozlov, claims that the choice of passport nationality involves a crystallization or fixing (*fiksatsiia*) of ethnic affiliation that makes subsequent change in self-identification highly improbable. Ethnic intermarriage, therefore, is probably an important route through which changes in subjective ethnic attachment occur in the USSR.[25]

Thus, in combination with other factors, the excessive war losses among the ASSR nationalities of the RSFSR could have set the stage for rapid assimilation of non-Russians in the postwar period.

Ethnic Reidentification

Assimilation of certain Soviet nationalities by others has often been noted. For example, Kozlov observes that the Jews have undergone some assimilation by Ukrainians and Russians; Poles—by Ukrainians; and Mordvinians, Karelians, Chuvash, and other ethnic groups in European Russia—by Russians.[26] Assimilation of the Chuvash, Mordvinians, Mari, and Udmurts by Russians, and of Bashkirs by Tatars, in both Tsarist Russia and the Soviet Union, has also been cited by Klavdiia I. Kozlova.[27] Bernard Comrie has commented on the ethnic Russification of members of small ethnic groups.[28]

Large nationalities have also experienced assimilation. Thus, Kozlov contends that the slow growth in the number of Ukrainians between 1926 and 1939 was partially due to their assimilation by Russians.[29] He further states that between 1959 and 1970, Ukrainians living outside their titular republic were being assimilated by Russians.[30] Robert Lewis, Richard Rowland, and Ralph Clem have also argued that many Ukrainians were assimilated by Russians in the nineteenth and twentieth centuries.[31]

Although several Western and Soviet scholars have been concerned with the role of assimilation or ethnic reidentification (we use the terms synonymously) in the changing population size of Soviet nationalities, only rarely have they produced quantitative estimates of the magnitude of the process.[32] Here we propose to estimate the magnitude of assimilation. We are able to do this because the measure of ethnic identity or nationality in Soviet censuses is *subjective*, with respondents not required to show their internal passports or other identification papers. Thus, a person's self-identified nationality can change between two censuses, even if his or her official nationality remains unchanged.

Our method is as follows. Standard demographic techniques for estimating the proportion of a cohort surviving from one census to another are applied in order to establish a baseline for the number of members of an ethnic group who would be *expected* to be alive at the second census date. The expected number of survivors to the second census date for each age cohort of a given ethnic group is then compared to the *reported* (actual) number of cohort members at the second census date to determine the net number who have changed their ethnic self-identification—that is, have ethnically reidentified between censuses.[33] Here we are concerned with survival from the 1959 to the 1970 census.[34]

The estimated difference between the actual and expected number of survivors of a nationality between census dates is a net number; it does not reflect the gross amount of shifting in ethnic identities. To take a hypothetical example, if a net 10% of Ukrainians aged 20–24 appear to have shifted away from calling themselves Ukrainian between 1959 and 1970, much more than 10% of the cohort may actually have changed their ethnic self-identification, but this may have been offset by a shift by 20–24-year-old members of other nationalities, such as Russians, Poles, or Jews to Ukrainian self-identification.

Without individual-level time series data, it is impossible to measure the gross amount of ethnic reidentification that occurs between census dates. Nevertheless, the net proportions among those changing their ethnic identification indicate the attractiveness of particular self-designations. Moreover, ethnic reidentification affects the long-term survival or disappearance of an ethnic group through the net shift rather than the total (gross) amount of reidentification.

The net estimates of ethnic reidentification show the overall loss or gain in members of a nationality by cohort, but in the case of net loss, the destination nationality is not stated. We believe that in most cases the destination nationality is Russian. This is supported by our evidence of a net gain by Russians through ethnic reidentification between the 1959 and 1970 censuses.

Members of some groups are probably shifting to ethnic identifications other than Russian. For instance, Bashkirs are probably assimilating to Tatars, Poles—to Ukrainians and Belorussians,[35] and Ossetians—to Georgians. In the non-Russian republics, the titular nationality may assimilate members of other groups residing in that unit. Assimilation of Lezghians by Azerbaidzhanis, and of Uighurs by Uzbeks and Kazakhs are examples. For such groups, caution must be exercised in interpreting our results. However, the main destination nationality for ethnic reidentifiers is Russian.

Our estimates of ethnic reidentification encompass eleven ASSR and fifteen SSR nationalities, including the Russians. Estimates are presented for all cohorts aged 38 or younger in 1959 (aged 11 to 49 in 1970). (There are specific complications in making estimates for people who were aged 39 or older in 1959.[36])

Gainers and Losers Through Assimilation

Figure 5 shows the estimated number of members of each of the twenty-six nationalities who changed their ethnic self-identification between 1959 and 1970 per every one thousand members of the group aged 0–38 in 1959. The estimate for each group is presented as a range across various estimation assumptions. The figure reveals marked intergroup differences in the pro-

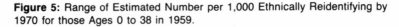

Figure 5: Range of Estimated Number per 1,000 Ethnically Reidentifying by 1970 for those Ages 0 to 38 in 1959.

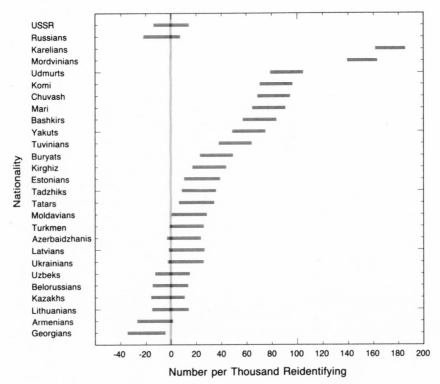

portions of those ethnically reidentifying between 1959 and 1970. The same information is presented in another way in Table 6. This table shows for each nationality our best estimate of the annual rate of decline in the size of the group and the number of years it would require for the group to fall to one-half its 1959 population size, given that rate of decline. Although a nationality with an estimated halving time of 2,954 years, such as the Uzbeks, has little to fear about its survival, a halving time of forty-six years, estimated for the Mordvinians, provides substantial reason for concern about the continued existence of the group as a distinct entity.

The twenty-six nationalities (including the Russians) may be classified into three main groupings: (1) "reidentifiers"; (2) "groups with little change"; and (3) "gainers."

Reidentifiers. The ethnic groups estimated to have the largest proportions of those reidentifying between 1959 and 1970 are ASSR nationalities whose official territories are located in the RSFSR. The two most extreme cases are the Karelians and the Mordvinians. Among the Karelians, between 16% and 18% of those aged 0–38 in 1959 are estimated to have reidentified

TABLE 6. Rates of Ethnic Reidentification and Halving Time for the Cohort
Aged 0-38 in 1959

	Annual Rate of Decline per 1,000	Halving Time in Years
A. Groups with Net Loss through Ethnic Reidentification between 1959 and 1970		
Karelians	17.2	40
Mordvinians	15.0	46
Udmurts	8.9	78
Komi	8.0	87
Chuvash	7.8	89
Mari	7.5	93
Bashkirs	6.8	103
Yakuts	5.9	118
Tuvinians	4.8	144
Buryats	3.4	203
B. Groups with Little Net Change in Ethnic Self-Identification between 1959 and 1970		
Kirghiz	2.9	241
Estonians	2.2	320
Tadzhiks	2.1	333
Tatars	1.9	370
Moldavians	1.4	505
Turkmen	1.3	525
Azerbaidzhanis	1.1	639
Latvians	1.1	655
Ukrainians	1.0	671
Uzbeks	.2	2,954
Belorussians	--	--
Kazakhs	--	--
Lithuanians	--	--
Armenians	--	--
C. Groups Gaining through Ethnic Reidentification between 1959 and 1970		
Georgians	--	--
Russians	--	--

Source: Barbara A. Anderson and Brian D. Silver, "Estimating Russification
of Ethnic Identity among Non-Russians in the USSR," Demography,
vol. 20, no. 4 (November 1983), pp. 461-89.

Note: Rates are not calculated (given as --) if estimated reidentification
was negative.

ethnically by 1970, and among the Mordvinians, between 14% and 16% of the cohort. These high rates of reidentification offer one explanation why, of the twenty-six groups for which estimates were made, only the Karelians and Mordvinians showed an absolute decrease in their total population between the censuses of 1959 and 1970 (as well as between 1970 and 1979, and between 1979 and 1989). For these groups, high rates of assimilation apparently occur not only in the youngest age cohorts but also among adults.

Several other groups display high estimated rates of ethnic reidentification. Like the Karelians and the Mordvinians, these are ASSR nationalities with homelands in the Russian republic and an Orthodox Christian religious tradition. The Chuvash, Komi, Mari, and Udmurts all are estimated to have lost between 6% and 10% of the 0–38 cohort through ethnic reidentification between 1959 and 1970.

These non-Muslim ASSR nationalities with high rates of ethnic reidentification are the same groups that showed very low sex ratios (very large male deficits) due to World War II. It is for these groups, especially, that we think ethnic intermarriage and the assumption of high status positions in their titular areas by Russians played an important role. The level of ethnic reidentification for all people aged 0–38 in 1959 in these groups is high, but for those aged 0–8 and those aged 9–18 in 1959 it is even higher.[37] Those aged 0–8 in 1959 would have included most of the children of women married shortly after World War II; those aged 9–18 in 1959 would have included most of the children of women who were married shortly before the war but became widowed during its course. Among the Mordvinians, 15% of those aged 0–8 and 28% of those aged 9–18 in 1959 had changed their ethnic self-identification by 1970, as did 22% of those aged 0–8 and 31% of those aged 9–18 among the Karelians—in both cases probably to Russian. These are extremely high rates of assimilation for such a short time.

The Tuvinians are estimated to have lost between 3.8% and 6.3% of the 0–38 cohort between 1959 and 1970. Because this relatively high estimated loss through ethnic reidentification is not consistent with their low propensity to adopt Russian as native language, it is doubtful that Tuvinians are actually Russifying in such proportions. It is plausible that the border between their ASSR and Mongolia was not completely closed to migration during that period, and a net emigration of only some 3,000 Tuvinians would account for the estimated reidentification of those aged 0–38 in 1959. The remaining ASSR nationalities of Siberia, the Yakuts and the Buryats, are marginal cases in the "reidentifier" category.

Of the ASSR nationalities, the Tatars show the lowest estimated proportion of those ethnically reidentifying. The Tatars are one of the two ASSR nationalities (of the eleven for which we have made estimates) who by tradition are Muslim. The other Muslim ASSR nationality, the Bashkirs, had a high reidentification proportion, comparable to that of the traditionally Orthodox, ASSR-level nationalities. But on the basis of census data on native language, as well as their historical patterns of assimilation, it is likely that most of the 6% to 8% of those Bashkirs in the 0–38 cohort who are estimated to have reidentified ethnically between 1959 and 1970 declared themselves Tatars. If this is true, then the low estimated proportion of "reidentifiers" among the Tatars is partially due to their absorption of Bashkirs.

Groups with Little Change. All nationalities whose official territories have the status of union republics—with the exception of the Armenians, Georgians, and Russians—have estimated rates of ethnic reidentification that are close to zero.

For the six Muslim nationalities in this group, the range between the low and the high estimated proportion of the 0–38 cohort that reidentified between 1959 and 1970 across the five survival assumptions was −1.5% and +4.3%. Since this range spanned the zero point, it is plausible that there was no net ethnic reidentification among the Azerbaidzhanis, Kazakhs, Kirghiz, Tadzhiks, Turkmen, and Uzbeks as a whole. If there is any assimilation among these nationalities, it is less likely to be by Russians than by other Muslim groups.[38]

The three Baltic nationalities (Estonians, Latvians, and Lithuanians) also have negligible proportions of those ethnically reidentifying in the 0–38 cohort, with estimates ranging between −1.4% and +3.8%. Thus, despite the increasing net migration of Russians to the Baltic republics, there appears to be little net ethnic Russification of their titular nationalities. This is consistent with the report by a Soviet scholar that even when marriages occur between Balts and Russians in these republics, the children tend to choose the non-Russian nationality.[39] The proportion of Moldavians reidentifying also appears to be negligible. Only between 0.1% and 2.8% of the Moldavian 0–38 cohort are estimated to have reidentified ethnically between 1959 and 1970.

The most surprising result of our analysis is the apparently low proportion of Belorussians and Ukrainians undergoing ethnic reidentification. Given the historical patterns of assimilation of these two Slavic nationalities by the Russians, particularly those of their members living outside their titular republics, as well as the evidence that Ukrainians and Belorussians readily intermarry with Russians, higher rates of ethnic reidentification would be expected.[40] Yet in the 0–38 cohort, only between −1.4% and +1.4% of the Belorussians, and only between −0.3% and +2.5% of the Ukrainians are estimated to have ethnically reidentified.

Perhaps one explanation of these low apparent rates of assimilation is that the Belorussians and Ukrainians were absorbing members of other groups, especially Poles and Jews. There were large numbers of Poles in both Belorussia and Ukraine in 1959. Almost one half of those in Belorussia, and over two-thirds of those in Ukraine reported the language of the titular nationality as their native language. Between 1959 and 1970 the number of self-declared Poles declined absolutely in both republics. Indeed, it is possible that many of the "Poles" in the 1959 census were actually Belorussians

TABLE 7. Estimated Contribution of Non-Russian Slavs and Non-Slavs
to the Gain in the Number of Russians through Ethnic
Reidentification between 1959 and 1970

	Number Reidentifying per 1,000	Number Reidentifying x 1000	Percentage of Russian Gain
Russians	-7.7	-599.9	
Non-Russian Slavs	11.8	357.3	55.5
Non-Slavs	8.4	286.3	44.5

Note: Non-Russian Slavs are Ukrainians, Belorussians, and Poles.
The figures refer to the estimated gains and losses by 1970
in the cohort aged 0-38 in 1959.

or Ukrainians who called themselves Poles because they were Roman Catholic
by religion.[41] The Jews also declined in absolute numbers in the USSR
between 1959 and 1970—before the beginning of substantial emigration in
the 1970s—and may also have helped to increase the number of Belorussians
and Ukrainians. However, given their pattern of language preference, it is
probable that most of the Jews who reidentified ethnically did so as Russians,
not Belorussians or Ukrainians.

To take the possible assimilation of Poles by Ukrainians and Belorussians
into account, we estimated the proportion of those ethnically reidentifying
among all three of these non-Russian Slavic groups taken together.[42] As
shown in Table 7, we estimate that about twelve out of every thousand
(1.2%) of the non-Russian Slavs in the 0–38 age cohort in 1959 were
ethnically Russified by 1970. This is comparable to our estimate of the
proportion of Ukrainians alone who became ethnically Russified between
1959 and 1970. Therefore, the absorption of Poles by Belorussians and
Ukrainians cannot explain the low estimated rate of ethnic Russification of
the Belorussians and Ukrainians.

Even though the non-Russian Slavs had a low *rate* of ethnic Russification
between 1959 and 1970, they contributed over half (55.5%) of the estimated
net gain in the number of Russians due to ethnic reidentification. This is
because the population size of the non-Russian Slavs is so large that even
a low rate of ethnic reidentification translates into a substantial absolute
number of newly self-declared Russians: 357 thousand.

Gainers. Three nationalities show definite "negative" rates of ethnic
reidentification, implying that they gained in group members. These three
are the Georgians, the Armenians, and the Russians.

The main source of the Georgian surplus is probably the Ossetians, who
have shown a strong tendency toward the adoption of Georgian as their
native language. Another source of the apparent surplus of Georgians could
be their unusually high survival rates.

TABLE 8.   Ethnic Reidentification of Synthetic Cohorts for Illustrative
           Cases, Based on Rates between 1959 and 1970

Nationality		Age Range			
		11-19	20-29	30-39	40-49
Ukrainians	100,000	97,918	96,813	95,495	95,495
Tatars	100,000	99,297	93,275	92,959	91,819
Chuvash	100,000	93,667	77,264	74,814	71,798
Karelians	100,000	78,893	56,428	49,885	46,789
All Non-Russians	100,000	99,887	97,575	97,031	96,118

Note: Synthetic cohorts begin with a standard initial population size
       of 100,000 at birth who belonged to the given nationality, with
       the numbers at successive ages representing the estimated number
       of those surviving from birth to the given age who still belonged
       to that nationality. If the estimated reidentification rate for
       a given age group between 1959 and 1970 is negative, as it is for
       the Ukrainians aged 29-38 in 1959 (= 40-49 in 1970), no ethnic
       reidentification is assumed to occur in the synthetic cohort as
       it passes through that age range.

Armenia is ethnically the most homogeneous republic in the USSR. In
1959, 88% of the republic's population consisted of Armenians. Intermarriage
between Armenians and non-Armenians in the Armenian SSR occurs extremely infrequently.[43] Assimilation of non-Armenians is, therefore, not a
likely source of the excess Armenians. Instead, the most likely source is
repatriation from abroad. Between 1946 and 1975, approximately 150,000
Armenians returned to Soviet Armenia, of whom 90,000 arrived in 1946–
49.[44] During the 1960s, an average of 2,000 to 4,000 Armenians per year
came to Soviet Armenia from abroad.[45] On net, only about 24,000 Armenians
who were aged 0–38 in 1959 needed to have immigrated to account for
the excess Armenians estimated in this cohort. Therefore, we consider
Armenians not to be gainers through ethnic reidentification, but rather as
belonging to the group of nationalities showing little change through ethnic
reidentification.

Another way to contrast the experiences of the "reidentifiers" and the
"groups with little change" is to use synthetic cohorts to calculate the
proportions of those who would have reidentified by a given age. These
estimates use a life table approach, in which the decline in population due
to mortality has already been taken into account. The experience is calculated
on the basis of what would happen to a hypothetical person who survived
from one age to the next but was subject to the reidentification rates for a
given age group between 1959 and 1970.

Table 8 presents such estimates for the entire non-Russian population of
the USSR and for four nationalities—two estimated to have undergone little
ethnic reidentification between 1959 and 1970 and two estimated to have

experienced substantial reidentification. The table shows that of a hypothetical initial cohort of 100,000 self-identified Ukrainians who survived to age 11–19, 97,918 would still call themselves Ukrainian. By the time the cohort reached age 40–49, 95,495 would still call themselves Ukrainian. In other words, the probability that an originally self-identified Ukrainian would still declare himself or herself as Ukrainian at age 40–49 is 0.95. For the Tatars, the probability of maintaining Tatar as a self-identification is 0.92. In contrast, only 72% of the originally self-identified Chuvash would still call themselves Chuvash by age 40–49. The figure of 47% for the Karelians is consistent with the estimated "halving time" of 40 years shown in Table 6.

Table 8 provides another basis for evaluating Kozlov's contention that national identification is unchanging after the teenage years. Of the initial cohort of all non-Russians aged 0–10 identifying themselves by a given ethnic label, 99.9% of those who survived would still use the same ethnic designation at age 11–19. By age 20–29, 97.6% of the survivors would still call themselves by their original ethnonym. By age 30–39 and 40–49, the percentages would be 97.0 and 96.1, respectively. Thus, for the non-Russians taken as a whole, there is evidence of steady net reidentification throughout the life cycle. But the largest net increase in reidentification occurs between ages 11–19 and 20–29, precisely the ages at which Kozlov suggested the change should occur.

For some nationalities the net shift in ethnic identification appears to be substantial even in the adult years. For example, while for the non-Russian population as a whole the proportion at age 30–39 who claim their original ethnic designation is less than half a percentage point lower than the proportion who claim that same designation at age 20–29, the corresponding proportion for the Karelians drops by 6.5 percentage points.

The differences in the estimated rates of ethnic reidentification are generally consistent with differences in linguistic Russification among the non-Russian nationalities. The groups showing the greatest propensity toward ethnic Russification are the traditionally Orthodox Christian nationalities, especially those whose official homelands in the Soviet state structure are below the level of union republic. All nationalities whose official homelands are of union republic status showed low estimated rates of ethnic reidentification between 1959 and 1970. The most surprising result of our estimates is the low rate of ethnic reidentification by Ukrainians and Belorussians. Although these kindred Slavic groups provide a large reservoir from which self-identified Russians have apparently been drawn in the past and might be drawn in the future, their propensity toward ethnic reidentification between 1959 and 1970 was not very strong.

Conclusion

Linguistic and ethnic affiliations of non-Russians have not changed mechanically as a result of policies introduced by the central Soviet authorities. Regime policies do play a role, but they have not been formulated or implemented without regard to social, cultural, and historical conditions. Nor have their outcomes always been those anticipated by the planners. Despite frequent assumptions to the contrary, the Soviet regime cannot easily change society.

But whether the result of policy or other factors, the observed changes in linguistic and ethnic affiliation among Soviet nationalities cannot be ignored. A change in an ethnic label reported to the census taker does not necessarily, of course, denote a change in everyday conduct, cultural orientation, or preferences for associating with members of particular groups. In some cases the choice of an ethnic label may be dictated more by expediency than by conviction—to avoid discrimination or persecution, for example. Still, Soviet scholars are undoubtedly correct in their assertion that a change in ethnic self-identification is generally not made lightly and that it typically implies a serious change in ethnic attachments.

Is everyone in the USSR becoming Russian? As our evidence shows, clearly not. For many groups—those of union republic status that account for the great majority of the non-Russian population—ethnic attachment, as measured by self-reported nationality, remains quite stable, surprisingly so for some (Ukrainians, Belorussians). For others—especially those Orthodox by tradition who have autonomous republic status—assimilation to the Russians, variously gradual or rapid, seems to be taking place. Erstwhile Karelians or Mordvinians, for example, who come to call themselves Russian may still maintain sentiments or habits that mark them as Karelians and Mordvinians. But if not they themselves, then more likely their children will come truly to regard themselves as Russians.

The trends in linguistic and ethnic assimilation that we have examined refer primarily to the period before Mikhail Gorbachev came to power. Gorbachev's policies of *perestroika, glasnost'*, and democratization helped to stimulate ethnic consciousness as well as the formation of organized popular fronts and other groups that openly sought greater cultural, economic, and political autonomy for the non-Russian peoples. We would expect this growing national self-awareness to retard and, in some cases, to reverse processes of linguistic and ethnic assimilation. Preliminary data from the 1989 Soviet census, we believe, provide some evidence of such change in the pace of assimilation. As more evidence becomes available from the census and from studies of changes in language and cultural policy in the non-Russian regions, we shall be able to determine more conclusively whether the pace of ethnic and linguistic assimilation has slowed, as well as the factors that may be responsible for it.[46]

Notes

1. These critical events include man-made calamities, such as wars, mass terror, and deportations. The effects of one such event, World War II, are discussed in some detail below. On the effects of other calamities on the Soviet population, see Barbara A. Anderson and Brian D. Silver, "Demographic Analysis and Population Catastrophes in the USSR," *Slavic Review*, vol. 44, no. 3 (Fall 1985), pp. 517–36; and "Tautologies

in the Study of Excess Mortality in the USSR in the 1930s," *Slavic Review*, vol. 45, no. 2 (Summer 1986), pp. 307–13.

2. The evidence and interpretation for the central parts of this analysis are developed in greater detail in: Barbara A. Anderson and Brian D. Silver, "Estimating Russification of Ethnic Identity among Non-Russians in the USSR," *Demography*, vol. 20, no. 4 (November 1983), pp. 461–89; "Equality, Efficiency, and Politics in Soviet Bilingual Education Policy: 1934–1980," *American Political Science Review*, vol. 78, no. 4 (December 1984), pp. 1019–39; and "Demographic Consequences of World War II on the Non-Russian Nationalities of the USSR," in Susan J. Linz, ed., *The Impact of World War II on the Soviet Union* (Totowa, NJ: Rowman & Allanheld, 1985), pp. 207–42. In using terms such as assimilation, Russification, and ethnic reidentification, we do not imply that this is an aspect, or intended outcome, of official policy. Instead, we use the terms to describe change in ethnic self-identification. Many different factors contribute to or impede such change.

3. Soviet sociological surveys have found that some non-Russians do not actually speak their "native language," which may for such individuals signify the language of their childhood or of their family. For further discussion of the measures of native language and second language in Soviet censuses, see Brian D. Silver, "The Ethnic and Language Dimensions in Russian and Soviet Censuses," in Ralph S. Clem, ed., *Research Guide to the Russian and Soviet Censuses* (Ithaca: Cornell University Press, 1986), pp. 70–97.

4. It seems likely that Russian was the response preferred by the census takers, even if the respondent knew another language equally well. Thus, the census data probably underestimate knowledge of second languages other than Russian. Whether the census figures actually overestimate the knowledge of *Russian* as a second language is not known. For more discussion, see Silver, "The Ethnic and Language Dimensions."

5. For a detailed analysis of the effects of these factors, see Brian D. Silver, "The Impact of Urbanization and Geographical Dispersion on the Linguistic Russification of Soviet Nationalities," *Demography*, vol. 11, no. 1 (February 1974), pp. 89–103; "Social Mobilization and the Russification of Soviet Nationalities," *American Political Science Review*, vol. 68, no. 1 (March 1974), pp. 45–66; and "Language Policy and the Linguistic Russification of Soviet Nationalities," in Jeremy R. Azrael, ed., *Soviet Nationality Policies and Practices* (New York: Praeger, 1978), pp. 250–308.

6. See Silver, "Language Policy."

7. K. Kh. Khanazarov, *Reshenie natsional'no-iazykovoi problemy v SSSR* (Moscow: Izdatel'stvo politicheskoi literatury, 1977), p. 133.

8. I. P. Tsamerian, *Teoreticheskie problemy obrazovaniia i razvitiia sovetskogo mnogonatsional'nogo gosudarstva* (Moscow: Nauka, 1973), pp. 241–42.

9. M. I. Isaev, *Iazykovoe stroitel'stvo v SSSR: Protsessy sozdaniia pis'mennostei narodov SSSR* (Moscow: Nauka, 1979), pp. 260–61.

10. John A. Armstrong, "The Ethnic Scene in the Soviet Union," in Erich Goldhagen, ed., *Ethnic Minorities in the Soviet Union* (New York: Praeger, 1968), pp. 3–49.

11. On the deported nationalities, see Robert Conquest, *The Nation Killers* (London: Macmillan, 1970); Alexander Nekrich, *The Punished Peoples* (New York: Norton, 1978); and S. Enders Wimbush and Ronald Wixman, "The Meskhetian Turks: A New Voice in Soviet Central Asia," *Canadian Slavonic Papers*, vol. 17, no. 2/3 (Summer/Fall 1975), pp. 320–40.

12. Yaroslav Bilinsky, "The Soviet Education Laws of 1958–59 and Soviet Nationality Policy," *Soviet Studies*, vol. 14, no. 2 (October 1962), pp. 138–57.

13. P. A. Avrorin, "Dvuiazychie i shkola," in P. A. Azimov, Iu. D. Desheriev, and F. P. Filin, eds., *Problemy dvuiazychiia i mnogoiazychiia* (Moscow: Nauka, 1972), pp. 56–57.

14. Although the pressrun for each book is recorded in our sources, we are not making explicit use of this information because its use is not straightforward. However, it is clear that even if textbooks are published in a certain language through a certain grade level, this does not necessarily mean that a large proportion of children of the given non-Russian nationality use textbooks in their national language. For example, while textbooks in Belorussian are published in math-science through the tenth grade, in the 1972/73 school year 97.6% of all urban schoolchildren in the Belorussian SSR attended schools where Russian was the medium of instruction, although at the time of the 1970 census Belorussians comprised nearly 70% of the republic's urban population (K. Kh. Khanazarov, *Reshenie natsional'no-iazykovoi problemy*, p. 137). It is likely that all urban schools in Belorussia, at least until recently, have had Russian as the medium of instruction. This is suggested also by the discussion in V. K. Bondarchik and V. N. Beliavina, "Etnokul'turnye protsessy v gorodakh Belorussii: Istoriia i sovremennoe razvitie," *Sovetskaia etnografiia*, 1987, no. 5, pp. 31–40.

15. For an explanation of the criteria for inclusion of nationalities in the analysis, see Anderson and Silver, "Equality, Efficiency."

16. In Table 2, for the entire 1934–85 period and for each subperiod, a nationality is considered to have had native-language schooling only if there were a textbook in the given language for grade one or higher; preschool texts alone do not suffice for inclusion.

17. Iu. D. Desheriev and I. F. Protchenko, *Razvitie iazykov narodov SSSR v sovetskuiu epokhu* (Moscow: Prosveshchenie, 1968), pp. 119–23.

18. Brian D. Silver, "The Status of National Minority Languages in Soviet Education: An Assessment of Recent Changes," *Soviet Studies*, vol. 26, no. 1 (January 1974), pp. 28–40.

19. M. I. Isaev, *Sto tridtsat' ravnopravnykh: O iazykakh narodov SSSR* (Moscow: Nauka, 1970), pp. 25–26.

20. The evidence for these findings is developed at greater length in Anderson and Silver, "Demographic Consequences."

21. In Table 5, the nationalities are collapsed into groupings: Balts—Estonians, Latvians, Lithuanians; Non-Muslim ASSR—Buryats, Chuvash, Karelians, Komi, Mari, Mordvinians, Ossetians, Udmurts; Tatar-Bashkir—Tatars, Bashkirs; Muslim SSR—Azerbaidzhanis, Kazakhs, Kirghiz, Tadzhiks, Turkmen, Uzbeks; Daghestanis—Avars, Darghins, Kabardinians, Kumyks, Lezghians; Deported—Balkars, Chechens, Ingush, Kalmyks.

22. V. I. Kozlov, *Natsional'nosti SSSR: Etnodemograficheskii obzor* (Moscow: Statistika, 1975), pp. 172–73.

23. Silver, "The Status of National Minority Languages."

24. Victor Zaslavsky and Yuri Luryi, "The Passport System in the USSR and Changes in Soviet Society," *Soviet Union*, vol. 6, pt. 1 (1979), pp. 137–53.

25. V. I. Kozlov, *Dinamika chislennosti narodov: Metodologiia issledovaniia i osnovnye faktory* (Moscow: Nauka, 1969), p. 298; idem, *Natsional'nosti SSSR*, pp. 230–31.

26. Kozlov, *Natsional'nosti SSSR*, pp. 115, 128, 214, and 245.

27. K. I. Kozlova, *Etnografiia narodov Povolzh'ia: Uchebnoe posobie* (Moscow: Izdatel'stvo Moskovskogo universiteta, 1964), pp. 25–27.

28. Bernard Comrie, *The Languages of the Soviet Union* (Cambridge: Cambridge University Press, 1980).

29. Kozlov does not mention the famine in Ukraine in 1932–33, which clearly took a heavy toll. It is difficult, however, to determine how much of the slow growth

in the number of Ukrainians between 1926 and 1939 was due to the famine. For further discussion, see Anderson and Silver, "Demographic Analysis."

30. Kozlov, Natsional'nosti SSSR, p. 115.

31. Robert A. Lewis, Richard H. Rowland, and Ralph S. Clem, Nationality and Population Change in Russia and the USSR: An Evaluation of Census Data, 1897–1970 (New York: Praeger, 1976), pp. 282–85.

32. On the approach of Soviet scholars to the study of assimilation processes, see, for example, Iu. V. Bromlei and V. I. Kozlov, "Etnicheskie protsessy kak predmet issledovaniia," in Iu. V. Bromlei, ed., Sovremennye etnicheskie protsessy v SSSR, 2d ed. (Moscow: Nauka, 1977). In current Soviet usage, assimilation is viewed as one of a set of processes of ethnic unification characterizing Soviet society. See S. I. Bruk and V. I. Kozlov, "Etnograficheskaia nauka i perepis' naseleniia 1970 goda," Sovetskaia etnografiia, 1967, no. 5, pp. 3–14; Kozlov, Natsional'nosti SSSR, pp. 196ff.; Bromlei and Kozlov, "Etnicheskie protsessy," pp. 18ff.

33. The expected number of survivors at the second census date depends on the mortality assumptions used. For a discussion of these, see Anderson and Silver, "Estimating Russification." The method also assumes that the census counts are complete, which is not entirely true. This, however, cannot account for our estimates of ethnic reidentification. See Barbara A. Anderson and Brian D. Silver, "Estimating Census Undercount from School-Enrollment Data: An Application to the Soviet Censuses of 1959 and 1970," Demography, vol. 22, no. 2 (May 1985), pp. 289–308.

34. It is not possible to make analogous estimates for the 1970–79 and 1979–89 intercensal periods because age distributions by nationality have not been published for the 1979 and 1989 Soviet censuses.

35. V. K. Bondarchik, ed., Etnicheskie protsessy i obraz zhizni: Na materialakh issledovaniia naseleniia gorodov BSSR (Minsk: Nauka i tekhnika, 1980), p. 206.

36. For a discussion of the choice of nationality and the age range for estimates of ethnic reidentification, see Anderson and Silver, "Estimating Russification."

37. See Anderson and Silver, "Estimating Russification."

38. Ia. R. Vinnikov, "Natsional'nye i etnograficheskie gruppy Srednei Azii po dannym etnicheskoi statistiki," in R. Sh. Dzharylgasinova and L. S. Tolstova, eds., Etnicheskie protsessy natsional'nykh grupp Srednei Azii i Kazakhstana (Moscow: Nauka, 1980), pp. 11–42.

39. L. N. Terent'eva, "Opredelenie svoei natsional'noi prinadlezhnosti podrostkami v natsional'no-smeshannykh sem'iakh," Sovetskaia etnografiia, 1969, no. 3, pp. 20–30.

40. L. V. Chuiko, Braki i razvody (Moscow: Statistika, 1975); Iu. A. Evstigneev, "Natsional'no-smeshannye braki v Makhachkale," Sovetskaia etnografiia, 1971, no. 4, pp. 80–85; A. Lapin'sh, "Brachnaia izbiratel'nost' v Latviiskoi SSR," in P. Gulian, ed., Sotsial'no-demograficheskie issledovaniia sem'i v respublikakh sovetskoi Pribaltiki (Riga: Zinatne, 1980), pp. 49–62; and Vinnikov, "Natsional'nye i etnograficheskie gruppy."

41. Bondarchik, Etnicheskie protsessy, pp. 202–3; and O. A. Gantskaia and L. N. Terent'eva, "Etnograficheskie issledovaniia natsional'nykh protsessov v Pribaltike," Sovetskaia etnografiia, 1965, no. 5, pp. 3–19.

42. For details of the method used, see Anderson and Silver, "Estimating Russification."

43. A. E. Ter-Sarkisiants, "O natsional'nom aspekte brakov v Armianskoi SSR," Sovetskaia etnografiia, 1973, no. 4, pp. 89–95.

44. V. A. Kuregian, "Nekotorye osobennosti formirovaniia i ispol'zovaniia trudovykh resursov Armianskoi SSR," in V. G. Kostakov and E. L. Manevich, eds.,

Regional'nye problemy naseleniia i trudovye resursy SSSR (Moscow: Statistika, 1978), p. 239.

45. *Bol'shaia sovetskaia entsiklopedia,* 3d ed., vol. 2 (Moscow: Izdatel'stvo Sovetskoi entsiklopedii, 1970), p. 643.

46. For an analysis of trends in the ethnic composition of the Soviet Union and the union republics based on preliminary data from the 1989 Soviet census, see Barbara A. Anderson and Brian D. Silver, "Demographic Sources of the Changing Ethnic Composition of the Soviet Union," *Population and Development Review,* vol. 15, no. 4 (December 1989).

APPENDIX

Nationalities by Status of Titular Areas in the Federal System in 1990
and by Population Size in 1926, 1959, and 1979

STATUS OF TITULAR AREA	Population 1926	Population 1959	Population 1979	Ever Had Native Schools 1934-1985
UNION REPUBLIC (SSR)				
Ukrainians	31,194,976	37,252,930	42,347,387	Yes
Belorussians	4,738,923	7,913,488	9,462,715	Yes
Uzbeks	3,988,740	6,015,416	12,455,978	Yes
Kazakhs	3,969,007	3,621,610	6,556,442	Yes
Azerbaidzhanis	1,712,921	2,939,728	5,477,330	Yes
Armenians	1,568,197	2,786,912	4,151,241	Yes
Georgians	1,821,191	2,691,950	3,570,504	Yes
Lithuanians	41,463	2,326,094	2,850,905	Yes
Moldavians	278,905	2,214,139	2,968,224	Yes
Latvians	151,410	1,399,539	1,439,037	Yes
Tadzhiks	981,441	1,396,939	2,897,697	Yes
Turkmen	763,940	1,001,585	2,027,913	Yes
Estonians	154,666	988,616	1,019,851	Yes
Kirghiz	762,736	968,659	1,906,271	Yes
AUTONOMOUS REPUBLIC (ASSR)				
Tatars[a]	3,311,241	4,764,504	6,317,468	Yes
Chuvash	1,117,419	1,469,766	1,751,366	Yes
(Peoples of Daghestan)[b]				
Avars	197,392	270,394	482,844	Yes
Lezghians	134,529	223,129	382,611	Yes
Darghins	125,764	158,149	287,282	Yes
Kumyks	94,549	134,967	228,418	Yes
Laks	40,380	63,529	100,148	Yes
Tabasarans	31,983	34,700	75,239	Yes
Noghais	36,274	38,583	59,546	Yes
Rutuls	10,495	6,732	15,032	No
Tsakhurs	19,085	7,321	13,478	Yes
Aguls	7,653	6,709	12,078	No
Mordvinians	1,340,415	1,285,116	1,191,765	Yes
Bashkirs	713,693	989,040	1,371,452	Yes
Udmurts	514,222	624,794	713,696	Yes
Mari	428,192	504,205	621,961	Yes
Chechens	318,522	418,756	755,782	Yes
Ossetians	272,272	412,592	541,893	Yes
Komi	226,383	287,027	326,700	Yes
Buryats	237,501	252,959	352,646	Yes
Yakuts	240,709	233,344	328,018	Yes
Karakalpaks	146,317	172,556	303,324	Yes
Karelians	248,120	167,278	138,429	Yes
Ingush	74,097	105,980	186,198	Yes
Tuvinians	---	100,145	166,082	Yes
Kalmyks	133,652	106,066	146,631	Yes
Abkhazians	56,957	65,430	90,915	Yes

AUTONOMOUS OBLAST (AO)

Jews	2,672,499	2,267,814	1,810,876	Yes
Kabardinians	139,925	203,620	321,719	Yes
Karachai	55,123	81,403	131,074	Yes
Adyghei	65,270	79,631	108,711	Yes
Khakas	45,608	56,584	70,776	Yes
Altai	50,951	45,270	60,015	Yes
Balkars	33,307	42,408	66,334	Yes
Cherkess	65,270	30,453	46,470	Yes

AUTONOMOUS DISTRICT (AD)

Komi-Permiaks	149,488	143,901	150,768	Yes
Evenki	39,488	24,151	27,294	Yes
Nenets	17,566	23,007	29,894	Yes
Khanty	22,306	19,410	20,934	Yes
Chukchi	13,037	11,727	14,000	Yes
Mansi	5,754	6,449	7,563	Yes
Koryaks	7,439	6,287	7,879	Yes
Dolgans	656	3,932	5,053	No

OTHER INDIGENOUS (IND)

Crimean Tatars[c]	179,094	203,197	305,921	Yes
Gagauz	844	123,821	173,179	Yes
Abaza	13,825	19,591	29,497	Yes
Veps	32,785	16,374	8,094	Yes
Shor	12,601	15,274	16,033	Yes
Muslim Tats	28,705	11,463	22,441	No
Even	2,044	9,121	12,523	Yes
Nanai	5,860	8,026	10,516	Yes
Karaim	8,324	5,727	3,341	No
Selkup	1,630	3,768	3,565	Yes
Nivkhi	4,076	3,717	4,397	Yes
Udin	2,455	3,678	6,863	No
Ulchi	723	2,055	2,552	No
Saami	1,720	1,712	1,888	Yes
Udegei	1,357	1,444	1,551	Yes
Itelmen	4,217	1,109	1,370	No
Izhora	16,137	1,062	748	Yes
Ket	1,428	1,019	1,122	No
Orochi	647	782	1,198	No
Tofa	2,829	586	763	No
Negidals[d]	683	537	504	No
Yukagirs	443	442	835	No
Aleuts	353	421	546	No

130

NONINDIGENOUS

Germans	1,238,549	1,619,655	1,936,214	Yes
Poles	782,334	1,380,282	1,150,991	Yes
Bulgarians	111,296	324,251	361,082	Yes
Koreans	86,999	313,735	388,926	Yes
Greeks	213,765	309,308	343,809	Yes
Hungarians	5,476	154,738	170,553	Yes
Gypsies	61,265	132,024	209,159	Yes
Rumanians	4,651	106,366	128,792	No
Uighurs	108,570	95,208	210,612	Yes
Kurds	69,184	58,799	115,858	Yes
Finns	134,701	92,717	77,079	Yes
Chinese	10,247	25,781	--	Yes
Czechs	27,123	24,557	17,812	Yes
Dungans	14,600	21,928	51,694	Yes
Assyrians	9,808	21,803	25,170	Yes
Iranians	53,159	20,766	31,313	Yes
Slovaks	27,123	14,674	9,409	No
Beluchi	9,974	7,842	18,997	Yes
Albanians	3,057	5,258	--	No
Khalkha-Mongols	559	1,774	3,228	No

Sources: Population totals are from the 1926, 1959, and 1979 Soviet
censuses. The information in this and other tables on which
nationalities had native-language schools is derived from
bibliographic data on the publication of school textbooks,
as described in Barbara A. Anderson and Brian D. Silver,
"Equality, Efficiency, and Politics in Soviet Bilingual
Education Policy, 1934-1980," American Political Science
Review, vol. 78, no. 4 (December 1984), pp. 1019-39.

[a]The 1959 population for the (Volga) Tatars is derived by subtracting
the estimated number of Crimean Tatars from the reported total number
of "Tatars" in the 1959 census.

[b]The Daghestani nationalities listed here are those reported separately
in the 1959 census. Although ten nationalities are listed here, only
the first seven are treated as "titular" nationalities of Daghestan.

[c]The population totals for the Crimean Tatars are derived as follows:
(1) for 1926, all persons reported as "Tatars" who lived in the
Crimean ASSR; (2) for 1959 and 1979, all persons reported as "Tatars"
who lived in the city of Tashkent or Tashkent oblast. Each of these
is only an approximation of the true number of Crimean Tatars.

[d]The Negidals are listed separately in the 1926, 1970, and 1979 censuses
but are omitted from the 1959 census report. The population figure
given here for 1959 is actually from the 1970 census.

CHAPTER 6

Readers, Writers, and Republics: The Structural Basis of Non-Russian Literary Politics

Paul A. Goble

Literary politics in the non-Russian republics of the USSR are shaped by three distinct sets of factors. The first set encompasses those factors, such as party control and bureaucratic management, that are endemic to the Soviet system as a whole; the second—those, like the dual subordination (to central and local officials) of literary life, that are common to all republics; and the third—those, like national culture, that are unique to each particular republic. Western observers have concentrated on the first and third of these sets; they have virtually ignored the second. While this omission is under-standable—sources of information were quite scarce before the era of *glasnost'* and the languages needed to exploit them extremely diverse—it is nonetheless doubly unfortunate, both because these republic-level commonalities explain much of what takes place in each republic, and because they provide the basis for assessing the relative impact of the other two.

Among the most important of these commonalities are the ideological imperatives operating at the republican level, the shared structural framework of non-Russian literary politics, and the political strategies available to the main actors on the literary scene. They, rather than the specific details of literary politics in one or another republic, are the focus of this chapter.

Ideological Imperatives

Most Western studies of non-Russian literatures in the USSR have concen-trated on their ideological aspects, with literature serving as a barometer of national self-assertiveness and Soviet pressure. This approach has yielded numerous important insights, but since the accession of Mikhail Gorbachev as general secretary it has become increasingly problematic. First of all, this approach understates the importance of the decline of ideological prescriptions in the era of *glasnost'*. Second, it tends to assume that we can know precisely what Moscow, on the one hand, and the various non-Russian nationalities, on the other, actually want. And third, it often presupposes that criticized literature is the best source of information on tendencies in non-Russian literary politics, thus ignoring the more general patterns of what gets published and what does not.

Both Moscow and the non-Russian writers have their own distinctive interests and concerns. In the past, leadership statements on ideology were commonly assumed to define the first, and various trends in the national past to circumscribe the latter. In fact, positions on both sides have been significantly more diverse and have become even more so under *glasnost'*. There is no single Uzbek or only one Moscow position at any particular time. Instead, there is an increasing diversity of views on both sides. Moreover, the notion that criticized literature constitutes the best source of such information is particularly misleading, both because it focuses on a very small part of the ideological spectrum, implicitly or explicitly dismissing the rest as simply a sellout, and because we frequently do not know enough to determine why specific items are written or criticisms made.

Given such difficulties with the earlier approach, it may be useful to explore the still important ideological constraints on republican writers and literary institutions, consider those factors within the ideology that both define and stimulate nationalist impulses in literature, and note those ideological factors that push some writers towards a Soviet rather than a nationalist position. This will provide the essential background for examining the increasingly important structural basis of non-Russian literary politics and the strategies its various participants have devised to cope with the new political situation.

"National in Form, Socialist in Content"

It is a commonplace that non-Russian writers in the Soviet Union have borne a double burden. On the one hand, they have had to conform to all-union literary norms such as socialist realism, which carries with it enormous Russian cultural baggage, and to approved literary forms such as the novel. (Seldom recognized as an ideological tool, this latter requirement has, in fact, played a far greater role in the transformation of literary life in non-Russian, and especially Central Asian, areas than the former.) On the other hand, they have had to obey dicta directed specifically at them as non-Russians: to promote the "friendship of peoples" under Soviet Russian suzerainty and produce works that are "national in form, socialist in content."

Soviet writers—and not only they—have often invoked the formula "national in form, socialist in content" as an explanation rather than something to be explained. At an intellectual level, such a position is deeply flawed: separating form and content may be possible analytically, but it is virtually impossible in practice. Nonetheless, the concept remains a powerful one for helping to understand the frequently shifting requirements Moscow has imposed on non-Russian writers. Under Stalin, this formula became a procrustean bed, one that eliminated all diversity, except for names and settings, and generated a literature striking only in its overwhelming dullness. Under Khrushchev and Brezhnev, the indefiniteness of the concept permitted a greater range of diversity in understanding and production. Moscow tolerated this greater diversity, and non-Russian writers continued to explore its limits. Now, under Gorbachev, many—both in Moscow and the periphery—have explicitly rejected the term. Still, its strictures that non-Russian literatures not promote nationalism or anti-Russian attitudes and that they serve to mold the "Soviet people"—even one marked by greater diversity than heretofore admitted—into a politically unified population remain strong and operative for most officials and many writers as well.

If Moscow is increasingly tolerant of diversity, non-Russian writers are increasingly interested in exploring just how far they can push the boundaries of the permissible. But today, as in the past, these writers have goals and interests far broader than simple national self-assertion, particularly if that is defined, as it often is in the West, as the recovery of a pre-Soviet past untouched by modernization. Some non-Russian writers may wish to experiment with particular genres or ideas taken from other cultures—Chingiz Aitmatov is an obvious but not isolated example—while others may be interested in the existential problems of modern life with little reference to nationality as such, and still others in looking to the past may in fact be seeking only the raw materials from which to fashion some new future. Such searches and the works they generate are undoubtedly more reflective of the national aspirations of most groups in the USSR than particular statements denounced as nationalistic by the Soviet press and regularly quoted with interest by Western observers.

Because of this complexity on both sides, conflicts in the ideological sphere should not be viewed as an either/or proposition, a "zero-sum game" in which one group "wins" while the other "loses." In reality, varieties of other outcomes, of compromise and conflict, are more likely. Approached from this perspective, the very formula "national in form, socialist in content" will appear to have had the more interesting and undoubtedly unintended consequence of both generating more nationalistic statements of a particular kind than might otherwise have been the case, and pushing many writers to develop within the Soviet context a far broader range of literary options.

The Push Toward the National

By reifying nationality in literary life and by setting a marker against which non-Russian writers must work, Moscow has unintentionally generated a particular form of nationalism in literature, one that might not otherwise exist. This constitutes yet another commonality among the republics. Part of the reason for this development is the universal nature of the literary process, a desire by writers to find new ways of expressing their ideas and finding a receptive audience for such expression. But part of the explanation lies in the specifically Russian tradition of the author as spokesman for national interests and concerns that Moscow has unwittingly taught non-Russian writers. Most of them now see themselves as spokesmen for their respective nations in the same way the more familiar Russian writers do.

It could be argued that this is the most successful transplant of Soviet Russian experience in non-Russian literary affairs.

More than that, the formula "national in form, socialist in content" has driven non-Russian authors not merely to adopt Soviet-prescribed literary forms and interests, but, whenever they chose to resist them, to adopt remarkably similar positions. Most of this similarity is obscured by terminology, but analytically and politically there is little substantive or ideological difference between the *mirasism* ("recovery of the past") of Central Asian and Islamic writers, the ruralist prose of the Russians, and the sometimes romantic interests of the Baltic nationalities. Failure by Western scholars to make comparisons in this area has obscured a remarkable Soviet "achievement"—the promotion of functionally and ideologically similar national, even nationalist, literatures on the periphery of the USSR. But this achievement entails a price that may be higher than Moscow can comfortably pay.

As a result, with the decline in coercion and ideological constraint under Gorbachev, national literatures worthy of the name have emerged; and non-Russian writers in their search for both self-realization and an audience are advancing national themes that have already touched a nerve.

The Push Toward the Soviet

If earlier ideological pronouncements have had the effect of pushing many non-Russian writers toward the national, other considerations—including ideological ones—have pushed some, and often the more widely read, authors toward Soviet values. Many Soviet values are attractive to non-Russian writers and their audiences, and even a rejection of some of them does not mean a rejection of them all. Many non-Russians take an understandable pride in the status of the USSR as a world power, and many accept both proclaimed Soviet values and actual guarantees—such as no unemployment and lifetime security, albeit at a low standard of living. Not surprisingly, many popular non-Russian writers reflect these themes, just as Yulian Semenov does among the Russians. And while the attractiveness of many aspects of official doctrine has diminished over time for non-Russians as well as Russians, many of its more general ideas have become so entrenched in the population that Gorbachev and the reformers face an enormous task uprooting them.

This pattern holds in non-Russian literatures as well. The notions of modernity and transformation, both as an ideal and as a partially accomplished fact, are widely shared by many non-Russian elites, literary and political. Socialism, at least in principle, and Soviet patriotism, in practice, are far more highly valued by many non-Russians than only a reading of literature criticized by the authorities would suggest. Indeed, many of the most famous non-Russian books in the West are virtually unknown in their native republics, as any conversation with non-literary specialists from those areas attests. Moreover, one should not discount the undoubted calculation of many non-Russian writers that they can reach an audience beyond their own, often small, nationality only by accepting certain views thought to be shared by that larger group. Opting out of such a system may be morally attractive, but this option is unlikely to win a large number of adherents at any one time. Consequently, this desire to reach out both to one's own nationality and to others leads many non-Russian writers to parrot and ultimately to believe many broader Soviet views.

Again, many observers in the West are tempted to see this pattern as a form of sellout to the authorities and a compromise of national dignity. But in fact, this very acceptance of Soviet-style ideology has often helped stimulate support for a new type of ethnic identity, one that may not challenge the territorial integrity of the system but still contributes to the rise of a kind of ethnic politics that may challenge Moscow's ability to promote significant reform.[1]

A Common Structural Framework

These ideological impulses are reinforced by the common structural framework within which non-Russian literary politics takes place. Soviet federal arrangements, rather than the national composition of the population, define the basic structure of non-Russian literary life. As the Nagorno-Karabakh dispute has underscored, the non-Russian republics are not ethnically homogeneous. This is so partly by design, since the central authorities have always wanted dependent minorities to assist them in non-Russian areas dominated by other groups; partly it is the result of accident, since much of the migration that has taken place since 1953 has been in response to economic stimuli rather than central direction. Nevertheless, this fact has given nationality politics a particular flavor, especially since in almost all instances Moscow has dealt with the periphery as a set of republics rather than as a collection of national groups. That is how the bureaucracies of the country are arranged, and bureaucratic realities determine much of what takes place on the periphery. Not coincidentally, these general structures determine the nature of the organizations involved with non-Russian literatures, the role of the non-literary elites in literary affairs, and the specific audiences available to non-Russian writers.

Literary Organizations

Like so many institutions that govern various spheres of Soviet life, literary organizations in the fourteen non-Russian republics replicate those in Moscow. Each union republic has its own Writers' Union, its own censorship office (*Glavlit*), and its own state publishing committee (*Goskomizdat*). More than that, all of these republic-level organizations have displayed characteristics familiar to any student of literary affairs in Moscow: tight party control, bureaucratization and hypercentralization, corruption, and the regular imposition of extra-literary standards on literary questions.[2] Even more to the point, *glasnost'* has highlighted these shortcomings without doing much to overcome them. As one senior USSR Ministry of Culture official observed, "In the cultural sphere, all the same structures of the administrative-command system and its offspring—various social organizations and creative unions—continue to operate."[3] But this is also where the similarities of these republic-level bodies with their all-union counterparts end and their specifically republic-level distinctions begin.

The most important difference, and the one from which all others flow, is that in the republics, all three of these institutions and the others that are involved with literary life are subordinate both to their parent organizations in Moscow and to the local political authorities. Thus, the all-union Writers' Union sets detailed standards for its republican affiliates; the central *Glavlit* determines the rules of prepublication review; and the Moscow *Goskomizdat* supervises virtually all regional publishing houses, allocates resources among them, and passes on all publication plans (*templans*).[4] Much has been said in the Soviet press recently about the traditional hypercentralization of all three—local officials could not make even the simplest decision without recourse to Moscow—but subsequent publications in the USSR show that the orders may have changed, but that the system of giving them generally has not. Indeed, in some critical respects, central policies are more restrictive now than they were, as will be seen below in the discussion of the impact of the drive for profitability in the publishing industry.

At the same time, the leaderships of both the republican Writers' Unions and publishing houses invariably fall within the *nomenklatura* of the republican Central Committees, giving senior party bosses in the republics ample room for interference. As a result, these literary institutions are subject to two kinds of outside meddling—a pattern that simultaneously restricts their autonomy in most spheres, but in others allows them to play off one group against another. All this affects who writes, what they write, and where they publish, and represents another structural commonality among the republics.

One surprising feature of the non-Russian literary landscape is that non-Russian writers appear to be, relative to population, slightly more numerous than Russian ones. According to one recent study—which, it must be cautioned, counted both Russians and non-Russians in the non-Russian republics—there is one writer for every 31,500 people in non-Russian areas, compared to one for every 33,200 in the country as a whole.[5] Not unexpectedly these figures conceal significant regional differences—the Transcaucasian and Baltic republics are vastly overrepresented, while those of Central Asia are significantly underrepresented.[6] This pattern reflects Moscow's longstanding policy of using writers to propagandize socialism and represents the opposite of the usual trend in modernizing societies toward increasing concentration of literary talent. Given the new messages many of these writers are carrying, that may create additional problems for Moscow.

But while they may be relatively more numerous, the non-Russian writers are also significantly more constrained by bureaucratic arrangements. Non-Russian writers typically have fewer opportunities than those in Moscow to engage in other kinds of quasi-professional work outside the confines of the Writers' Union. This is reflected in the fact that in non-Russian areas the republican Writers' Unions themselves employ a far higher share of writers within their own bureaucracies than does the Writers' Union at the center. A study of the Writers' Union in Lithuania showed, for example, that bureaucratic growth there exceeded numerical growth in membership between 1960 and 1980.[7] The same pattern holds elsewhere: all republics have reported an expansion of both central staffs and local branches during the last two decades. As a result, republican Writers' Unions tend to exercise even greater control over non-Russian writers than is the case at the center.

Another effect of this bureaucratic incorporation of local writers is the widespread "protectionism" that pits the leaderships against the members and members against outsiders. In every republic, the leadership of the Writers' Union has made it extremely difficult for new writers to get published, as an examination of the table of contents in any republican literary journal will confirm; and writers inside the Union have done little to help outsiders, something for which they have recently drawn criticism by a few established authors. As a result, according to the then chief of the all-union *Goskomizdat*, Mikhail F. Nenashev, the republican Writers' Unions continue to exceed even that in Moscow in their structural conservatism.[8] Efforts to remedy the situation have generally failed.[9]

These bureaucratic constraints have been most clearly in evidence in what non-Russians write. The literary forms of what gets written (fiction, poetry, and criticism), the outlets where it is published (journals and books), and the languages in which it appears have been decided by the republican Writers' Unions, *Glavlits*, and *Goskomizdats* operating within the tight constraints imposed by Moscow.[10] And despite the diversity of the country, Moscow has generally imposed a relatively common mix for each republic as to genre, language, and access. Because such decisions have been made for political rather than literary reasons, they at times have become a source of conflict among Moscow, the republican literary establishments, and local party elites, but—for reasons discussed below—these are conflicts in which the literary establishments and the republican political elites have held far fewer cards than Moscow and hence generally have lost.

Regarding language in particular, Moscow has imposed two kinds of strictures within which the republics operate. First of all, the central authorities determine—either directly by order or indirectly through controls on paper allocation and demands for profitability—just how much is to be published in each language. In general, these decisions reflect the pattern of language use Moscow wishes to promote rather than the popularity of particular literatures or the actual size of potential readerships.[11] For small nationalities, such policies often benefit the few writers chosen as representative; but for larger republican nationalities, this policy works very much as a constraint, linguistically and artistically. Moscow's decisions on these questions apparently are regularly appealed, but *samizdat* novels, such as Semen Lipkin's *Dekada*, suggest that such appeals have a chance of succeeding only if local party officials intervene, a pattern likely to be true in all republics and one that may explain the rise of a new set of bureaucracies in republican party apparatuses intended to coordinate literary questions.[12]

Second, Moscow has imposed universal rules regarding the publication of translations—a major issue in and of itself, since it determines just which audiences a non-Russian author can reach. One key aspect of this that has received extensive media attention under *glasnost'* is a new rule prohibiting the publication of a translation of a work that has not been published in its original language. This step was taken apparently to prevent a widespread form of fraud whereby "translators" in fact write their "authors'" works.[13] Nevertheless, the decision has enormous consequences for non-Russian literary life: it gives republican Writers' Union bosses and publishing house heads tremendous power as gatekeepers, forcing non-Russian writers to comply with their wishes, opt out of literature, or change their language. The rule has been extended union-wide,[14] despite some reports in the West that it was being imposed only on certain republics.[15] Whether it will be maintained, however, remains to be seen.

The most potent institutional matrix for control and competition has been the republican publishing industry itself. Its most important characteristic for the present discussion is the enormous range of opportunities it provides for outside interference. But of increasing significance is its role as the balancing point between command decisions and market forces, a role likely to grow as Moscow pushes for profitability.[16]

In the republics, as in Moscow, political decisions rather than profitability have typically determined the capacity of publishing houses, the selection of authors to be published, and the pressrun of specific books. (This last is especially important because it, rather than sales, determines the incomes of authors.[17]) But three factors set book publishing in the republics apart. First, because republican political elites are closer to the situation and because some of their number are writers themselves—Uzbekistan's late first secretary, Sharaf Rashidov, is the classic case—they are more likely to interfere in the publication process.[18] Second, because bribery is less expensive and the risk of exposure smaller, republican publishing houses and *Goskomizdats* are more likely to be the victims of or willing participants in longstanding corruption arrangements, a pattern recently exposed in Kirghizia.[19] And third, because decisions emanating from Moscow often fail to match the publishing capacity to the production of manuscripts, republican publishers often find themselves with "excess" capacity on the one side or the other. When there is "excess" capacity to publish, publishing house officials apparently seek to publish themselves to supplement their incomes, a practice recently decried by the Kazakh writer Olzhas Suleimenov.[20] When the "excess" is on the side of manuscript production, the doors to the more usual forms of corruption are thrown wide open.

Market forces, too, operate differently in the republics. While in Moscow book publishing has often been profitable, many publishers in the republics operate at a loss and have to be subsidized from the state budget.[21] The reasons for their losses are obvious: low pressrun publications, the need to issue a disproportionate number of low-priced texts, and a market typically limited to a single republic. The textbook requirement is especially onerous in the Muslim national republics. According to 1988 figures, up to 65 percent of the total pressrun in Central Asia was devoted to textbooks, while in the Baltic republics, with their low birthrates and relatively small numbers of schoolchildren, only 20 percent of the publications were texts, thus allowing more room for other types of works.[22] Moreover, as the reading public has become "all-unionized," republican publishers are sometimes forced and sometimes lured to publish part of the printruns of "big" books like Chingiz Aitmatov's *The Executioner's Block*, Anatolii Rybakov's *Children of the Arbat*, and Vladimir Dudintsev's *White Coats*. The budget situation came to a head in 1985 when the central *Goskomizdat* ordered publishing houses in the republics to improve their balance sheets and seek profitability. In 1986 the new requirements were enacted in the RSFSR and Belorussia, and have since been extended, in fits and starts, to the other republics.[23]

This decision has already made its mark. The central publishing houses have generally been able to improve their profitability by raising prices—rather than reducing the number of titles published—or by expanding pressruns.[24] The non-Russian houses have been less fortunate. According to a Latvian study, republican publishers will have to respond by increasing pressruns of sure-fire winners, at the expense of the number of titles in their inventories.[25] In Lithuania, the republican houses have already cut publication of poetry, often a poor seller.[26] And all republics have been told to increase the percentage of profitable reprints from the current 5–6 percent to 15 percent.[27] All these decisions restrict still further non-Russian writers' opportunities for publication,[28] especially since Moscow simultaneously dropped its affirmative action program in key central journals and publishing houses.[29]

The Role of Non-Literary Elites

Both central and republican party officials have routinely interfered in non-Russian literary life. While at the center party interference has been long evidenced, it has been more rarely documented at the republican level, and the continuing involvement of party functionaries in the literary process in the republics has seldom been exposed. Now, under conditions of *glasnost'*, that has begun to change, and the emerging picture is even more unattractive than the more familiar scene in Moscow.

Lionginas Šepetys [*Russ.* Shepetis], a party secretary in Lithuania, has revealed just how crude this interference can be and suggested some of the reasons.[30] He notes that party involvement in the arts in Moscow is generally the domain of professionals who have worked in this area for many years, while in the republics it is likely to devolve on officials lacking any background in the arts and hence any understanding of the literary process. Moreover, few such officials expect to be "guiding the arts" for long and so are not inclined to acquire these skills.

Other writers now echo similar complaints. The following comment is typical:

> Much that has been prohibited in Voronezh has been printed in Moscow and elsewhere. We tell workers at the *obkom* culture section: "Here you are, cancelling things while Moscow prints them." And we get the self-confident answer: "That is Moscow. This is Voronezh!" And that's it. Hold your tongue and figure out what this could mean! How much further can we go in the "administrative enthusiasm" of petty autocrats? . . . But somehow nothing has been seen or heard regarding journals and their chief editors, or the artistic advisory boards of publishing houses located outside the capital. Maybe something is being done somewhere, but so far I personally have not seen anything.[31]

Three recent novels by insiders—one set in the North Caucasus, another in Kazakhstan, and a third concerning a publishing house in an unspecified region—provide additional telling details.[32] They document continuing petty interference by party officials at all stages of the literary process, and the continuing insidious self-censorship by authors in anticipation of their activities. More than that, they suggest that the further the distance from Moscow—both geographically and psychologically—the worse the situation is likely to be. Several recent academic studies and publicistic works confirm this pattern, clearly documenting that party committees in the republics still are involved in virtually every literary decision, meet regularly with editors and writers to guide them, control travel and other perquisites, and frequently make decisions on literary questions without the benefit of any expert knowledge.[33]

These books and articles reveal that such interference is especially brutal and blatant in the non-Russian republics. First, as has already been suggested, there is considerably more overlap between literary and political elites there, particularly in the smaller republics. Hence, personal scores add to political ones. Second, literary elites in the republics are more defenseless than those in Moscow, lacking access to alternative bases of support from the bureaucracies or a large readership, and are subject to interference from both republican and central officials. As a result they can easily become a political football between the two, with little possibility of escape. And third, republic-based writers lack regular access to the Western media and to significant *samizdat* channels—defense mechanisms regularly deployed by Moscow-based authors.

Moreover, republican political elites probably have a greater interest in interfering in the literary process. Some may use actions in the literary sphere to appease or please Moscow, or at least to anticipate Moscow's reaction to anything that could be labelled as nationalistic. As the Ukrainian writer Borys Oliinyk has written, it is often convenient for non-Russians to blame Moscow for distortions that "for the most part are perpetuated by local, native, home-grown enthusiasts of our political orthodoxy, who obviously inherited this servile psychology from those who were given allotments of their own native land at the price of speaking broken Russian."[34] Other national elites may have additional reasons to intervene, ranging from complex political games to a desire to reform the incredibly conservative literary organizations in their republics.

Moscow, too, has a special interest in the literary life of the republics: the prevention of any encouragement of centrifugal forces based on nationality. Usually it has relied on the general organizational matrix described above, intervening directly only when that system breaks down, from the center's point of view. With the decentralization and *glasnost'* promoted by Gorbachev, that may change: Moscow may have to use both the economic levers mentioned above and direct intervention. The former will probably be preferred: many in the republics will not be conscious of the political calculations behind them, though enough national elites are likely to understand and to act accordingly, possibly forcing the central political authorities to intervene more often.

The special vulnerability of non-Russian literary life to outside interference has left its mark in the conservatism and arbitrariness of local cultural bodies. In the last several years, case after case has come to light of republic-level publishers and Writers' Unions violating contracts or otherwise treating authors shabbily because of outside pressures or simple bureaucratic inertia.[35] The most famous of these concerned a Ukrainian writer who successfully sued his publisher in court;[36] but other cases have shown that the protectionist republican elites can still defend themselves against any attack.[37]

Available Audiences

Underlying all of the above considerations is the problem of the remarkably segmented quality of the potential audiences for republic-level publications. In addition to the normal divisions by consumer preference for genres and subject matter—and these vary markedly from one republic to another[38]—writers in the non-Russian republics must confront at least four different possible audiences for their works. They may target their works in

- non-Russian-language publications directed only at their co-nationals;
- Russian-language publications directed only at their co-nationals and Russian speakers in their home areas;
- Russian or native-language publications aimed at other, closely related republics (as in Central Asia or the Baltic states); and
- Russian-language publications directed at an all-union audience, either by virtue of where they are published or how they are distributed.

The ability of a writer to maneuver among these various audiences is constrained by personal factors, such as literary skill and political acceptability, and by institutional factors, such as pressrun policies and the actions of editors and officials. The differential impact of editorial decisions, for example, on what may be published where is illustrated by the policies of three analogous journals in the Baltic republics. In Lithuania, the local Russian-language literary journal has undertaken to propagate the republic's national literature in translation; in Estonia, the analogous journal attempts to promote new names, whether these be Estonians or Russians; and in Latvia, the editorial policy is to seek out the best, regardless of who wrote it and where it was produced.[39]

Most of the time this segmentation of audiences functions simply as a constraint. In at least some instances, however, it may allow non-Russian writers a flexibility that Russian authors generally lack. As is well known, some literary products that could never be published in Moscow have appeared in Estonia; conversely, central publishers may issue works that a local agency would proscribe. Clever non-Russian authors, such as Chingiz Aitmatov or Rasul Gamzatov, can and do take advantage of this fact.

There is yet another new "wild card" in this deck—the rise of all-union "best sellers" at the expense of local publishing houses. Promoted by media publicity and serials like *Roman-gazeta*, these books attract readers throughout the USSR. For most non-Russians the consequences of this are negative.[40] Increasing numbers of non-Russians are reading the centrally produced books and ignoring local publications; republican publishers throughout the country— with the exception of the Baltic states—report a loss of readership.[41] And the number of locally published books in the republics now pulped because they cannot find a reader is four to six times that of books published in Moscow.[42] The disparity would be even greater, but several republics have successfully forced local libraries to buy up the surpluses in order to improve the numbers.[43] As Moscow continues to push for greater cost accounting in the publishing industry, this pattern could ultimately drive many republican presses off the markets. This would reduce yet again the opportunities for non-Russians to be published, and so a process advertised as decentralization may in fact lead to just the opposite result.[44]

Yet another audience exists for a special kind of non-Russian literature— that which for political or artistic reasons cannot be published. In contrast to the situation in Moscow and Leningrad, however, this audience is very small and the *samizdat* channels generally much more restricted and ir- regular—a reflection of greater official pressure against such literature, non- literary concerns, and the absence of ready outlets or markets for such works abroad. In those republics where opportunities are relatively greater— such as Ukraine and the Baltics—literary *samizdat* can be expected to grow even under conditions of *glasnost'*.

Political Strategies

These institutional arrangements and their ideological underpinnings define the range of possible strategies for the three major participants in literary politics in the republics—the non-Russian writers, the non-Russian political elites, and Moscow. They do not determine specific choices, but an awareness of the limits they impose is especially important in assessing Soviet literary life in a time of change. Moreover, an awareness of how the system works to impose these limits provides another vantage point from which to view and assess various reform proposals.   .

The Strategies of Non-Russian Writers

As has already been suggested, non-Russian writers find themselves caught between a desire to express themselves as they would personally and professionally prefer and a desire to publish and find an audience. In their endeavors, the writers must contend with the two other participants in this politics—the local political elites and Moscow. And in their maneuverings they have a variety of options. They may collaborate to one or another degree, or seek to use the multiple publishing opportunities they have. They may play off one group against another, now allying with Moscow against their own republican elites, now using republican ties to protect themselves against central directives. Or they may simply drop out of the system. (According to one study, this last option is increasingly exercised. The writers do not go into *samizdat;* they simply stop seeking to publish their works. As a result, republican publication plans in the early 1980s were seldom more than 70 percent filled.[45]) All these possibilities exist in all republics. But, as we have seen, in this game the writers have the fewest cards— except for those with a large audience, an attentive foreign public, or a powerful political patron—and consequently must make the best of a bad situation and expect to achieve minimal results.

The Strategies of National Elites

The position of non-Russian political elites is stronger and more interesting. They are constrained by the twin requirements of their position: to satisfy Moscow by fulfilling its demands, and to mobilize the local populations by at least partially meeting their desires. As the use of coercion has declined, the latter has become the more important consideration in many cases, forcing non-Russian elites into the possibly uncomfortable position of siding with the non-Russian writers in order to hold onto power. But the power of Moscow remains considerable, and its past ability to impose its will throws a powerful shadow in non-Russian areas. This has led to some unexpected strategies. Some republics have entered into regional agreements to supply each other with books to circumvent Moscow's limitations.[46] Others have sought to promote their publications outside by setting up special stores to promote the local product.[47] Or the republics may evade Moscow's will in other ways.[48]

But all too often, the complaint of the Kazakh writer Olzhas Suleimenov still holds true:

> . . . in some oblasts and republics, the regime of prohibitions operates more strongly than in Moscow. If V. Bykov, Ch. Aitmatov, or V. Rasputin depended entirely on local publishing, they would write differently. Or they would not write at all. . . . [Moreover] the pace and quality of the development of national

culture depends at times on the personal qualities, preparation, and intelligence of the leadership.[49]

In this connection, republican political elites may seek to manipulate literature and cite their treatment of it as a display of loyalty to Moscow—one thinks of Shcherbitsky's crackdown on Ukrainian writers in 1973. Or they may allow the expression of certain radical views in order to warn Moscow of the problems the center would face if a particular republican leader were sacked. This is a most dangerous game, but many republican elites have played it. Republican elites may also allow a certain amount of what might be called nationalist writing as a safety valve, a trial balloon for ideas, or even a political weapon in intrarepublican conflicts. (Sometimes, as in Uzbekistan and Tadzhikistan, writers may be enlisted in interrepublican conflicts as well.) Republican elites may even seek to exaggerate the nationalist character of certain works, just as antireligious specialists do with certain Churches in order to justify their own existence. And they may sanction certain works for reasons of corruption or even personal conviction.

This diversity of motives and strategies undoubtedly characterizes elites in all non-Russian republics, though we seldom have the data necessary to determine exactly which one is operative at a particular time and place. The essential point, however, is that such features and calculations are common to all republics and set limits on the nature of literary politics in all of them. Their very range also serves as a warning against a simplistic counterposing of nationalistically inclined writers and Soviet authority. If the conflict were that simple, it would have ended long ago.

Moscow's Strategies

Moscow's goals in the republics—loyalty and support—have been promoted through the various ideological strictures and institutional arrangements described above; they need not be recapitulated here. Two general observations, however, are in order. First, Moscow has largely exercised its control through certain institutional instruments—sometimes obvious, like the *Glavlit* system, often more recondite, like the drive for profitability—rather than through micromanagement of particular cases; the latter are more famous, but they represent a response to a breakdown in the system rather than its normal operation. And second, Moscow will undoubtedly retain the instruments to maintain and perhaps even enhance its influence in non-Russian literary politics as a result of Gorbachev's reforms. Just how far this process goes will depend on the actions of all three sets of actors.

Yet another, more general observation may be useful. Namely, Moscow's decisions regarding particular republics are usually made within the context of a general calculation about the national republics as a whole and their role in the Soviet system. In short, Moscow generally makes decisions about *national republics* and much more rarely about *nationalities* as such.

This pattern has important consequences for literary politics in non-Russian areas. For example, if one knew nothing about a republic except its relative size, one could predict with a high degree of probability certain things about Moscow's relationship to its literary affairs, as well as others. The larger the republic and the more important to the economy, the more concerned is Moscow about the ideological soundness of its elites and masses. At the same time, the larger the republic, the more differentiated are its political and literary elites, with the latter thereby more exposed than elsewhere. In such a situation Moscow is more concerned about what is written, more willing to take steps against particular writers, and better able to secure the cooperation of republican elites, who have a relatively distant relationship with the literary elites in their charge. Conversely, the smaller the republic and the less important to the economy, the less worried is Moscow about its ideological soundness. And the less differentiated the republican political and literary elites, the greater the latitude and influence of the latter. Thus, Moscow is significantly less concerned about what is published in the smaller republics—a situation that allows literary elites greater opportunities than elsewhere and a more favorable attentiveness on the part of the local political elites. Ukrainian literary politics represents the first instance, and Estonian literary politics—the second.

Obviously, such a schema needs refinement for any particular case. But this schema and the structural elements described above play a far larger role in non-Russian literary politics in the USSR than is generally acknowledged. Keeping these factors in mind, Western observers of nationality processes will be in a better position to assess the actual role of specifically national factors, on the one hand, and generically Soviet ones, on the other.

Notes

1. For a broader discussion of these possibilities, see Paul A. Goble, "Gorbachev and the Nationality Problem," in Maurice Friedberg and Heyward Isham, eds., *Soviet Society under Gorbachev* (Armonk, NY: M. E. Sharpe, 1987), pp. 76–100.

2. See Harold Swayze, *The Political Control of Literature in the USSR* (Cambridge, MA: Harvard University Press, 1962); and John and Carol Garrard, *The Organizational Weapon: Russian Literature and the Union of Soviet Writers* (Washington: NCSEER, 1986).

3. Viacheslav Rodionov, "Kul'tura i struktura," *Komsomol'skaia pravda*, 2 August 1988.

4. *Normativnye materialy po izdatel'skomu delu: Spravochnik* (Moscow: Kniga, 1987), pp. 75–77 and passim.

5. Iu. V. Arutiunian and Iu. V. Bromlei, eds., *Sotsial'no-kul'turnyi oblik sovetskikh natsii: Po rezul'tatam etnosotsiologicheskogo issledovaniia* (Moscow: Nauka, 1986), p. 300. Interestingly, the most overrepresented group of writers are those in the autonomous republics of the RSFSR. In those territories, there is one writer for every 21,400 people.

6. One measure of this is the number of writers who publish primarily in a given language. According to 1981 data, of the members of the Union of Writers 641 published in Ukrainian; 294 in Georgian; 265 in Armenian; 258 in Azerbaidzhani; 221 in Belorussian; 218 in Kazakh; 152 in Uzbek; 147 in Latvian; 130 in Lithuanian; 111 in Kirghiz; 110 in Estonian; 95 in Moldavian; 94 in Tadzhik; 80 in Turkmen;

and 744 in the non-Russian languages of the RSFSR. 3448—including many non-Russians—published in Russian. (*Sed'moi s"ezd pisatelei* [Moscow: Gosizdat, 1983], p. 587. Cf. *Kommunist Uzbekistana*, 1988, no. 4, p. 52.)

7. E. Vaitiekienė, "Lietuvos TSR kurybinių sajungų struktūra 1960–1980 m.," *Lietuvos TSR Mokslų akademijos darbai/Trudy Akademii nauk Litovskoi SSR*, ser. A, 1988, no. 4 (97), pp. 70–83.

8. *Komsomol'skaia pravda*, 19 February 1987.

9. On successes and failures, see A. Zaripova, "Tvorcheskim soiuzam—tvorcheskii impul's," *Kommunist Tatarii*, 1988, no. 7/8, pp. 134–40.

10. V. Beekman's comments to the 1986 Writers' Union Congress in *Literaturnaia gazeta*, 2 July 1986. Cf. Mira Blinkova, "Natsional'naia po forme, sotsialisticheskaia po soderzhaniiu," *Obozrenie* (Paris), no. 15 (1985), pp. 19–23.

11. Blinkova, p. 21; and *Kommunist Azerbaidzhana*, 1986, no. 6, pp. 49–55.

12. For details on the new body in Uzbekistan, see *Komsomolets Uzbekistana*, 22 July 1988.

13. See Lev Druskin's recollections in his *Spasennaia kniga: Vospominaniia leningradskogo poeta* (London: Overseas Publications Interchange, 1984).

14. *Literaturnaia Rossiia*, 28 February 1986. Not all non-Russians felt this to be a bad decision; the Daghestani poet Rasul Gamzatov even suggested that it was "dangerous" to publish a Russian translation if the original had never been printed. (*Literaturnaia gazeta*, 2 July 1986).

15. Julia Wisnevsky, "Getting Published in the Ukraine," *Radio Liberty Research Bulletin*, RL 29/86 (16 January 1986).

16. For a useful discussion of its impact on a particular non-Russian publishing house, see the articles on the Uzbek "Esh Gvardiia" publishers in *Komsomolets Uzbekistana*, 12 February 1988.

17. *Literaturnaia gazeta*, 23 April 1986.

18. See Valentin Semenov in *Sovetskaia kul'tura*, 4 October 1986.

19. *Sovetskaia Kirgiziia*, 24 January 1986.

20. *Literaturnaia gazeta*, 23 April 1986.

21. *Planovoe khoziaistvo*, 1986, no. 7, p. 122.

22. *Knizhnoe obozrenie*, 12 August 1988.

23. *Planovoe khoziaistvo*, 1986, no. 7, pp. 93–94.

24. *Sotsiologicheskie issledovaniia*, 1986, no. 3, p. 122. The last time Moscow withdrew subsidies from the local press (January 1922), the number of Russian-language newspapers dropped from 803 to 382, but the number of non-Russian newspapers fell from 108 to 23. (*Kommunist Tatarii*, 1986, no. 5, p. 85.)

25. Dzintra Bungs, "Book Publishing in Latvia," *Radio Free Europe Research*, RAD Background Report/99 (Latvia) (15 July 1986), pp. 1–8.

26. *Komsomol'skaia pravda* (Vilnius), 30 January 1988.

27. *Sovetskaia kul'tura*, 12 January 1988.

28. And the smaller the republic and nationality involved, the more severe the impact. Nationalities lacking an official territory have been especially hard hit. See Eino Karkhlu, "'Malaia literatura' v obshcheistoricheskom kontekste," *Sever*, 1988, no. 10, pp. 110–20.

29. The conservative Russian writer Sergei Mikhalkov denounced the old practice as "impermissible." (*Moskva*, 1987, no. 10, p. 194.) The editors of the pace-setting *Roman-gazeta* said they had eliminated any provision for preferences to non-Russian authors. (*V mire knig*, 1987, no. 10, p. 30.)

30. See his remarkable statement, "The Art of Guiding the Arts," in *USSR: A Time of Change* (Moscow: Progress, 1987), pp. 146–55.

31. *Sovetskaia kul'tura*, 4 October 1986. Cf. Ion Drutse, "Otkrytoe pis'mo," *Kodry* (Kishinev), 1988, no. 9, pp. 148–52; and the various cases described in *Knizhnoe obozrenie*, 4 December 1987, p. 5, and 1 April 1988, pp. 14–15.

32. Semen Lipkin, *Dekada* (New York: Chalidze Publications, 1983); Vladimir Ermenchenko, *Mednoe miloserdtse* (Alma-Ata: Zhazhus, 1985); and Arkadii Arkanov, "Rukopisi ne vozvrashchaiutsia," *Iunost'*, 1986, no. 12, pp. 30–78.

33. A. V. Tykheshkin, "Partiinoe rukovodstvo deiatel'nost'iu Soiuza pisatelei Buriatskoi ASSR," *Partiinoe stroitel'stvo v Sibiri* (Novosibirsk: Nauka, 1984), pp. 125–30, and sources cited therein.

34. *Literaturna Ukraina*, 3 July 1986. This passage was mangled in the Russian *Literaturnaia gazeta*, 2 July 1986. That such distortions may be common is suggested by Roy Medvedev (*Knizhnoe obozrenie*, 28 October 1988, p. 2). He reports that editors often insert phrases that he had not said or written.

35. Pavel Botsu of Moldavia (*Literaturnaia gazeta*, 2 July 1986) noted that republican Central Committee intervention had saved many books from their editors.

36. *Literaturnaia gazeta*, 29 October 1986.

37. *Sovetskaia kul'tura*, 9 September 1986.

38. On the preferences of these various groups, see Arutiunian and Bromlei, *Sotsial'no-kul'turnyi oblik*, pp. 201–20; L. M. Drobizheva, *Dukhovnaia obshchnost' narodov SSSR* (Moscow: Nauka, 1982); F. E. Sheregi, "Struktura chitatel'skikh predpochtenii," *Sotsiologicheskie issledovaniia*, 1986, no. 3, pp. 116–27; and A. Asinkanov, "Internatsionalizatsiia chteniia v kirgizskikh selakh," *Izvestiia Akademii nauk Kirgizskoi SSR*, 1988, no. 2, pp. 45–50.

39. *Literaturnaia gazeta*, 25 May 1988.

40. *Sovetskaia kul'tura*, 9 September 1986.

41. Cf. *Literaturnoe obozrenie*, 1988, no. 1, pp. 93–94; *Ogonek*, 1988, no. 11, p. 8; and, in particular, the poll results in *Leninskaia smena*, 14 October 1988.

42. *Knizhnoe obozrenie*, 5 August 1988.

43. *Komsomolets Turkmenistana*, 1 November 1988.

44. *Literaturnaia gazeta*, 4 June and 2 July 1986.

45. *Kommunist* (Erevan), 18–20 May 1985.

46. *Partiinaia zhizn'* (Tashkent), 1988, no. 8, pp. 95–96; and *Knizhnoe obozrenie*, 5 August 1988.

47. *Kommunist Ukrainy*, 1987, no. 10, p. 5.

48. *Agitator Tadzhikistana*, 1987, no. 13, pp. 5–7.

49. *Literaturnaia gazeta*, 2 July 1986.

CHAPTER 7

Nationalities and Soviet Religious Policies

Bohdan R. Bociurkiw

There has been a close relationship, especially since World War II, between the Soviet perception and treatment of the nationalities problem on the one hand and the Kremlin's religious policies on the other. This relationship, noted by Walter Kolarz and some other scholars, has eluded many students of religion in the Soviet Union, who have either proceeded from a single ideological premise ("communism vs. religion") or approached the problem through the experience of the country's largest religious community—the Russian Orthodox Church, which they sometimes mistook for an ethnically homogeneous "Church of the Russians."[1] Thus, close parallels can be established between the twists and turns of Soviet nationalities policy and the meandering course of the Kremlin's religious policy, especially in the non-Russian borderlands of the USSR.

The Ideological and Political Context

The interdependence of the two policies cannot be understood without considering their larger ideological and political context, in which the changing relationship between Marxism-Leninism and Russian nationalism has played a central role. The Kremlin's dilemma of reconciling internationalism with Russian nationalism finds parallel in the recurrent contradiction between the party's ideological commitment to atheism and the practical advantages of utilizing the state-controlled Moscow patriarchate as an instrument of imperial integration and Russification of Ukrainians, Belorussians, and Moldavians. The increasing, if not exclusive, role assigned to Russian nationalism in domestic self-legitimation during the late Stalinist and post-Khrushchev periods offered special advantages to the Russian Orthodox Church as the only surviving institutional link to the imperial past and credible bearer of

---

This chapter draws in part on the author's study, "Institutional Religion and Nationality in the Soviet Union," in S. Enders Wimbush, ed., *Soviet Nationalities in Strategic Perspective* (New York: St. Martin's Press, 1985), pp. 181–206.

traditional Russian national values and legitimizing myths. These advantages were not without inherent dangers for the Church, as illustrated by Khrushchev's antireligious campaign. Above all, there was the danger that the Church might be perceived as a catalyst for the political mobilization of an anti-Soviet variety of Russian ethnonationalism.

Underlying the contradictions besetting Soviet religious policies has been the shifting "correlation of forces" within the Soviet elite over nationalities policy. There has been an ongoing debate between advocates of a Soviet melting-pot (*sliianie*) and adherents of the Russian imperial model who, while pressing for the Russification of Ukrainians, Belorussians, and Moldavians, would stop short of absorbing the rapidly growing Muslim peoples, in order to preserve the political continuity and distinct ethno-cultural character of the Russian nation. Until recently, the adherents of a third model—the "flourishing" (*rastsvet*) of Russian and non-Russian nations in a supranational political entity, with its concomitant bona fide exclusion of the party from the religious realm[2]—could be encountered only outside the top decision-making groups. They were to be found either within the Russian cultural intelligentsia or, more frequently, among the "national Communist" party cadres and cultural elites in the non-Russian republics.

The advocates of the Soviet, linguistically Russian, melting-pot concept (who in recent times have increasingly borrowed from American ethno-demographic models) find support not only among Russians, but, even more so, in the assimilated non-Russian elements of the elite. They have adopted the "Leninist" position that religious and ethnonational loyalties represent the main obstacles to the molding of a new "Soviet man," while atheism and internationalism are indispensable for integrating and legitimizing the Soviet political system and, by extension, the *Pax Sovietica* in Eastern Europe.

The adherents of the Russian imperial model, despite their criticism of Stalin's pre-1939 domestic policies, have essentially embraced Stalin's discriminatory approach to nationalities and religious groups. That approach sought to relegitimize the Soviet state in terms of its continuity with Imperial Russia, Muscovy, and Kievan Rus'; its defense of the national legacy and imperial unity; its "recovery" of the "Russian lands"; and its transformation of Russia from an isolated continental power into a global superpower. In this context, the quasi concordat with the Russian Orthodox Church, formalized in September 1943, as well as the classification of other religious groups along a continuum ranging from recognition to mere toleration to prohibition, appeared to be a logical extension of the Stalinist nationalities policy. Only Khrushchev's limited and short-lived de-Stalinization ("re-Leninization") of Soviet nationalities and religious policies seriously challenged, but failed to displace completely, the Stalinist pattern of relations between the Kremlin and the Moscow patriarchate. This discriminatory pattern, while ultimately based on assessments of a present or future threat to Soviet internal security posed by a given religious group, was closely linked to the Kremlin's perception of the intimate historical relationship between religion and nationality.

Patterns of Relationship Between
Religion and Nationality

The relationship between institutional religion and nationality, which is of central interest to Soviet religious policy makers, varies not only from one nationality to another and among different religions, but also within individual nationalities. Four indicators help to identify the principal patterns linking institutional religion and nationality in the USSR:

1. the (positive or negative) historical relationship between a given nationality's predominant religion and its ethno-cultural persistence and nation-building;
2. the extent to which particular religions or religious institutions have been employed by the imperial (Tsarist or Soviet) regime as vehicles for Russification or integration and for destruction of the subject peoples' ethnic, cultural, and linguistic distinctiveness;
3. the impact (including the duration and intensity) of Sovietization (i.e., Soviet political resocialization, modernization, interrepublican migration, etc.) on the traditional interdependence between religion and nationality;
4. the specific features of a given religion, including its attitude toward the state, the nature of its organization, and the location of its ultimate spiritual authority (within or outside the Soviet sphere of control); the numbers, strategic location, and political influence of its cobelievers abroad; the extent of its adaptability to political and social change; and the degree of its vulnerability to Soviet penetration and control.[3]

On the basis of these indicators it is possible to classify the institutional religions represented in the Soviet Union under the following principal categories: (1) the imperial Church; (2) national Churches; (3) traditional native sects; (4) transnational religious communities; (5) ethnoreligious diasporas; and (6) modern cosmopolitan sects.

The Imperial Church

Since World War II the Russian Orthodox Church, while restricted and closely controlled by the authorities, has outwardly resumed its historical symbiotic ("symphonic") relationship with the state. Already at the time of the Soviet annexation of the western regions of Ukraine and Belorussia, the Baltic states, and Bessarabia and Bukovina in 1939–40, the Kremlin recognized its importance as an "imperial Church." The regime relied upon the then nearly moribund Russian Orthodox Church to help integrate the Orthodox Ukrainians, Belorussians, and Moldavians within the state-controlled Moscow patriarchate. This function greatly expanded and became even more important during and after the German wartime occupation.

In return for limited concessions and protection against internal schisms (the Renovationist Church and the Autocephalous Orthodox Churches in

Ukraine and Belorussia) and competing faiths (the Ukrainian Uniate—or Greek Catholic, as it was also called—Church), the "imperial Church" helped to legitimize the Soviet war effort in traditional nationalist and religious terms. It employed ecclesiastical sanctions against Ukrainian and other churchmen in the occupied territories who challenged the legitimacy and integrity of the empire. As the Germans retreated, the Moscow patriarchate assisted in the reintegration and "patriotic" resocialization of the reoccupied and newly annexed territories. It absorbed the autocephalous and autonomous Churches established under German occupation and joined the authorities in forcibly "converting" to Russian Orthodoxy some four million Ukrainian Uniates. Thus, since 1950, with the single exception of the Georgians (whose self-proclaimed 1917 autocephaly was recognized by the Moscow patriarchate only in 1943, under Stalin's pressure), all Orthodox non-Russians (Ukrainians, Belorussians, and Moldavians, as well as the Turkic Chuvash and Gagauz, the Finnic Mordvinians, Mari, Udmurts, and Komi, and other groups) are integrated with the dominant Russians in a single, indivisible, centralized Russian Orthodox Church. The latter is the only union-wide institution that has retained its prerevolutionary epithet "Russian" (allegedly for historic reasons), as well as its monarchic (patriarchal) structure.

The loyalty of the Moscow patriarchate to the Soviet regime was put to a severe test between 1959 and 1964, when Khrushchev unleashed a massive antireligious campaign that closed down some 10,000 of the 17,500 Orthodox churches, five of the eight seminaries, and fifty-three of the sixty-nine monasteries and convents. Outwardly the patriarch and the majority of bishops cooperated with the authorities in "voluntarily" reducing the Church's institutional strength and relinquished the control over the management and finances of parishes hitherto exercised by pastors to the state.[4] But the humiliation, harassment, and persecution of some recalcitrant bishops, clergy, monastics, and believers, as well as vandalism and destruction of some churches and the transformation of others into antireligious museums—all left a legacy of lasting bitterness. This later turned into religious dissent when the Brezhnev leadership refused to restore to the Church its 1959–64 losses. Increasingly, religious dissent in Russia acquired nationalist connotations, attracting support from the cultural intelligentsia, which came to view antireligious vandalism as the destruction of Russia's national heritage and her aesthetic and ethical values. Some Orthodox dissent turned against the subservient leadership of the Church, eventually calling (as did the priest Gleb Yakunin in 1979) for the development of a parallel catacomb Church.[5]

Khrushchev's assault on the Church apparently persuaded the leading hierarchs of the Moscow patriarchate that, while the Church should maintain outward domestic passivity, it must intensify its external propaganda in behalf of the regime (primarily in the form of ecumenical "peace-making" activities) in hope that by performing this function the Church would become indispensable to the Kremlin. The replenishment and education of the clergy and rejuvenation of the episcopate were henceforth justified by the patriarchate almost entirely in terms of the external benefits derived by the Soviet regime from the Church's activities.

It can be assumed that Khrushchev's antireligious campaign sought to prevent religion from filling the ideological vacuum that developed in the wake of de-Stalinization by radically reducing the points of contact between the clergy and the population. If that was indeed the ultimate purpose of this campaign, it merely succeeded in delaying the process. During the late 1960s and 1970s a religious revival occurred among the intelligentsia and student youth, associated in many cases with the rise of ethnonationalism. Religious and nationalist themes, severely attacked in the non-Russian republics, acquired a relative legitimacy in Russian literature and the visual and performing arts. Possibly, this phenomenon was connected with the renewed emphasis during the Brezhnev era on "patriotic-military education," serving to counterbalance both centrifugal religio-nationalism in the borderlands and "cosmopolitan" Western-derived sectarianism. It is, however, as the "national Church" of the Russians and the repository of national values and morality that Russian Orthodoxy has attracted converts within the Russian intelligentsia. As the country slid deeper into corruption and hypocrisy, the shared perception of a profound demographic, social, and moral crisis of the Russian ethnos brought the religious Russian intelligentsia, the Orthodox Church, and some elements of the Soviet political elite closer to each other.[6]

The National Churches

While in the consciousness of Russians the Russian Orthodox Church is perceived as their national Church, this Church itself never restricted its membership to Russians. On the contrary, it always sought to extend its sway in parallel with the expanding borders of the Russian Empire and to bring into its fold all of the empire's subject peoples. This is what constitutes its essence as an "imperial Church." National Churches, on the other hand, as a rule restrict their membership to faithful of a particular nationality, usually excluding, unlike an imperial Church, other ethnic groups. Thus, they represent a unique symbiosis of religious and national identities that sustain and reinforce each other. This religio-ethnic symbiosis is expressed institutionally through an independent or autonomous ecclesiastical structure based in the nation's territorial homeland and integrating members of that nationality at home and in dispersion. This integrating function acquires additional dimensions and special significance for a subject nationality that has lost its independence or aspires to its own nation-state. In the absence of other autonomous ethnic institutions, a national Church becomes a haven for national traditions and culture: it legitimizes the struggle for their preservation and, at least implicitly, for national liberation, and assumes the role of spokesman for the national interest. For these reasons, both the imperial government and the imperial Church strive to break up the religio-ethnic symbiosis by a variety of means, ranging from conversion through co-optation of the ecclesiastical elite to severe restrictions or even the proscription of the national Church's activities.

Within the USSR, the model of a national Church is presently exemplified by the ancient Armenian Gregorian Church (which unifies Armenians within and outside the USSR), the Georgian Orthodox Church, the Lithuanian Roman Catholic Church, and the Ukrainian Catholic (Uniate) Church. As branches of Catholicism, the latter two Churches may also be subsumed under the category of transnational religious communities, but given the intimate interdependence of religion and nationality in Lithuania and Western Ukraine, they have to be classified in the first instance as national Churches; because of their association with Lithuanian and Ukrainian nationalism, respectively, they certainly have been treated as such by the Soviet regime.

Implicitly recognized by the regime as a national institution, the Armenian Gregorian Church dates its long association with Armenian nationhood to the adoption of Christianity as the official state religion of Armenia in A.D. 301. Split from the rest of Christendom over the Monophysite controversy since the fifth century, the Armenian Church turned inward and developed into a classic national institution. The bond between religion and ethnicity was cemented over the long periods of statelessness, especially the centuries of Ottoman Turkish domination. The head of the Church, the "Catholicos of All Armenians," has, indeed, been encouraged by Soviet authorities to maintain extensive external relations, competing with the rival Lebanon-based catholicos of Cilicia not just for the ecclesiastical but also political loyalties of Armenians abroad.[7] While its loyal leadership has enjoyed material benefits and other privileges reserved for the Soviet elite, the Armenian Church in the USSR has been kept under close control by the state authorities. Despite a widespread identification of Armenian ethnicity with the national religion, the Church's domain in the Armenian SSR has been reduced to a mere shadow of its pre-revolutionary strength—some forty active churches and six monasteries by 1977.[8] Given the geographical location of Armenia on the frontier with Turkey and the depth of Armenian-Turkish hostilities, Armenian religious nationalism was not, apparently, perceived by the Kremlin as a significant threat to its rule over Transcaucasia.

In contrast, the Georgian Orthodox Church still retains a living memory of oppression under the Russian Empire and the imperial Church. Dating its origins to about A.D. 330, and with its own catholicos since the fifth century, the Church of Georgia—unlike the Armenian Gregorian Church—ultimately adhered to the Orthodox positions in the theological controversies of the time. It remained the established Church and a dominant national institution down to the end of the Georgian monarchy and the annexation of Georgia by the Russian Empire. In 1811 the Georgian Orthodox Church was forcibly absorbed into the Russian Church. In place of the catholicos, St. Petersburg appointed exarchs, all but the first of whom were Russians, and introduced the completely alien Church Slavonic instead of Georgian as the liturgical language.[9] Only after the 1917 Revolution did the remaining Georgian bishops declare the restoration of Georgian autocephaly. A small fraction of Georgian monasteries and churches survived Stalinist rule and Khrushchev's antireligious campaign of 1959–64. Though unpublished sociological surveys showed that nearly fifty percent of the population in Georgia are believers, by the early 1970s only some sixty churches (of the 2,455 before 1917) were still functioning in the republic.[10] Stories of vandalism, desecration, and looting of the national Church treasures by corrupt party and ecclesiastical leaders surfaced in *samizdat* during the 1970s.[11] Religious and national sentiments in Georgia have taken a stronger anti-Russian direction than in Armenia. Without a numerous and prosperous foreign constituency, the Georgian Church, unlike the Armenian, has been more vulnerable to Soviet pressures. Since the 1970s, however, it has received strong support from the ranks of Georgian intellectuals and even from some officials.[12]

The Lithuanian Roman Catholic Church, having come under Soviet rule during World War II, did not experience, as had the Georgian and Armenian Churches, the antireligious terror of 1929–38. Although the Lithuanians were officially converted to Catholicism in 1387, the symbiotic relationship between the Church and Lithuanian national consciousness dates back not more than two hundred years.[13] The interwar period of independence completed the process of religio-ethnic consolidation. After Soviet occupation, the Church remained the only ethnic Lithuanian institution in the USSR still able to speak for the national interest, not only in relation to the Soviet regime, but to the Vatican as well. It suffered severe repressions for its refusal to condemn the nationalist resistance movement after the war. Early attempts by the regime to separate the Lithuanian Church from Rome failed, despite the massive use of force against its hierarchy and clergy,[14] while the Church's continued canonical subordination to the pope frustrated Soviet efforts to penetrate the hierarchical core of Lithuanian Catholicism. As of January 1984, the Catholic Church in Lithuania had 630 parishes, served by 693 priests, and 104 students in the single seminary in Kaunas.[15] At the time there were three (since 1987, four) bishops allowed to exercise their office, of whom Bishop Vincentas Sladkevičius became the first publicly proclaimed Lithuanian cardinal of the Roman Catholic Church in July 1988. The pervasive religio-ethnic solidarity of Lithuanians helped compensate for the banning of monastic, educational, and publishing institutions through an underground ecclesiastical substructure operating in the shadow of the legal but heavily circumscribed Church. The underground *Chronicle of the Catholic Church in Lithuania* [Lietuvos Katalikų Bažnyčios Kronika], the main Lithuanian *samizdat* periodical appearing since 1972, epitomized the close interdependence of religion and nationalism in Lithuania and the continuing nation-integrating (and, conversely, empire-disintegrating) role of the Lithuanian Catholic Church.[16]

The Ukrainian Catholic (Uniate) Church in Western Ukraine represents a similar symbiotic relationship between religion (in this instance also a distinct religious rite) and ethnicity in those areas of Ukraine that had never been part of the Russian Empire. This Church dates to the end of the sixteenth century, when within the confines of the Polish-Lithuanian Commonwealth a substantial part of the once common Ukrainian-Belorussian ("Ruthenian") Orthodox Church, itself tracing its origins to the conversion of Kievan Rus' in 988, accepted union (hence, Uniate) with Rome, while keeping its Eastern liturgy and customs. The Uniate Church was wiped out in Belorussia and most of Ukraine through joint action by the Russian imperial government and the Russian Orthodox Church after the partitions of Poland. It survived only in the Austrian-occupied province of Galicia (and in Transcarpathia, part of the Hungarian crown) where it played a role of decisive importance in the Ukrainian nation-building process. The Uniate Church supported the strivings for Ukrainian independence in the wake of World War I and, after Galicia was occupied by the reconstituted Polish state, provided support for the Ukrainian national movement in the interwar period. The Church's primate, Metropolitan Andrei Sheptytsky, for more than forty years (1901–44) served as the most widely recognized spokesman for Ukrainian national interests. After the Soviet occupation of Galicia in 1944, having failed to force the Church into condemning Ukrainian nationalist resistance, the Kremlin proceeded to suppress this national Church in 1945–46, imprisoning and exiling its entire hierarchy and several hundred clergymen who refused to join the Russian Orthodox Church.[17] The intertwined religious and national consciousness among the Ukrainians of Galicia proved stronger than expected by the Soviet authorities. Clandestinely surviving nearly a decade of Stalinist persecution, the Uniate Church managed to rebuild its organization and hierarchy in conditions of illegality and harassment.[18] The post-Stalin detente between the Vatican and Moscow evoked considerable bitterness among the Ukrainian Uniates, leading a fraction of them to break away from the Catholic Church and form an eschatological Penitent (*pokutnyky*) sect. The election of Pope John Paul II contributed to a resurgence of the illegal Uniate Church and a marked intensification of demands for its legalization.[19] Ukrainian Uniates in the USSR derive considerable inspiration not only from their ecclesiastical link with the papacy, but also from the existence of a numerous Ukrainian Catholic Church in diaspora, with its own institutional structures and hierarchy, headed by the archbishop-major of Lviv in exile and cardinal, now resident in Rome.

The Armenian Gregorian, Georgian Orthodox, Lithuanian Roman Catholic, and Ukrainian Uniate Churches are the main, but not the only, national Churches in the USSR. The Lutheran Churches of Latvia and Estonia, however, for a variety of reasons (particularly, their German origin and traditional deference toward political authority) have not displayed as close a linkage between religion and ethnicity until the dramatic upsurge in the Latvian and Estonian national movements since 1988.[20] By contrast, Lutheranism among the exiled Germans in the Asiatic part of the USSR has been a rallying point for ethno-cultural maintenance.[21]

Roman Catholicism in Latvia represents a mixed pattern. Not a national Church, it is still firmly rooted in history and clearly differentiates its Latvian adherents from the Russians. More than the Lithuanian or Uniate Churches, it illustrates the role of Catholicism as a transnational religion. Thus, the Riga archbishopric and seminary serve as a focal point for Soviet Catholics union-wide—Poles, Germans, and others. The importance of the Riga see was highlighted when its apostolic administrator, Bishop Julijans Vaivods, was elevated by the pope to cardinal in 1983, the first resident cardinal on Soviet territory.

Traditional Native Sects

Several religious groups in the USSR may be categorized as traditional native sects. These trace their direct or indirect origin to the seventeenth-century protest against perceived innovations in Muscovy's Orthodox ritual (the Old Believers) or to a rejection of the hierarchical and sacramental structures of the state Church (the "Spiritual Christians"—in particular, the *Khlysty* [Flagellants], *Dukhobors* [Spirit-Wrestlers], and *Molokans* [Milk-Drinkers]). They share such characteristics as a close association with Russian ethnicity; non-proselytism and self-isolation, combined in many instances with a communal way of life; and a traditional distrust of state authority. Such features have caused great difficulties for the traditional native sects in adapting to Soviet political, economic, and social conditions and have contributed to their rapid decline; their descendants have largely either joined the pietist current within Russian Orthodoxy or moved into the "modern cosmopolitan sects" of Western origin.

The doctrinally and organizationally divided Old Believers (*Popovtsy* [Priestly], *Beglopopovtsy* [Fugitive-Priest], and *Bezpopovtsy* [Priestless]) overlap the categories of "national Churches" and "traditional native sects." In sharp contrast to the fundamentalist sects of Western origin, they have not been perceived as a political threat by the Soviet authorities in the last decade and have, on occasion, received sympathetic treatment in Soviet Russian literature as preservers of "genuine" Russian values, customs, and art.[22]

Transnational Religions

Islam in the Soviet Union represents a transnational religion that, without destroying or impeding the ethnic loyalties of its Turkic- and Iranian-speaking adherents, integrates them into the *ummah*—the community of believers. It sharply differentiates them from the dominant Russians and other European nationalities while linking them with Islamic nations outside the USSR. The Soviet regime attempted to break up a pan-Islamic and pan-Turkic con-sciousness of its Muslims through the formation of six union republics and a number of autonomous republics and oblasts.[23] In fact, this *divide et impera* policy, along with far-reaching destruction of *institutional* Islam during the 1930s, contributed to a potent synthesis of those elements of Islam that were not seriously affected by modernization with the emergent ethnic consciousness of the Turkic and Iranian peoples. Thus, the religious and secular components of the new "socialist nations" became inseparably linked in the historically Islamic areas of the USSR under the overarching self-

designation *musul'manin* (Muslim).[24] In recent years, the simultaneous processes of a demographic explosion among the Muslim peoples of the Soviet
Union and a dramatic rise in the strategic, economic, and political importance
of the Islamic nations of the Third World have given Soviet Muslims a
sense of optimism about their future.[25]

Four muftiates (spiritual administrations) have been established with the
Soviet government's approval after World War II to direct official Muslim
activities in, respectively, Central Asia and Kazakhstan; European Russia
and Siberia; Azerbaidzhan; and the North Caucasus.[26] Closely controlled
by the regime, they have been used to confine the religious fervor of believers
within the narrow limits prescribed by Soviet laws. The institutional strength
of "official" Islam was sharply reduced in the course of Khrushchev's
antireligious campaign. The number of registered mosques declined from
about 1,500 in 1959 to 300 in 1976, with some 700 existing ouside the
law.[27] Apparently some mosques have been reopened over the last decade,
however. In 1986, according to an official statistic, there were 751 Muslim
communities active in the USSR.[28] Together with other officially recognized
religious centers in the USSR, the muftiates have been employed by the
Kremlin for external propaganda activities among Muslims abroad in support
of Soviet foreign policy objectives. The four administrations, led by the
chief mufti for Central Asia and Kazakhstan, have provided theological
rationalizations for Soviet restrictions on Muslim religious practices, as well
as for the many contradictions between Islam and Soviet norms and policies.
By helping to adapt Muslim doctrines and practices to Soviet conditions,
however, they also facilitated the survival of Islamic values in modernized
form.[29] The Muslim establishment, nevertheless, has not been able to cope
with tradition-bound "unofficial" Islam and faces a growing challenge from
the secret *Sufi* brotherhoods, which condemn Soviet Russian policies towards
Islam and charge the muftiates with betrayal of the basic tenets of the faith.
Most vocal in the North Caucasus and Turkmenia, the brotherhoods have
stressed the transnational unity of all Muslims.[30] The Soviet invasion of
Afghanistan and the resistance of the Muslim guerrillas tested the political
loyalty of the muftiates and their credibility with believers, and deepened
the tension between official Islamic leaders and their fundamentalist opponents. The arrests and sentencing of Islamic "extremists" reflected the
extent of the regime's concern over the fusion of religious and nationalist
resistance, especially in Muslim areas adjoining Afghanistan and Iran.[31]

Ethno-Religious Diaspora

Soviet Jewry constitutes the principal example of an ethno-religious diaspora
in the USSR.[32] Once religiously defined, Jewish identity has survived in
conditions of territorial dispersal and a high degree of social mobilization
for three main reasons: the adoption of a secularized notion of Jewish
nationality; the growing resistance on the part of the dominant nationality
to the absorption of assimilated Jews; and those Soviet policies (especially
passportization) that made it almost impossible to change one's nationality,

except for children from ethnically mixed marriages.[33] Only among the Oriental Jewish communities in Central Asia and the Caucasus and among Holocaust survivors in the western areas annexed by the USSR since the war has religion preserved its dominance in the shaping of Jewish national consciousness.[34]

Since World War II only remnants of institutional Judaism have survived in the USSR. By 1975 a mere 62 synagogues were known to exist, only a few of them served by a rabbi,[35] and by 1980 this total had declined even further to 57.[36] Apparently inflated, 1986 data supplied by the chief Soviet official in charge of religious affairs list 109 Judaic communities active in the USSR (down from 130 in 1981).[37] In aggregate terms, Soviet Jewry displays the highest level of modernization among Soviet nationalities and— not surprisingly for Soviet conditions—the lowest indicators of religiosity.[38]

The establishment of the State of Israel had a profound impact on the perception of their own nationality among Soviet Jews, which intensified especially after the Seven-Day War in 1967, just as these developments significantly affected Soviet policies towards the Jews.[39] A resurgent Zionist current among Jewish youth made synagogues a rallying point for the manifestation of their Jewishness on major holidays, though this did not immediately translate into a religious revival.[40] While a Soviet specialist on Judaism maintained in 1980 that believers constituted just over 3% of Soviet Jews,[41] a 1976 survey had put the figure at 7%, reporting as well that 51% of the 1,215 Jews interviewed observed some Jewish holidays.[42] Since then, until the mid-1980s the number of Judaic religious activists and prisoners of conscience increased, especially among those refused emigration visas, the refuseniks.[43]

Modern Cosmopolitan Sects

In contrast to the rapidly declining old Russian sects, modern sects of Western origin—with their egalitarian and activist orientation, strict doctrinal and moral norms, and conversionist propensities uninhibited by Soviet legal restrictions or ethno-cultural barriers—have been the most rapidly growing religious communities in the USSR. These sects—particularly the Evangelical Christians-Baptists, the Pentecostalists, and the Seventh-Day Adventists— have in many ways been the unintended beneficiaries of Soviet policies promoting the breakdown of traditional linkages between nationality and religion on the one hand, and the penetration and corruption of traditional Church hierarchies on the other.

In Ukraine, where reportedly half of all their congregations are located,[44] these sects have spread most in the industrialized urban areas, where Khrushchev's antireligious campaign closed the great majority of Orthodox churches. The sectarians' reliance on Russian as the lingua franca and their indifference to indigenous languages and ethno-cultural values may be explained as much by Evangelical "cosmopolitanism" and practical missionary considerations as by the effects of Soviet political socialization. Only within the dissident Council of Churches of Evangelical Christians-Baptists (CCECB), with a strong following in Ukraine, have concessions been made in the 1970s to the Ukrainian language in its *samizdat* publications.[45]

Characteristically, Soviet policies have aimed to maximize centralization and institutionalization of sectarianism in the interests of state control. Internal tensions beween the co-opted leaders of the official All-Union Council of Evangelical Christians-Baptists and fundamentalist members erupted into schism in the early 1960s, when Khrushchev used the former to enforce restrictions on Baptist conversionist activities. The secessionist Council of Churches of the Evangelical Christians-Baptists was denied governmental registration and subjected to repeated waves of persecution, with some 143 dissident Baptists imprisoned in the USSR as of January 1985.[46] By December 1988 all of them had been released, according to CCECB foreign representative Georgii Vins.

Nationalities and Soviet Antireligious Propaganda

Soviet religious policy and antireligious propaganda have long displayed an acute awareness of the mutually supportive and protective roles of national and religious sentiments. The overlap of ethnic and religious loyalties was viewed as the main obstacle to Soviet political socialization in the national republics and as an opportunity for anti-Soviet diversions by émigré "bourgeois nationalists" and Western propaganda agencies. The symbiotic relationship between religion and nationality became a special target for Soviet "internationalist, patriotic" indoctrination.[47]

The highly selective treatment of this problem in the Soviet mass media can be illustrated by a 1981 study of atheist indoctrination in seven oblasts of Western Ukraine.[48] The survey showed that only 13.3% of the antireligious articles published in the seven Ukrainian oblast newspapers from 1971 to 1979 were directed against Orthodoxy, which claims the overwhelming majority of religious congregations in these regions. Significantly, most of these anti-Orthodox articles attacked the national Church that has been long suppressed—the Ukrainian Autocephalous Orthodox Church (nearly 30% of all articles in the Volyn oblast newspaper and over 20% in the Rovno oblast organ). Only a few articles were directed against the Russian Orthodox Church, but solely for its reactionary activities before 1917. The main target of Soviet antireligious press campaigns has been the officially non-existent Ukrainian Uniate Church—23.7% of all articles (including over 47% of antireligious articles in the Lviv daily, over 31% in Ivano-Frankivsk, 25.5% in Ternopil, and 23.3% in Transcarpathia). Between 1957 and 1977, the Ivano-Frankivsk *Prykarpats'ka pravda* alone published 200 anti-Uniate and anti-Catholic articles. The other targets of the seven newspapers were, in the order of space devoted to them, Jehovah's Witnesses (14%), Baptists (8.4%), Judaism (7.2%), Pentecostalists (3%), and Adventists (3%).[49]

Analysis of the targeting of articles in the Soviet Ukrainian antireligious monthly, *Liudyna i svit*, during 1973–83, shows a similar pattern of selectivity: while the Russian Orthodox Church, which claims an overwhelming majority of believers in the republic, was attacked in 27 articles, the Ukrainian Uniates were attacked in 65, Roman Catholics in 36, Evangelical Christians-Baptists and Jehovah's Witnesses—29 each, Judaism—25, Adventists and Pentecostalists—12 each, and the Ukrainian Autocephalous Orthodox Church—in 9 articles.[50] This striking partisanship in the party's antireligious propaganda underlined once more the appreciation by the Soviet authorities of the integrating, "patriotic" role performed by the imperial Church in the non-Russian parts of the USSR and, conversely, demonstrated their special hostility to the disintegrative "bourgeois nationalist" national Churches, "disloyal" cosmopolitan sects, and religious Zionism.

Reorientation of Soviet Religious Policy

Toward the end of Brezhnev's rule and into the regime of his successors, a number of external and domestic factors compelled the Soviet leadership to reassess and redirect its religious policy. A series of events abroad, especially, were perceived by the Kremlin to have important implications for policy on religion.

In the fall of 1978 the Polish Cardinal Karol Wojtyła was elected pope, assuming the name of John Paul II. His election had an immense emotional impact on Poland, helping to destabilize the unpopular Warsaw government, as well as on the adjoining Catholic regions of the USSR. John Paul II soon proceeded to revise the Vatican's *Ostpolitik*. The pope's frequent expressions of concern for the Catholic faithful in the Soviet Union were coupled with attempts to improve the status of the Church and to bolster the embattled hierarchies. In 1983 the pope publicly elevated to the rank of cardinal the Latvian Julijans Vaivods, and in 1988 the Lithuanian Vincentas Sladkevičius. The Polish pope was also quick to demonstrate his support for the Ukrainian Uniate Church. In what the Kremlin and the Moscow patriarchate perceived as a direct challenge, the pope convened a world synod of Ukrainian bishops in 1980 and confirmed the synod's choice, Archbishop Myroslav Ivan Lubachivsky, as coadjutor-successor to Cardinal Slipyj, the exiled archbishop-major of Lviv.[51] On Cardinal Slipyj's death in 1984, Lubachivsky succeeded him as archbishop-major, and was himself named cardinal in 1985. Pope John Paul II aroused profound anxieties in the Kremlin as a powerful and clever instigator of a "clerical crusade" against the USSR and its client regimes in Poland and Czechoslovakia, working hand-in-hand with Western human rights "crusaders," "international Zionism," and other hostile forces abroad.

Developments across the USSR's Asian frontiers also had implications for the twin issues of religion and nationality. In Iran, the overthrow of the monarchy in January 1979 and its replacement by the militant theocratic regime of Khomeini called for increased vigilance against the spread of Islamic propaganda into the Soviet Union's adjoining Muslim regions. In the event, the fundamentalist Shiite message found little resonance among the USSR's more modernized and (except for the Azerbaidzhanis) largely

Sunni Muslim nationalities. At the same time, a pro-Soviet regime in Afghanistan was seriously threatened by bloody factional struggles and Muslim guerrilla resistance. By the fall of 1979, the Soviet leadership had made the decision to invade Afghanistan, a decision whose domestic implications vis-a-vis Soviet Muslims must have entered into consideration.

Domestically, the expanding scope of religious activism and protest—in particular, by Orthodox, Lithuanian Catholic, fundamentalist Protestant, and Ukrainian Uniate dissenters—could not but alarm the internal security, propaganda, and military establishments in Moscow. The siege mentality that took hold in the Kremlin in the early 1980s was reflected in the redirection of Soviet antireligious propaganda. Its sharp edge turned primarily against the linkage between religion and non-Russian nationalism at home, and "clerical anti-communism" abroad. The former was singled out as one of the main concerns at an all-union conference in Riga in June 1982 devoted to the problems of nationality relations, while the latter figured prominently at a Tallinn conference in October of that year that focused on the worldwide "sharpening of the ideological struggle" and the redirection of political indoctrination at home.[52] The June 1983 ideological Plenum of the Central Committee claimed that in the course of the "global struggle of the two ideologies," "many ideological centers of imperialism seek not only to support but also to implant religiosity and to give it an anti-Soviet, nationalist orientation."[53]

The linkage of religion and nationalism continued to come under attack by Soviet propaganda despite the accession to power of Mikhail Gorbachev. Thus, in mid-1986 the first deputy chairman of the KGB, Filipp Bobkov, noted "an intensification of subversive actions against the USSR involving the use of religion":

> An important place in the subversive activities of imperialist states is assigned to the Vatican, which, seeking the role of "leader" of clerical anti-communism, fosters the idea of creating a so-called "Religious International" for the struggle against atheism, in essence—against socialism.
>
> Lately, one can detect in the tactics of the Vatican and other clerical organizations attempts to utilize illegal forms of activity. In particular, efforts are made to create various "groups" and "communities" in our country among the reactionary Catholic clergy, as well as "secular" persons, to galvanize the Uniates, who could serve as a basis for a subsequent religious confrontation with the state.[54]

At the same time, an intensification in anti-Islamic propaganda was evident in Central Asia in 1986–87, clearly aiming to break the links between local religious and national sentiments.[55] The tone for this campaign was set by Gorbachev himself. In a major speech to the republican leadership of Uzbekistan in November 1986,

> Mikhail Sergeyevich Gorbachev focused attention on the need to improve ideological work, the enhancement of the human factor's role in solving urgent

socioeconomic tasks, the resolute and uncompromising struggle against religious manifestations, and the stepping up of mass political work and atheistic propaganda. Even the slightest divergence between words and deeds is impermissible here. Communists and leaders above all must be held strictly to account, and particularly those who pay lip service to our morality and ideals while in practice pandering to obsolete views and personally participating in religious rituals.[56]

The growing Soviet concern about the impact of centrifugal, "alien" religions on interethnic relations at home could not but offer special advantages and opportunities to the Russian Orthodox Church, perceived by the Kremlin as a natural ally against the "anti-Russian" forces of Catholicism, Islam, fundamentalist Protestant "extremists," and "international Zionism."

The Millennium and Rapprochement Between the Kremlin and the Moscow Patriarchate

The approach of the one-thousandth anniversary of Christianity in Kievan Rus' in 1988 provided an opportune occasion for a rapprochement between the Soviet regime and the Russian Orthodox Church.

The symbolic and political importance of the Millennium went far beyond its religious significance or its implications for Soviet religious policy and external propaganda. It touched upon an issue central to Soviet nationalities policy: the sense of Russian national identity—or, to be more precise, the relationship between Russian and Ukrainian (as well as Belorussian) identity and historical-cultural consciousness. From the prevailing Russian point of view, officially maintained both by the Tsarist and (since the 1930s) Soviet regimes—and shared by most Russians at home and abroad—the events of 988 and the entire legacy of Kievan Rus' are integral parts of Russian, or "Old Russian," history, in which the yet "unseparated" ancestors of modern Ukrainians and Belorussians participated as part of the "Old Russian people." In Ukrainian national and religious consciousness the event belongs to Ukrainian history, of which Kievan Rus' is seen as the early period. Progressive Russification of the Orthodox Church in Ukraine in the confines of the Russian Empire had disrupted the Church's links with the Ukrainian national revival in the nineteenth century, and the secessionist Ukrainian Autocephalous Orthodox Church formed after the Revolution had only a brief existence in Ukraine before its suppression in the 1930s. The sense of historical continuity, however, has been strongly maintained by the clandestine Ukrainian Catholic (Uniate) Church. The Millennial polemics, therefore, emanating both from the Moscow patriarchate and from official Soviet sources, were primarily aimed at the Ukrainian Catholics and their Vatican and "bourgeois-nationalist" supporters.[57]

While the marking of the Millennium by the Russian Orthodox Church offered definite advantages for the regime, certain questions had to be resolved: the scale on which religious celebrations would be allowed; the degree of the state's involvement; the message to be conveyed by the occasion;

the implications of the Millennium for Soviet religious, nationalities, and foreign policies; and the treatment to be accorded the anniversary in Soviet antireligious media. Vacillation over these issues within the Brezhnev leadership appears to have been broken by developments abroad: the announcement in 1978 of Russian émigré preparations to mark the Millennium and, above all, a letter by Pope John Paul II in 1979 to the exiled primate of the Ukrainian Uniate Church, Cardinal Josyf Slipyj, calling upon Ukrainian Catholics to celebrate the Millennium of the Christianization of Kievan Rus'—in unity with the Holy See, and without any reference to the Russians or the Russian Orthodox Church.[58] The convening by the pope in the fall of 1980 of a synod of the Ukrainian Catholic episcopate and its condemnation of the forcible incorporation of the Uniates into the Russian Orthodox Church in 1946 apparently greatly strengthened the Moscow patriarchate's hand in pleading with the Kremlin for its own Millennial celebrations on a scale that would defeat the Vatican-Uniate and Ukrainian nationalist designs on this historic occasion.

In December 1980, in the midst of the Moscow-Vatican confrontation over the Ukrainian Catholic Church, came the announcement from the Russian Orthodox Church of the formation by the Holy Synod of a thirty-four-member commission for the preparation of celebrations marking the Millennium.[59] At the same time, a special commission to oversee the Millennial preparations and the actual program is said to have been established at the Central Committee (Secretariat) level by the party.[60] As the site of the celebrations the regime strategically chose Moscow, the symbol of the continuity of Russian statehood, rather than Kiev, the Ukrainian capital, where the historic event occurred and where the nine-hundredth anniversary was celebrated in 1888. In May 1983 the new Andropov leadership returned to Church ownership the sixteenth-century Danilov monastery, the oldest in Moscow, now designated the centerpiece of the Millennial celebrations and the future spiritual and administrative center of the Russian Orthodox Church. A special patriarchal commission undertook a major renovation and building program in the monastery complex.[61]

Since 1985, and largely timed to coincide with the Millennial preparations and celebrations, concessions unprecedented since Stalin's wartime quasi concordat have been accorded the Russian Orthodox Church. In 1987, for the first time since the early 1950s, the Church experienced a net increase of sixteen parishes; 1244 more parishes were registered during 1988.[62] Late in 1987 the authorities restored to the Church the Optina monastery (in Kaluga oblast) and the Tolga convent (in Yaroslavl oblast), and in 1988 returned to the patriarchate part of the Kievan Pecherska Lavra monastery complex, including the famous caves, as well as several monasteries in Moscow, Riazan, and Novgorod oblasts and in Moldavia. Precious relics of saints, confiscated during the Civil War, were also restored to the Church.[63] Enrollments were allowed to increase significantly in the theological schools at Zagorsk and Leningrad, and additional facilities were returned to them, as also to several existing monastic institutions. Seminaries were reopened during 1988–89 in Zhirovitsy, Belorussia, and in Kiev, and psalmists' courses were established in Kolomna, Smolensk, Chernihiv, and Stavropol.[64] A large-scale publication program was initiated in connection with the anniversary. This included a five-volume history of the Russian Orthodox Church; a multi-volume "encyclopedia" for priests; a three-volume illustrated Bible; picture and record albums; and 75,000 prayer books and a New Testament in Ukrainian. In addition, the patriarchate was permitted to receive from abroad 500,000 Russian prayer books, 150,000 Russian and 100,000 Ukrainian Bibles.[65]

For its part, the Soviet state marked the Millennium with a series of commemorative coins and stamps. Central Soviet periodicals opened their pages to Church representatives, and since November 1987 *glasnost'* markedly transformed the tone of the principal antireligious periodical, *Nauka i religiia*, which for the first time published selected statistical data on a number of religious groups in the USSR.[66] In an unprecedented move, in April 1988 Soviet television carried the Easter service at the patriarchal cathedral in Moscow, and *Izvestiia* published a full-page interview with Patriarch Pimen. On 29 April General Secretary Gorbachev held a publicized meeting with the patriarch and the permanent members of the Holy Synod that received lengthy coverage on the front pages of *Pravda, Izvestiia,* and other newspapers on 1 May. Representatives of the Moscow patriarchate were appointed to the boards of several new official bodies, including the Cultural Foundation, the Children's Fund, and the (Peace) Foundation for the Survival and Development of Mankind.

The official celebrations of the Millennium in June 1988, centered in Moscow and Zagorsk, were held on a lavish scale. On the occasion, the Russian Orthodox Church convened a Local Council, only the fourth in the Soviet period.[67] Nine new saints were canonized, and the gathering adopted a new statute for the Church that restored (obviously with prior government approval) the priests to the leadership of executive parish committees. Large foreign delegations attended the festivities, and their most prominent representatives were received by Secretary General Mikhail Gorbachev and the Chairman of the Presidium of the Supreme Soviet Andrei Gromyko. Government officials and prominent public figures, including Gorbachev's wife Raisa, were highly visible at the concerts and artistic events held in conjunction with the religious celebrations.[68]

During the summer of 1988, unofficial celebrations of the Millennium were organized by groups of Ukrainian Orthodox and Catholics in Kiev, Kharkiv, and other places in Ukraine. In Western Ukraine they turned into mass gatherings of Uniates, with the open participation of illegal clergy and hierarchy, and demands for the relegalization of their Church. These were met with administrative harassment, police interference, fines, and threats of criminal proceedings, as well as attacks in the Soviet media. Emblematic of the newly evolving type of Church-state relations was the seizure by the authorities of several hundred churches used by the clandestine Ukrainian Catholic Church and their transfer to hastily organized Russian

Orthodox parishes.[69] A striking feature of this anti-Uniate campaign was the involvement of spokesmen for the Moscow patriarchate in attacks against the "nationalist" and "separatist" nature of the Ukrainian Catholic Church.[70] In part, at least, such attacks were meant to counteract the Ukrainian observances of the Millennium abroad, especially the week-long celebration in Rome in July, with the conspicuous participation of Pope John Paul II.

References to any distinctly Ukrainian and Belorussian aspects of the Millennium, however, were virtually absent in what, in fact, turned out to be joint Church-state Soviet celebrations of "Russian Orthodoxy" and "Russian statehood." The dominant themes elaborated by Patriarch Pimen and other ecclesiastical spokesmen were the tremendous positive contributions of the Church to the development of "Russian national awareness, culture and statehood," "the integrity of the Russian state" and "national unity," and the benevolence shown by the Soviet state to the Church.[71] These themes echoed Patriarch Pimen's message of 12 May 1986 on the fortieth anniversary of the liquidation of the Uniate Church that emphasized the common interest of the Church and the Soviet state in the ecclesiastical and political indivisibility of the Russian, Ukrainian, and Belorussian peoples:

> Reaffirmation of our confessional and cultural unity, unity of origin of our three peoples, is especially important in connection with the approaching Millennium of the Baptism of Rus'. . . . Our membership in the fraternal family of Soviet peoples encourages the growth of this confessional unity; and the unity of the Church also serves to strengthen the friendship of peoples of [the USSR].[72]

It is undoubtedly in view of this "patriotic," integrative function of the Russian Orthodox Church that the huge apparatus of Soviet propaganda, in a manner reminiscent of Stalin's quasi concordat with the Moscow patriarchate in the 1940s, promoted, especially abroad, the new image of church-state harmony, even at the expense of distorting Lenin's pronouncements on the subject.[73]

Gorbachev's Reforms and Religion: Trends and Prospects

In the continuing internal polemics within the Soviet political elite over the course, direction, and extent of change necessary to reverse economic and social decay, Mikhail Gorbachev has taken a pragmatic approach to religion and nationality problems. This was reflected in the differences that surfaced in connection with the adoption of a new Party Program at the Twenty-seventh Party Congress in February 1986.[74] The new line essentially follows the principle of rewarding the regime's friends and punishing its enemies. The Kremlin's lenience toward the Russian Orthodox Church was compensated by intensified attacks on Islamic "survivals," especially their linkage with "reactionary nationalism," as well as by counteracting foreign attempts to use minority religions to weaken or subvert Soviet power.[75]

Apart from concessions to the Russian Church in connection with the Millennium, Gorbachev has relaxed certain other administrative restrictions on all loyal, recognized religious groups. These concessions include the relaxation of a "binding interpretation" of the current laws on religion issued by the Council on Religious Affairs in late 1985. Typically vague in its wording, this ruling suggested some broadening of the Churches' right to acquire and own certain types of property (by some interpretations, to "own *newly built* houses of prayer"), as well as religious objects within churches; however, the ruling arbitrarily set ten years as a minimum age for children's participation in religious rites.[76] Further reforms in religious legislation were promised, in particular a new law on freedom of conscience and religious organization, which has become a matter of controversy between liberal and conservative elements in the Soviet leadership.[77]

Since early 1987, some visible concessions have been made by the Kremlin to foreign and domestic demands for Jewish emigration, with well-known refuseniks allowed to leave the USSR. In the course of negotiations with Western Jewish delegations in the spring of 1987, Soviet officials promised improvements in the situation of Judaic religious communities, including permission for six rabbinical students to study in the United States, provided that they return to lead Soviet synagogues.[78] The long-standing ban on the teaching of Hebrew, it was announced in November 1988, had been allowed to lapse.[79]

Some concessions were also made to the Lithuanian Catholics, apparently in response to the major nationalist upsurge in the Baltic republics. Commemorations—albeit low-key in comparison with the Russian Orthodox Millennial festivities—were allowed in 1987 to mark the six-hundredth anniversary of Lithuania's conversion to Christianity; no official delegation, however, attended the solemn commemoration of this event in Rome with the pope presiding. In July 1988 Bishop Sladkevičius was allowed to travel to Rome for his installation as cardinal at the papal consistory, and in October Bishop Steponavičius was released from internal exile and, after a visit to the Vatican, to resume his duties in the archdiocese of Vilnius. The long-confiscated cathedral in Vilnius was restored for church use in October, and in November the authorities returned to the faithful the church in Klaipėda that had been built with believers' contributions in the 1950s and immediately appropriated by the state as a concert hall.[80] In 1989 the Lithuanian bishops, who had functioned as apostolic administrators, were named residential ordinaries of their sees.

In June 1988 the Russian Orthodox exarch of Ukraine, Metropolitan Filaret, announced that the Ukrainian Uniate issue would be on the agenda of discussions between the Moscow patriarchate and the Vatican. Representatives of the illegal Uniate Church, including two bishops, were allowed to meet with members of the Vatican delegation attending the Russian Orthodox celebrations in Moscow.[81] Despite several subsequent meetings between Ukrainian Catholic bishops and officials of the Council on Religious Affairs, there was no evidence until mid-1989 that the regime seriously contemplated lifting the ban on the Ukrainian Catholic Church. Since then, however, several factors have evidently persuaded the Soviet leaders to adopt a more conciliatory posture. These factors included the mounting pressure from the Ukrainian popular movement (Rukh) for the restoration of Ukrainian rights; a well-publicized, four-month-long hunger protest in Moscow by rotating groups of Ukrainian Catholics and their effective lobbying of deputies to the People's Congress; and the increasingly vocal support for the legalization of the Uniate Church in pro-reform Soviet periodicals, such as *Moscow News* and *Ogonek*. Greater urgency was given to this issue by mass demonstrations by Ukrainian Catholics in September 1989 (over 100,000 protested in Lviv alone). With the removal of Shcherbitsky from the Ukrainian party leadership in September, there were more and more indications that some form of legal status for the Uniates was being contemplated.[82] During the unprecedented meeting between Mikhail Gorbachev and Pope John Paul II at the Vatican in early December 1989, the Soviet leader affirmed that the new law on freedom of conscience would soon be passed. At the same time, officials in Ukraine announced that Uniate congregations would be allowed to register with the authorities; although this did not yet constitute full-scale legalization—the question of hierarchy, church institutions, and property remained unresolved—it was an important step in that direction. Significantly, the Moscow patriarchate's authority in Western Ukraine was also challenged since the summer of 1989 by the defection of some clergy and congregations who declared themselves part of the proscribed Ukrainian Autocephalous Orthodox Church.[83]

In the course of 1986–89, the majority of religious prisoners were released from camps and internal exile, though most were first compelled to pledge not to resume "anti-Soviet activities."[84] Among those released were most well-known Orthodox dissidents, including Vladimir Poresh, Irina Ratushinskaia, Aleksandr Ogorodnikov, Father Gleb Yakunin, and Deacon Vladimir Rusak.[85] While it is still difficult to gauge what lay behind these releases, Gorbachev's wooing of the intelligentsia and the need to impress the Kremlin's liberal critics abroad were all important factors.

Unlike his opponents in the lower levels of the bureaucracy, Gorbachev is inclined to take political risks by challenging established institutional and policy patterns and seeking allies in social groups that for a variety of reasons are dissatisfied with the status quo. The overlapping constituencies of the Russian Orthodox and Russian nationalists appear to be among those who may benefit most from Gorbachev's policies. Lately, however, the independent dynamics of national movements in the Baltic and Transcaucasian republics, in Ukraine and Moldavia, as well as in Central Asia,[86] have prompted the authorities to offer new concessions to local Churches in the hope that they may exercise a moderating influence on nationalist "extremists."[87] Given the multinational and multi-confessional nature of the Soviet population, the sources of the party's claim to legitimacy in the non-Russian republics, and the Kremlin's bloc-wide and international roles, there are distinct limitations and risks involved in a much closer identification of the Soviet regime with Russian ethnonationalism and, especially, with Russian Orthodoxy.

Notes

1. Compare Walter Kolarz, *Religion in the Soviet Union* (London: St. Martin's Press, 1969); Richard H. Marshall, Jr., ed., *Aspects of Religion in the Soviet Union, 1917–1967* (Chicago: University of Chicago Press, 1971); and Pedro Ramet, ed., *Religion and Nationalism in Soviet and East European Politics* (Durham, NC: Duke University Press, 1984), on the one hand; and John S. Curtiss, *The Russian Church and the Soviet State, 1917–1950* (Boston: Little, Brown & Co., 1953); Matthew Spinka, *The Church in Soviet Russia* (New York: Oxford University Press, 1956); and Dimitry Pospielovsky, *The Russian Church under the Soviet Regime, 1917–1982*, 2 vols. (Crestwood, NY: St. Vladimir's Seminary Press, 1984), on the other hand. On the dimension of the problem, see Bohdan R. Bociurkiw, "Institutional Religion and Nationality in the Soviet Union," in S. Enders Wimbush, ed., *Soviet Nationalities in Strategic Perspective* (New York: St. Martin's Press, 1985), pp. 181–206.

2. Yugoslavia, with its "federalized" party structure and "privatization" of religion, offers perhaps the closest analogy to this model.

3. Bociurkiw, "Institutional Religion and Nationality," pp. 182–83.

4. On Khrushchev's antireligious campaign and its effects on the Russian Orthodox Church, see Pospielovsky, *The Russian Church*, vol. 2, esp. pp. 336–40.

5. Father Gleb Yakunin, "On the Present State of the Russian Orthodox Church and the Prospects for a Religious Rebirth of Russia," *Russia* (New York), 1982, no. 5–6, pp. 51–54. For an extensive analysis of Orthodox dissent in the USSR, especially Fr. Yakunin's "Christian Committee for the Defense of Believers' Rights," see Jane Ellis, *The Russian Orthodox Church: A Contemporary History* (Bloomington: Indiana University Press, 1986), part 2 (pp. 285–454).

6. See, for example, John B. Dunlop, *The Faces of Contemporary Russian Nationalism* (Princeton: Princeton University Press, 1983), esp. chap. 7; and Dimitry Pospielovsky, "The Neoslavophile Trend and Its Relation to the Contemporary Religious Revival in the USSR," in Ramet, *Religion and Nationalism*, pp. 41–58.

7. Vahakn N. Dadrian, "Nationalism in Soviet Armenia: A Case Study of Ethnocentrism," in George W. Simmonds, ed., *Nationalism in the USSR and Eastern Europe in the Era of Brezhnev and Kosygin* (Detroit: The University of Detroit Press, 1977), pp. 216–53. See also Eduard Oganessyan, "The Armenian Church in the USSR," *Religion in Communist Lands* (henceforth *RCL*), vol. 7, no. 4 (Winter 1979), pp. 238–42, with a comment by Rev. R. Oppenheim, ibid., pp. 242–43. Cf. Mesrob K. Krikorian, "The Armenian Church in the Soviet Union, 1917–1967," in Marshall, *Aspects of Religion*, pp. 253–56.

8. *Internationale Kirchliche Zeitschrift* (Bern), vol. 67 (1977), p. 89, cited in Eugen Voss, ed., *Die Religionsfreiheit in Osteuropa* (Zollikon: G2W-Verlag, 1984), p. 167.

9. Kolarz, *Religion in the Soviet Union*, pp. 97–99.

10. Information gathered during the author's 1972 visit to Georgia. Cf. Elie Melia, "The Georgian Orthodox Church," in Marshall, *Aspects of Religion*, pp. 223–37. By early 1989, seventy-two more churches, some monasteries, and a theological academy in Tbilisi were opened in Georgia. (*Keston News Service*, no. 332 [24 August 1989], p. 20.)

11. Peter Reddaway, "The Georgian Orthodox Church: Corruption and Renewal," *RCL*, vol. 3, no. 4–5 (July–October 1975), pp. 114–23.

12. On protests against repression of the Georgian Orthodox Church, see *RCL*, vol. 9, no. 1 (Spring 1985), p. 78.

13. See Stanley V. Vardys, *The Catholic Church, Dissent and Nationality in Soviet Lithuania* (Boulder, CO: East European Monographs, 1978).

14. Ibid., pp. 70–72, 74–79.

15. Classified report by the Council for Religious Affairs (henceforth CRA) commissioner for Lithuania, Petras Anilionis, reproduced in the *Chronicle of the Catholic Church in Lithuania*, no. 66 (7 April 1985) (Brooklyn, NY: Franciscan Fathers Press, 1986), pp. A12–A13.

16. See Kęstutis K. Girnius, "Nationalism and the Catholic Church in Lithuania," in Ramet, *Religion and Nationalism*, pp. 82–103, 252–55.

17. See *First Victims of Communism: White Book on the Religious Persecution in Ukraine* (Rome: [Analecta OSBM], 1953); and Bohdan R. Bociurkiw, "The Uniate Church in the Soviet Ukraine: A Case Study in Soviet Church Policy," *Canadian Slavonic Papers*, vol. 7 (1965), pp. 95–111.

18. See Vasyl Markus, "Religion and Nationality: The Uniates of the Ukraine," in Bohdan R. Bociurkiw and John S. Strong, eds., *Religion and Atheism in the USSR and Eastern Europe* (London: Macmillan, 1975), pp. 101–22; Bohdan R. Bociurkiw, "The Catacomb Church: Ukrainian Greek Catholics in the USSR," *RCL*, vol. 5, no. 1 (Spring 1977), pp. 4–12; and Ivan Hvat', "The Ukrainian Catholic Church, the Vatican and the Soviet Union during the Pontificate of Pope John Paul II," *RCL*, vol. 9, no. 3 (Winter 1983), pp. 264–80.

19. See Ivan Hvat', *The Catacomb Ukrainian Catholic Church and Pope John Paul II* (Cambridge, MA: Ukrainian Studies Fund, Harvard University, 1984), including the appended documents. The *samizdat* publication *Chronicle of the Catholic Church in Ukraine* [Khronika Katolyts'koi Tserkvy v Ukraini] appeared irregularly since 1984 and has merged with the new Uniate publication, *Khrystiianskyi holos* in 1988. For a review of the first eight issues, see Andrew Sorokowski, "The Chronicle of the Catholic Church in Ukraine," *RCL*, vol. 13, no. 3 (Winter 1985), pp. 292–97.

20. Christel Lane, *Christian Religion in the Soviet Union* (London: Allen & Unwin, 1978), pp. 192–200. See also Tönu Parming, "Nationalism in Soviet Estonia since 1964," in Simmonds, *Nationalism in the USSR*, p. 128. In Latvia, however, such factors as Russification and the influx of migrants, as well as the alleged subservence of the local Lutheran Church's consistory to Soviet authorities, generated religious ferment with nationalist undertones. (See dissident Janis Rozkalns' report of 29 April 1987, published in *Glaube in der 2. Welt* [hereafter *G2W*], vol. 15, no. 7–8 [1987], pp. 16–17.) In April 1989, the Latvian Lutheran Synod replaced the entire consistory as too subservient to the state. New consistory members, headed by Karlis Gailitis, represent the "rebirth and renewal" movement, and are allied with the National Movement for Latvia's Emancipation from Moscow. (*Keston News Service*, no. 324 [27 April 1989], pp. 2–3.)

21. See Edgar C. Duin, "Soviet Lutheranism after the Second World War," *RCL*, vol. 8, no. 2 (Summer 1980), pp. 113–18; and "Lutheraner in der Sowjetunion," *G2W*, vol. 19, no. 7–8 (1981), pp. 255–326.

22. On the native sects, see Kolarz, *Religion in the Soviet Union*, chap. 4 ("The Old Believers") and chap. 11 ("Genuine Russian Sects"); A. Katunskii, *Staroobriadchestvo* (Moscow: Politizdat, 1972); I. Malakhova, *Dukhovnye khristiane* (Moscow: Politizdat, 1970); and, in particular, *Voprosy nauchnogo ateizma* (hereafter *VNA*), vol. 24 (1979), devoted to the theme "Evolution of Christian Sectarianism in the USSR."

23. See Bohdan R. Bociurkiw, "The Changing Soviet Image of Islam: The Domestic Scene," *Journal of the Institute of Muslim Minority Affairs* (Jeddah), vol. 2, no. 2/vol.

3, no. 1 (Winter 1980/Summer 1981), pp. 9–25; and E. G. Filimonov et al., eds., *Islam v SSSR: Osobennosti protsessa sekuliarizatsii v respublikakh sovetskogo Vostoka* (Moscow: Mysl', 1983).

24. See Azade-Ayşe Rorlich, "Notes on the Dynamics of Religion and National Identity in Central Asia," in Davie Nalle, ed., *Conference on the Study of Central Asia, March 10–11, 1983* (Washington: The Wilson Center, 1983), p. 34; and Alexandre Bennigsen and S. Enders Wimbush, *Muslims of the Soviet Empire: A Guide* (London: Hurst, 1985), pp. 31–35.

25. See Hélène Carrère d'Encausse, *Decline of an Empire: The Soviet Socialist Republics in Revolt* (New York: Harper & Row, 1981), chaps. 7 and 8.

26. Bennigsen and Wimbush, *Muslims of the Soviet Empire*, pp. 14–20.

27. According to a May 1976 briefing given by Vasilii Furov, deputy chairman of the CRA, to the staff members of the *Bol'shaia sovetskaia entsiklopediia*, as reported by the *Chronicle of Current Events*, no. 41 (dated 3 August 1976), published abroad by Amnesty International (London, 1979), p. 125. Cf. Bennigsen and Wimbush, *Muslims of the Soviet Empire*, pp. 17–18, who compare the exaggerated figures cited to foreigners by officials of the four directorates with unofficial Soviet sources; according to the latter, only 143 mosques were operating in 1976 in Central Asia and Kazakhstan, 45 in the North Caucasus in 1974, and only 16 in Azerbaidzhan.

28. "Garantii svobody" (an interview with K. M. Kharchev, chairman of the CRA), *Nauka i religiia*, 1987, no. 11, p. 23. The figure for Muslims includes, apparently, at least some of the unregistered communities.

29. Rorlich, "Notes on the Dynamics," pp. 31–33.

30. See Alexandre Bennigsen and S. Enders Wimbush, *Mystics and Commissars: Sufism in the Soviet Union* (London: Hurst, 1985).

31. According to Keston College records, there were sixteen Muslim religious prisoners in the Soviet Union (mostly from Uzbekistan) arrested and sentenced in 1986–87. See "Religious Prisoner Update," no. 1 (August 1987), appended to *Keston News Service*, no. 281 (6 August 1987).

32. With qualifications, one may also speak of Armenian (outside the Armenian SSR), German and Polish diasporas as displaying that particular interdependence of religion and ethnicity in conditions of demographic dispersal.

33. Zvi Gitelman, "Moscow and the Soviet Jews," *Problems of Communism*, vol. 29, no. 1 (January–February 1980), pp. 18–34; Kolarz, *Religion in the USSR*, chap. 20; see also Bohdan R. Bociurkiw, "Soviet Religious Policy and the Status of Judaism in the USSR," *Bulletin on Soviet and East European Jewish Affairs*, no. 6 (December 1970), pp. 13–19.

34. Joshua Rothenberg, "The Jewish Religion in the Soviet Union since World War II," in Marshall, *Aspects of Religion*, pp. 352–53; cf. I. Shapiro, "Iudaizm v SSSR," *Nauka i religiia*, 1980, no. 9, pp. 38–39.

35. National Conference on Soviet Jewry (New York), "Synagogues in the USSR," a list dated July 1975.

36. *The Position of Soviet Jewry, 1977–1980*. Report on the Implementation of the Helsinki Final Act since the Belgrade Follow-up Conference (London: World Conference on Soviet Jewry, 1980), pp. 18–19.

37. See "Garantii svobody," p. 23.

38. Surveying post-1971 Soviet Jewish immigrants to the United States, Zvi Gitelman found only 8% identifying themselves as religious. ("Soviet Immigrant Resettlement in the United States," *Soviet Jewish Affairs*, vol. 12, no. 2 [May 1982], p. 16.) On the other hand, a much higher proportion of religious believers was found by Gitelman among Soviet Jewish immigrants to Israel in 1971–72: 46% of his random

sample, and among Georgian Jews the proportion was 77%. ("Judaism and Modernization in the Soviet Union," in Denis J. Dunn, ed., *Religion and Modernization in the Soviet Union* [Boulder, CO: Westview, 1977], p. 302.)

39. Rothenberg, "Jewish Religion," pp. 343–51; Gitelman, "Moscow and the Soviet Jews," pp. 25–34.

40. Moshe Davis, "Jewish Spiritual Life in the USSR: Some Personal Impressions," *RCL*, vol. 4, no. 4 (Winter 1976), pp. 20–23.

41. According to I. Shapiro, a senior Jewish official of the CRA, there were by the late 1970s some 60,000 practicing religious Jews in the USSR, a number that amounts to slightly over 3% of the officially reported Soviet Jewish population in the 1979 census. See Havdallah Wein, "A Religious Minority among Soviet Jewry," *RCL*, vol. 6, no. 4 (Winter 1978), pp. 244–47.

42. Allan L. Kagedan, "The Condition of Soviet Jews," in G. Brunner and A. Kagedan, eds., *Minorities in the Soviet Union under International Law* (Cologne: Markus Verlag, 1988), pp. 134–35.

43. Keston College's *Religious Prisoners in the USSR* (1985) listed eighteen Jewish prisoners of conscience, all but one (Anatol Shcharansky) sentenced in the 1980s (pp. i–iv).

44. "Krizis khristianskogo sektantstva i osobennosti ego proiavleniia v razlichnykh raionakh strany," *VNA*, vol. 24 (1979), p. 46.

45. A *samizdat* collection of religious songs and poetry in Ukrainian, *Pisni spasennykh*, was published by the Baptist underground press "Khristianin" in the 1970s; since 1975 the latter published in Ukrainian the New Testament and several songbooks. *Pislanets' Pravdy*, vol. 60, no. 5–6 (May–June 1986), p. 50.

46. The January 1985 figure was listed in the annual report of the Council of Relatives of the ECB prisoners, *Otchetnoe pis'mo za 1985 god*, p. 10; a copy of this report was circulated abroad by the CCECB Foreign Representation headed by Georgii Vins.

47. See *VNA*, vol. 22 (1978), as well as A. V. Shuba, "Leninskie printsipy kritiki soiuza religii i natsionalizma," *Voprosy ateizma* (Kiev), vol. 16 (1980), pp. 122–29, and M. G. Mustafaeva, "Mezhnatsional'noe obshchenie, internatsionalisticheskoe i ateisticheskoe vospitanie," *VNA*, vol. 26 (1980), pp. 51–66. An All-Union Scientific-Practical Conference on "Development of National Relations in Conditions of Mature Socialism: The Experience and Problems of Patriotic and Internationalist Upbringing" was held in Riga on 28–30 June 1982, and selected materials of its Section XI (focusing on domestic "counterpropaganda") were published in a separate volume: *Neprimirimost' k burzhuaznoi ideologii, perezhitkam natsionalizma* (Moscow: Mezhdunarodnye otnosheniia, 1982). Several papers were devoted to the struggle against religion and nationalism in the non-Russian regions, in particular in Western Ukraine, Lithuania, the Muslim republics, and among Soviet Jewry; see, especially, L. M. Kravchuk, "Ateisticheskoe vospitanie trudiashchikhsia i zadachi kontrpropagandy" (pp. 35–50), and M. A. Gol'denberg, "Natsionalizm i religiia v planakh sovremennogo klerikal'nogo antikommunizma" (pp. 153–62).

48. *Stanovlennia i rozvytok masovoho ateizmu v zakhidnykh oblastiakh Ukrain'skoi RSR*, ed. Iu. Iu. Slyvka et al. (Kiev: Naukova dumka, 1981).

49. Ibid., pp. 183–84; see also pp. 144–45.

50. The survey, covering *Liudyna i svit* from January 1973 to October 1983, was conducted with the assistance of Nestor Woychyshyn. The totals exclude multi-targeted articles (66).

51. See Ivan Hvat', "The Ukrainian Catholic Church, the Vatican, and the Soviet Union during the Pontificate of Pope John Paul II," *RCL*, vol. 11, no. 3 (Winter 1983), pp. 269–70.

52. See L. K. Shepetis, "Ateisticheskomu vospitaniiu—deistvitel'nost' i nastupa-tel'nost'," *VNA*, vol. 32 (1985), p. 36. See also Carolyn Burch, "Religious Policy under Andropov and Chernenko," *RCL*, vol. 12, no. 2 (Summer 1984), pp. 198–201.

53. Cited in *VNA*, vol. 33 (1985), p. 26.

54. F. Bobkov, "Politicheskaia bditel'nost'—trebovanie vremeni," *Politicheskoe sa-moobrazovanie*, 1986, no. 6, p. 31. Conspicuously missing among General Bobkov's targets was the largest religious organization in the USSR, the Russian Orthodox Church.

55. See, for example, reports on anti-Islamic propaganda in Central Asia in *Keston News Service*, no. 262 (30 October 1986), pp. 8–9, and no. 277 (11 June 1987), pp. 11–13.

56. *Pravda vostoka*, 25 November 1986, translated in Foreign Broadcast Information Service, *Daily Report: Soviet Union*, 4 December 1986, p. R2. The text of the speech itself was not published. That it was aimed particularly at Central Asia and Islam is evidenced, among other things, by the fact that even its substance was not mentioned in the central press reports of the meeting. See *Pravda* and *Izvestiia*, 25 November 1986.

57. See, for example, P. Iarots'kyi, "Pravda istorii i vyhadky," *Pid praporom leninizmu*, 1986, no. 11, pp. 67–73; Kievan Metropolitan Filaret's address in Lviv on 17 May 1986, *Zhurnal Moskovskoi-patriarkhii* (henceforth *ZhMP*), 1986, no. 8, pp. 5–9; *Argumenty 86* (Moscow: Politizdat, 1986), pp. 172–73; M. Kotliar, "'Scholarly' Guise for a Hopeless Cause," *News from Ukraine* (Kiev), 1987, (January); and an interview with Metropolitan Filaret of Kiev, "1000-richchia khreshchennia Rusi—sviato vsioho khrystyians'koho svitu," *Visti z Ukrainy* (Kiev), 1987, no. 23 (June). TASS and Novosti Press Agency regularly carried dispatches on the patriarchate's preparations for the celebration of the Millennium of Christianity "in Russia"; unlike Soviet publications aimed at Ukrainian émigrés, such as *News from Ukraine*, the all-union media dispensed with the term "Rus'" in this connection.

58. See "Letter of His Holiness Pope John Paul II to Josyf Cardinal Slipyj on the Occasion of the Announcement of the Millennium of Christianity in Ukraine," 19 March 1979, reprinted as an appendix to Ivan Hvat', *The Catacomb Ukrainian Catholic Church and Pope John Paul II* (Cambridge, MA: Ukrainian Studies Fund, Harvard University, 1984).

59. *Pravoslavnyi visnyk* (Lviv), 1981, no. 3, pp. 3–5.

60. According to a fourteen-page *samizdat* article by Kirill Golovin, "Griadet den' . . ." (on the situation of the Russian Orthodox Church under Gorbachev), *Arkhiv samizdata*, AS 5899, in *Materialy samizdata*, no. 7/87 (13 March 1987), p. 6.

61. *ZhMP*, 1985, no. 11, p. 39. For a detailed discussion of Moscow's Millennium program, see Jane Ellis, "Preparations for the Official Celebrations of the Millennium of the Baptism of Kievan Rus'," *RCL*, vol. 15, no. 2 (Summer 1987), pp. 195–99.

62. Metropolitan Vladimir of Rostov, cited by *Keston News Service*, no. 304 (7 July 1988); *Liudyna i svit*, 1989, no. 9, p. 11.

63. *Radio Liberty Research Bulletin*, RL 223/88 (27 May 1988).

64. *Liudyna i svit*, 1989, no. 9, p. 11.

65. *Literaturna Ukraina*, 5 May 1988.

66. "Garantii svobody," p. 23.

67. A Local Council (*pomestnyi sobor*) is the supreme authority of an independent (national) Orthodox Church. The three earlier Local Councils of the Soviet period were held in 1917–18, when the patriarchate was restored; 1945, when Patriarch Alexei was elected; and 1971, when Pimen was elected his successor. See Ellis, *The Russian Orthodox Church*, p. 233.

68. The Moscow celebrations received heavy coverage in the foreign media. See, for example, *New York Times*, 16 June 1988.

69. *Keston News Service*, no. 304 (7 July 1988); "Millennium Celebrations in Ukraine," *Ukrainian Press Service* (Rome), no. 7–8 (31–32) (Summer 1988), pp. 4–7; *Ukrainian Weekly*, 12 and 19 June, 21 August, 11 September, and 9 October 1988; *Izvestiia*, 1 February 1989.

70. Note, for example, a speech by Archbishop Kirill of Smolensk at the Catholic Academy in Naurod/Wiesbaden, West Germany, on 7 May 1988 (transcript of tape).

71. I. Troyanovsky, "Patriarch Pimen Greets Perestroyka," APN dispatch (17 May 1988); "Marking Christian Jubilee," and "To Mark Historic Dates," APN dispatches (13 June 1988).

72. "Zvernennia do Prezydii Verkhovnoi Rady SRSR i Rady Ministriv SRSR," *Pravoslavnyi visnyk*, 1986, no. 7–8, p. 26.

73. See "Secretary General Meets Pimen . . . ," APN dispatch (3 May 1988), and Patriarch Pimen's reply to Gromyko's greetings during the Millennial celebrations (*Izvestiia*, 11 June 1988). For a comprehensive treatment of Gorbachev's policy toward the Russian Orthodox Church, see John B. Dunlop, "Gorbachev and Russian Orthodoxy," *Problems of Communism*, vol. 38, no. 4 (July–August 1989), pp. 96–116.

74. The Draft Program, prepared by a special Program committee headed by Gorbachev, eliminated a sentence of the 1961 Program on the "dissemination of the scientific-materialist world view" to "overcome religious prejudices," while introducing a passage: "The Party condemns attempts to utilize religion to the detriment of the interests of society and the individual." (*Radians'ka Ukraina*, 26 October 1986.) In the final version of the new Program, the omitted 1961 sentence was restored. (See *The Programme of the Communist Party of the Soviet Union: A New Edition* [Moscow: Novosti Press Agency Publishing House, 1986], p. 58.)

75. See Gorbachev's report to the Twenty-seventh Party Congress (*Pravda*, 26 February 1986) attacking "reactionary nationalistic and religious survivals"; the editorial in *Pravda*, 14 August 1986, pointing out the "certain role of religion in inciting nationalistic prejudices"; and A. Tursunov, "Ateizm i kul'tura," *Pravda*, 16 January 1987, specifically attacking the linkage of religion and nationalism in Islamic areas of the USSR.

76. "Prava i obiazannosti religioznogo obshchestva," *ZhMP*, 1986, no. 1, p. 80.

77. See the interview with the former chairman of the CRA, Konstantin Kharchev, in *Ogonek*, 1989, no. 44, pp. 9–12.

78. *New York Times*, 24 May 1987. A similar promise made in the 1970s had never been acted upon.

79. *New York Times*, 4 November 1988.

80. On some of these developments, see *New York Times*, 23 July and 27 October 1988, and *Globe and Mail* (Toronto), 22 October 1988. The authorities also permitted the Lithuanian Church to reopen its seminary in Telšiai and to launch a periodical, *The Catholic World* [Katalikų Pasaulis]. See *G2W*, vol. 17, no. 9 (1989), p. 11.

81. On Filaret's announcement, see *New York Times* and *Los Angeles Times*, 5 June 1988; on the Uniate meeting with cardinals Casaroli and Willebrands in Moscow, see *New York Times*, 11 June 1988.

82. See the interview with the new CRA chairman, Yurii Khristoradnov, in *Pravitel'stvennyi vestnik*, no. 20 (October 1989), pp. 8–9; the interview with his predecessor, Konstantin Kharchev, in *Ogonek*, 1989, no. 44, p. 12; and V. Razuvaev, "Brat'ia razdelennye," *Novoe vremia*, 1989, no. 45, p. 36.

83. *Novyi shliakh* (Toronto), 18 November 1989.

84. In all, 84 religious prisoners are known to have been released during the first seven months of 1987, including 21 Evangelical Christians-Baptists, 14 Russian Orthodox, 13 Pentecostalists, 10 Jews, 10 Roman Catholics, 7 Hare Krishna, 3 Ukrainian Catholics, 2 Jehovah's Witnesses, and 4 others. (See *Keston News Service*, no. 277 [11 June 1987], p. 24, and no. 281 [6 August 1987], appendix: "Prisoner Update no. 1.") As of 30 March 1989, there were reportedly still 76 known religious prisoners in the USSR, including 18 Christians, 23 Jehovah's Witnesses, and 31 Muslims; among the Christians and Jehovah's Witnesses many were conscientious objectors. (See *Keston News Service*, no. 327 [30 March 1989], pp. 19–20.)

85. Fr. Gleb Yakunin has since resumed his pre-arrest role of leading a "loyal opposition" to Soviet religious policies; see the May 1987 petitions to Gorbachev and Patriarch Pimen, signed by Yakunin and eight other Orthodox dissidents (on the former, see *Keston News Service*, no. 277 [11 June 1987], pp. 3–5; a copy of the petition to the patriarch was made available to the author in June 1987). On 31 July 1987, a religious *samizdat* journal called *Bulletin of the Christian Community* [Biulleten' khristianskoi obshchestvennosti] was launched openly in Moscow by a group of former religious prisoners, including Aleksandr Ogorodnikov. (See *Keston News Service*, no. 281 [6 August 1987], p. 3, and no. 312 [3 November 1988], pp. 2–3.)

86. In March 1989, following a public demonstration by the "Islam and Democracy" movement in Tashkent, the leadership of the Muslim Board for Central Asia and Kazakhstan was replaced. Some mosques were reopened in Central Asia and officials promised to print 50,000 copies of the Koran. (*Keston News Service*, no. 323 [13 April 1989], pp. 7–8.) In Azerbaidzhan, an Islamic academy (medrese) was opened for the Shiites. In Moldavia, under pressure from the Moldavian Popular Front, the corrupt Russian metropolitan of Kishinev, Serapion, was replaced by a Moldavian bishop, Vladimir (Cantareanu); 265 Orthodox churches were reopened in the republic during 1988–89. (*Keston News Service*, no. 332 [24 August 1989], pp. 11–12; *G2W*, vol. 17, no. 6 [1989], p. 11.)

87. The CPSU Central Committee Plenum on nationalities, which met on 19 September 1989, noted the important role of religion in internationality relations, but except for condemning the "incitement of national hatred on religious grounds," failed to offer concrete policy guidance in this realm. *Keston News Service*, no. 336 (5 October 1989), p. 5.

CHAPTER 8

Ukraine, Belorussia, and Moldavia: Imperial Integration, Russification, and the Struggle for National Survival

Roman Solchanyk

Ukraine, Belorussia, and Moldavia, together wih the Baltic states, form part of a specific geographical and, less perceptibly, political and cultural entity within the USSR that has conveniently come to be known as the Soviet West. The common geographic denominator that runs through this area is obvious: these are the westernmost republics of the Soviet Union. Ukraine shares a common border with Poland, Czechoslovakia, Hungary, and Romania; Belorussia with Poland; and Moldavia with Romania. Much less evident but considerably more important are certain shared circumstances of historical development that have contributed to the formation of a Western or European political culture that, in turn, sets the region apart from the remainder of the Soviet multinational conglomerate. Most important is the fact that historically the peoples of the Soviet West have been linked—at various times and in varying degrees—to their immediate neighbors in Eastern Europe or Scandinavia. Moreover, it was only in the course of World War II and its direct aftermath that the Soviet West assumed its present form with the integration of territories that previously lay outside the borders of the USSR.[1]

This combination of factors—the historical link to the West, the permanent exposure to "alien" ideological influences, and the relatively recent experience of Sovietization throughout much of the region—has constituted a formidable challenge to Soviet nationalities policy. Briefly stated, this policy sought to translate into reality a fiction that was proclaimed ex cathedra and gained wide currency since the late 1960s—namely, that the nations of the Soviet Union constitute a unified supranational "new historical community" called the "Soviet people" (*sovetskii narod*). Increasingly, Soviet theoreticians came to focus their attention on the "attributes of memory" as a determining factor in the success or failure of this policy. In the words of two leading Soviet experts on the nationality question, "National consciousness is always historical consciousness, forming a continual linkage of the present and future with the past."[2] If historical memory is indeed the key to national awareness, then the nations of the Soviet West have been in a relatively favorable position to maintain their national identities in the face of determined efforts to mold a uniform "Soviet people."

Those factors common to the historical development of the Soviet West that permit us to treat it as a distinct entity should not obscure the diversity of its component parts. Ukraine, Belorussia, and Moldavia exhibit considerable variation in their demographic and socioeconomic structures. The political experience of the three republics under the Soviet system has also been varied. And, of course, the cultural dimension, particularly its linguistic component, remains unique in each case. Ukraine, with a population of 51.4 million in 1989, is the second largest republic in the USSR, with a highly developed industrial and agricultural economy. By contrast, the population of Belorussia was 10.1 million and that of Moldavia only 4.3 million. Whereas two-thirds of the population of Ukraine and Belorussia was urban in 1989, more than half of Moldavia's inhabitants still lived in rural areas. Ukrainian and Belorussian, like Russian, are East Slavic languages. Moldavian is in fact Romanian, which belongs to the Romance language group, artificially distinguished largely by the Soviet-imposed use of the Cyrillic script and a significant infusion of Russian vocabulary and Soviet neologisms. Indeed, the Soviet argument that Moldavian is a separate language and that its speakers constitute a full-fledged nation distinct from the Romanians underlines a political issue that has no equivalent in the Ukrainian and Belorussian cases. At the heart of the matter is the longstanding dispute between Russia and Romania over the historical province of Bessarabia, which was ceded to the Soviet Union in 1940 and formed the territorial basis for the creation of the Moldavian SSR.[3] Finally, the existence of a lively dissident movement in Ukraine in the 1960s and 1970s, focusing both on national and religious rights, contrasted sharply with the situation in Belorussia and Moldavia, where dissident activities were much less in evidence. However, hasty judgments often made on this basis about the relative levels of national consciousness among Ukrainians, Belorussians, and Moldavians were certainly premature, as evidenced by the developments of the late 1980s.

Political Developments

When Leonid Brezhnev was chosen to replace Nikita Khrushchev as head of the CPSU in October 1964 the Belorussian party first secretary, Kirill Mazurov, had already been in office since 1956; Ivan Bodiul had been party leader in Moldavia since 1961; and the Ukrainian party was led by Petr (*Ukr.* Petro) Shelest since mid-1963. Brezhnev himself had personal links to both the Ukrainian and Moldavian party organizations. His first party posts in the 1930s were in the industrial Dnipropetrovsk region, and later he also served briefly as first secretary of the Zaporizhia oblast party committee. In 1950–52 he headed the Moldavian party organization.

Shortly after becoming first secretary, Brezhnev was confronted with a political challenge in Ukraine stemming from a growing cultural revival that evidently enjoyed the support of elements within the Ukrainian party leadership. The national self-assertiveness that began to gain momentum in the late 1950s and early 1960s was most easily discernible in Ukrainian belles lettres, particularly in the works of the younger generation of writers, poets, and literary critics collectively known as the "Sixties Generation" (*shestydesiatnyky*). This was a literary-cultural phenomenon that perhaps, in its initial stages, only implied demands for loosening ideological controls over Ukrainian national life, and as such it must be seen within the context of the cultural thaw that accompanied the Khrushchev de-Stalinization. At about the same time, several clandestine groups were formed that, for the most part, limited their activities to discussion and criticism of the regime's Russification policies and Ukraine's subordinate political and economic status within the USSR. However, in August–September 1965 the authorities reacted by arresting about two dozen Ukrainian intellectuals who were tried for "anti-Soviet" activities during the first few months of the following year. This, in turn, gave rise to a full-fledged human rights movement in the republic that produced such classic *samizdat* texts as Ivan Dzyuba's *Internationalism or Russification?* and Vyacheslav Chornovil's *The Chornovil Papers.*[4] Ukrainian dissidents also began to issue a *samizdat* journal, *Ukrainian Herald* [Ukrains'kyi visnyk], eight issues of which are known to have been compiled in 1970–74.

Moscow's concern over developments in Ukraine led to the removal of Shelest in May 1972. He was replaced by the chairman of the Ukrainian Council of Ministers, Vladimir Shcherbitsky (*Ukr.* Volodymyr Shcherbyts'kyi), one of the main figures in Brezhnev's coterie of clients and patrons known as the Dnipropetrovsk group. Initially, Western observers were inclined to view Shelest's dismissal as the outcome of a disagreement with the Politburo majority over foreign policy issues, an interpretation that still finds its way into the literature. Authoritative Soviet publications, however, have made it abundantly clear that the Ukrainian party leader was ousted for failing to deal satisfactorily with the growing national ferment in the republic, a fact that has been confirmed by Shelest himself in recent interviews.[5]

In January 1972, shortly before Shelest's removal from office, the security organs carried out widespread political arrests throughout Ukraine. The next several years witnessed a systematic purge of both political and cultural elites. In the party, high-level functionaries responsible for ideological and cultural affairs were particularly hard hit. In addition to the arrests and subsequent incarceration of numerous representatives of the intelligentsia, the authorities launched a campaign emphasizing ideological orthodoxy in literature, the arts, and scholarship, especially the social sciences, that took a severe toll of both the leadership and rank and file in the cultural sphere. An important and symbolic aspect of this campaign was the editorial criticism of Shelest's book *O Ukraine, Our Soviet Land* [Ukraino nasha Radians'ka] (1970) in the April 1973 issue of *Komunist Ukrainy*, which clearly served to define the issues that, from the party's standpoint, required "normalization."[6] The clampdown was supervised by Shcherbitsky's new ideological secretary, Valentin (*Ukr.* Valentyn) Malanchuk, a scholar-apparatchik whose specialization in nationality affairs was buttressed by practical experience in ideological work in the Lviv oblast in Western Ukraine.[7] By mid-1976, Shcherbitsky largely completed the consolidation of his position in the Ukrainian party with two important personnel appointments. In February of that year Ivan Sokolov replaced Ivan Lutak as second secretary of the Central Committee. Sokolov was a Russian, and his appointment to this important post broke a long-standing tradition in cadre selection in the republic—since 1949 the second secretary in Kiev had always been Ukrainian.[8] The second important personnel shift involved the transfer of Aleksei (*Ukr.* Oleksii) Vatchenko, first secretary of the Dnipropetrovsk oblast party committee, to the capital as chairman of the Presidium of the Supreme Soviet.

The relative calm that had settled over the Ukrainian party organization by the mid-1970s was abruptly broken in April 1979 when Malanchuk was unexpectedly removed from his post as the ideological chief. The reasons for his dismissal and removal from party work have remained largely a mystery. He had played a crucial role in the post-Shelest purge of the Ukrainian cultural intelligentsia, and there were no indications of serious shortcomings in the work of the party's ideological apparatus during his tenure in office. It may well be that the party leadership had decided that the time had come to establish a working relationship with its cultural elites, who were left alienated and badly demoralized by the purges within their ranks, and that the price for such an accommodation was Malanchuk's departure from the scene. This explanation is supported by the signs of "cultural detente" between the party and the intellectuals that more or less coincided with Malanchuk's removal. It was also at this time that preparations were under way for two major celebrations—the 325th anniversary of Ukraine's "reunification" with Russia in 1979 and the 1500th anniversary of Kiev in 1982—that were to play an important role in the party's approach to the nationality question in Ukraine. Both of these undertakings, if they were to be even minimally successful, required the cooperation of writers, filmmakers, journalists, historians, and other representatives of the Ukrainian intelligentsia.

The dramatic changes at the very top of the Ukrainian party leadership in the early 1970s contrasted sharply with the political tranquility in Belorussia and Moldavia; although subsequently the first secretaryship of the Belorussian party organization changed hands several times within a relatively short space of time, this was occasioned by deaths in office and promotions. In March 1965, not long after Brezhnev took over in Moscow, Mazurov, the Belorussian party chief, was transferred to Moscow as first deputy chairman of the USSR Council of Ministers and promoted from candidate to full member of the Presidium (later Politburo) of the CPSU Central Committee. His place was taken by Petr Masherov, whose death in an automobile accident in October 1980 ended a fifteen-year term of office at the head of the Belorussian party. Since then there have been three turnovers in the post of first secretary. Tikhon Kiselev, who served as chairman of the Belorussian Council of Ministers from 1959 to 1978 and was subsequently promoted to deputy chairman of the USSR Council of Ministers, was brought back to Minsk as Masherov's successor. But little more than two years later Kiselev died after what was described as a serious and prolonged illness. His place was taken in January 1983 by Nikolai Sliunkov, a former first secretary of the Minsk city party committee who had served as deputy chairman of the USSR Gosplan for almost ten years. In January 1987, however, Sliunkov was made a secretary of the CPSU Central Committee and was later promoted to full membership in the Politburo. His successor, chosen in February 1987, was Efrem Sokolov, formerly first secretary of the Brest oblast party committee. In Moldavia, Bodiul served as head of the republican party organization for almost twenty years, until he too was promoted to a Moscow post as deputy chairman of the USSR Council of Ministers in December 1980. He was succeeded by Semen Grossu, until then the chairman of the republic's Council of Ministers.

It is interesting to note that in recent years the Belorussian party organization has played an important role in Soviet-Polish relations by serving as a source of Soviet ambassadors to the troublesome Warsaw Pact ally. Three of the four Soviet ambassadors to Warsaw in the two decades since 1970 have come from Belorussia: Stanislav Pilotovich (1971–78), who held various posts in the Belorussian party; Aleksandr Aksenov (1983–85), who previously served as chairman of the Belorussian Council of Ministers; and Vladimir Brovikov (1986–), who had succeeded Aksenov as Belorussian "premier." Certainly the fact that the highest concentration of Poles in the USSR—35% of their total number, according to the 1979 census—is in Belorussia must be taken into account when looking at Moscow's choice of personnel in this area. There is also another dimension to Belorussia's ties to Poland, one that it shares with the remainder of the Soviet West—namely, the often expressed concern about ideological contagion from across the border. Savelii Pavlov, head of the Propaganda and Agitation Department of the Belorussian Central Committee, posed the problem in figurative terms almost two decades ago when he cautioned that Belorussia is the "Western gate to our land," that is, the USSR.[9] The danger of exposure to undesirable influences assumed special urgency during the heyday of the Solidarity movement in Poland, and in its aftermath the current Belorussian party leader, Efrem Sokolov, then first secretary of the Brest oblast party committee, reiterated these concerns on the pages of Moscow's *Kommunist*.[10] Moldavia has also been the focus of Soviet apprehension with regard to relations with an East European partner, but in a rather different context. The main issue here is the controversy over Bessarabia, which has intermittently served as a source of tension between Moscow and Bucharest, particularly after Romania declared its independent course in East-bloc affairs in 1964.[11] Although the polemics had subsided in recent years, the issue has been raised again by so-called informal groups in Moldavia, resulting in official warnings about the internal dangers of "immature opinions about the so-called 'Bessarabian question.'"[12]

The question that has intrigued many Western observers of the Soviet scene is the role of former Ukrainian party chief Shcherbitsky in the context of the policies of *perestroika* and his relations with Soviet party and state leader Mikhail Gorbachev. Not long after Gorbachev's election as general secretary in March 1985, the Western media began to speculate that Shcher-bitsky—a "Brezhnevite," a member of the "old guard," and a "leftover"— would soon be sacked and lose his seat on the Politburo. This notion gained wide currency particularly after the dismissals of Politburo members Viktor Grishin, Grigorii Romanov, Nikolai Tikhonov, and, especially, the Kazakh party first secretary, Dinmukhamed Kunaev. Yet, Shcherbitsky was reelected first secretary at the Twenty-seventh Congress of the Ukrainian party in early February 1986 and retained his seat on the Politburo in Moscow at the conclusion of the CPSU Congress several weeks later. The disaster at the Chernobyl nuclear power plant in Ukraine in April 1986 seemed to remove any lingering doubts about Shcherbitsky's future. Virtually without exception, Western commentators assumed that Gorbachev would utilize the opportunity to oust the Ukrainian party leader. The prediction failed to materialize.[13] Moreover, Shcherbitsky apparently emerged unscathed in the aftermath of the Berkhin Affair in Voroshylovhrad, a scandal that came to the surface at the end of 1986 stemming from the illegal arrest and detention of a journalist by the local KGB. The scandal was reported in *Pravda*, perhaps the first time since the early 1950s that the security organs were criticized in the Soviet press, and Gorbachev himself made an oblique reference to the affair at the January 1987 Plenum of the Central Committee. It resulted in the dismissal of the first secretary of the Voroshylovhrad oblast party committee, and probably also explains the retirement of the Ukrainian KGB chief in May 1987.

First secretaries were also removed in three other oblasts (Dnipropetrovsk, Lviv, and Volyn) under circumstances that leave no doubt that they were sacked for political failings. Overall, however, there have been comparatively few personnel changes in the upper levels of the Ukrainian party organization, and the majority of these have been routine in nature. In the spring of 1987 Shcherbitsky confirmed that only "over one-fifth of the [party] workers who are confirmed by the Central Committee of the Communist Party of Ukraine" were replaced since Gorbachev came to power. And in early 1988 Shcherbitsky revealed that the proportion of party workers confirmed by the Central Committee who were removed for shortcomings since the Twenty-seventh Party Congress (February–March 1986) amounted to "about 6%" of all personnel changes in this category—i.e., 110 of a total of 1,912 individuals.[14]

Clearly, developments in the Ukrainian party organization did not follow the scenario posited by many observers of the Kremlin scene, who seemed convinced of a Shcherbitsky-Gorbachev struggle and were puzzled by the Soviet leader's "failure" to unseat the Ukrainian party boss. In this connection, it is noteworthy that in an interview with the Associated Press in April 1989 Shcherbitsky asserted that he had supported Gorbachev's election as CPSU general secretary. At the same time, he sidestepped a direct response to the question whether or not he agreed entirely with Gorbachev's program, maintaining that "there have not been and there are no disagreements on questions of principle" in the Politburo and Central Committee.[15] When Shcherbitsky, after almost five years, was finally replaced as Ukrainian party leader by Vladimir (*Ukr.* Volodymyr) Ivashko in September 1989, he was highly praised by Gorbachev, who attended the Central Committee session in Kiev. Directly afterwards *Pravda* published back-to-back interviews with Gorbachev, Shcherbitsky, and Ivashko that projected an image of near full unanimity.[16] All this calls into question traditional Western assumptions about Soviet politics with regard to relations between Moscow and the republics and requires a reevaluation of the impact of ethnic politics on the center-periphery relationship. Certainly in the case of Ukraine Gorbachev's concern about serious potential problems stemming from "nationalist" discontent were readily apparent.[17]

The turnover of party leaders in all fourteen non-Russian republics was completed in November 1989 when Semen Grossu was replaced by Petr Luchinsky in Moldavia. The new party leader, a Moldavian, previously served as second secretary of the Tadzhik Central Committee. Grossu's "transfer to other work" came in the aftermath of violent demonstrations in Kishinev in early November, which resulted in the imposition of a state of emergency in the republic and the dispatch of troops from the center. Ethnic tension had been growing in Moldavia, with controversy over a proposed law on languages in mid-1989 leading to frequent mass demonstrations led by the Moldavian Popular Front and counter-strikes organized by activists of groups representing the republic's Russian-speakers.[18]

Demographic and Social Trends

In the 1960s, 1970s, and 1980s Ukraine, Belorussia, and Moldavia registered some of the largest proportional increases in Russian population among the union republics. As Table 1 shows, between 1959 and 1989, the number of Russians increased in Ukraine by 59.9%, in Moldavia by 91.1%, and in Belorussia by 103.2%—the latter figure being the highest for all of the union republics. In addition, Moldavia has a significant number of Ukrainians, who increased at about the same rate as the Moldavians. The relative growth of the Russian population was particularly rapid in the 1960s, and continued to outdistance corresponding increases in most of the other union republics during the following decade. In all three republics the proportion of Russians in the total population increased steadily, while the share of indigenous groups registered small decreases. Nonetheless, Ukrainians and Belorussians still constitute large majorities in their republics—72.6% and 77.8%, respectively—while Moldavians are over 64% of the population of Moldavia.

One of the prominent features of the ethnodemographic structure of the Ukrainian republic is the large Russian element, almost 11.5 million in 1989,

TABLE 1A. Demographic Trends among Ukrainians, Belorussians, and Moldavians in the USSR, 1959-1989

	Total Population (in thousands)				Population Increase
	1959	1970	1979	1989	1959-89
USSR	208,827	241,720	262,085	285,689	76,862
Russians	114,114	129,015	137,397	145,072	30,958
Ukrainians	37,253	40,753	42,347	44,136	6,883
Belorussians	7,913	9,052	9,463	10,030	2,117
Moldavians	2,214	2,698	2,968	3,355	1,141

	Percent Increase				Percent of Population			
	1959-70	1970-79	1979-89	1959-89	1959	1970	1979	1989
USSR	15.7	8.4	9.0	36.8	100	100	100	100
Russians	13.1	6.5	5.6	27.1	54.65	53.37	52.42	50.78
Ukrainians	9.4	3.9	4.2	18.5	17.84	16.86	16.16	15.45
Belorussians	14.4	4.5	6.0	26.8	3.79	3.74	3.61	3.51
Moldavians	21.9	10.0	13.0	51.5	1.06	1.12	1.13	1.17

TABLE 1B. Percentage Concentration Rates of Nationalities in Their Titular Republics, 1959-1989

	1959	1970	1979	1989	Change 1959-89
Russians	85.8	83.5	82.6	82.6	- 3.2
Ukrainians	86.3	86.6	86.2	84.7	- 1.6
Belorussians	82.5	80.5	80.0	78.7	- 3.8
Moldavians	85.2	85.4	85.1	83.2	- 2.0

TABLE 1C. Ethnodemographic Trends in Ukraine, Belorussia, and Moldavia, 1959-1989

	Total Population (in thousands)				Population Increase
	1959	1970	1979	1989	1959-89
Ukraine	41,869	47,127	49,609	51,449	9,580
Ukrainians	32,158	35,284	36,489	37,370	5,212
Russians	7,091	9,126	10,472	11,340	4,249
Jews	840	777	634	488	- 352
Belorussia	8,055	9,002	9,533	10,149	2,094
Belorussians	6,532	7,290	7,568	7,898	1,366
Russians	660	938	1,134	1,341	681
Poles	539	383	403	418	- 121
Moldavia	2,884	3,569	3,950	4,332	1,448
Moldavians	1,887	2,304	2,526	2,791	904
Ukrainians	421	507	561	600	179
Russians	293	414	506	560	267

	Percent Increase				Percent of Population			
	1959-70	1970-79	1979-89	1959-89	1959	1970	1979	1989
Ukraine	12.6	5.0	3.7	22.9	100	100	100	100
Ukrainians	9.7	3.4	2.4	16.2	76.81	74.87	73.55	72.64
Russians	28.7	14.7	8.3	59.9	16.94	19.37	21.11	22.04
Jews	- 7.5	-18.4	-23.0	-41.9	2.01	1.64	1.28	0.95
Belorussia	11.8	5.9	6.5	26.0	100	100	100	100
Belorussians	11.6	3.8	4.4	20.9	81.09	80.97	79.39	77.82
Russians	42.1	20.9	18.2	103.2	8.19	10.42	11.90	13.21
Poles	-28.9	5.4	3.6	-18.3	6.69	4.25	4.23	4.12
Moldavia	23.7	10.7	9.7	50.2	100	100	100	100
Moldavians	22.1	9.6	10.5	47.9	65.40	64.56	63.95	64.42
Ukrainians	20.4	10.7	7.0	42.5	14.59	14.19	14.20	13.84
Russians	41.5	22.2	10.8	91.1	10.16	11.61	12.81	12.94

Sources: Derived from 1959, 1970, 1979, and 1989 Soviet census data. Itogi Vsesoiuznoi perepisi naseleniia 1959 goda: SSSR; ... Ukrainskaia SSR; ... Belorusskaia SSR; ... Moldavskaia SSR (Moscow: Gosstatizdat, 1962). Itogi Vsesoiuznoi perepisi naseleniia 1970 goda, vol. 4 (Moscow: Statistika, 1974). Chislennost' i sostav naseleniia SSSR: Po dannym Vsesoiuznoi perepisi naseleniia 1979 goda (Moscow: Finansy i statistika, 1984). Data for 1989 are from preliminary unpublished results of the 1989 census, and are subject to correction.

TABLE 2. Language Patterns among Ukrainians, Belorussians, and Moldavians Residing
in Their Titular Republics, 1959-79 (in percent)

Nationality	National Language as Native Language			Russian as Native Language			Russian as Second Language	
	1959	1970	1979	1959	1970	1979	1970	1979
Ukrainians in Ukraine	93.5	91.4	89.1	6.5	8.6	10.9	35.8	51.8
Belorussians in Belorussia	93.2	90.1	83.5	6.8	9.8	16.5	52.3	62.9
Moldavians in Moldavia	98.2	97.7	96.5	1.3	2.0	3.3	33.9	46.2

Source: Calculations based on 1959, 1970, and 1979 census data, as given in Table 1.

which represents 22.0% of the population. Between 1979 and 1989, the
number of Russians grew by almost 900,000—or about 8%. An important
factor influencing the national composition of the population has been
migration. Throughout the 1960s Ukraine registered net increases of population through migration which reached a peak in the latter half of the
decade, and this trend continued in the first half of the 1970s, although on
a smaller scale. In the period 1959–72, residents of the RSFSR accounted
for 75% of the total migrants to Ukraine.[19] From the mid-1970s, however,
the balance of migration began to yield net losses of population, which
have continued throughout the 1980s.

In Belorussia, although the number of Russians increased by over 18%
between 1979 and 1989, their share in the republic's population was only
13.2%. A similar situation can be observed in Moldavia, where the Russian
population grew by 10.8% and constituted 12.9% of the population. But
Moldavia also has more than half a million Ukrainians, whose share in the
republic's population is 13.8%; taken together, Ukrainians and Russians form
almost 27% of the republic's population. Belorussia belongs to that category
of republics where the balance of migration in the 1970s has resulted in
net losses of population, although in decreasing numbers as the decade
wore on. By the mid-1980s the situation was reversed, with the balance of
migration showing small increases. Moldavia experienced large net gains of
population in the 1960s through migration. This trend came to a halt in
the first half of the 1970s, and since then migration has resulted in net
losses, which have been particularly large in the early 1980s. In the first
half of the 1980s the natural increase of the population in Ukraine has been
among the lowest in the Soviet Union, ranking with that of Latvia and
Estonia. The data for Belorussia are more favorable, but still below the all-
union average. In Moldavia, the natural increase of the population was
greater than the Soviet average.[20]

In the 1970s the Russian language continued to make inroads in all three
republics. As Table 2 indicates, the overwhelming majority of Ukrainians,
Belorussians, and Moldavians in their republics continued to identify with

their national languages, although the proportion doing so in each case decreased. While the change was insignificant among Moldavians, it was considerable among Belorussians. At the same time, there was a corresponding increase in the proportion of the population in each of the republics claiming Russian as their native language. In Belorussia, it almost doubled during the nine-year period between 1970 and 1979. Linguistic Russification has taken a heavy toll among Belorussians residing in the republic's cities. According to a Soviet source, urban Belorussians claiming Russian as their native language was 40.5% in 1979, while in the rural areas it was only 7%.[21] Perhaps the most revealing data concern the significant proportional increases in knowledge of Russian as a second language.

In contrast to the overall trends in the republics, in the capital cities of Kiev and Minsk the proportion of the indigenous nationalities grew slightly, continuing a development evident in the previous decade and reflecting the further urbanization of Ukrainians and Belorussians. Both Minsk and Kishinev claim to be the fastest growing republican capitals in the Soviet Union. The share of Ukrainians in Kiev's population increased from 64.8% to 68.7% between 1970 and 1979, and the share of Belorussians in Minsk from 65.6% to about 68.5%. Moreover, in Kiev the percentage of the population claiming Ukrainian as their native language grew from 50.7% to 52.8%, while at the same time the proportion claiming Russian dropped from 47.5% to 44.8%.[22] In this connection, it is interesting to note that although the proportion of mixed-nationality families in Ukraine is among the highest in the Soviet Union—21.9% as compared to the all-union average of 14.9% in 1979—it seems that the children of Ukrainian-Russian families in the republic's cities usually opt for Ukrainian nationality.[23] The proportion of mixed marriages is also considerable in Belorussia (20.1%) and Moldavia (21%). In Minsk, in contrast to Kiev, the percentage of Belorussians claiming Russian as their native language apparently increased from 35.4% in 1970 to 39.3% in 1979, as did the percentage of Belorussians claiming knowledge of Russian as a second language—from 51.1% to over 54%.[24]

Ukrainians, Belorussians, and Moldavians are underrepresented in their respective party organizations. The disproportions are particularly glaring in Moldavia, where the share of Russians in the party is almost twice as large as their share in the general population; the overrepresentation of Ukrainians in the Moldavian party is also considerable. The proportion of "leading cadres" in the Ukrainian party organization is slightly lower than the Ukrainian share of the general population. According to Shcherbitsky, in 1987 Ukrainians accounted for 72% of the functionaries in the Central Committee *nomenklatura*, while Russians were 25%. Several years earlier, in 1983, Ukrainians constituted 80% of the secretaries of oblast, city, and raion party committees, while Russians formed 19% of the total.[25] Although the samples are not identical—the Central Committee *nomenklatura* includes government officials, directors of large enterprises and academic institutions, heads of public organizations and creative unions, and others—the contrast between the two years is noteworthy. In this connection, it should be pointed

TABLE 3.   National Composition of Republican Communist Party Organizations
Compared with National Composition of Population (in percent)

Nationality	Ukraine		Belorussia		Moldavia	
	Party 1988	Population 1989	Party 1986	Population 1989	Party 1988	Population 1989
Titular Nationality	67.0	72.6	71.1	77.8	47.2	64.4
Russians	27.3	22.0	19.1	13.2	22.5	12.9
Others	5.7	5.4	9.8	9.0	30.3[a]	22.7[b]

Sources: "Vyprobuvanyi zahin KPRS. Kompartiia Ukrainy v tsyfrakh," Komunist
Ukrainy, 1988, no. 6, p. 20;   Kommunisticheskaia Partiia Belorussii
(Minsk: Belarus', 1986), p. 21;   and Sovetskaia Moldaviia, 6 July 1988.

[a]Of which 20.9% were Ukrainian.

[b]Of which 13.8% were Ukrainian.

out that Mark Beissinger's study of oblast first secretaries in Ukraine and the RSFSR shows that in the immediate post-Brezhnev period there was a reversal of the trend toward nativization of the provincial party elite in Ukraine.[26] In Moldavia, on the other hand, Moldavians are overrepresented in the category of "leading cadres," constituting 71% of the first secretaries of the city and raion party committees, while Russians and Ukrainians together account for 24%.[27]

Systematic data on the national composition of scientific personnel in the union republics has not been published after 1973. At that time, in their respective republics, Ukrainians constituted 50.6% of the total, Belorussians 47.6%, and Moldavians 39%. In 1975, the proportion of Moldavian scientists in the republic increased to 48.8%.[28] Data on the national composition of students at institutions of higher education in the republics are also not readily available. However, one Soviet source revealed that in the academic year 1980–81 Belorussians in the republic's institutions of higher learning formed 70.2% of the student body, a lower proportion than the Belorussian share of the general population; Russian students accounted for 20.9%, at a time when Russians formed about 12% of the population. In Moldavia, the proportion of Moldavians in the contingent of first-year university students was 64.3% in 1988, a figure almost identical with the Moldavian share of the overall population. In Ukraine, data for 1989 reveal that Ukrainians accounted for approximately 62% of the student body, which is below the Ukrainian share of the republic's population, while Russians constituted 32%. Moreover, there are significant regional differences. In the eastern oblasts, the proportion of Ukrainian students was 46%, while in the western oblasts the corresponding figure was 86%. The teaching staff at Ukrainian universities was 54% Ukrainian and 40% Russian.[29]

The Ukrainian economy has long been plagued by serious problems in two of its most important industries, ferrous metallurgy and coal mining, both of which are significant in all-union terms as well. The issues here are no different than those that characterize the Soviet economy in general, which can be briefly summed up in the formula: high investments = low outputs. In the coal industry, the situation has been exacerbated by the dangers to miners forced to move deeper and deeper into old seams in order to meet planned targets. Already at the end of the 1960s the unsafe working conditions in the Donbas prompted a group of thirty miners to address an appeal to Moscow, which resulted in the dismissal and arrest of their leader, Aleksei Nikitin. Continued abuses and the evident lack of official concern led to the emergence at the end of 1977 of the Soviet Union's first independent trade union since the 1920s. The group was led by Vladimir Klebanov, a mining engineer from the Donbas, who was incarcerated in a psychiatric institution for his troubles. By the summer of 1989, striking coal miners in Ukraine, as elsewhere in the Soviet Union, were joining political demands to longstanding economic and social grievances.

The year 1986, of course, was the year of the Chernobyl nuclear power plant disaster. The Soviet press has provided ample evidence that the disaster at Chernobyl served to intensify ecological concerns in Ukraine, most visibly among the intelligentsia. This, in turn, may account for the recent emergence of the concept of "ecology of culture," which includes elements such as awareness of one's historical past and purity of language. It cannot be excluded that Chernobyl may develop, or already has, into a Ukrainian-Russian issue, although this would be difficult to gauge accurately even under the conditions of *glasnost'*. It might be noted, however, that a leading Polish weekly took pains to point out that the defendants at the trial of Chernobyl's top management were all Russians, a fact that could not be determined from the Soviet press.[30] Certainly, the Chernobyl disaster and Moscow's continued insistence on the further development of nuclear energy in Ukraine in the face of widespread public opposition have brought into focus the outlines of a confrontational scenario that can easily transcend purely ecological issues. This was illustrated by the speeches at a demonstration in Kiev on 13 November 1988 attended by some 10,000 to 20,000 people, the first major ecological gathering in the republic.[31]

Cultural Developments

Cultural politics in Ukraine, Belorussia, and Moldavia, as elsewhere in the non-Russian republics, have been conditioned by the Soviet determination to forge a single "Soviet people." But there is an added dimension to Soviet nationalities policy in the two Slavic republics. Because for long historic periods large portions of Ukrainian and Belorussian territories had been joined to Russia, and because of the similarity of the languages, Soviet ideologists have increasingly come to view Ukrainians and Belorussians in terms of a special relationship with the Russians, a link that is often characterized as "inviolable unity." An important factor contributing to this view has its roots in certain peculiarities of the historical development of Russian national identity—not the least of which is that in Russia empire-building was completed before Russians had become a modern nation—

which may well explain why many Russians, whether left or right on the political spectrum, have had such inordinate difficulties distinguishing between "us" and "them" where Ukrainians and Belorussians are concerned.[32]

In the context of Soviet nationalities policy during the past few decades, it may be useful to consider this Russian-Ukrainian-Belorussian nexus as representing a Slavic bloc based on shared linguistic and historical features, real and imagined, that functions as the nucleus or foundation for a single "Soviet people."[33] From the standpoint of Soviet policy makers, such an approach to the nationality question is not without its merits, particularly in view of the perceived challenge, both ethnodemographic and ideological, emerging from the Muslim Soviet south. The operative tools are language and historical memory.

Ethnolinguistic processes in Ukraine and Belorussia, as we have seen, have resulted in formidable inroads into the linguistic homogeneity of the two republics, a fate they share to a greater or lesser degree with the other non-Russian republics. These processes were set in motion by conscious efforts designed to establish the Russian language as the "second native language" throughout the USSR, a formula that went beyond the practical need for a lingua franca in a multinational state and incorporated a distinct ideological undercurrent. In the recent past, there has been no lack of examples from the writings of Soviet experts to the effect that the Russian language serves "to cement the unity of Soviet culture" or functions as an "effective accelerator of the convergence of nations," all of which illustrate the fact that the Russian language in the non-Russian republics was seen to perform a *political* function.[34] The impact of Soviet language policy has been felt in the schools and universities, in press and book publication practices, in the theaters and cinema, and in the daily business of the party and state bureaucracies. In Ukraine, it has even produced a new "language" within segments of the Ukrainian urban and rural population who wish to improve their standing in society by attempting to speak Russian. The result, the so-called *surzhyk*, is a bastardized form of both Russian and Ukrainian.

Concern about the fate of the Ukrainian language was particularly evident during the debate over Khrushchev's school reform of 1958–59, which was correctly perceived as a serious threat because it deprived the national language of its status as an obligatory subject of study. In the 1960s language issues were raised by the intelligentsia, who benefited from the tacit support of Shelest and like-minded party officials. There was even a plan to Ukrainianize the system of higher education in Ukraine from above. The arrests of Ukrainian intellectuals and Shelest's dismissal in early 1972 inaugurated what might be termed the Ukrainian stagnation. Shcherbitsky and his ideological secretary launched a cultural pogrom that included attacks on supporters of the Ukrainian language. Ukrainian *samizdat* sources reported a high-level decision gradually to transform scholarly journals into Russian-language publications. Whereas in the past the congresses of the Ukrainian Writers' Union served as important forums for criticism of official language policy, the 1976 meeting was conspicuously silent on this issue. Although on occasion individuals such as Oles' Honchar did not shrink from arguing that the Ukrainian language would continue to remain a viable literary and scientific tool, the 1970s were but a pale reflection of the preceding decade. At the end of 1978 the USSR Council of Ministers adopted a decree on improving the teaching of Russian in non-Russian schools, and in 1979 a second all-union conference on the subject was held within a four-year period. In Ukraine, among other measures, the teaching of Russian was now to begin with the first grade in all schools with Ukrainian as the language of instruction. At the end of 1982, Yurii Andropov placed the notion of merger (*sliianie*) of nations on the agenda, and in 1983 the Politburo considered additional measures to improve the study and teaching of Russian in Soviet schools, with an appropriate party and government decree following.

What have been the results of these policies? Whereas in the mid-1960s the proportion of schoolchildren in Ukraine being taught in Ukrainian was 62%, even then a proportion significantly lower than the share of Ukrainians in the republic's population, by 1987 this figure had dropped to 50.5%. At the same time, instruction in Russian encompassed 48.7% of the school-children, while two decades earlier it had accounted for 37.2%. In the capital of Kiev only about 23% of the children were taught in Ukrainian—this while 68.7% of the capital's population claimed Ukrainian nationality and 52.8% designated Ukrainian as their native language in the 1979 census. Of the total of 274 schools in Kiev, only thirty-four were Ukrainian-language institutions. In twenty-four of the twenty-five oblast centers, including the city of Kiev, Russian-language schools accounted for 72% of the total, while the remainder were Ukrainian and mixed Ukrainian-Russian schools. If one considers that in practice the mixed schools were actually Russian-language schools slated for official reorganization as such, then Russian-language schools accounted for 84% of the total, leaving 16% of the schools with Ukrainian as the language of instruction in the republic's twenty-four major cities. By 1988, according to ideological secretary Yurii Il'chenko, 50.6% of the schoolchildren in the republic were taught in Russian, while the proportion of pupils taught in Ukrainian had slipped to "almost half."[35]

In Belorussia, the situation has become even more precarious from the standpoint of the Belorussians. In the mid-1960s, the proportion of school-children taught in Belorussian was only 51.6% at a time when the Belorussian share of the population was about 81%. By the 1972–73 school year, the proportion shifted in favor of Russian, which was now the language of instruction for 51.4% of the pupils. In the republic's urban centers, however, 97.6% of the schoolchildren were taught in Russian—that is, practically all urban schools in Belorussia were Russian-language schools. It is important to note that this was at a time when the republic's Belorussian population was moving in large numbers to the cities. In 1979, the Belorussian minister of education reported a further proportional increase in Russian-language instruction, which now encompassed 61% of the schoolchildren. The same year, a noted Russian linguist was able to assure members of the USSR Academy of Sciences that there was no Belorussian-language teaching in

TABLE 4.   Percentage of Single-Issue Print Runs of Newspapers in Language of Titular
Nationality Compared with National Composition of Population (in percent)

Republic	Print Run		Titular Nationality	
	1960	1982	1959	1979
Ukraine	72.5	66.1	76.8	73.6
Belorussia	52.2	32.4	81.1	79.3
Moldavia	57.3	55.1	65.4	63.9

Source: Ann Sheehy, "Belorussian Scholar Upholds Importance of Nationhood and
National Languages," Radio Liberty Research Bulletin, RL 204/84
(23 May 1984).

Minsk. As of early 1989, 77.7% of the schoolchildren in Belorussia were taught in Russian and only 20.6% in Belorussian.[36]

In the mid-1960s, 66% of Moldavia's schoolchildren were being taught in Moldavian, at the time a higher figure than in Ukraine or Belorussia, and almost identical to the Moldavian share of the general population. By early 1989 this figure had dropped to 59.5%. In the schools of Kishinev the corresponding figure was even lower, 34.3%. A similar situation prevailed in the preschool institutions, where 52.6% of the children were taught in Moldavian.[37]

A picture similar to that in education emerges from a survey of press and book publication policies. Between 1960 and 1982, for example, the share of single-issue press runs of newspapers in the indigenous language in Ukraine, Belorussia, and Moldavia experienced the largest proportional decreases of all the non-Russian republics. In 1987, the proportion of books and brochures published in the national language was: Ukraine 22.1%, Belorussia 12.5%, and Moldavia 35.3%. At the end of the 1970s and in the early 1980s Belorussia ranked lowest among all the non-Russian republics in per capita publication of books and brochures in the language of the titular nationality. Indeed, Belorussia was the only union republic where the total edition of books printed in the indigenous language was lower in 1982 than in 1940. In Ukraine, the percentage of scholarly journals published by the Academy of Sciences in Russian increased from 19% to 76.2% between 1969 and 1980, while the proportion of Ukrainian-language journals decreased correspondingly. By 1989, only eight out of forty-nine academic journals, or 16.3%, were published in Ukrainian. Circulation of the local-language periodical press suffered from restrictions imposed on non-Russian publications in 1975 throughout the Soviet Union.[38]

Although language policies have always been a sensitive and sometimes volatile issue, the encroachment on the historical memories of the non-Russian peoples probably posed a more serious threat to their national consciousness. As noted earlier, this issue is particularly significant for the Ukrainians and Belorussians. It is instructive to recall that one of the major charges leveled at Shelest in 1973 was his alleged glorification of the pre-Soviet Ukrainian past. After Shelest's fall, there was a major campaign to root out "glorification of the past" and "one-sided portrayals of historical figures and events" in Ukrainian literature and scholarship. A number of non-periodical historical journals ceased publication, books were suppressed, scholarly institutions were "restructured," and there were dismissals from institutes and universities. At the same time, a major effort was made to emphasize the important role played by the Russian language and the Russian people in the historical development of Ukrainians and Belorussians. In Ukraine, the celebrations in 1979 marking the 325th anniversary of "reunification" with Russia and Kiev's 1500th jubilee in 1982 were conducted as major cultural events. The main themes of these extravaganzas were "eternal unity" with the Russian nation and the common origins of Ukrainians, Belorussians, and Russians from the "single ancient Rus' nationality" with its own language and state. The notion that Russians, Ukrainians, and Belorussians are bonded in a special relationship was widely propagated again during the official celebrations marking the Millennium of Christianity in the summer of 1988. Yet, at the same time the authorities and the Russian Orthodox Church made it plain that there was no room for distinct Ukrainian or Belorussian dimensions to the Millennium. Indeed, the main celebrations were held in Moscow rather than in Kiev, focusing heavily on *Russian* Christianity and its role in the development of *Russian* culture and *Russian* statehood.[39] This, in turn, provoked a reaction from Ukrainians, who organized unofficial millennial celebrations and voiced their dissatisfaction in the press.[40]

Although there were some signs of a relaxation in cultural policies in Ukraine after 1979, it was not until *glasnost'* and *perestroika* became the order of the day under Gorbachev that there has been any serious movement in this direction. This was reflected first and foremost in the wide-ranging criticism, primarily by writers and other intellectuals, of the existing situation with regard to the national languages. In the summer and fall of 1986 the literary and cultural press in Ukraine and Belorussia began to devote increasingly more attention to language issues. Demands were raised for revision of existing legislation governing public education; Ukrainianization and Belorussianization of the entire educational system, from kindergarten through university; and constitutional guarantees for the national language similar to those in the Transcaucasian republics. In December 1986 a group of Belorussian cultural figures sent a letter to Gorbachev emphasizing the threat to the existence of the Belorussian language and proposing a long list of reforms. Another appeal from Belorussia with 134 signatures was addressed to Gorbachev and *Pravda* in June 1987. Several prominent Russian writers publicly voiced their support for the concerns of their Ukrainian and Belorussian colleagues, and Russians in Ukraine have organized a group in support of the Ukrainian language and culture. Pressure for language reform in Moldavia, particularly the demand to replace the Cyrillic alphabet with Latin, initially resulted in two joint party and government decrees in 1987 providing for the improvement of the study of Moldavian and Russian in the republic. The following year the Bureau of the Central Committee of the Moldavian party issued a decree "On Measures to Intensify the Study of the History and Development of the Moldavian Language," and the

Presidium of the Moldavian Supreme Soviet formed a special Interdepartmental Commission to implement this decision. Steps were also taken to
satisfy the cultural and language demands of the Turkic-speaking Gagauz
and the Bulgarian minorities, including bi-weekly inserts in these languages
to the party and government daily *Sovetskaia Moldaviia*.[41] Although no action
was taken in either Kiev or Minsk along the lines of the Moldavian language
decrees, in August 1987 the Central Committee of the Ukrainian party
adopted a resolution on the nationality question that devoted considerable
attention to the language issue and promised measures for improvement.
At about the same time, the Belorussian ideological secretary met with
writers and outlined a long list of improvements affecting the teaching and
study of the Belorussian language in the republic's schools.

The literary intelligentsia in all three republics consistently publicized the
language issue through the press organs of their respective Writers' Unions,
focusing, among other things, on the need for state status for the native
language and, in Moldavia, on the reinstitution of the Latin script. By 1988–
89, the authorities in all three republics, faced with mounting pressure, were
making concessions. At the May 1988 Plenum of the Belorussian Central
Committee, party leader Sokolov cited a decree of the party's Bureau on
improving the study of Belorussian language and literature in schools,
technical schools, and institutions of higher learning, and in September the
Bureau approved a long-range program for raising the status of Belorussian
in the educational system and popularizing the Belorussian cultural heritage.
In Ukraine, two commissions of the Supreme Soviet, citing appeals from
the citizenry, resolved in November 1988 to approach the Presidium of the
Supreme Soviet in Kiev regarding an amendment to the republic's constitution
that would grant Ukrainian state language status. Two months later, the
Central Committee of the Ukrainian party issued a wide-ranging decree on
nationality relations that was almost entirely devoted to the language question.
Soon thereafter, in February 1989, it was announced that the Ukrainian
Supreme Soviet had formed a "working group" to prepare a draft amendment
to the republican constitution as well as a draft law on languages. In both
Ukraine and Belorussia, mass organizations in support of the native language—the Taras Shevchenko Ukrainian Language Society and the Belorussian Language Society—convened their founding congresses in February
and June 1989, respectively.[42] The draft "Law on Languages in the Ukrainian
SSR," which recognized Ukrainian as the state language, was published in
September and enacted into law essentially unchanged after a two-month
republic-wide discussion. In Belorussia, a Supreme Soviet commission on
the preparation of language legislation was formed only in August and was
still in the process of preparing drafts in October.[43]

Developments in Moldavia took a rather different turn. Although authorities had made some initial concessions, in December 1988 the Moldavian
party Central Committee issued a set of lengthy Theses that rejected the
three main demands of language activists—namely, state status; recognition
that Moldavian and Romanian are identical languages; and the switch to

the Latin alphabet. In the aftermath of protests and public demonstrations, the party leadership was forced to retreat and the official position was repudiated. On 30 December it was announced that the Interdepartmental Commission had resolved to propose state status for the Moldavian language; the drafting of laws and decrees on language; and the transfer to the Latin script.[44] In early 1989, Kishinev witnessed several large demonstrations in support of the language issue, which continued after the first set of draft laws was published for discussion at the end of March. By late summer, however, after the publication in May of the draft law on the changeover to the Latin alphabet, Russian-speakers organized protest strikes in an attempt to influence the voting in the republic's Supreme Soviet, while supporters of the proposed legislation staged counter-rallies. In the final analysis, however, the draft legislation and constitutional amendments were passed into law.[45]

A new development, reviving practices of the 1920s and early 1930s, has been the increased attention devoted to the linguistic and cultural needs of national minorities in the republics, which is evident throughout the Soviet Union and has been formalized in the CPSU's platform on nationalities policy adopted at the September 1989 Central Committee Plenum. In Ukraine and Belorussia, representatives of the Polish and Jewish minorities were among the first to establish their social-cultural societies. In Ukraine, there were about thirty such organizations in mid-1989. At the same time, Ukrainians in Moscow, Leningrad, and Riga have organized groups to promote national traditions. The language concessions to the Gagauz and Bulgarians in Moldavia have already been noted. Similar steps have been taken in Ukraine, particularly with regard to the Crimean Tatars. The Hungarian, Moldavian, and Polish minorities in the republic are served by more than 160 schools with native-language instruction, and more than five hundred groups have been formed for the elective study of other minority languages.[46] The national and cultural rights of Ukraine's minorities were unequivocally recognized by the burgeoning Popular Movement of Ukraine for *Perestroika*, or "Rukh." At its constituent congress in September 1989, Rukh adopted special resolutions to this effect addressed "To All Non-Ukrainians in Ukraine" and "To the Russian Population of Ukraine." A separate resolution "Against Anti-Semitism" advocated full civic and religious rights for Jews, the right to teach and study Yiddish and Hebrew, and the creation of Jewish societies and schools, a scholarly research institute for Jewish history and culture, theaters, publishing houses, and synagogues.[47]

Significant progress has been made with regard to a more honest portrayal of historical events and personalities, which was perhaps inevitable in view of the ferment among Russian intellectuals that was set in motion by the renewed criticism of Stalin. It must be emphasized, however, that *glasnost'* on historical themes in Ukraine, Belorussia, and Moldavia is still weaker than in Moscow, Leningrad, or the Baltic republics. Nonetheless, the press has raised the sensitive issues of "excesses" in the course of collectivization and dekulakization, and the famine in Ukraine in 1932–33 is frequently characterized as "artificial." At the end of 1987, even Shcherbitsky referred to "serious food supply difficulties in late 1932–early 1933, and famine in a number of rural areas."[48] In Belorussia, the discovery in the spring of 1988 of mass graves of hundreds of thousands of victims of Stalin's NKVD executioners in the Kurapaty woods near Minsk had the effect of rapidly mobilizing public opinion in the republic. The widespread demands for a full accounting of the physical and spiritual devastation wrought by Stalinism resulted in mass demonstrations in the streets and open conflict between the Belorussian intelligentsia and the party.[49] Cultural figures in Moldavia also called for a fuller and more forthright account of the Stalin period, recalling also the deportations of the local population after 1940. In Kiev, articles have been devoted to such important and controversial literary and political figures as Volodymyr Vynnychenko, Mykola Khvyl'ovyi, and Mykhailo Hrushevs'kyi, who were ignored or harshly criticized in the past, and their works are being published with increasing frequency. At the same time, it must be emphasized that filling in the "blank pages" of the non-Russian past has not been an easy process, particularly in the first years of *glasnost'*. Thus, a book of essays on Belorussian history from the earliest times to the mid-nineteenth century was severely criticized in 1986 in the crudest fashion on the pages of *Kommunist Belorussii* for a variety of ideological sins. Among them were the author's alleged "denial of the single origin of the Belorussian and Russian peoples"; his purported attempt to prove that "the reunification of Belorussia with the Russian state was historically unjustified and did not have a progressive character"; and, according to the reviewer, the author's emphasis on "the tyranny of Tsar Nicholas I and Russification", while remaining silent about "the progressive forces of Russia and their influence on [the development of] free thought and culture in Belorussia."[50] Moreover, while in Moscow it was possible to publish the works of Tsarist historians like Karamzin in mass editions without any apparent difficulties, in Kiev both the party and establishment historians were determined to prevent the rehabilitation of Mykhailo Hrushevs'kyi, a socialist and a member of the Soviet Academy of Sciences, who is universally recognized as the architect of modern Ukrainian historiography. At a meeting of Ukrainian historians in Kiev in early 1988, one of the participants roundly criticized attempts to rehabilitate Hrushevs'kyi, referring specifically to the decision releasing his works from the *spetsfond* of the Central Scientific Library of the Ukrainian Academy of Sciences. A major article criticizing attempts to rehabilitate the Ukrainian historian was published in the party and government daily *Radians'ka Ukraina*, and it was later praised by Shcherbitsky at a session of the Ukrainian Central Committee.[51]

Dissent

Dissent focusing on national and human rights has been a more or less permanent feature of the Ukrainian political scene since the late 1950s. Although dealt a severe blow by what has become known as the General

Pogrom of 1972–73, the protest movement in Ukraine was not suppressed. Individuals and underground groups continued their activities, including the preparation and circulation of *samizdat*. Indeed, in the spring of 1974 activists succeeded in bringing out no. 7–8 of the underground journal *Ukrainian Herald*. It was prepared by a different group of editors and was more radical in tone than the first six issues (1970–72), reflecting the impact of the General Pogrom. The bulk of Ukrainian *samizdat*, however, was now coming from the labor camp writings of Ukrainian political prisoners such as Vyacheslav Chornovil, Valentyn Moroz, Vasyl' Stus, Ievhen Sverstiuk, Ivan Svitlychnyi, Danylo Shumuk, and scores of others. The 1970s witnessed a significant influx of Ukrainians into the Gulag, and by the end of that decade the well-known Russian human rights activist Yurii Orlov reported that 30–40 percent of political prisoners in the Mordvinian and Ural camps were Ukrainians.

The situation in Ukraine following the arrests, trials, and purges of the early 1970s is described in a thoughtful essay by Yurii Badz'o, written in the form of an open letter to Soviet authorities shortly before his arrest in April 1979. His analysis of the consequences of Soviet nationalities policy in Ukraine ranks with Dzyuba's essay as one of the most important contributions to Ukrainian underground literature. But unlike Dzyuba, Badz'o is not burdened by the Marxist-Leninist approach to nationalities policy. His conceptual framework is defined by the conviction that the historical existence of nations has three aspects—the past, present, and future. Taken together, these "three parameters of reality" form a single psychological entity. Badz'o argues that Soviet nationalities policy, by destroying memory of Ukraine's past and eliminating its language and culture, set out to preclude the future existence of the Ukrainian nation, which was now in a "state of siege."[52] His pessimism was entirely justified. In 1979, Ukrainian rights activists were in the midst of another major KGB frontal attack directed primarily against members and sympathizers of the Ukrainian Helsinki Group.

The group was formed in November 1976 by nine persons headed by the writer Mykola Rudenko. Their representative in Moscow was General Petro Grigorenko. It was the second such organization set up in the Soviet Union to monitor implementation of the 1975 Helsinki Accords after the Moscow Helsinki Group, and most of its members were former political prisoners. Its membership represented various generations and included individuals with very different backgrounds ranging from veteran activists in clandestine organizations to youthful newcomers. The establishment of the Ukrainian Helsinki Group marked a new stage in the development of Ukrainian dissent: from a spontaneous movement in defense of cultural and national identity to an organized forum for the pursuit of human and national rights.[53] The authorities reacted very quickly. In February 1977 Rudenko and Oleksii Tykhyi were arrested and subsequently sentenced to long terms in the camps. Two other founding members of the group were arrested in April and a fourth in December of that year and later sentenced.

In the meantime, the group's membership was replenished by new adherents. The well-known writer Oles' Berdnyk, also a founding member, succeeded Rudenko as chairman. But Berdnyk, too, was arrested and sentenced in 1979. By mid-1980, the Ukrainian Helsinki Group was essentially destroyed through a systematic campaign of arrests, persecution, and exile. Of its thirty-seven members, twenty-seven had been arrested, seven had emigrated, and only three were at liberty. Later, many group members were arrested and sentenced either while still serving their terms or in internal exile. Unlike its Moscow counterpart, however, the Ukrainian Helsinki Group did not declare its dissolution and continued to exist in the camps. The editors of the renewed *Ukrainian Herald*, the first issue of which appeared in August 1987, announced that they had also joined the group and that their journal was its official organ.

The repressions of the late 1970s and early 1980s affected not only the Helsinki monitors, but anyone who fell into the broad and arbitrarily interpreted category of engaging in "anti-Soviet" activities. A case in point is the writer Helii Sniehir'ov, who was expelled from the Writers' Union and later arrested for preparing a documented study of the Stalinist persecution of Ukrainian intellectuals in the late 1920s and 1930s. In December 1978 he died in a clinic while in custody. In May 1979 the immensely popular young composer and lyricist Volodymyr Ivasiuk was found dead near Lviv, his badly mutilated body hanging from a tree. The Moscow-based *Chronicle of Current Events* reported that he had conflicts with the authorities and had been summoned by the KGB. Ivasiuk's funeral is reported to have turned into a massive demonstration of national solidarity by about 10,000 people. In the same year, the authorities broke up an underground organization in Western Ukraine called the Ukrainian National Front, which numbered about forty people. This group put out two issues each of a journal also called the *Ukrainian Herald* and an almanac entitled *Insight* [Prozrinnia]. Another conspiratorial group, the Ukrainian Patriotic Movement, surfaced in January 1980, and the following year five young intellectuals were arrested in Kiev for distributing leaflets marking the anniversary of the mass arrests in 1972.[54] The harsh conditions in the camps resulted in the deaths of a number of Ukrainian political prisoners, among them Valerii Marchenko (38), Vasyl' Stus (47), and Oleksii Tykhyi (57) in 1984–85. Some activists were either exiled abroad or permitted to emigrate, including Leonid Plyushch (1976), Nadia Svitlychna (1978), Valentyn Moroz (1979), Sviatoslav Karavans'kyi (1979) and his wife Nina Strokata (1979), Danylo Shumuk (1987), Mykola Rudenko and his wife Raisa (1987), Petro Ruban (1988), and Fr. Vasyl' Romaniuk (1988).

In the early 1980s, the authorities in Ukraine were also confronted with a new challenge in the form of an organized movement for the legalization of the Ukrainian Catholic (Uniate) Church, which had been forced to "reunite" with the Russian Orthodox Church in 1946. Ukrainian Catholics are largely concentrated in the western regions of the republic, where the "Catacomb Church" has been functioning illegally for many years. The struggle for legalization took a new turn in September 1982 with the formation of the Initiative Group for the Defense of the Rights of Believers and the Church, led by Yosyp Terelia. Terelia was arrested soon thereafter, but after his release at the end of 1983 the group began to circulate the *Chronicle of the Catholic Church in Ukraine* [Khronika Katolyts'koi Tserkvy v Ukraini]. Certainly a major factor in the activist position taken by the Initiative Group has been the continued support for Ukrainian Catholics from the Slavic Pope, John Paul II, support that has also proven to be a major stumbling block in relations between the Vatican and the Russian Orthodox Church. In June 1987 the Vatican released a document signed by Terelia and twenty others addressed to Gorbachev expressing the hope that relations between Moscow and the Ukrainian Catholics could be improved in the context of "the new political policy of the Soviet government." Not long after, the Western press reported a statement addressed to the Vatican and signed by two Ukrainian underground bishops, a group of clergy, and 174 laymen announcing that they had abandoned their conspiratorial existence. In September 1987 Terelia was permitted to leave for the West, presumably in the hope that this would weaken the Initiative Group. However, his place was taken by Ivan Hel', a veteran political prisoner, who subsequently presented the USSR Supreme Soviet with still another petition pleading the Ukrainian Catholic cause. The campaign of the Ukrainian Catholics for the restoration and legalization of their Church received support from several Russian Orthodox activists and, in the summer of 1988, from Andrei Sakharov. Pope John Paul II is believed to have raised the issue once again in his letter to Gorbachev, delivered by the Vatican's secretary of state, Cardinal Casaroli, during the Millennium celebrations in Moscow in June 1988. At that time representatives of the Vatican, including Cardinals Casaroli and Willebrands, held an unprecedented meeting with two bishops and three priests of the underground Church in a Moscow hotel. Yet, despite the improved atmosphere in Vatican-Kremlin relations and the liberalization of religious life in the USSR, until recently the Soviet government and especially the Moscow patriarchate appeared determined in their refusal to yield on the issue of a legal status for Ukrainian Catholics.[55] Only in the fall of 1989—in the wake of more frequent and increasingly massive public demonstrations, open rejection of the Russian Orthodox Church's authority by individual priests and entire parishes, and a meeting on 1 December 1989 between Pope John Paul II and Mikhail Gorbachev at the Vatican—did some movement toward legalization of the Uniate Church appear possible.

The relative lack of dissident activity and the paucity of *samizdat* in Belorussia, combined with the widespread linguistic Russification of the indigenous population, frequently led outside observers to conclude that Belorussian national consciousness is essentially nonexistent. Recent events in that republic have clearly proven this assumption to be false. Moreover, although in the past dissident activity had been sporadic at best, it was not altogether absent from the Belorussian political scene. In the 1960s and 1970s, reports reached the West about conspiratorial student groups and petitions, and in 1972 it was learned that a *samizdat* periodical called *Leaflet*

[Listok] had begun to appear irregularly. There have also been reports in the *Chronicle of Current Events* about arrests and demonstrations.[56] A partial list of Belorussian political prisoners presented to the 1977 U.S. Congressional hearings on the implementation of the Helsinki Accords identified fifty-eight individuals. The best known among them was Mikhail Kukobaka, a worker who was first arrested in 1970. Kukobaka had defended workers' rights and had also spoken out on national issues. He is the author of several *samizdat* texts, including "The Stolen Fatherland."[57] The anonymous essay *Letter to a Russian Friend*, which addresses the language question, was completed in early 1977 and later published in the West. The same issue is at the center of Aleh Bembel's *Native Language and Moral-Aesthetic Progress*, which appears to have been compiled in 1979–81 and was made available in the West in 1985. More recent contributions to Belorussian *samizdat* are the two letters to Gorbachev concerning language and cultural grievances.

Under the impact of *glasnost'*, dissident or unofficial activities have found a new vehicle for expression through so-called "informal groups," many of which occupy a precarious position in the gray area between legality and illegality. Several such groups focusing on nationality issues have been formed in Ukraine, Belorussia, and Moldavia. In Kiev, the Ukrainian Culturological Club, which emerged in August 1987, was subjected to severe criticism in the press. Led by Serhii Naboka, who was active in dissident activities in the latter half of the 1970s, its members organized discussions and seminars on topics that continued to remain beyond the scope of *glasnost'*. The activist core of the Ukrainian Culturological Club included well-known dissidents and former political prisoners. This, together with the group's independent-minded and iconoclastic approach to contemporary national issues, earned it the ire of the authorities. Other groups, like Zelenyi Svit (Green World), which was concerned with ecology, and Tovarystvo Leva (Lion Society) in Lviv, which focused on the preservation of historical and cultural monuments, were affiliated with official organizations and therefore enjoyed a measure of support from the party. Among the organizers of the previously mentioned mass demonstrations in Kiev were the Spadshchyna (Heritage) Club and a student group at Kiev University called Hromada (Community).

The most dramatic confrontations between proponents of change and the authorities have been in Lviv in Western Ukraine, which has been the scene of a series of mass public demonstrations since mid-June 1988. Veteran activists and former political prisoners Vyacheslav Chornovil, the brothers Mykhailo and Bohdan Horyn', Iryna Kalynets', and others have been joined by newcomers like Ivan Makar and Yaroslav Put'ko in mobilizing public sentiment in defense of national rights. The first of these rallies, on 13 June, coincided with the selection of delegates to the Nineteenth Party Conference in Moscow, which quickly emerged as one of the major issues dividing the public and local authorities. A much larger demonstration was held on 7 July. The party responded with police action and harassment of activists. Criminal proceedings were initiated against Chornovil and the Horyn' brothers in July. On 4 August, the militia and special units brutally dispersed Lviv residents who had gathered once again to hear speakers near the Ivan Franko monument. Earlier in the day authorities arrested Makar, who had played a prominent role in the Lviv meetings. This, in turn, led to additional protests, and Makar was released in early November.[58]

Lviv is also the organizational center of the newly formed Ukrainian Helsinki Union, a confederation of human rights groups founded on the basis of the Ukrainian Helsinki Group in the summer of 1988.[59] Its leader is the long-time political prisoner Levko Lukianenko, who was released from internal exile in the RSFSR in December 1988. Ukrainian activists have also played a leading role in coordinating the national democratic movements in the republics. On 11–12 June 1988 the Inter-Nationality Committee in Defense of Political Prisoners convened a conference in Lviv attended by representatives from Estonia, Latvia, Lithuania, Georgia, and Ukraine; a second conference was held in Riga on 24–25 September.

In Belorussia, the Talaka Historical-Cultural Association and the Tuteishyia Society of Young Writers have been in the forefront of unofficial patriotic activities. The two groups organized a public meeting in Minsk in November 1987, prompting a warning against the dangers of "nationalism" from *Sovetskaia Belorussiia*. And in Kishinev the local press launched an attack on the Alex Mateevici Literary-Musical Club and the Democratic Movement to Support *Perestroika* in August 1988, accusing their leaders of stirring up anti-Russian attitudes. The Belorussian and Moldavian unofficial groups have focused on language and cultural rights and, increasingly, have taken the lead in the anti-Stalin campaign in their republics.[60]

But the most important new groups to make their appearance on the political scene in all three republics are the popular fronts. These crystallized in 1989 and held their founding congresses in the course of the summer and early fall. The authorities in Kiev, Minsk, and Kishinev viewed these fronts with suspicion and hostility as contenders in the struggle for power. Indeed, the Belorussian "Renewal Popular Front" was forced to hold its constituent congress in Vilnius, Lithuania, because of opposition from the Belorussian party leadership. Having come into being, however, the three popular fronts are now admitted by the republican authorities to be political realities.[61]

Conclusion

In May 1972 Ukrainian party leader Shelest was ousted because he was either unable or unwilling to implement Moscow's policies. Under the new conditions of *glasnost'* and *perestroika*, the conventional wisdom had been that Shcherbitsky faced the same prospect and for the same reason. The circumstances, of course, were different. Then it was a question of eliminating a movement from below that sought to publicize the effects of a "braking mechanism" on the development of the nation that was directed from above.

More recently the former first secretary of the Ukrainian party was having difficulties with a movement initiated from above that had been enthusiastically embraced from below. Although the settings were different, the issues remained the same—language, culture, history, and, ultimately, the fate of the ethnos.

Thus, it is not surprising that now, as then, the intelligentsia, whether established writers or harassed "informals," is preoccupied first and foremost with nationality issues. During the period of "stagnation," the cultural elites were effectively silenced, although many continued to work under the difficult conditions imposed by the regime. The dissidents, as they came to be known, never ceased pressing that regime with their concerns, appeals, and demands. In 1972, Chornovil was compiling and editing material for the *Ukrainian Herald*, an enterprise that he has resumed once again. Then it was a highly conspiratorial affair; now the *Ukrainian Herald* seeks recognition from the party, and its editors openly assume responsibility for its contents. In a very real sense, the "new thinking" has served to highlight the old issues. This is no less true for Belorussia and Moldavia, where it was casually assumed that because problems were not readily apparent they did not exist.

The continuities do not end here. As the Soviet Union moves into the 1990s, a solution to the nationality question remains as elusive as it was ten or twenty years ago. True, references to the mythical "Soviet people" have become muted and are heard much less frequently. The first steps have been taken to reverse linguistic Russification and pave the way for genuine bilingualism. And, of course, Gorbachev and his adherents have, in effect, admitted that the theoretical baggage of Soviet nationalities policy has proven to be a monumental failure. Nonetheless, thus far the party has failed to come up with a response to what is increasingly becoming a paramount problem. Moreover, developments in Ukraine, Belorussia, and Moldavia, where the party leadership has been largely successful in resisting the kinds of changes articulated by local elites, justify raising the question to what extent Moscow is in fact interested in having these issues on the agenda in these republics. Could it be that the present CPSU leaders, like their predecessors, consider the "inviolable unity" of the Russians, Ukrainians, and Belorussians as non-negotiable? At this juncture, it is impossible to suggest a definitive answer. However, developments demonstrate that *glasnost'* and *perestroika* in nationality affairs can vary radically in terms of results from region to region. Stated differently and at the risk of gross oversimplification, the historical experience of the Estonians, Latvians, and Lithuanians has made possible advances in national mobilization and consolidation that are still beyond the reach of Ukrainians or Belorussians. In Kiev, Lviv, and Minsk the intelligentsia is currently in the process of building national coalitions with which to confront the center, a stage that has very likely been completed in Tallinn, Riga, and Vilnius. Clearly, Moscow is aware of these differences, and they will continue to be reflected in Soviet nationalities policy.

Notes

1. The concept of the Soviet West is utilized in the case studies assembled in Roman Szporluk, ed., *The Influence of East Europe and the Soviet West on the USSR* (New York: Praeger, 1975), and Ralph S. Clem, ed., *The Soviet West: Interplay between Nationality and Social Organization* (New York: Praeger, 1975). See also Roman Solchanyk, "Poland and the Soviet West," in S. Enders Wimbush, ed., *Soviet Nationalities in Strategic Perspective* (New York: St. Martin's Press, 1985), pp. 158–80.

2. Iu. V. Bromlei and M. I. Kulichenko, "Natsional'noe i internatsional'noe v obraze zhizni sovetskogo cheloveka," in Ts. A. Stepanian and A. K. Karypkulov, eds., *Internatsional'noe i natsional'noe v sotsialisticheskom obraze zhizni sovetskogo naroda* (Moscow: Nauka, 1985), p. 52.

3. On the historical and political aspects of the "Bessarabian question," see, for example, Robert R. King, *Minorities under Communism: Nationalities as a Source of Tension among Balkan Communist States* (Cambridge, MA: Harvard University Press, 1973), chap. 11 ("'Historical' Debates: Bessarabia"). On the linguistic dimension, see Michael Bruchis, *One Step Back, Two Steps Forward: On the Language Policy of the Communist Party of the Soviet Union in the National Republics (Moldavian: A Look Back, a Survey, and Perspectives, 1924–1980)* (Boulder, CO: East European Monographs, 1982).

4. See the documentation compiled by Michael Browne, ed., *Ferment in the Ukraine* (London and Basingstoke: Macmillan, 1971).

5. See Roman Solchanyk, "Politics and the National Question in the Post-Shelest Period," in Bohdan Krawchenko, ed., *Ukraine after Shelest* (Edmonton: Canadian Institute of Ukrainian Studies, 1983), pp. 5ff; and Dmytro Tabachnyk's interview with Shelest, "Bez kul'tury nemaie narodu," *Kyiv*, 1989, no. 10, pp. 90–110.

6. For a discussion of this review, see Lowell Tillett, "Ukrainian Nationalism and the Fall of Shelest," *Slavic Review*, vol. 34, no. 4 (December 1975), pp. 752–68. See also Jaroslaw Pelenski, "Shelest and His Period in Soviet Ukraine (1963–1972): A Revival of Controlled Ukrainian Autonomism," in Peter J. Potichnyj, ed., *Ukraine in the Seventies* (Oakville, Ont.: Mosaic Press, 1975), pp. 283–305.

7. For a detailed analysis of these and related developments, see Borys Lewytzkyj, *Politics and Society in Soviet Ukraine 1953–1980* (Edmonton: Canadian Institute of Ukrainian Studies, 1984), pp. 147–68.

8. Yaroslav Bilinsky, "Politics, Purge, and Dissent in the Ukraine since the Fall of Shelest," in Ihor Kamenetsky, ed., *Nationalism and Human Rights in the USSR: Processes of Modernization* (Littleton, CO: Libraries Unlimited, 1977), pp. 168–70.

9. Quoted by Jan Zaprudnik, "Developments in Belorussia since 1964," in George W. Simmonds, ed., *Nationalism in the USSR and Eastern Europe in the Era of Brezhnev and Kosygin* (Detroit: The University of Detroit Press, 1977). p. 106.

10. Solchanyk, "Poland and the Soviet West," p. 169, and E. Sokolov, "Za klassovuiu zorkost'," *Kommunist*, 1984, no. 4, pp. 27–36. See also Sokolov's article "Vykhovuiemo perekonanykh patriotiv-internatsionalistiv," *Komunist Ukrainy*, 1984, no. 8, p. 36. The Brest region forms part of the western Belorussian territories annexed from Poland in 1939.

11. See Stephen Fischer-Galati, "The Moldavian Soviet Republic in Soviet Domestic and Foreign Policy," in Szporluk, *Influence of East Europe*, pp. 246–48.

12. See the speech by Viktor Smirnov, the former Moldavian party second secretary, at a plenum of the Central Committee of the Moldavian Komsomol as reported in *Sovetskaia Moldaviia*, 31 May 1987.

13. For details, see Roman Solchanyk, "Chernobyl: The Political Fallout in Ukraine," *Journal of Ukrainian Studies*, vol. 11, no. 1 (Summer 1986), pp. 20–34.

14. *Radians'ka Ukraina*, 25 March 1987 and 23 January 1988; and V. V. Shcherbitskii, "Kadry v usloviiakh perestroiki: Opyt, problemy," *Voprosy istorii KPSS*, 1988, no. 2, p. 5.

15. *Pravda Ukrainy*, 21 May 1989.

16. See Roman Solchanyk, "Ukrainian Party Plenum Emphasizes Continuity," Radio Liberty, *Report on the USSR*, vol. 1, no. 42 (20 October 1989), pp. 17–19.

17. See Roman Solchanyk, "Red Storm Rising in the Ukraine," *Wall Street Journal*, 6 June 1989.

18. On developments in Moldavia, see Vladimir Socor, "Politics of the Language Question Heating Up in Soviet Moldavia," Radio Liberty, *Report on the USSR*, vol. 1, no. 36 (8 September 1989), pp. 33–36.

19. *Natsional'nye otnosheniia v SSSR na sovremennom etape: Na materialakh respublik Srednei Azii i Kazakhstana* (Moscow: Nauka, 1979), p. 81.

20. Iu. V. Arutiunian and Iu. V. Bromlei, eds., *Sotsial'no-kul'turnyi oblik sovetskikh natsii: Po rezul'tatam etnosotsiologicheskogo issledovaniia* (Moscow: Nauka, 1986), p. 20; Ann Sheehy, "Population Trends in the Union Republics, 1979–1984," *Radio Liberty Research Bulletin*, RL 166/85 (21 May 1985); Ann Sheehy, "Migration to RSFSR and Baltic Republics Continues," *Radio Liberty Research Bulletin*, RL 478/87 (30 November 1987).

21. Iu. V. Arutiunian and L. M. Drobizheva, *Mnogoobrazie kul'turnoi zhizni narodov SSSR* (Moscow: Mysl', 1987), p. 134.

22. The 1979 data for Kiev are taken from *Prapor komunizmu*, 10 January 1980. The national composition of Minsk in 1979 has been derived from the census data. Unfortunately, it has not been possible to derive national or linguistic affiliation for Kishinev.

23. A. A. Susokolov, *Mezhnatsional'nye braki v SSSR* (Moscow: Mysl', 1987), p. 140, and *Pravda Ukrainy*, 10 January 1981.

24. G. I. Kasperovich, *Migratsiia naseleniia v goroda i etnicheskie protsessy: Na materialakh issledovaniia gorodskogo naseleniia BSSR* (Minsk: Nauka i tekhnika, 1985), p. 109.

25. *Radians'ka Ukraina*, 25 March 1987 and 25 March 1983.

26. Mark Beissinger, "Ethnicity, the Personnel Weapon, and Neo-Imperial Integration: Ukrainian and RSFSR Provincial Party Officials Compared," *Studies in Comparative Communism*, vol. 21, no. 1 (Spring 1988), pp. 75–76.

27. *Sovetskaia Moldaviia*, 6 July 1988.

28. *Vestnik statistiki*, 1974, no. 4, p. 93, and V. P. Tomin, *Uroven' obrazovaniia naseleniia SSSR* (Moscow: Finansy i statistika, 1981), p. 81.

29. *Kritika fal'sifikatsii natsional'nykh otnoshenii v SSSR* (Moscow: Izdatel'stvo politicheskoi literatury, 1984), p. 280; *Kommunist Moldavii*, 1989, no. 6, p. 93; and *Radians'ka Ukraina*, 26 January 1989.

30. *Polityka*, 15 August 1987. I would like to thank Roman Szporluk for calling this article to my attention.

31. David Marples, "Mass Meeting in Kiev Focuses on Ecological Issues, Political Situation," *Ukrainian Weekly*, 4 December 1988. See also *Visti z Ukrainy*, 1988, no. 48 (November).

32. For a full exposition of this view, see Roman Szporluk, "The Ukraine and Russia," in Robert Conquest, ed., *The Last Empire: Nationality and the Soviet Future* (Stanford: Hoover Institution Press, 1986), pp. 151–82.

33. See Roman Solchanyk, "Molding 'the Soviet People': The Role of Ukraine and Belorussia," *Journal of Ukrainian Studies*, vol. 8, no. 1 (Summer 1983), pp. 3–18.

34. See Roman Solchanyk, "Russian Language and Soviet Politics," *Soviet Studies*, vol. 34, no. 1 (January 1982), pp. 23–42.

35. Roman Solchanyk, "Language Politics in the Ukraine," in Isabelle T. Kreindler, ed., *Sociolinguistic Perspectives on Soviet National Languages: Their Past, Present and Future* (Berlin: Mouton de Gruyter, 1985), pp. 77–78; *Literaturna Ukraina*, 9 April and 9 July 1987; and *Radians'ka Ukraina*, 9 April 1988.

36. Iu. D. Desheriev, *Razvitie obshchestvennykh funktsii literaturnykh iazykov* (Moscow: Nauka, 1976), pp. 94–95; K. Kh. Khanazarov, *Reshenie natsional'no-iazykovoi problemy v SSSR*, 2d enl. ed. (Moscow: Izdatel'stvo politicheskoi literatury, 1982), p. 174; *Russkii iazyk—iazyk druzhby i sotrudnichestva narodov SSSR: Materialy Vsesoiuznoi nauchno-teoreticheskoi konferentsii "Russkii iazyk—iazyk druzhby i sotrudnichestva narodov SSSR," 22–24 maia 1979 g., g. Tashkent* (Moscow: Nauka, 1981), p. 115; "O dal'neishem razvitii issledovanii po problemam funktsionirovaniia i izucheniia russkogo iazyka, prepodavaniia russkoi literatury v soiuznykh i avtonomnykh respublikakh, avtonomnykh oblastiakh i okrugakh SSSR," *Vestnik Akademii nauk SSSR*, 1979, no. 5, p. 10; and *Nastaŭnitskaia hazeta*, 8 April 1989.

37. Desheriev, *Razvitie obshchestvennykh funktsii*, p. 283; and *Sovetskaia Moldaviia*, 12 January 1989.

38. *Narodnoe khoziaistvo SSSR v 1987 g.* (Moscow: Finansy i statistika, 1988), p. 536; Ann Sheehy, "Belorussian Scholar Upholds Importance of Nationhood and National Languages," *Radio Liberty Research Bulletin*, RL 204/84 (23 May 1984); Solchanyk, "Language Politics in the Ukraine," p. 89; *Visnyk Akademii nauk Ukrains'koi RSR*, 1989, no. 6, p. 11; Roman Szporluk, "The Press and Soviet Nationalities: The Party Resolution of 1975 and Its Implementation," *Nationalities Papers*, vol. 14, nos. 1–2 (Summer–Fall 1986), pp. 47–64.

39. See Bohdan Nahaylo, "Moscow Manipulates the Millennium," *American Spectator*, March 1988, pp. 16–18.

40. On unofficial observances of the Millennium in Ukraine—Kiev, Kharkiv, and the village of Zarvanytsia, where a mass gathering of adherents, clergy, and hierarchy of the illegal Ukrainian Catholic (Uniate) Church took place—see the reports in *Ukrainian Weekly*, June through October 1988. See also Bohdan Nahaylo, "Ukrainians Object to Moscow Patriarchate's Depiction of Millennium Jubilee as Solely 'Russian' Affair," *Radio Liberty Research Bulletin*, RL 476/88 (12 October 1988).

41. See Ann Sheehy, "Moldavians Gain Some Language Concessions," *Radio Liberty Research Bulletin*, RL 353/87 (23 August 1987); *Sovetskaia Moldaviia*, 8 and 14 July 1988; Ann Sheehy, "Cultural Concessions but No Autonomy for Gagauz," *Radio Liberty Research Bulletin*, RL 456/87 (12 November 1987); and *Sovetskaia Moldaviia*, 7 and 30 July 1988.

42. Language issues in Ukraine and Belorussia in 1987–89 are discussed in numerous issues of *Radio Liberty Research Bulletin*, 1987–88, and Radio Liberty, *Report on the USSR*, vol. 1 (1989).

43. See *Radians'ka Ukraina*, 5 September and 3 November 1989, and *Sovetskaia Belorussiia*, 4 August, and 18 and 19 October 1989.

44. Jonathan Eyal, "Soviet Moldavia: History Catches Up and a 'Separate Language' Disappears," Radio Liberty, *Report on the USSR*, vol. 1, no. 8 (24 February 1989), pp. 25–29.

45. Socor, "Politics of the Language Question," and idem, "Moldavian Proclaimed Official Language in the Moldavian SSR," Radio Liberty, *Report on the USSR*, vol. 1, no. 38 (22 September 1989), pp. 13–15.

46. *Visti z Ukrainy,* 1989, no. 34 (August), and *Izvestiia,* 7 October 1989.

47. *Literaturna Ukraina,* 5 October 1989. For an English translation of the resolution "Against Anti-Semitism," see *Ukrainian Weekly,* 29 October 1989.

48. *Radians'ka Ukraina,* 26 December 1987.

49. See Kathleen Mihalisko, "Mass Grave of Stalin's Victims Discovered in Minsk," *Radio Liberty Research Bulletin,* RL 288/88 (26 June 1988); and idem, "The Archeology of Stalinist Genocide in Belorussia," ibid., RL 452/88 (3 October 1988).

50. A. Zalesskii, "Ne v ladakh s faktami istorii," *Kommunist Belorussii,* 1986, no. 5, pp. 91–94.

51. See *Radians'ka Ukraina,* 3 March 1988; "Istorychna nauka i suchasnist' (Materialy 'kruhloho stolu')," *Ukrains'kyi istorychnyi zhurnal,* 1988, no. 8, p. 35; and *Radians'ka Ukraina,* 27 August and 11 October 1988.

52. Iurii Badz'o, *Vidkrytyi lyst do Prezydii Verkhovnoi Rady Soiuzu RSR ta Tsentral'noho Komitetu KPRS* (New York: Vydannia Zakordonnoho Predstavnytstva Hrupy Spryiannia Vykonanniu Hel'sinks'kykh Uhod, 1980). A German translation was published in Munich in 1981.

53. See Yaroslav Bilinsky and Tönu Parming, "Helsinki Watch Committees in the Soviet Republics: Implications for Soviet Nationality Policy," *Nationalities Papers,* vol. 9, no. 1 (Spring 1981), pp. 1–25; and Bohdan Nahaylo, "Dissent and Opposition after Shelest," in Krawchenko, *Ukraine after Shelest,* pp. 30–54. Documents pertaining to the Ukrainian Helsinki Group have been compiled by Osyp Zinkewych, ed., *Ukrains'ka Hel'sinks'ka Hrupa 1978–1982: Dokumenty i materiialy* (Toronto-Baltimore: Ukrains'ke Vydavnytstvo "Smoloskyp" im. V. Symonenka, 1983).

54. Ludmilla Alexeyeva, *Soviet Dissent: Contemporary Movements for National, Religious, and Human Rights* (Middletown, CT: Wesleyan University Press, 1985), pp. 56–58.

55. See Roman Solchanyk and Ivan Hvat, "The Catholic Church in the Soviet Union," in Pedro Ramet, ed., *Christianity under Stress,* vol. 2 (Durham, NC: Duke University Press, 1990).

56. Jan Zaprudnik, "Inakodumstvo v Bilorusi," *Suchasnist',* vol. 19, no. 7–8 (July–August 1979), pp. 158–69.

57. See Victor Swoboda, "Prospects for Soviet Slavs in Conditions Favourable to the Establishment of National Freedom" (Paper presented at the Second International Congress of Professors' World Peace Academy, Geneva, 13–18 August 1985), pp. 31–32.

58. On the demonstrations and political activities in Lviv, and their repercussions, see the series of reports in *Ukrainian Weekly,* beginning with 3 July 1988, and the coverage in the *Radio Liberty Research Bulletins.*

59. The Ukrainian Helsinki Union's "Declaration of Principles" was published in *Svoboda* (Jersey City, NJ), 30 and 31 August and 1 September 1988, and its "Statutory Principles" in the 13 September issue of the newspaper.

60. The activities of the Belorussian groups have been described in the *Radio Liberty Research Bulletins.* On the Moldavian groups, see *Sovetskaia Moldaviia,* 27 and 29 July 1988.

61. On the Moldavian group, see Vladimir Socor, "Popular Front Founded in Moldavia," Radio Liberty, *Report on the USSR,* vol. 1, no. 23 (9 June 1989), pp. 23–26. On the Belorussian front, see Kathleen Mihalisko, "Belorussian Popular Front Holds Founding Congress in Vilnius," ibid., vol. 1, no. 28 (14 July 1989). For extensive coverage of the Ukrainian front, "Rukh," see the reports in *Ukrainian Weekly,* 17 and 24 September, and 8 and 22 October 1989.

CHAPTER 9

The Baltic Republics: Stagnation and Strivings for Sovereignty

Romuald J. Misiunas

The three Baltic republics—Estonia, Latvia, and Lithuania—form a unique westernized corner of the USSR. Their historical ties have been primarily with their western neighbors—Scandinavia and Germany in the case of Estonia and Latvia, Poland and Central Europe in the case of Lithuania—and their cultures predominantly European in orientation. The modern nation-state traditions of all three republics developed outside the Soviet context: they are the only national entities of the USSR to have experienced membership in the international community of sovereign states in the twentieth century. Independent existence during the interwar period spared the Baltic states from the upheavals that shook the Soviet Union in the 1930s—collectivization, famine, and terror—while allowing them to develop an autonomous political and cultural life that remains a living memory for many Balts in the USSR today.

Beyond such commonalities and the regional solidarity they have engendered, the Baltic peoples differ in significant ways. Linguistically, Estonian is a Finno-Ugric tongue closely related to Finnish, and access to Finnish media, especially television, has given the Estonians in the Soviet period exposure to non-Communist-bloc sources of information unavailable to other Soviet nationalities; Lithuanian and Latvian, on the other hand, together form the Baltic branch of the Indo-European language family. In terms of traditional religion, the Estonians and Latvians largely adhere to Lutheranism, though its association with the nationalism of the two peoples has been historically weak; the Lithuanians are overwhelmingly Roman Catholic, and their religion has become an important element in their national identity while the Church remains perhaps the dominant national institution.

These religious differences reflect the broader varieties of historical experience among the Baltic peoples. Estonia and Latvia, since their conquest by the crusading Teutonic knights in the Middle Ages and through the nineteenth century, were dominated by a local German elite, no matter what the changes in ultimate sovereignty over the region: Danish, Swedish, or, since the eighteenth century, Imperial Russian. The Reformation, Renaissance, and later Western intellectual and cultural movements left a strong imprint in the area. The abolition of serfdom in the Estonian and Latvian provinces in the early nineteenth century paved the way for industrialization, urbanization, and mass education among the indigenous nationalities sooner than in other parts of the Russian Empire. By the beginning of the twentieth century, these provinces were the most developed and their populations the most literate and skilled in the empire; they were also characterized by those modern patterns of demographic behavior, especially greatly reduced birth rates, that account in large measure for the low rates of natural increase among the Estonians and Latvians in the USSR today. At the same time, the emergence of a native professional and middle class stimulated a cultural renaissance and rapid growth in national awareness. These gains were finally consolidated in the period of independence.

Unlike its two northern neighbors, medieval Lithuania emerged as a separate state, with a native dynasty and ruling elite. It not only successfully withstood the onslaught of the German knights, but expanded into the Slavic lands to its southeast. At its apogee, the Lithuanian realm extended to the Black Sea and included all of Belorussia, most of Ukraine, and even some ethnically Russian territories. In the late fourteenth century the Lithuanians accepted Western Christianity as part of a political arrangement by which the Lithuanian dynasty acceded to the crown of Poland. This personal union was transformed two centuries later into a federation known as the Polish-Lithuanian Commonwealth. With the partitions of the Commonwealth in the late eighteenth century, the bulk of Lithuania fell under Russian rule, though Polish cultural influences continued to be felt into the twentieth century. Under the Russian Empire, Lithuania remained economically undeveloped, and its population overwhelmingly rural and rapidly growing. More than in Estonia and Latvia, the national literary and cultural movement was impeded by the Tsarist policy of Russification, and—in the absence of a sizable urban middle class—prominently featured clerical figures and religious issues. Despite advances in the period of independence, Lithuania at the time of its annexation by the USSR was at a significantly lower level of socio-economic development than Latvia and Estonia, but with a considerably larger population and a national consciousness that drew much of its inspiration from a perceived glorious historical tradition.

The traumatic events of the 1940s that accompanied the incorporation of Estonia, Latvia, and Lithuania into the USSR—occupation, mass deportations, war, large-scale flight to the West, guerrilla resistance, and collectivization—had, by the time of Stalin's death, effectively numbed national life in the three republics. Nevertheless, Baltic nationalism remained a strongly entrenched force which the regime was unable to eliminate or fully coopt. The Thaw triggered a veritable political and cultural renaissance that developed throughout the Khrushchev and Brezhnev periods and emerged as an openly significant force with the advent of Gorbachev's policies of *perestroika* and *glasnost'*.

On the political level, attempts began during the Thaw to nativize the republican Communist parties. These were most successful in Lithuania, where the local Communists did not have to contend with a large body of functionaries who, though of the titular nationality, had during the period of independence lived abroad in the USSR and immigrated after the Soviet occupation. In Latvia, on the other hand, such efforts backfired and triggered a purge in 1959–60. As a result, leadership positions in that republic continued to be dominated by the immigrant element. Estonia differed from the other two by having experienced a party purge while Stalin was still alive. Nativization of the Estonian Communist party has therefore been slow, but a trend favoring the ascendancy of its indigenous element can be clearly noted since the 1970s.

The nativization of the Communist party of Lithuania was particularly significant in that it coincided with the industrialization of the republic. Unlike Estonia and Latvia, Lithuania had remained overwhelmingly agricultural well into the 1950s. The decentralized *sovnarkhoz* system of economic organization that operated in the late 1950s allowed considerable autonomy to local administrators. The rising native element in the Lithuanian party was able to take advantage of the situation and effect industrialization in such a way as to utilize local labor resources. Lithuania, as a result, did not experience the massive immigration of workers from outside the republic (mainly from Russia) that altered the demographic profile of the other two republics.

The Thaw also ushered in a remarkable rebirth in cultural life. The relaxation of controls and the renewal, albeit circumscribed, of foreign contacts were accompanied by efforts to redirect cultural life in the three republics as much as possible toward their traditional European orientation. In many ways life in the Baltic rapidly acquired a level of modernity that quite distinguished it from the rest of the USSR.

A chill during the last years of Khrushchev's rule put a curb on such developments. The frequent economic reorganizations augured ill for republican autonomy. A new campaign against nationalism and religion was particularly intense in Lithuania. It was rumored that First Secretary Antanas Sniečkus (*Russ.* Snechkus), who had in effect received a public rebuke from Khrushchev for sanctioning the restoration of a medieval monument of considerable national sentiment, the capital fortress at Trakai, was on the verge of replacement.

Politically, the change in leadership in Moscow in 1964 favored the incumbents in the republics and the stability of the political machines they had created. The first secretaries of Estonia, Johannes Käbin (*Russ.* Ivan Kebin), in office since 1950, and of Lithuania, Antanas Sniečkus, in office since 1936 (then still in the underground), remained in place. Latvia's first secretary, Arvīds Pelše (*Russ.* Arvid Pelshe), who had assumed office during the purge in 1959, was promoted to the Politburo in 1966. He was succeeded as first secretary by Augusts (*Russ.* Avgust) Voss, but no other notable change in the Latvian leadership accompanied this transition.

While on the all-union level the ascendancy of Brezhnev marked a clear departure from the liberalizing policies of the Thaw, no pronounced change was noted immediately in the Baltic. The ouster of Khrushchev was actually followed by a temporary lull in the various all-union campaigns and therefore appeared to some in the Baltic republics as a welcome reprieve on the cultural scene. In this situation the Baltic party organizations, especially in Lithuania, pushed for national causes whose implementation could contribute to a greater acceptance of the system. The new atmosphere in the Kremlin allowed the adoption of some measures that had been blocked during the late Khrushchev period. The most notable was the introduction in the three Baltic republics of an eleven-year primary and secondary educational system, ostensibly to facilitate study of the native languages, while a ten-year system was operative throughout the rest of the USSR.

Widespread hopes for continued political and cultural liberalization did not abate until the end of the decade. While no dramatic events occurred in the Baltic itself, the Soviet invasion of Czechoslovakia can be described as a psychological watershed. Prior to that time, expectation of within-system change predominated. After 1968, such hopes diminished significantly. Dissent and *samizdat*, never totally absent in the postwar period, began to acquire a more notable presence. But continued economic growth, presenting a choice between an increasingly comfortable life and the risk of repression, served effectively to dampen much of the potential opposition.

Political Developments

The gerontocratic *immobilisme* that began to set in at the center of the Soviet state in the late 1960s under Brezhnev was paralleled on the Baltic political scene during the 1970s and into the 1980s, despite the fact that during this period all three republics received new first secretaries. The death in office of the Lithuanian party chief, Antanas Snieckus, in 1974 was the first such occurrence among republican first secretaries in the history of the USSR. In many ways, Snieckus had been an unusual phenomenon among these officials. No one exceeded his longevity in office—thirty-four years, plus an additional four while in the prewar underground—perhaps because no one could match his astute ability to foresee and profit from changes in the Kremlin. Presiding over the nativization of the Lithuanian party during the 1950s and 1960s, he transformed it into his personal political machine and even managed to secure an almost Kadaresque degree of native acceptance. Snieckus was not only aware of the intense nationalism of the Lithuanians, but was able to turn it to his political advantage in the Kremlin, citing it as proof of the difficulty of his job rather than his inability to handle it.[1] The selection of Petras Griškevičius (*Russ*. Piatras Grishkiavichus) as successor to Snieckus came as a surprise. A rather mediocre functionary with some literary pretensions and a career that spanned positions in the press and the Vilnius city party committee, he may well have been a compromise choice.

When the long-term Estonian first secretary, Käbin, retired in 1978, he was replaced by another immigrant from Russia, the lackluster Karl Vaino (born in Tomsk in the RSFSR and originally named Kirill Voinov), a man of limited ability who had scarcely managed to learn the Estonian language. As in the case of Griškevičius, the selection of Vaino came as a surprise, and some Estonians considered it an insult. The consumer goods and food product shortages that set in soon after were readily ascribed to his eagerness to please his patrons in Moscow by shipping local produce outside the republic. An attempt on his life is said to have taken place in 1979.[2]

A more consequential leadership change occurred in Latvia in 1984 under Konstantin Chernenko, underscoring the paramount role of personal connections in the all-union apparatus as well as the efficacy of a position in the KGB as a stepping-stone to power in the Soviet hierarchy. Augusts Voss, first secretary since 1966, was elevated to the ceremonial post of chairman of the Soviet of Nationalities of the USSR Supreme Soviet in Moscow. His replacement, Boris Pugo, reputedly the stepson of Pelše, also came from immigrant background. Born in 1937, most likely in Moscow, he represented a younger generation of non-native-born administrators. Pugo's family connections may have played a significant role in his rapid rise through the Latvian Komsomol and party apparatus. In 1976, while a candidate member of the republican party Bureau, he went to Moscow for a year, probably to prepare for his assumption of leadership posts in the Latvian KGB. At the time of his selection as first secretary he was still only a candidate member of the Bureau, an unprecedented situation. Unlike his colorless colleagues in Estonia and Lithuania, Pugo acquired a reputation for ruthless efficiency and absence of moral scruple, gaining considerable notoriety during the crackdown in 1983 on dissident activity in Latvia.[3]

During this period as well, all three Baltic republics received new second secretaries, all of them Russians. The marked turnover began in the late 1970s. In 1978 the Latvian party second secretary, in office since 1963, was replaced by a functionary who held the post only until 1980; yet another second secretary was appointed in September 1986. In Estonia, the incumbent in that position since 1971 was replaced in 1982, and was in turn replaced in December 1985. The post of second secretary in Lithuania was likewise held by the same individual for a long time, from 1967 to 1978; his successor was himself replaced in the fall of 1986. Such a reduction in the length of tenure of republican second secretaries may reflect an attempt by Moscow to forestall the corruption which long service in the republican apparatus has tended to foster.

The policy of appointing republican second secretaries from within the central bureaucracy came under open attack in 1988. While the incumbent in Estonia, Georgii Aleshin, enjoyed some local approbation for his purported role in the dismissal of Vaino as first secretary (see below), his colleague in Lithuania, Nikolai Mitkin, became a symbol of the most objectionable facets of the system; by November 1988 he had resigned, reportedly under pressure, and left the republic. His replacement, named in December, was Vladimir Berezov, a local Russian with a favorable reputation in Lithuania.

Changes in the composition of party membership in the Baltic republics proceeded only slowly. The nativization of the party rank and file in Estonia and Latvia that could have been expected with the retirement of older immigrants and an influx of new local cadres was not markedly pronounced. Despite the steady growth of overall party membership in all three republics, the natives remained significantly underrepresented. Thus, in Estonia as of 1980 the proportion of Estonians in the party stood at 50.8%, while their share in the population in 1979 was 64.7%. Figures on the national composition of the Communist party of Latvia have not been published in recent times, as they would doubtlessly prove embarrassing to the regime: in 1965 it was estimated that Latvians formed 39% of the party membership, although in 1959 their weight in the republic's population was 62.0%. The Lithuanian party organization grew at a faster pace than the CPSU as a whole and registered the second highest rate of growth among all union republics. Nevertheless, in 1984 the percentage of party members in the population of Lithuania (5.25%) was still below the corresponding USSR average (6.74%). The proportion of Lithuanians in the republican party organization increased from 67.1% in 1970 to 70.4% in 1985—a figure, however, still far below their weight in the republic's population, which in 1979 was almost 80%.[4] Party membership evidently did not enjoy unreserved approbation among considerable segments of the indigenous population. Indeed, a clear lack of confidence in the Communist party was demonstrated by the dramatic events that have occurred since the summer of 1988.

The new atmosphere of *glasnost'* and the promises of *perestroika* and democratization which followed the accession of Mikhail Gorbachev to power in Moscow in 1985 had a profound effect in the Baltic republics.[5] Manifestations of dissatisfaction with the status quo and affirmations of nationalism became more and more frequent during the summer of 1987, first led by unofficial dissident elements. In June 1987 Latvians openly commemorated the deportations of 1941 at the Independence Monument in Riga. In August all three Baltic capitals saw commemorations of the anniversary of the Molotov-Ribbentrop Pact of 1939 which had paved the way for Soviet occupation in the following year. These demonstrations, still modest in size, were reluctantly tolerated by the local authorities, though media attacks on them were launched and some of their leaders were forced to emigrate. Tolerance changed into active attempts to obstruct observances of the independence days of the prewar states—on 18 November 1987 in Latvia and 16 February 1988 in Lithuania. Only the anniversary in Estonia on 24 February 1988 passed without obvious interference.

Events took a more radical turn on 1–2 April 1988 when a plenum of the Estonian Creative Societies passed a resolution calling for sweeping changes within the republic and in its relationship with the central authorities in Moscow—changes that if effected would be tantamount to far-reaching economic and political autonomy. The resolution, moreover, explicitly expressed no confidence in the republic's first secretary, Vaino, and his "cohorts of stagnationists." Two weeks later, an initiative group launched a mass quasi-political organization, a "popular front," to press, within the framework of all-union *perestroika*, for the changes enumerated in the resolution. By June the Estonian Popular Front claimed a membership of 40,000 and was growing at a very fast rate. That same month, in the wake of analogous resolutions by the Writers' Unions in Latvia and Lithuania, similar organizations—the Latvian Popular Front and the Lithuanian Restructuring Movement (Sajūdis)—made their appearance.

As the summer progressed, the national movements gathered further momentum. The Baltic capitals witnessed increasingly large demonstrations, some numbering hundreds of thousands of participants. The proclaimed goal of all three movements was real autonomy for their republics, usually expressed in the term "sovereignty." This envisaged a thorough restructuring of the Soviet political system, with all political and economic decision making transferred to the republics and only foreign policy and defense remaining the preserve of Moscow. Calls for republican diplomatic representation abroad also emerged, as did proposals to turn the three republics into open economic zones with their own foreign trade policies and convertible currencies. In such a reformed system, the three republics would become true masters of their house, dealing with the issues of greatest concern to their populations. Among these, ecology, immigrant labor, and language rights figured most prominently.

The appearance and activity of the popular front movements, which held their founding congresses in the fall of 1988, led to a palpable change in the mood and psychology of the Baltic nationalities. Expressions of national pride, which had been under a total ban, emerged with force. During the summer the flags and anthems associated with the interwar period of independence were rehabilitated as national symbols. Many localities and streets were rechristened with their prewar names.

The national mass movements had a significant effect on the local party elites. While the popular fronts explicitly eschewed the role of a political opposition, and had significant representation of party members in their ranks, they nevertheless assumed the role of a de facto opposition. All three fronts expressed the intention of running candidates for government office in future elections. All vigorously protested the selection of delegates to the Nineteenth Party Conference, held in Moscow in June 1988, by the local party machines—a process that resulted in the usual delegations of handpicked bureaucrats out of touch with the rising national ebullience of the masses. The mood of disorientation among the republican party leaderships in the face of developments beyond their control can be clearly seen in a transcript of the June Plenum of the Latvian party.[6]

Unprecedentedly, the mass movements triggered leadership changes in all three republics. The first occurred in Estonia. Two days before the opening of the party conference in Moscow, the incumbent first secretary, Karl Vaino, was replaced by Vaino Väljas (*Russ.* Vialias), USSR ambassador to Nicaragua. Väljas had been in the Soviet diplomatic service after losing out in a power struggle during the late 1970s. At the September Plenum of the Estonian party Väljas admitted that the party faced a crisis of confidence and called for renewal.

A split occurred in the leadership of the Lithuanian party. Ringaudas-Bronislovas Songaila, first secretary only since December 1987 when he replaced Griškevičius, who had died in office, visibly distanced himself from the popular movement and was on record criticizing it. However, Central Committee secretary Algirdas Brazauskas addressed a mass gathering on 9 July, and at the commemoration of the Molotov-Ribbentrop Pact on 23 August was joined by another secretary, Lionginas Šepetys (Russ. Shepetis). In October, in the aftermath of a police action on 28 September against a dissident demonstration that had evoked extensive public protest, Songaila, whose removal had become an espoused goal of many in the movement, was replaced as first secretary by Brazauskas.

The leadership change in Latvia was not as dramatic. During the September CPSU Central Committee Plenum, the Latvian first secretary, Boris Pugo, was transferred to Moscow as head of the Party Control Committee. He was not, however, succeeded by the party leader most closely identified with the goals and aspirations of the Latvian Popular Front, the secretary for ideology Anatolijs Gorbunovs (Russ. Anatolii Gorbunov), but by the more conservative Jānis (Russ. Yan) Vagris, chairman of the republican Supreme Soviet. Gorbunovs moved into Vagris's old position.

Gorbachev's planned constitutional changes in the fall of 1988, perceived in the Baltic as a threat to some of the formal independence the republics enjoyed, galvanized political activity in October and November. The popular fronts pressed the republican Supreme Soviets to pass legislation affirming national sovereignty. The Supreme Soviet of the Estonian SSR passed a constitutional amendment affirming Estonian sovereignty and republican veto power over any central decision affecting its territory. The USSR Supreme Soviet in its turn pronounced this declaration unconstitutional and invalid, and the Estonian leadership was summoned to Moscow for consultations. Nevertheless, the Estonian legislature reaffirmed its stand on sovereignty, and at the end of 1988 the constitutional crisis remained unresolved. With the Estonian imbroglio before them, the Supreme Soviets of Latvia and Lithuania did not follow suit, despite publicized expectations, but they did express reservations about possible dilution of republican sovereignty in the forthcoming revision of the USSR constitution.[7] The Lithuanian legislature used the occasion to declare the prewar flag and anthem, which had already been legalized as symbols of the nation during the summer, as official state insignia. The failure of the Supreme Soviets in Lithuania and Latvia to follow the Estonian example led to mass demonstrations and calls for new elections. Mass petition drives affirming national sovereignty were launched. The one in Lithuania claimed over 1,800,000 signatures.[8]

The strivings for sovereignty continued to gather even greater momentum during 1989. The appearance of the popular fronts in 1988, indeed, marked the return of political life, in the normally accepted sense of the term, to the Baltic lands. In less than a year, the political scene in the three republics changed almost beyond recognition. Although, as in the rest of the vast Soviet realm, one-party rule in theory continued, de facto pluralism had made significant inroads. In addition to the three major popular fronts, other political groups—some of them resurrected prewar parties, others new organizations unwilling to concede any legitimacy whatsoever to the existing system—have sprung up and achieved a modicum of toleration by the regime.

The resulting situation pushed the republican Communist parties into a more clearly nationalist direction in order to avoid their total discredit among the populace. In the fall of 1989 the proposed new party platforms in Lithuania and Estonia envisaged Communist party organizations with only loose ties to the center. The Lithuanian draft coined a new term, "self-standing," to describe the republican party in the proposed new relationship. The declaration of independence of the Lithuanian party from the CPSU at the party congress in December 1989 provoked a new crisis in relations with the center. The republican Komsomol had already split off from the all-union body in the summer.

The elections in the spring of 1989 to the new Congress of People's Deputies provided the first significant demonstration of these tendencies. The results in all three republics underscored the resurgence of national sentiment and a turn away from the traditional political establishment. The shift was most evident in Lithuania, where Sąjūdis won thirty-six of forty-two seats; it would very likely have carried two more, but for tactical reasons chose not to oppose the first and second secretaries of the republican party, who were considered positive figures. The results in Estonia and Latvia were equally telling. In Estonia the battle lines were drawn not so much between the party and the popular front as between anti-sovereignty conservatives—supported by the so-called Inter-movement, a largely Russian immigrant-labor group—and the popular front. Proponents of sovereignty won thirty-one of the thirty-six seats at stake. The electoral struggle in Latvia was not as clearly drawn between proponents and opponents of sovereignty. However, about three-fourths of the contested seats were carried by candidates supported by the popular front. The most graphic example of dissatisfaction with the status quo came in a largely Russian district in Riga: there the republic's first secretary, Vagris, was able to garner only 51% of the vote, although he was opposed only by two members of the Total Independence Party.

What began in 1988 as a push for within-system change, including a vague and ill-defined notion of "sovereignty," developed in 1989 into an all-embracing alternative movement for a fundamental transformation of the political status quo. The earlier reticence to advocate the goal of independence disappeared. In May, the Supreme Soviet of Lithuania adopted a sovereignty declaration similar to that which it had refused to pass the previous fall. In June, the Supreme Soviet of Latvia followed suit. The public statements of the Lithuanian Communist party first secretary, Brazauskas, at the June commemoration ceremony for Stalin-era deportees could have been written by Sąjūdis speechwriters.

The Baltic delegations to the Congress of People's Deputies in Moscow, composed overwhelmingly of nominees of the popular fronts and individuals supported by them, were among the most outspoken at the session. The Lithuanian delegation, in particular, proved to be a coherent group with clearly defined goals. Their vocal opposition to the nomination of Nikolai Ryzhkov as chairman of the Council of Ministers stemmed from that body's opposition to devolution of control over economic management to the republican level. On two occasions the majority of Lithuanian delegates, joined by several other Balts, walked out of the televised proceedings. The walkouts were in protest against the procedures for election of deputies to the standing Supreme Soviet and the formation of a USSR Committee for Constitutional Oversight before its functions had been clarified. In both cases, a threat to republican sovereignty was perceived. The Baltic delegations, moreover, succeeded in having a parliamentary commission formed to study the question of the Molotov-Ribbentrop Pact.

The question of independence also figured prominently in several nongovernmental events. It formed a clear leitmotif in the program and resolutions of the first Baltic Assembly in Tallinn on 12–13 May 1989, a joint gathering of the assemblies of the three popular fronts. And it surfaced most dramatically in August, when a human chain of between one and two million people stretched over the three republics, a six-hundred-kilometer distance from Tallinn to Vilnius, to commemorate the anniversary of the Nazi-Soviet Pact which sealed the fate of Baltic independence in 1939. A signature campaign denouncing the pact and its consequences yielded results analogous to those of the similar campaign in the fall of 1988.

The push for independence appeared impervious to a much publicized reaction from the Kremlin in the aftermath of the human chain. This was a statement specifically condemning Baltic nationalism and separatism, and carrying vague threats to the very existence of the Baltic nations. To many these appeared threats without substance and an open insult. Indeed, the Kremlin statement conveniently provided a focus for the opposition, and by explicitly ruling out Baltic independence placed that very question on the agenda for discussion. A resolution of the congress of the Popular Front of Latvia, adopted on 8 October 1989, provided an explicit and detailed program calling for independence after a transitional period of autonomy. Thus, in the fall of 1989 the question of independence—of how and when—had emerged as a fact of Baltic political life.

Demographic, Economic, and Social Trends

The slow but steady rise in the quality of life in all three Baltic republics that had characterized the 1960s came to a visible end by the 1970s with the appearance of shortages of food products and consumer goods. Russian immigration, which had slowed during the early 1970s, again increased and even began to acquire significance in Lithuania.

Russian immigration has been perceived by the Baltic peoples as the principal threat (real in Estonia and Latvia, potential in Lithuania) to their national existence. The immigrants were attracted to the Baltic lands largely by the higher standard of living. The launching of grandiose construction projects frequently served as a catalyst for increased immigration. While many newcomers were so-called ruble immigrants, constantly roaming the USSR in search of better pay, others stayed after the completion of the projects that initially attracted them or managed to change employment after arrival.

In Latvia and Estonia postwar immigration, coupled with low native birth rates, has led to a decrease in the proportion of the indigenous nationalities in the population. (The main demographic developments among the Baltic nationalities are shown in Table 1.) In Estonia this dropped from 88.2% before the war to 74.6% in 1959 and 61.5% in 1989. In Latvia, the decrease was from 75.5% to 62.0% to 52.0%, respectively. Only Lithuania has managed to maintain a relative equilibrium: 80.6% before the war, 79.3% in 1959 and 79.6% in 1989.[9]

The patterns of immigration have drastically altered the population structure in Estonia and Latvia. The national composition of these two republics by district and town has not been openly published. Such information, however, became available through copies of restricted bulletins smuggled out of the USSR. In both republics in 1979 the total population was divided almost equally among the capital cities, other urban centers, and rural areas. In Latvia, the titular nationality formed 38.3% of the population in Riga, 51.5% in other cities, and 71.9% among the rural population. In Estonia the proportions were 51.9% in Tallinn, 56.9% in the other cities, and 87.6% in the rural areas.[10] Of the larger cities in Lithuania, only Vilnius and Klaipėda have sizable groups of non-Lithuanians; however, the Lithuanian percentage of both is considerably higher than in prewar times.

During the 1970s there was a notable drop in the absolute numbers of immigrants into the three republics. That trend apparently was reversed during the early 1980s in Estonia and Lithuania as both republics became sites for large construction projects. In Estonia, the undertaking was a gargantuan transshipment harbor at Muuga near Tallinn. In Lithuania, it was the ferry harbor in Klaipėda for a sea link with the German Democratic Republic, and a nuclear power plant at Ignalina. Such projects, undertaken under conditions of a rapidly increasing labor shortage in the Baltic republics, were questioned from the purely economic standpoint and castigated as covert methods of Russification in the *samizdat* press of both republics. Estonian *samizdat* literature ascribed former First Secretary Vaino's assiduousness in courting such projects to his insecurity in office; an earlier letter in May 1977 expressed concern over the expansion of oil-shale and phosphorite mining.[11] Similar apprehensions were expressed in Latvia and Lithuania. The effects of the massive hydroelectric project at Pļaviņa in Latvia caused concern among ecologists and the intelligentsia. In Lithuania, the construction of the atomic power plant at Ignalina, the largest such facility in the USSR, manned by immigrant labor and planned for a capacity far exceeding the needs of the republic, became a sensitive issue in the aftermath of the accident at Chernobyl. Another project planned on a massive scale, oil extraction along the Baltic littoral, aroused considerable opposition among the republic's intelligentsia. Ecological arguments against the venture were published in the official press. The success in Russia of grass roots opposition to the planned diversion of northern rivers to Central Asia fired the Lithuanian opposition, which managed to block the plan, at least temporarily.[12]

Control of immigration has emerged as a primary concern for the national movements and provides the rationale for their call for a republican citizenship. In Latvia proposals have surfaced for legislation requiring enterprises to pay a substantial fee for every worker they hire from outside the republic, but that is viewed by many as insufficient.[13] As most of the immigration is migrant labor in search of higher pay, there is a constant turnover of residents, placing a particular strain on social resources. The increase in immigration exacerbates the chronic housing shortage. The unexpected influx in June 1986 of over 10,000 Ukrainian and Belorussian refugees from the Chernobyl disaster aggravated the situation. Although the refugees were ostensibly only temporary settlers, the general population, already sensitive to Russian immigration, did not welcome their arrival, fearing that the higher standard of living would attract their permanent presence and the eventual arrival of their relatives.

Overall, interaction between the indigenous populations and the immigrants remained limited. If knowledge of the indigenous language can be taken as an indicator of the integration of immigrants into the local culture, this was highest in Lithuania (37.4% in 1979), where the immigrant population was by far the smallest, both in absolute and percentage terms. The analogous figures were 20.1% for Latvia and 12.9% for Estonia. Mixed marriages between natives and immigrants increased, but were still not very widespread. More than half of the offspring of such marriages tended to opt for the republican nationality if residence was maintained in the republic.[14]

The Baltic republics continue to enjoy the highest living standards in the USSR. However, they have not remained unaffected by the general economic decline that set in throughout the USSR as a whole since the mid-1970s. This became particularly notable in the area of consumer goods, and especially food supply. Although productivity in the region continues to be higher than in the rest of the USSR, shortages have become endemic. And expectations in the Baltic are perhaps higher than elsewhere in the USSR.

The introduction of full cost-accountability, mandated by the all-union *perestroika* plans in 1988, led to discussions of the possible establishment of a Chinese-style free economic zone in the region. Such proposals first appeared in Estonia, but soon surfaced in Lithuania and Latvia as well. Several joint meetings by Baltic economists took place throughout 1988 and 1989. A meeting in Riga in early October 1988, called to work out common principles of republican cost-accounting, seems to have gone beyond that

216

TABLE 1A. Demographic Trends among the Baltic Nationalities in the USSR, 1959-1989

	Total Population (in thousands)				Population Increase
	1959	1970	1979	1989	1959-89
USSR	208,827	241,720	262,085	285,689	76,862
Russians	114,114	129,105	137,397	145,072	30,958
Lithuanians	2,326	2,665	2,851	3,068	742
Latvians	1,400	1,430	1,439	1,459	59
Estonians	989	1,007	1,020	1,027	38

	Percent Increase				Percent of Population			
	1959-70	1970-79	1979-89	1959-89	1959	1970	1979	1989
USSR	15.7	8.4	9.0	36.8	100	100	100	100
Russians	13.1	6.5	5.6	27.1	54.65	53.37	52.42	50.78
Lithuanians	14.6	7.0	7.6	31.9	1.11	1.10	1.09	1.07
Latvians	2.2	0.6	1.4	4.2	0.67	0.59	0.55	0.51
Estonians	1.9	1.2	0.7	3.8	0.47	0.42	0.39	0.36

TABLE 1B. Percentage Concentration Rates of Nationalities in Their Titular Republics, 1959-1989

	1959	1970	1979	1989	Change 1959-89
Russians	85.8	83.5	82.6	82.6	- 3.2
Lithuanians	92.5	94.1	95.1	95.3	+ 2.8
Latvians	92.7	93.8	93.4	95.1	+ 2.4
Estonians	90.3	91.8	92.9	93.8	+ 3.5

TABLE 1C. Ethnodemographic Trends in the Baltic Republics, 1959-1989

	Total Population (in thousands)				Population Increase	Percent of Population			
	1959	1970	1979	1989	1959-89	1959	1970	1979	1989
Lithuania	2,711	3,128	3,391	3,673	962	100	100	100	100
Lithuanians	2,151	2,507	2,712	2,924	773	79.32	80.13	79.95	79.60
Russians	231	268	303	344	113	8.52	8.57	8.93	9.35
Poles	230	240	247	258	28	8.49	7.68	7.28	7.02
Latvia	2,093	2,364	2,503	2,667	574	100	100	100	100
Latvians	1,298	1,342	1,344	1,388	90	62.00	56.76	53.70	52.04
Russians	556	705	821	906	350	26.58	29.80	32.80	33.96
Belorussians	62	95	112	120	58	2.94	4.01	4.46	4.49
Estonia	1,197	1,356	1,464	1,566	369	100	100	100	100
Estonians	893	925	948	963	70	74.59	68.22	64.71	61.52
Russians	240	335	409	475	235	20.07	24.68	27.92	30.33
Ukrainians	16	28	36	48	32	1.32	2.07	2.46	3.08

	Percent Increase			
	1959-70	1970-79	1979-89	1959-89
Lithuania	15.4	8.4	8.3	35.5
Lithuanians	16.6	8.2	7.8	35.9
Russians	16.0	13.1	13.2	48.9
Poles	4.4	2.8	4.4	12.2
Latvia	12.9	5.9	6.5	27.4
Latvians	3.4	0.2	3.2	6.9
Russians	26.6	16.5	10.2	62.9
Belorussians	54.1	17.5	7.4	93.5
Estonia	13.3	8.0	6.9	30.8
Estonians	3.6	2.5	1.6	7.8
Russians	39.3	22.1	16.2	97.9
Ukrainians	78.1	28.3	33.9	200.0

Sources: Derived from 1959, 1970, 1979, and 1989 Soviet census data. Itogi Vsesoiuznoi perepisi naseleniia 1959 goda: SSSR; ... Litovskaia SSR; ... Latviiskaia SSR; ... Estonskaia SSR (Moscow: Gosstatizdat, 1962). Itogi Vsesoiuznoi perepisi naseleniia 1970 goda, vol. 4 (Moscow: Statistika, 1974). Chislennost' i sostav naseleniia SSSR: Po dannym Vsesoiuznoi perepisi naseleniia 1979 goda (Moscow: Finansy i statistika, 1984). Data for 1989 are from preliminary unpublished results of the 1989 census, and are subject to correction.

limited question. Proposals were entertained for foreign capital investment on a wide scale, independence from central control in taxation and price-formation policies, and the issuance of local convertible currencies.[15]

Through the end of 1989 all such plans and proposals still remained basically in the discussion stage. Some practical changes could be noted in the introduction of cooperative enterprises in the service sector, particularly taxis and restaurants, and the appearance of a household leasing system in agriculture. Both remained circumscribed by a host of regulations which, it can be expected, will be diluted or eliminated in the future. The need to focus on agriculture was expressed by the new Estonian first secretary, Väljas, at the 9 September 1988 Plenum of the Estonian Central Committee, and he also hinted at the return of private farming. "We must create without delay equal possibilities for all forms of production in rural areas, for all producers, large and small. We must legally guarantee the equal rights of all forms of ownership."[16] On 27 July 1989, the Supreme Soviet of the USSR endorsed in principle the Estonian and Lithuanian plans to develop market-oriented economies independent of the central planning institutions in Moscow. The resolution approved, in a general way, laws already passed in these republics providing for local control over the budgets, tax policies, prices, financial markets, and foreign trade, and specifically exempted these republics from all-union legislation interfering with the development of their economic independence. The specific legislation on this resolution was enacted in November 1989.

Cultural Developments

Despite the increasing reassertion of central control and outward ideological orthodoxy during the Brezhnev years, the renaissance in national cultural life that had begun during the Thaw was not curtailed. Instead, an equilibrium between increasing modernization and westernization on the one hand and periodic exhortation to ideological vigilance on the other hand has been the hallmark of Baltic cultural development. By the late 1960s, Lithuania had already developed a rich and distinctive national cultural life within Soviet strictures. During the subsequent decade, Estonia and Latvia followed suit.

The Russification campaign, which intensified in the late 1970s following the conferences at Riga and Tashkent on the need to increase knowledge of the Russian language among non-Russians in the USSR, continued through the mid-1980s. While the brunt of this all-union effort was aimed at Central Asia, where knowledge of Russian was extremely low, and at the Slavic republics, to promote more rapid assimilation of Ukrainians and Belorussians, the Balts have also felt its impact. Increased Russian-language instruction in the school system, including kindergarten, and the growing Russian-language presence in the media and public life of the three republics were its most typical manifestations. Illustrative of the tenor of this campaign was the statement by Mirdza Karkliņš, then minister of education of the

Latvian SSR, on the benefits of teaching Russian to young people. "[It] safeguards the effectiveness of patriotic internationalist education, promoting the development of high moral and ideological-political qualities among pupils." She reproached Latvians for not appreciating sufficiently the benefits of speaking Russian among themselves.[17] The campaign was abruptly halted in the Baltic republics in the late 1980s under pressure from the national movements. The indigenous languages were declared official languages in 1988 and the teaching of Russian to children in kindergarten and the early grades was discontinued.

It is difficult to gauge the impact, apart from a rise in resentment, of this campaign on the Baltic populations. In 1979 self-declared knowledge of Russian among the titular nationalities of the union republics had increased in all but Estonia. In Latvia the proportion of the titular nationality claiming knowledge of Russian as a second language rose from 45.2% in 1970 to 56.7% in 1979, and in Lithuania from 35.9% to 52.1%, while in Estonia the figure dropped from 29.0% to 24.2%. But these data must be viewed with caution. According to one Lithuanian *samizdat* source, the student census takers in Vilnius were instructed to report knowledge of Russian, whatever the actual response, for anyone with a secondary education acquired in Soviet times. Ostensibly this was done to prevent a repetition of such cases as occurred in 1970, when respondents listing "teacher of Russian" under occupation also indicated "no knowledge of Russian" in answer to the question on language.[18] The Russification campaign also stressed the need to inject Soviet political themes into public events not intrinsically connected with politics. Such politicization was particularly evident during the traditional song festivals held in all three republics in the summer of 1985, when the theme of victory in World War II figured prominently.

A Western cultural orientation and continuing foreign contacts mitigated the effects of ideological campaigns and the Russification drive. Fads in youth culture, styles of dress, and patterns of social behavior modelled on the West reach the Baltic republics after only a short delay. Official reaction has typically been initial opposition followed by acquiescence to the inevitable. At the same time, as in other republics, restoration work has become a prominent feature of the effort to preserve the national cultural heritage. Considerable pride is taken in its achievement. Special occasions, such as the 400th anniversary of the University of Vilnius in 1979 and the yachting events of the 1980 summer Olympics in Tallinn, were preceded by large-scale, though hasty and superficial, renovations of the old towns of Vilnius and Tallinn.

As earlier, literature and theater continued to test the limits of acceptability. The occasional ideological reprimands did not result in wholesale cultural reaction, and each successful overstepping of the bounds expanded the limits of the permissible. Ideological cant ebbed and flowed in cycles, while cultural life became almost oblivious to it. Works of quality tended to appear in relatively small editions insufficient to satisfy demand, quickly becoming black market items. Historical fiction frequently provided a means to discuss sensitive contemporary questions. Surprisingly open literary-sociological investigations of contemporary urban life became extremely popular. The novels of the Lithuanian Lenin-prize winner, Jonas Avyžius, *The colors of a chameleon* [Chemeleono spalvos] (1979) and *Burnings* [Degimai] (1982), were praised by some for their daring and castigated by others as little better than sensationalized imitations of American soap operas, but in any case provide intriguing glimpses into contemporary life and problems of Soviet Lithuanian society. The work of some younger avant-garde writers became entirely emancipated from any ideological strictures.[19]

Similar trends were apparent in theatrical life. Some productions have enjoyed immense staying power. The most notable example is the Lithuanian play *Barbora Radvilaitė* (1972) by Juozas Grušas, the story of a sixteenth-century queen that contains numerous allusions to contemporary conditions. The original production continues to be staged—perhaps the longest run in the Baltic—even though its director now lives in emigration. The Estonian play *Responsibility* [Vastutus] (1985) by Valter Udam, a district party secretary, achieved immense popularity for its open depiction of bureaucratic tangles.[20]

Since the accession of Gorbachev, the policy of *glasnost'* has seemingly removed virtually all strictures from cultural life in the Baltic. This has become strikingly evident in historiography, the last bastion of the earlier conservatism. That fortress fell with the all-union recall of history textbooks in 1988. The secret protocols of the Molotov-Ribbentrop Pact of 1939, which paved the way for Soviet annexation in 1940, have been published in all three republics. Works questioning the "revolutions" of 1940 that accompanied the entry of ˙the Red Army have appeared, as have reminiscences by perpetrators and victims of the deportations of 1941 and 1948–51. Perhaps the most notable of such memoirs are those of the last minister of foreign affairs of independent Lithuania, Juozas Urbšys, published in a very large edition in the fall of 1988; the volume was nevertheless still graced with an ideological disclaimer noting that in the opinion of the publishers some of the author's statements are disputable.[21]

The 1980s witnessed considerable shifts in the regime's relations with organized religious bodies, especially the Catholic Church of Lithuania which, unlike the predominant Lutheran Churches in Latvia and Estonia, had assumed the position of a national institution. By the beginning of the decade, the propaganda line that religion was a dying vestige of the past had become untenable. At the same time the patent identification of Catholicism with Lithuanian nationalism was cause of evident concern to the Lithuanian ideological establishment, which increasingly stressed the theme that the historic relationship between Catholicism and Lithuania was accidental. This was especially pronounced in 1984, on the occasion of the 500th anniversary of the death of St. Casimir, the patron saint of the country. The regime prevented a joint celebration with the Vatican from taking place, and Pope John Paul II revealed that the Soviets had not allowed him to attend the celebrations in Lithuania.[22] While denigrating the historic identification of Catholicism with Lithuanian nationalism, some publications began to stress the "national," as opposed to religious, significance of certain holidays, in particular Christmas, which are widely celebrated.[23]

The regime's ideological problem with the Lithuanians' religious-national symbiosis increased in intensity with the approach of the 600th anniversary of the baptism of Lithuania. Celebrations were held at the Vatican in June 1987, but again the pope was prevented from attending the observances in Vilnius. Nevertheless, despite efforts by the authorities to downplay and limit the anniversary commemorations, signs began to appear that the regime wished to reach a modus vivendi with the Church. It was announced that the church in Klaipėda, which had been built during the Thaw with donations from the faithful, but was then confiscated and turned into a concert hall, would be returned to the Church. In the fall of 1988, the cathedral of Vilnius, which had also become a concert hall, and the church of St. Casimir, converted into a museum of atheism, were likewise returned. The acting head of the Lithuanian Church, Bishop Vincentas Sladkevičius, who had been repressed in the early 1960s, was allowed to go to Rome in July 1988 to be invested as cardinal and was received by the party leadership on his return. Restrictions were lifted from the other repressed prelate, Bishop Julijonas Steponavičius of Vilnius, who was allowed to visit the Vatican in the fall of 1988 and at the end of December was invited by the authorities to resume his pastoral duties. For the first time since 1940 mass public religious services were allowed. The open air Mass celebrated in the cathedral square in Vilnius on the occasion of the founding congress of the Lithuanian Restructuring Movement in October 1988 was, unprecedentedly, broadcast live on television.

While not as dramatic as in Lithuania, analogous developments in the regime's relations with religious bodies also occurred in the other two republics. In the fall of 1988 the Riga cathedral was returned to the Lutheran Church, and an open air service took place on the occasion of the founding congress of the Popular Front of Latvia.

Opposition and Dissent

Opposition to the political status quo has been an undercurrent in the Baltic republics since their occupation and incorporation into the USSR. During the immediate postwar years opposition, in anticipation of an imminent Soviet break with the West, took the form of guerrilla warfare, particularly in Lithuania. As these hopes waned, accommodation with the occupation became the norm. But accommodation did not necessarily imply permanent acceptance. With the Thaw and Khrushchev's de-Stalinization campaign, overt manifestations of dissatisfaction with Soviet rule in the Baltic reappeared.

In Lithuania, mass demonstrations took place in Vilnius in the fall of 1956 and in Kaunas in 1960. A full-scale riot broke out in Kaunas in 1972, occasioned by the self-immolation of a young man, Romas Kalanta, in protest against the regime. The local militia proved unable to cope with the crowds of youths, numbering in the thousands and shouting nationalist slogans; special army and KGB troops had to be flown in to quell the riots. In Latvia, disturbances took place in Liepāja, and there were unconfirmed reports of a riot in Riga in May 1985: students gathered for an official convention staged a demonstration, carrying posters reading "Down with the Party—Down with the Russians." They were in turn attacked by Russian youths. Three hundred participants reportedly were detained, and three Russians who were thrown into the Daugava River drowned.[24] That fall, hundreds of Estonian youths clashed with Russians in Tartu during preparations for the Day of the Soviet Constitution. Earlier in Estonia there were disturbances in Tartu in 1977, and, most notably, a series of demonstrations by high school and university students in Tallinn and other cities in the fall of 1980. Such sporadic youth outbursts became common, especially in Estonia and Latvia where they frequently involved confrontations between the natives and immigrant Russian workers.

Other types of dissident activity, never absent, also increased during the 1970s.[25] These were most pronounced in Lithuania, where much opposition has been religiously motivated. During the early 1970s mass petition drives were successfully conducted on questions of Church-state relations. Lithuania achieved a record in the production of known *samizdat* literature, on a per capita basis more than any other Soviet republic. The *Chronicle of the Catholic Church in Lithuania* [Lietuvos Katalikų Bažnyčios Kronika], which systematically recorded instances of harassment of clergy and believers by the authorities, was the longest running *samizdat* periodical in the USSR, appearing since 1972. In November 1976, a Helsinki Watch Committee, paralleling similar groups in Moscow and in other republics, was formed in Lithuania to monitor Soviet compliance with the newly signed Helsinki Accords. Of its original five founders, two have since died, two emigrated, and one, Viktoras Petkus, the most prominent Lithuanian dissident, was arrested and sentenced in 1977; he was released only in 1988.

In Estonia, the early 1970s saw the formation of two small resistance groups, the Estonian National Front and the Estonian Democratic Movement. Their memorandum to the secretary general of the United Nations in 1972, calling for Estonian self-determination, led to arrests and prison sentences in 1974 and 1975. Dissident activities continued, however, in the form of letters, petitions, and *samizdat* publications, most prominently *Some Additions to the Free Flow of Thoughts and News in Estonia* [Lisandusi mõtete ja uudiste vabale levikule Eestis], which began to appear in 1978. Political and cultural issues, especially language rights and the immigration of Russians, as well as ecology were the main concerns. These concerns also featured prominently in Latvian dissent, which, however, was less widespread and more pessimistic in tone than in Lithuania and Estonia.

In contrast to the situation elsewhere in the Soviet Union, dissidents in the three Baltic republics cooperated with each other and coordinated their activities. Thus, a joint statement, dated 23 August 1979, protested the Molotov-Ribbentrop Pact of 1939 and demanded the publication of its full text in the USSR, including the secret protocols on the division of Eastern Europe. Signed by forty-five individuals, the statement demanded that the pact be declared void by the USSR and the two German states, which were requested "to assist the Soviet government to nullify the consequences of that Pact; namely, to withdraw foreign troops from the Baltic states." It has been claimed that the petition gathered some 35,000 signatures in Lithuania, but that cannot be confirmed. A similar statement, dated January 1980, was signed by twenty-one persons from all three republics condemning the Soviet invasion of Afghanistan. The repression that followed only seemed to increase the protest. In October 1981 an open letter signed by thirty-eight Balts "Concerning the Establishment of a Nuclear-Free Zone in Northern Europe" called for the inclusion of the Baltic republics in such a zone.[26]

The events in Poland during the early 1980s caused reverberations throughout the Baltic region, especially in Lithuania, two-thirds of which can receive Polish television. To stem a possible contagion, regime apologists began privately, though seemingly in concert, to revive anti-Polish sentiments in Lithuania, where they were strong in prewar times. The most evident echo of Solidarity, however, came from Tallinn, where a call was issued in December 1981 for a "silent half-hour"—a brief work stoppage, to be repeated once a month until several demands, mostly economic, had been met.

A crackdown on dissident activities took place in 1983, possibly connected with the elevation of the KGB chief, Yurii Andropov, to the post of general secretary. For the first time since 1971, clergymen in Lithuania were arrested and placed on trial. Other prominent religious activists were repressed or subjected to assault. One, the Rev. Juozas Zdebskis, was killed in February 1986 in an automobile accident which, according to several sources, showed signs of having been arranged.[27] The repression succeeded in reducing the volume of Lithuanian *samizdat*. The only such publications to come out in 1984 were the *Chronicle of the Lithuanian Catholic Church* and *Dawn* [Aušra]. Both continued to appear, though for a while they faced greater difficulty in reaching the West.

The wave of repression also affected Estonia and Latvia. The Latvian Gunārs Astra, for example, received the unusually harsh sentence of seven years in a strict regime labor camp, to be followed by five in exile, for dissemination of a *samizdat* novel and possession of George Orwell's *1984*. An even harsher sentence, by Soviet standards, was meted out in 1984 to the Estonian Enn Tarto, who received ten years in a strict regime labor camp for signing appeals labelled as "anti-Soviet agitation and propaganda." These included the above-mentioned letter on a nuclear-free zone.[28]

As in Lithuania, visible dissent was not eliminated in either Latvia or Estonia. In 1984, a letter on world disarmament and the abolition of censorship signed by eight individuals appeared. In early 1986, an anonymous group of Estonian scientists issued a protest against the ongoing Russification of the republic stimulated by the massive port construction at Muuga and the phosphate mining operations. The twenty-third issue of the Estonian *samizdat* journal *Lisandusi . . .* appeared in 1986.

The mass demonstrations that have taken place since 1987 have fundamentally altered the role and rationale of dissident activity in all three Baltic republics. The role of dissent has been preempted to a large extent by the mass national movements. While the Latvian commemoration of the 1941 deportations in June 1987 and the demonstrations in the three capitals in August of that year noting the anniversary of the Molotov-Ribbentrop Pact were still organized by elements prominent in the dissent movement, these demonstrations were allowed by the authorities. The mass demonstrations in the summer of 1988 even drew the participation of regime officials. The Lithuanian dissidents planning the 23 August 1988 demonstration opted to join in the mass event called by the Lithuanian Restructuring Movement, as the goals of both coincided. However, dissident activity did not entirely disappear and continued to play some role on the evolving scene. A hunger strike in the cathedral square of Vilnius in August–October 1988 protesting continued political repression of some individuals drew considerable public support from republican notables. Public reaction to the suppression of an unsanctioned demonstration in Vilnius in September 1988 contributed to the change in republican party leadership. Nevertheless, the line between dissident and sanctioned political activity has grown exceedingly thin. If present policies of *perestroika, glasnost'*, and democratization continue and genuinely take root, that line is bound to disappear.

Conclusion

The period from 1968 to the accession of Gorbachev was marked by basic contradictions in the three Baltic republics. On the one hand, the Brezhnev years saw a continuing centralization of political and economic life. The *immobilisme* of party leadership at the republican level paralleled the gerontocratic stagnation at the center. Large-scale economic projects involving massive construction and the use of immigrant labor continued, despite their increasingly deleterious effect on the society and ecology of the Baltic republics and in the face of growing opposition. On the other hand, the expansion of a Western-oriented culture, begun in the late 1950s, outlasted the Thaw. Ideological cant proved insufficient to homogenize Baltic cultural life, which steadily expanded the limits of the acceptable. Contacts with the outside world increased steadily. A slow but real rise in living standards through the late 1970s somewhat mollified local discontent. By the end of the decade and into the 1980s, however, economic growth slowed, and this was accompanied by a fresh wave of Russification and renewed immigration. Perceived as the main threat to national survival, immigration engendered particular resentment.

Soviet authorities expected that with the passage of time and the change of generations, the benefits of the new social system would mitigate native opposition. Support for the regime, originally limited to a tiny minority, would spread to ever larger numbers, whose positions and material comfort would depend upon the maintenance of the existing order. Modernization and rising standards of living would legitimize the regime. The presence of a large population of Russian settlers in Latvia and Estonia would serve as further insurance for the preservation of the status quo.

Such expectations proved illusory, even in Lithuania, where industrialization has by any calculation considerably improved the quality of life in comparison with prewar days, to an extent greater than in Estonia or Latvia. By Soviet standards, the three Baltic republics are in the forefront of economic development and modernization. They enjoy the highest standard of living in the USSR outside of Moscow and Leningrad. Yet for the indigenous populations the real measure of comparison remained the West, and their relatively extensive exposure to the outside world continued to underscore the backwardness of the region in their minds.

In the final analysis, economic issues have not proved to be the paramount question in the Baltic republics. It may well be that Gorbachev, sensing that his program of *perestroika* was being subverted by conservative bureaucrats at the all-union level, realized a need to circumvent the entrenched bureaucracy with the help of grass roots movements. The Baltic republics, a traditional arena for Soviet economic experimentation (most of it ill-conceived), appeared particularly suited for such a venture. It cannot be known whether the initiative for the mass movements led by the creative and technical intelligentsia of the three republics merely received the sanction of the Kremlin, or whether they were part of a larger centrally conceived design on the part of Gorbachev and his reformist supporters.[29] It is clear, however, that the hundreds of thousands of Baltic demonstrators who had taken to the streets since 1987 were concerned primarily with a fundamental transformation of the political system rather than with economic mismanagement. The loyalty of the Baltic populations is to their national groups, not to the USSR or to the Soviet regime. The espousal of the national cause by the new leaders of the Baltic republics accorded them some genuine popularity. That, however, may prove to be short-lived. Expectations among the Balts have been aroused, and the return of national symbols has proved inadequate. As Politburo member Aleksandr Yakovlev is reputed to have said to the Lithuanians with whom he met during a publicized visit to Vilnius in August 1988, "We have let the genie out of the bottle." It is too early to speculate how the issue of sovereignty-independence, on which all other desiderata of the national movements depend, will be decided. But hopes of genuine self-determination are strong, and it is doubtful whether a form of autonomy can any longer be designed that would both satisfy the Baltic populations and still preserve the Soviet state.

Notes

1. T. Ženklys [pseud.], "Su A. Sniečkaus mirtimi pasibaigusi Lietuvos gyvenimo epocha," *Akiračiai* (Chicago), March 1974; republished in Russian translation as "Dve stat'i T. Zhenklisa: Proshchaias' s Antanasom Snechkusom; Chego my zhdem ot emigratsii?" with an introductory note by A. Shtromas, *Kontinent*, vol. 14 (1977), pp. 229–50.

226 ROMUALD J. MISIUNAS

2. *USSR News Brief* (Munich), 31 May 1981, pp. 4–5.

3. Sergei Zamascikov, "The Ascent of Boriss Pugo or Voss's Long Road to Moscow," *Baltic Forum*, vol. 1, no. 1 (Fall 1984), pp. 67–73.

4. Romuald J. Misiunas and Rein Taagepera, *The Baltic States: Years of Dependence, 1940–1980* (Berkeley and Los Angeles: University of California Press, 1983), p. 284; Pranas Vaitkūnas, "Lietuvos komunistų partija," *Švyturys*, 1986, no. 2, pp. 5–6; *Kommunisticheskaia partiia Estonii v tsifrakh, 1920–1980* (Tallinn: Eesti raamat, 1983), pp. 109, 181–82.

5. The events in the Baltic republics since the summer of 1987 have been extensively reported in the Western press, and increasingly openly in the Soviet media. For day-by-day Soviet press coverage, see the relevant issues of U.S. Foreign Broadcast Information Service, *Daily Report: Soviet Union*.

6. A transcript of the meeting circulated in Latvian translation in *samizdat*. Extensive sections of it appear in *Baltic Forum*, vol. 5, no. 2 (Fall 1988). Highlights have been reported in a news bulletin of the World Federation of Free Latvians (Rockville, MD), 23 June 1988. An extensive description and summary also appeared in *Dagens Nyheter* (Stockholm), 16 October 1988.

7. On the debates and votes on the sovereignty issue in Estonia, Lithuania, and Latvia, respectively, see *New York Times*, 17, 19, and 23 November 1988.

8. *Gimtasis kraštas*, 17 November 1988.

9. For a discussion of demographic developments through 1979, see Misiunas and Taagepera, *Baltic States*, pp. 272–73.

10. *Chislennost', sostav i razmeshchenie naseleniia Latviiskoi SSR po gorodam i raionam po dannym perepisi naseleniia 1979 goda* (Riga, 1980), reproduced in "National Composition of Population in Latvia," *World Federation of Latvians Press Release* (Rockville, MD), 24 September 1984; *Baltic Forum*, vol. 2, no. 1 (Spring 1985), pp. 145–49; *Itogi perepisi naseleniia po Estonskoi SSR, 1979* (Tallinn, n.d.), reproduced in Rein Taagepera, "Size and Ethnicity of Estonian Towns and Rural Districts, 1922–1979," *Journal of Baltic Studies*, vol. 13, no. 2 (Summer 1982), pp. 105–27.

11. Toomas Ilves, "An Open Letter of Protest from Estonian Scientists," *Radio Free Europe Research*, Baltic Area/SR 4 (18 July 1986), pp. 5–6.

12. *Baltic Forum*, vol. 3, no. 2 (Fall 1986), pp. 52–55; *Literaturnaia gazeta*, 5 November 1986.

13. See Vera Tolz, "The USSR This Week," *Radio Liberty Research Bulletin*, RL 485/88 (4 November 1988), p. 4.

14. Misiunas and Taagepera, *Baltic States*, p. 207.

15. TASS, 10 October 1988.

16. *Sovetskaia Estonia*, 10 September 1988.

17. *Sovetskaia Latviia*, 6 January 1979.

18. *Aušra*, no. 15 (February 1979).

19. *Baltic Forum*, vol. 3, no. 2 (Fall 1986), pp. 113–17.

20. "An Interview with Arthur Miller," *Baltic Forum*, vol. 3, no. 1 (Spring 1986), pp. 13–15; see also pp. 80–86 for Udam.

21. Juozas Urbšys, *Lietuva lemtingaisiais 1939–1940 metais* (Vilnius: Mintis, 1988).

22. *New York Times*, 26 August 1984.

23. See, for example, *Gimtasis kraštas*, 18–24 December 1986.

24. *Die Welt*, 5 July 1985.

25. For a detailed survey of dissent in the Baltic republics, see Ludmilla Alexeyeva, *Soviet Dissent: Contemporary Movements for National, Religious, and Human Rights* (Middletown, CT: Wesleyan University Press, 1985), pp. 60–85 (on Lithuania), pp. 86–96 (on Estonia), and pp. 97–105 (on Latvia).

26. Misiunas and Taagepera, *Baltic States*, pp. 258–59; Rein Taagepera, "Inclusion of the Baltic Republics in the Nordic Nuclear-Free Zone," *Journal of Baltic Studies*, vol. 16, no. 1 (Spring 1985), pp. 33–51.

27. "Catholic Committee Member Killed in Lithuania," *Lithuanian Information Center Bulletin* (New York), 10 February 1986; also noteworthy is the TASS comment on the case (18 February 1986).

28. *Information Bulletin of the Estonian Centre for Relief of Prisoners of Conscience* (Stockholm), 1984.

29. See, for example, the evaluation of Alex Milits in *Svenska Dagbladet* (Stockholm), 27 October 1988.

CHAPTER 10

Transcaucasia:
Cultural Cohesion and Ethnic Revival
in a Multinational Society

Ronald Grigor Suny

Of the various ethnic peripheries of the Soviet Union—the European West, the Baltic, Central Asia—the most linguistically and culturally diverse is certainly Transcaucasia. Historic attempts to link Armenians, Azerbaidzhanis, and Georgians politically have invariably faltered, and the cultural orientations of the three major nationalities of the region remain focused in very different directions. Azerbaidzhanis, though far more secularized than their neighbors and kinsmen across the Soviet borders, are part of the Eurasian Turkic and Muslim worlds. Armenians pride themselves on their cosmopolitan horizons and see themselves as tied to an international Armenian community with deep historic roots in a land lost to many of them. The Georgians, more insular than the Armenians and as reluctant as the Azerbaidzhanis to migrate from their homeland, remain intent on maintaining their traditions no matter what the thrust of current Soviet policy. In the decades since the fall of Khrushchev, the history of Transcaucasia has been one of recurring attempts by central authorities to make the area conform to the norms of Soviet life. Yet the internal cohesion of each of the local nationalities has permitted effective resistance to outside interference, and Transcaucasia continues to be one of the most culturally and socially independent parts of the Soviet Union. In 1988 that very diversity precipitated an explosion that constituted the most serious challenge to Soviet state authority over the border republics since the early postrevolutionary years.

By the early 1960s the republics of Transcaucasia had undergone a long and complex process of national state-building. Though the Armenians and Georgians looked back on a past that included numerous state formations stretching back into classical times, the Azerbaidzhanis had never had an independent political existence. All three peoples had experienced national awakenings in the nineteenth century—the Georgians and Armenians first, the Azerbaidzhanis toward the end of the century. All three had briefly formed independent national republics at the end of World War I and before the establishment, by the Red Army, of Soviet power. But it was in the early Soviet period that the state policy of *korenizatsiia* (nativization) within a federal system based on ethnic units permitted the three republics eventually to establish solid demographic bases (with the in-migration of Armenians into the Armenian republic and out of the other two republics), build up national cultural institutions, and educate Communist and intellectual cadres from the dominant nationality. The peculiar process of Soviet state-building occurred without the exercise of full sovereignty or unlimited nationalist expression and simultaneously with state-promoted economic development that transformed a predominantly agrarian society of small towns and villages into a more mobile and potentially diverse urban and industrial society.

With the end of the police regime of Stalin and the loosening of central control under Khrushchev, the national political elites exercised greater power in the republics, and the extraordinary restrictions on ethnic expression of the Stalinist past were modified. But in Transcaucasia this period of "indirect rule" from Moscow was used by local party elites to extend favoritism toward their respective nationalities.[1] Along with the rise of complex networks of patrons and clients, "family circles," and the widespread development of a "second economy," there was a perceptible and chronic slowdown in the official economy.

Through the 1960s the Moscow leadership was concerned about the poor economic performances by the Transcaucasian republics, particularly by Azerbaidzhan. In national income growth Azerbaidzhan was in fifteenth place among the fifteen union republics; Georgia was twelfth; and only Armenia, at third place, was above the all-union average. In industrial labor productivity Armenia and Azerbaidzhan tied for twelfth place, well below the USSR average, and Georgia finished in ninth place. Azerbaidzhan was fourteenth in overall industrial productivity, Georgia twelfth, and Armenia fifth.[2] Moreover, the well-known and only slightly hidden underground economic activities were becoming a national scandal. Party leaders, like Veli Akhundov in Azerbaidzhan, Anton Kochinian in Armenia, and Vasilii Mzhavanadze in Georgia, men who had enjoyed Khrushchev's favor, were themselves known to be involved in the corruption and favoritism that characterized normal Transcaucasian political and economic practices. Their tenures were marked by extraordinary longevity. Mzhavanadze was first secretary of the Georgian Communist party for nineteen years (1953–72). Kochinian had served as chairman of the Council of Ministers of Armenia (1952–66) before being tapped by Brezhnev to be first secretary (1966–74). Akhundov had succeeded Imam Mustafaev (1954–59), who had been ousted for corruption and national "isolationism," and spent ten years as first secretary of the Azerbaidzhani party. The longevity of these national leaderships had by the early 1970s led to consolidated local elites which placated the local populations with moderate concessions to national feelings and a high degree of economic permissiveness. But by the end of the 1960s the Brezhnev regime, which in general backed the entrenched party cadres, could no longer tolerate the continued frustration of its economic plans.

Political Developments

In order to break through the complex networks of friends, clients, and relatives which local party bosses had erected, the central party leaders turned to new personnel outside the dominant party apparatuses. On 14 July 1969, Geidar (*Azer.* Heidar) Aliev, a career KGB officer, was selected as first secretary of the Azerbaidzhani Communist party. Three years later, in September 1972, his colleague in the Georgian security forces, Eduard Shevardnadze, was named leader of the Georgian party. That same year Russians were brought into Armenia to serve as second secretary of the Central Committee and head of the KGB, and in November 1974 Karen Demirchian, a young Armenian engineer educated outside the republic, became party chief in Armenia. The mandate given these men was the same: to end economic and political corruption, to stimulate economic growth, to end ethnic favoritism and contain the more overt expressions of local nationalism, and to promote a new governing elite able to carry out the policies of the Communist party.

Once Akhundov had been "retired" to the Azerbaidzhani Academy of Sciences, Aliev began an extensive purge of high party and state officials. Within the first five years of his administration, two-thirds of the Council of Ministers, eight of the ten members of the party Bureau, three of the four Central Committee secretaries, thirteen of the fourteen heads of Central Committee departments, and forty-five of the fifty-seven district party committee first secretaries had been replaced by new people.[3] Personal associates of the former KGB chief were placed in the great majority of the posts in the Bureau, in the Secretariat of the Central Committee, and at the head of the Central Committee departments. In order to prevent the re-formation of "family circles," a policy of frequent cadre rotation was instituted, and the party chief emphasized the need for party members to be moral exemplars and disciplined organizers.

In Georgia Shevardnadze attacked the dismal state of Georgian agriculture where "instances of embezzlement, report padding, bribery, extortion, deception and hoodwinking have been uncovered."[4] Little pride could be taken in the oft-repeated claim that the Georgian republic held first place in the world in the number of physicians per 10,000 people. One of the first officials to be dismissed was the notorious rector of the Tbilisi Medical Institute, who had tampered with entrance examinations, excluding qualified students and admitting those who paid bribes or were well connected.[5] In the next few years Shevardnadze replaced over three hundred high party and state officials, arrested hundreds of underground businessmen, restricted the free flow of farm produce out of Georgia (the source of a great deal of black market revenue), and used the considerable powers at his disposal to drive out the entrepreneurs who had transformed Georgia into a model of petty capitalism. With the police moving in to break up their illegal activities, some "speculators" struck back with bombings and arson in Tbilisi. The Moorish-style opera house on Rustaveli Prospekt was badly damaged by a deliberately set fire, and the first secretary himself was threatened with assassination.

Like that of Aliev in Azerbaidzhan, Shevardnadze's political style was a combination of toughness mixed with frank public criticism, energetic prosecution of wrongdoing tempered with moralism and calls for discipline—a style not unlike that adopted in the post-Brezhnev period by Andropov and Gorbachev. Even the first secretary himself was not above criticism, at least self-criticism, and in 1983 Shevardnadze publicly apologized for making the "serious mistake" of not heeding earlier warnings about the illegal activities of the Georgian finance minister.[6] Rather than rely simply on the power of the police, Shevardnadze was determined to base his programs on a degree of popular support. Earlier, as minister of internal affairs, he had organized an Institute for the Study of Public Opinion (1966) in order to learn more about public attitudes toward state policies. In this instance Aliev followed Shevardnadze and in the early 1970s established the Republican Center for the Study of Public Opinion in Azerbaidzhan.

Though economic problems and corruption also plagued the Armenian republic, the purges of party and state personnel were not as extensive as in Georgia and Azerbaidzhan. Shortly after Demirchian came to power, a number of ministers were dismissed (most importantly, Minister of the Interior Volodia Darbinian, replaced by Evgenii Badalov), along with the leaders of the Erevan and Leninakan party committees, the chairman of the Presidium of the Supreme Soviet, the head of the Komsomol, and the first and second secretaries of the Writers' Union. The new party leaders considered the rise in dissident nationalism and ideological laxness to be as much a failing of the previous leadership as the underground economy. Kochinian and Darbinian were accused of "delusions of grandeur," idealization of the past, as well as moral turpitude. Central party authorities were concerned that renewed interest in the Armenian national Church was competing with the official ideology for young hearts and minds.[7]

The underground economy and corrupt political practices in Transcaucasia were difficult, if not impossible, to eradicate precisely because of their connection to the traditional Caucasian reliance on close ties with family and friends. Since among Armenians, Georgians, and Azerbaidzhanis primary loyalty is centered on kinship groups or intimate friends, the sense of personal worth stems more from the honor or shame one brings on one's circle than from a successful career or great accumulation of wealth.[8] Favors done or received are the operative currency of both social and political relations, and the networks built up through favors and personal ties make it possible to circumvent the official state economy and legal forms of political behavior. So powerful are the obligations to one's relatives and friends that the shame incurred by non-fulfillment is, for most Caucasians, much more serious than the penalties imposed by law. Since the political and police structures have also been penetrated by such personal networks, protection from punishment was a frequent favor, and non-compliance with the law held fewer risks before the 1970s than breaking family codes. Even after the state came down hard on the "second economy" and the risks involved in circumventing the law increased, the networks persisted, an effective form of national resistance against the ways of doing business imposed by the Soviet polity.

The personnel changes and enforcement of discipline and legality in the economy began to have positive results by the mid-1970s. Azerbaidzhan's recovery was the most spectacular. As early as 1970–74 it ranked fourth among union republics in industrial labor productivity and national income growth, and sixth in industrial productivity. At that point Armenia was second in national income growth, but ninth in industrial productivity and thirteenth in industrial labor productivity. Georgia, however, was at the very bottom (fifteenth) in industrial productivity, with slightly better showings in industrial labor productivity (twelfth) and national income growth (thirteenth).[9] Through the decade labor productivity in Georgia and Azerbaidzhan rose faster than the USSR average, and in Armenia it ended the 1970s only slightly lower than the all-union figure.[10]

As the Brezhnev era drew to a close and reform-minded leaders tightened their hold on the central government, the achievements of the Transcaucasian parties were noted by the younger generation of Soviet party leaders. The experiments in economic organization undertaken in Georgia were widely reported. As early as 1973 Shevardnadze had promoted the efforts of Guram Mgeladze, first secretary of the Abasha district party committee in western Georgia, to institute a new system of agricultural management loosely based on the Hungarian reforms. A regional production association was set up that included collective and state farms as well as all the services and organizations involved in agriculture. Instead of each branch of the rural economy reporting separately to the corresponding republican or all-union authority, all aspects of local agriculture were controlled by the production association. This horizontal integration facilitated decision making, increased local initiative and coordination, and resulted in higher productivity and incomes for farmers. In 1981 Shevardnadze announced that the Abasha model would be applied throughout Georgia. With much of Soviet agriculture in crisis, Abasha attracted the attention of the Central Committee secretary in charge of agriculture, Mikhail Gorbachev, who visited Georgia on several occasions and pronounced the experiment "worthy of approval."[11]

Politically the 1970s were a period in which Moscow ended its laissez-faire policy toward Transcaucasia that had allowed local elites enormous discretion within their republics. But instead of imposing central control primarily through Russian officials or native Communists from the central apparatus, the choice was made to use dependable and energetic figures from within the republic but outside the circles of the former elites. The renewal of the party organizations and the economy was carried out by Communists whose programs had to balance skillfully the interests of the central party leadership and the needs of the local population. The success of the native Communists was reflected in the promotion of Aliev and Shevardnadze to the Politburo in 1982 and 1985 respectively, the appointment of Shevardnadze as foreign minister of the Soviet Union in 1985, and the retention of Demirchian as first secretary of the Armenian Communist party after more than twelve years in power. Aliev's replacement as first secretary of Azerbaidzhan was Kiamran Bagirov, and Shevardnadze's in Georgia— Dzhumber Patiashvili, both with experience in their republics' party apparatus. Political survival in the Gorbachev years, however, required new skills and an unusual degree of initiative and flexibility in order to adapt to and promote the far-reaching economic and social reforms of the new leadership. By the end of 1987 Aliev had been removed from the Politburo, and Demirchian's leadership had been repeatedly criticized for retarding the progress of *perestroika*. Both he and the Azerbaidzhani leader, Bagirov, were simultaneously removed in May 1988 in the midst of the explosion of protest over the fate of Nagorno-Karabakh. Their replacements—Suren Arutiunian (*Arm.* Harutiunian) in Armenia and Abdul-Rakhman (*Azer.* Abdul-Rahman) Vezirov in Azerbaidzhan—had both spent part of their careers outside their home republics, Arutiunian working in Moscow, Vezirov as a diplomat abroad. In April 1989 Patiashvili was dismissed as first secretary of Georgia, also in the wake of mass upheaval in that republic. His successor, Givi Gumbaridze, in contrast to the new Armenian and Azerbaidzhani leaders, had spent his entire career in his home republic. His rise was extremely rapid: from a district party committee first secretary he was promoted in the mid-1980s to serve on the republican Central Committee; in 1988 he became first secretary of the Tbilisi city party committee, and after only six months was tapped to head the republican KGB; four months later he was elected first secretary of the Communist party of Georgia.

Transcaucasia is part of what might be called "the Soviet Middle East," a strategically important salient into one of the most volatile and vulnerable parts of the world. The Iranian revolution, with its Shiite fundamentalism, had little visible reverberation in Azerbaidzhan, though Western analysts expected the new vigor of Islam in the Middle East to incite nationalism among Soviet Muslims. The persecution of Azerbaidzhanis in Iran—the closing of Turkic-language newspapers and reports of forced acceptance of Persian nationality—insulated Soviet Azerbaidzhanis from the influence of Khomeiniism. The Soviet Union reportedly opened its border with Iran to permit refugees from Khomeini's rule to move to the USSR.[12] The growing interest in the Islamic factor in Middle Eastern politics encouraged the Azerbaidzhani Institute of Peoples of the Near and Middle East to begin investigation of this phenomenon. But the most immediate consequence of Khomeini's revolution for Transcaucasia was the cutting off of natural gas, which was used extensively in Armenia for heating. Only in mid-1986 did Iran agree to renew exports of gas to the USSR.

The Arab-Israeli conflict has had reverberations in Transcaucasia. The Jewish community in Georgia, which dates back to the Middle Ages, began at the end of the 1960s to petition for emigration to Israel. Although they had rarely been victims of anti-Semitism and were well-integrated into Georgian society, the Georgian Jews were motivated by a new sense of

Jewish identity and the opportunity to better their material prospects. Eventually more than five thousand left for Israel, with hundreds of others settling in the United States.[13] In the same period that Jewish emigration was permitted from the Soviet Union, those Armenians who had been repatriated to Soviet Armenia in the 1940s or who had relatives abroad were permitted to leave for Europe or America. Some tens of thousands chose to emigrate to the West.

Armenians were concerned with two issues in Middle Eastern politics— the ongoing civil war in Lebanon and the campaign by the government of Turkey to deny the Armenian genocide of 1915. In November 1978 protests by the catholicos of the Armenian Apostolic Church (centered in Echmiadzin, Soviet Armenia) and the well-known writer Marietta Shahinian were directed against the attacks on Armenians in Lebanon.[14] But the issue that stirred Armenians most, both in Armenia and throughout the world, was the state-directed effort by Turkish scholars and diplomats to deny the Ottoman government's massacres and deportations of Armenians in eastern Anatolia in 1915. Beginning in January 1975 Armenian revolutionary groups abroad (first the Armenian Secret Army for the Liberation of Armenia and later the Justice Commandos of the Armenian Genocide) launched armed attacks on Turkish diplomats. Whatever the reaction of ordinary people in Soviet Armenia, the official attitude of the Soviet government was to condemn terrorism as well as the campaign of denial. Armenians were caught between their own ethnic interest in preserving the memory of the genocide and the Soviet state's interest in improving relations with Ankara. At the seventieth-anniversary commemorations of the genocide in 1985 anti-Turkish attacks were muted and the achievements of Soviet Armenia stressed. Only in the realm of scholarship were the Armenian concerns subtly expressed. A collection of documents on the genocide appeared, as well as a monograph on the Kars region, considered by Armenians to be part of their irredenta lost to Turkey.[15]

Demographic and Social Trends

Whatever the ultimate aims of Soviet nationalities policy—acculturation and bilingualism, assimilation, or the creation of a multinational "Soviet people"— the dominant process in Transcaucasia has been the ethnic consolidation and growing internal cohesion of the major nationalities. High birth rates for Armenians and Azerbaidzhanis, the out-migration of Russians and Georgian Jews, and the movement of Armenians—and more recently Azer-baidzhanis—from other Transcaucasian republics to their own have resulted in greater ethnic homogeneity in each republic. (The main demographic trends among the Transcaucasian nationalities since 1959 are shown in Table 1.) In the USSR overall, Azerbaidzhanis grew in number from 1959 to 1989 by 131.0%, Armenians by 66.0%, and Georgians by 48.0%. Within their respective republics all have increased their ethnic dominance. Georgians are over 70% of the population in Georgia, Azerbaidzhanis nearly 83% in

Azerbaidzhan, and Armenians, with the highest hegemony of any Soviet nationality, make up over 93% of their republic's population. At the same time the percentage of Russians in the population of Transcaucasia has steadily fallen—to 5.6% in Azerbaidzhan, 6.3% in Georgia, and 1.6% in Armenia—and there has been an absolute drop in the number of Russians in Georgia since 1959, in Azerbaidzhan since 1970, and in Armenia since 1979.

The nativization policies promoted in the 1920s were modified in the following decades as programs favoring Russian language and culture were implemented. Yet the demographic and cultural developments set in motion by *korenizatsiia* continued and by the 1960s had largely achieved their goals in Transcaucasia. The republics had become national in character, not only demographically, but politically and culturally as well. What have been in effect "affirmative action" programs promoted cadres from the titular nationalities, often to the detriment of the more urbanized and educated Russian (and in Azerbaidzhan and Georgia—Armenian) population. In Georgia, for example, the Communist party was 76.1% Georgian in membership in 1970, though in that year Georgians made up only 66.8% of the republic's population; Armenians made up 9.7% of Georgia's population but only 8.0% of the party membership, while Russians constituted 8.5% of the population and 5.5% of the party members.[16] At the same time ethnic Georgians accounted for 82.6% of the students in higher education in the republic, while Russians made up only 6.8% and Armenians 3.6%.[17]

The national consolidation of the Transcaucasian nationalities differed from republic to republic. For Azerbaidzhanis, with very high birth rates characteristic of the Soviet Muslim peoples, dominance is primarily the result of natural growth, assisted by the out-migration of Armenians from Baku and Nagorno-Karabakh. The number of Armenians in Azerbaidzhan declined by 19.4% between 1970 and 1989, from 484,000 to 390,000. By 1989 Azerbaidzhanis made up almost 83% of the republic's population. Relatively few of them migrate, and in 1989 85% of all Soviet Azerbaidzhanis lived within their titular republic.

The Georgians as well tend to stay within their homeland and have the highest concentration in the home republic (95.1%) of any Soviet nationality. Fearful about their birth rate, which is below that of both Azerbaidzhanis and Armenians, the Georgians have benefitted from the Russian and Armenian out-migration and the predilection of some non-Georgians to adopt Georgian endings for their names and assimilate into the dominant population. Still, in 1989 Georgians made up only 70.2% of the republic's population, with Armenians holding at 8.1% and Russians at 6.3%. In November 1983 Shevardnadze warned that the demographic situation in Georgia had worsened "catastrophically," and he spoke out forcefully against the prevalent practice of abortion as birth control. The rate of natural population growth had declined by 50% in recent years, and in thirty-five districts population had fallen. In 1981 alone abortions in Georgia had numbered 100,000, while live births were only 90,000.[18]

TABLE 1A. Demographic Trends among the Transcaucasian Nationalities in the USSR, 1959-1989

| | Total Population (in thousands) | | | | Population Increase |
	1959	1970	1979	1989	1959-89
USSR	208,827	241,720	262,085	285,689	76,862
Russians	114,114	129,015	137,397	145,072	30,958
Georgians	2,692	3,245	3,571	3,983	1,291
Armenians	2,787	3,559	4,151	4,627	1,840
Azerbaidzhanis	2,940	4,380	5,477	6,791	3,851

| | Percent Increase | | | | Percent of Population | | | |
	1959-70	1970-79	1979-89	1959-89	1959	1970	1979	1989
USSR	15.7	8.4	9.0	36.8	100	100	100	100
Russians	13.1	6.5	5.6	27.1	54.65	53.37	52.42	50.78
Georgians	20.6	10.0	11.6	48.0	1.29	1.34	1.36	1.39
Armenians	27.7	16.6	11.5	66.0	1.33	1.47	1.58	1.62
Azerbaidzhanis	49.0	25.1	24.0	131.0	1.41	1.81	2.09	2.38

TABLE 1B. Percentage Concentration Rates of Nationalities in Their Titular Republics, 1959-1989

	1959	1970	1979	1989	Change 1959-89
Russians	85.8	83.5	82.6	82.6	- 3.2
Georgians	96.6	96.5	96.1	95.1	- 1.5
Armenians	55.7	62.0	65.6	66.6	+10.9
Azerbaidzhanis	84.9	86.2	86.0	85.4	+ 0.5

TABLE 1C. Ethnodemographic Trends in the Transcaucasian Republics, 1959-1989

	Total Population (in thousands)				Population Increase
	1959	1970	1979	1989	1959-89
Georgia	4,044	4,686	4,993	5,396	1,352
Georgians	2,601	3,131	3,433	3,789	1,188
Armenians	443	452	448	437	- 6
Russians	408	397	372	339	- 69
Armenia	1,763	2,492	3,037	3,304	1,541
Armenians	1,552	2,208	2,725	3,082	1,530
Azerbaidzhanis	108	148	161	85	- 23
Russians	56	66	70	52	- 4
Azerbaidzhan	3,698	5,117	6,027	7,020	3,322
Azerbaidzhanis	2,494	3,777	4,709	5,801	3,307
Russians	501	510	475	392	- 109
Armenians	442	484	475	390	- 52

	Percent Increase				Percent of Population			
	1959-70	1970-79	1979-89	1959-89	1959	1970	1979	1989
Georgia	15.9	6.5	8.1	33.4	100	100	100	100
Georgians	20.4	9.7	10.4	45.7	64.31	66.81	68.76	70.23
Armenians	2.1	- 0.9	- 2.5	- 1.4	10.95	9.65	8.97	8.09
Russians	- 2.7	- 6.3	- 8.9	-16.9	10.09	8.46	7.45	6.28
Armenia	41.3	21.9	8.8	87.4	100	100	100	100
Armenians	42.3	23.4	13.1	98.6	88.01	88.62	89.73	93.27
Azerbaidzhanis	37.5	8.8	-47.2	-21.3	6.11	5.95	5.30	2.57
Russians	17.1	6.1	-25.7	- 7.1	3.20	2.65	2.30	1.56
Azerbaidzhan	38.4	17.8	16.5	89.8	100	100	100	100
Azerbaidzhanis	51.4	24.7	23.2	132.6	67.46	73.81	78.13	82.64
Russians	1.8	- 6.9	-17.5	-21.8	13.56	9.97	7.88	5.59
Armenians	9.4	- 1.9	-17.9	-11.8	11.96	9.45	7.88	5.56

Sources: Derived from 1959, 1970, 1979, and 1989 Soviet census data. Itogi Vsesoiuznoi perepisi naseleniia 1959 goda: SSSR; ... Gruzinskaia SSR; ... Armianskaia SSR; ... Azerbaidzhanskaia SSR (Moscow: Gosstatizdat, 1962). Itogi Vsesoiuznoi perepisi naseleniia 1970 goda, vol. 4 (Moscow: Statistika, 1974). Chislennost' i sostav naseleniia SSSR: Po dannym Vsesoiuznoi perepisi naseleniia 1979 goda (Moscow: Finansy i statistika, 1984). Data for 1989 are from preliminary unpublished results of the 1989 census, and are subject to correction.

The Armenian situation is at the opposite pole from that of the Georgians. While Armenia is the most ethnically homogeneous of the union republics (93.3% Armenian in 1989), only 66.6% of Soviet Armenians live in Armenia, and millions more Armenians live in the diaspora outside the Soviet Union. Though the percentage of Soviet Armenians living in the republic has improved since 1959, when it was only 55.7%, Armenians are still the Soviet people least likely to live in their union republic. Given the small size of their republic (the smallest of the fifteen union republics), their history as a dispersed and often stateless people, and the loss of the greater part of historic Armenia (now in present-day Turkey), the Armenians have maintained the traditional patterns of migration and adaptation to other cultures. While Armenia and Georgia ranked highest among all republics in the proportion of the population with some secondary education, as well as in per capita number of highly educated specialists, more than half (51%) of Armenia's specialists were "exported" to other parts of the Soviet Union.[19] Since Armenians who leave the republic are more likely to intermarry with non-Armenians and lose their sense of national identity, there has been apprehension about this tendency to lose half of the most talented young Armenians to other republics.

Yet from the standpoint of all-union interests, the high birth rates and educational attainments of Transcaucasia have created a pool of reserve labor, much of it highly skilled, for the Soviet Union's economic development plans. The population of Transcaucasia is younger than that of the USSR as a whole. In 1970, 49% of Armenians in Armenia were under twenty years of age; in Azerbaidzhan the figure was 58% for Azerbaidzhanis, in Georgia 39% for Georgians, while for the Soviet population overall it was only 38%.[20] Clearly, Transcaucasia contains an economic potential which the central authorities will want to tap, yet only the Armenians have so far shown any willingness to migrate. In the future the Soviet government may have to respond to ethnic preferences to remain in the national homelands by locating industry and research facilities closer to the available work forces.

As for intermarriage between ethnic groups, the rates are very low within Transcaucasia, both because of the preferences for endogamous marriages among Azerbaidzhanis and Georgians—one Soviet authority argues that there is less prejudice toward intermarriage among Armenians—and the high ethnic homogeneity of the republics, especially Armenia.[21] In general, marriages between Muslims and non-Muslims are rare. Though figures are sparse, all indications are that over 90% of marriages in Transcaucasia are between members of the same ethnic group. In 1969, for example, 93.5% of Georgians married other Georgians and only 6.5% intermarried.[22]

Despite the inroads made on traditional patterns of life by urbanization, industrialization, and secular education, the distinct ethnic cultures of the region have grown in strength over the years of Soviet rule. But those cultures have adapted significantly to Soviet social reality. A majority of Azerbaidzhanis (51.3%) and Armenians (59.1%) and 40.9% of Georgians were workers, by Soviet definitions, by 1970. Azerbaidzhanis and Georgians were less "proletarian" than the Soviet population as a whole (56.7% workers), and the Azerbaidzhani percentage of white-collar employees (20.1%) was also lower than the all-Soviet figure of 22.6%. Georgia had the highest proportion of white-collar employees of any titular nationality (26.4%), while Armenia at 23.6% just surpassed the all-union average. The collective farm peasantry, which in all three republics had been the majority of the population in 1939, now made up 32.6% in Georgia, 28.4% in Azerbaidzhan, and 16.9% in Armenia.[23] By 1970 a majority of the people in Transcaucasia lived in urban settlements. A decade later Armenia, which had been 80% peasant in the 1920s, reached a level of two-thirds urban population, a figure higher than that for the Soviet Union as a whole (62%). Azerbaidzhan and Georgia were just over the 50% mark, well below the USSR average. Of the Transcaucasian peoples, however, Armenians alone had a majority living in cities (63%). Only 41% of ethnic Georgians and 43% of Azerbaidzhanis lived in cities.[24]

Armenians and Russians continued to make up a significant proportion of the populations of Baku and Tbilisi, and their long demographic dominance of these two cities was broken only in the 1960s when the titular nationalities finally became a majority in their respective capitals. This achievement, perhaps more graphically than any of the less palpable trends, pointed out the ironic result of Soviet nationality processes and policies in Transcaucasia. A largely Russian leadership in Moscow, with an ostensibly internationalist ideology, has overseen the demographic and cultural renationalization of the southern republics. One hundred years earlier Erevan had a Muslim majority, while in the early years of Soviet rule Tbilisi and Baku were largely Russian and Armenian cities. As the Soviet Union entered its seventh decade, these cities had become in the full ethnic sense the capitals of national states.

Cultural Developments

Ethnic consciousness continues to mediate in different ways how Soviet norms of behavior and consciousness are assimilated by various nationalities. But adaptation to Soviet society, through education and urbanization, is not the same as the assimilation of major nationalities into the culture of the dominant Russian nationality. A number of dominant ethnic cultures are coexisting uneasily in Transcaucasia. At the same time the noted process of ethnic homogenization has led to a certain amount of discrimination toward ethnic minorities, and this in turn has led to protest and resistance.

One of the key indicators of possible Russification are the figures on native-language retention and bilingualism. Brian D. Silver made an important study of the 1970 census to determine for non-Russians the percentages of those who knew only their national language (parochials), those who knew both Russian and the national language (bilinguals), and those who had lost the national language altogether (assimilated). Table 2 is based on Silver's figures.[25]

TABLE 2. Language Patterns among the Transcaucasian Nationalities
Residing in Their Titular Republics in 1970

Nationality	Rural	Urban	Capital City
Georgians in Georgia			
Parochials	91.4	63.3	56.4
Bilinguals	8.3	36.2	43.1
Assimilated	0.0	0.5	0.5
Armenians in Armenia			
Parochials	90.5	68.1	63.1
Bilinguals	9.5	31.8	36.7
Assimilated	0.0	0.1	0.1
Azerbaidzhanis in Azerbaidzhan			
Parochials	95.1	68.5	50.0
Bilinguals	4.5	30.4	47.7
Assimilated	0.1	1.0	2.2

What is clear from these figures is the low level of Russian-language knowledge among the rural population of Transcaucasia, the higher levels of knowledge among the urban population, especially in the capital cities, and the extremely low levels of fully assimilated people. The knowledge of Russian is positively correlated with the process of urbanization. Many Transcaucasians, despite their early introduction to Russian-language courses in school, do not really attain a speaking knowledge of Russian until they either migrate to the cities or (in the case of males) enter the armed forces.

While the titular nationalities of the Transcaucasian union republics have full native-language schooling right through the university, the minorities within the republics do not enjoy this privilege. Abkhazians, who have an autonomous republic within the Georgian SSR, for example, have only four years of native-language schooling before the language of instruction is changed to Russian. At this point Abkhaz and Georgian are taught as separate subjects. This aspect of language policy also in part accounts for the relatively higher levels of bilingualism among the South Ossetians (37.4% according to Silver), another minority—with an autonomous oblast—in Georgia. Some very small ethnic groups have lost their national-language schools altogether and learn their mother tongue from the first day of school only as a subject. Other larger groups, like the Armenians in Azerbaidzhan, have their own schools, at least in Baku and Nagorno-Karabakh, but since the Khrushchev reform of 1959 they have tended to choose Russian-language or Azerbaidzhani-language schooling for their children.[26]

In the cultural sphere the three major nationalities of Transcaucasia enjoyed broad support from the state as long as cultural expression was kept within the strict political limits set by official policy. At times tensions developed between party authorities and the national intelligentsias. Shortly after coming to power Shevardnadze attacked the party cadres in the South Ossetian Autonomous Oblast for their lack of internationalism. Writers were idealizing "outmoded traditions" and glorifying "moribund attributes of antiquity."[27] Though religion plays far less central a role in the life of people than it did in the pre-Soviet period, the press frequently carried reports of religious ceremonies, ostentatious feasting, funerals that continue for days, and even blood feuds in the Svaneti, Khevsureti, and Adzharia regions of Georgia. In Azerbaidzhan a 1982–83 poll showed that most Azerbaidzhanis observe both Soviet and Islamic marriage and funeral customs. Young people between the ages of 16 and 20 were even more likely to invite a mullah or priest to a funeral (88.6%) than the oldest group surveyed, those over sixty (79.2%).[28] The Armenian Apostolic Church and its catholicos since 1955, Vazgen I, have been symbols of national continuity and connection with the homeland for many Armenians outside the Soviet Union, and within the USSR many ordinary people view the Church as a cultural institution rather than a specifically religious one. But periodic waves of interest in Christianity aroused the Central Committee of the CPSU to issue a stern warning to the Armenian party in June 1983 about its ideological and mass political work. Although the Armenians were congratulated in October 1984 for improving their "work in internationalist upbringing," especially in the teaching of Russian, "serious shortcomings" were noted in atheistic education. A "non-class approach to the evaluation of historical events" was observed.[29] For all three major nationalities in Transcaucasia, and for many of the smaller ones as well, national culture is nearly indivisible from their historical religious self-definition. Yet it was precisely the weeding out of religious elements within these cultures that the Soviet government was most anxious to achieve.

Dissent and the Management of Ethnic Tensions

While the "negative phenomena" associated with the underground economy are especially powerful in Transcaucasia because of their cultural base, equally disturbing and persistently problematic for the state are the recurring manifestations of extralegal nationalism and interethnic conflict. Three distinct forms of nationalism emerged in the 1960s and 1970s: a pervasive "official nationalism" within the party and state bureaucracy, and sanctioned among the intelligentsia and population; a dissident or "unorthodox nationalism" expressed by a few human rights activists and even revolutionary separatists; and the counternationalisms of the minorities within the republics, aroused by their perception of discrimination by the ethnic majority. "Official nationalism," or what has been defined by Soviet authorities as "patriotism," became a permissible form of expression in the more laissez-faire atmosphere of the 1950s–1960s, but central authorities, fearing the growth of ethnic chauvinism or political separatism, periodically tried to rein in the more vocal proponents of local nationalism. With the new regimes of 1969–74, a renewed emphasis was placed on the need for Russian-language education and the curbing of what Shevardnadze called "national narrow-mindedness and isolation." Artists, writers and filmmakers were chided for exploiting themes with nationalist overtones, while the strongest attacks were reserved for that most ideological of sciences, history. Ushangi Sidamonidze and Akaki Menabde, two historians who had insufficiently condemned the Georgian Mensheviks in their work, were taken to task for their softness toward the enemies of Bolshevism.[30] Aramais Mnatsakanian, a prolific writer on Armenian party history, was attacked frequently for his idealization of the Armenian past.[31] In 1983 the once powerful and well-connected former director of the Institute of Party History in Erevan, Gevorg Gharibdzhanian, was accused of a nationalist approach in his discussions of the Armenian independence movement. He was criticized for attempting to rehabilitate several party members of the past without the sanction of central authorities.[32] Rather than collapse before this criticism, however, many intellectuals in Transcaucasia continued to push against the limits on national and political expression. Mnatsakanian, for example, continued to write and managed to insinuate his views into his texts. Azerbaidzhan's historians were considerably more cautious than those in Georgia and Armenia, but some of their orthodox interpretations of the past have also been modified in the direction of greater sensitivity to Islamic aspects.[33]

The most impressive examples of the tugging back and forth of state and society over the definition of national rights took the form of open defiance of state preferences. The different outcomes of three protest demonstrations illustrate the changing relationship in Soviet Transcaucasia between state and society. In March 1956 students in Tbilisi took to the streets to protest the removal of a monument to Stalin and were met by gunfire from the army. Dozens were killed, and only in the aftermath were quiet concessions made to the cult of Stalin in Georgia. Almost a decade later, on 24 April 1965, thousands of Armenians marched in an unofficial demonstration to mark the fiftieth anniversary of the genocide. The then first secretary, Zakov Zarobian, rejected the use of force, tried to calm the crowds, and ultimately made concessions to Armenian national sentiments. A monument to the victims of the massacres and deportations of 1915 was built on a hill in Erevan, Tsitsernakaberd, and each year on 24 April a spontaneous procession of people files up to the eternal flame to lay flowers. Most meaningful of all, the music which somberly plays includes the hymn "Soorp, soorp" [Holy, holy] from the Armenian liturgy. But Zarobian, who had achieved considerable popularity in Armenia for his conciliatory attitude toward Armenian national sentiments, was removed from power within a year after the demonstration.

The third protest occurred in Georgia, where great anxiety about the inroads of the Russian language had arisen because of Shevardnadze's open promotion of Russian. Suggestions by the Georgian minister of education that schools teach history, geography, and other subjects in Russian accompanied instructions from Moscow that all textbooks for higher educational institutions were to be in Russian, and Georgian dissertations were to be published and defended in Russian. Outraged by these challenges to Georgian as a language of learning and science, the writer Revaz Dzhaparidze made a forceful speech at the Eighth Congress of Georgian Writers (April 1976) in which he expressed his fear over the gradual erosion of Georgian. The audience greeted Dzhaparidze with nearly a quarter hour of applause and prevented the Georgian minister of education from answering him. Even Shevardnadze's attempts to allay fears of Russification were interrupted repeatedly by shouts from the audience.[34] But even more dramatic events occurred in Tbilisi in April 1978 when hundreds of students and others took to the streets to protest a government plan to change the clause in the Georgian constitution which proclaimed Georgian to be the state language of the republic. Shevardnadze twice addressed the crowd, estimated at five thousand, before the building of the Council of Ministers. The second time he informed them that he had recommended recognition of Georgian as the state language.[35] Not only was Georgian retained, but similar proposed changes in the constitutions of Armenia and Azerbaidzhan were prudently abandoned. No party leaders suffered from this open manifestation of anti-Russian sentiment.

Much more ominous for the state was the extralegal dissident nationalism which appeared potently in Armenia and Georgia, though not in Azerbaidzhan, in the mid-1970s. A small group of nationalists in Armenia had secretly formed the National Unity Party in 1967, but it was only in 1974 that they published an illegal journal and had one of their members set fire to a portrait of Lenin in the main square of Erevan. The founder of the group, Stepan Zatikian, and his associates were quickly rounded up, and in prison Zatikian broke with his more moderate followers and began to advocate terrorism. On 8 January 1977 a bomb exploded in the Moscow metro, killing seven and injuring thirty-seven. Two years later TASS announced that Zatikian and two other Armenians had been secretly tried, found guilty of the bombing, and summarily executed.[36] But the idea of an independent Armenia did not disappear with the NUP; in 1981 five members of a "Union of Young Armenians" were sentenced to twelve years in prison for circulating poems glorifying the idea of independence. On 24 April 1985, the most important political holiday in the Armenian calendar, the nationalist Ishkhan Mkrtchian died in a labor camp. It was widely believed that he had committed suicide to commemorate the anniversary of the genocide.

More typical of "unorthodox nationalism" than the revolutionary separatists were the intellectuals who formed human rights organizations. Though short-lived, the various Helsinki Watch Committees attempted to attract the attention of the international community to the violations of national rights within the Soviet Union.[37] The dissidents in Georgia were at first interested in the seemingly anodyne pursuit of preservation of Georgia's historic and religious monuments. Some of the more daring soon took up the plight of the Meskhetians, Muslim Georgians who had been forcibly moved in 1944 from their homes along the border with Turkey to Central Asia and wanted to return. Early in the summer of 1974, three Georgian intellectuals—Zviad Gamsakhurdia, son of the prominent writer Konstantin Gamsakhurdia; Merab Kostava, a writer and musicologist; and Viktor Rtskhiladze, art historian and later Director of Historical Monuments in the Georgian Ministry of Culture—formed the Initiative Group for the Defense of Human Rights in Georgia. Within a year they published the first *samizdat* literary journal in Georgian, *Golden Fleece* [Okros satsmisi], followed a year later by the political journal *Georgia's Herald* [Sakartvelos moambe]. This core group reorganized in 1977 as the Group for the Implementation of the Helsinki Accords. Within months they had all been arrested, along with a similar group in Armenia. Though Gamsakhurdia and Rtskhiladze later repented for their actions, Kostava refused, and nearly ten years later he was still in prison. Released in May 1987, Kostava, with Gamsakhurdia, founded the unofficial Ilia Chavchavadze Society, which soon emerged as the spearhead of a powerful nationalist revival. In November 1988 demonstrations were held in Tbilisi to protest proposed limits on Georgian sovereignty. Early in 1989 Georgian separatists, angered by renewed Abkhazian calls for secession of their autonomous republic from Georgia, organized hunger strikes and demonstrations in Tbilisi. On April 9, Soviet troops clumsily and brutally broke up the demonstrations, leaving at least nineteen dead. Patiashvili fell from power, but the disaffection from the Soviet regime continued to grow. Calls for Georgian independence became a dominant theme in the nationalist discourse that swept the republic.

If official nationalism was the legally sanctioned expression of the newly confident national majority in each republic, and unorthodox nationalism the desperate attempt to extend the bounds of national expression beyond the tolerance of Soviet authorities, the third form of nationalism in Transcaucasia arose from the frustrations and discriminations experienced by ethnic minorities within each of the republics. The ethnic mosaic of the region includes more than a dozen small groups: in Armenia—the Kurds, Yezidis, and Azerbaidzhanis; in Azerbaidzhan—the Christian Udins, the Jewish and Muslim Tats, Ingilos (Georgians), Armenians, and the Talyshes; and in Georgia—Armenians, Adzhars, Abkhazians, Ossetians, Greeks, and Azerbaidzhanis. Conflicts have occurred between many of these groups, but the two major ongoing confrontations are between the Abkhazians and the Georgians, and the Karabakh Armenians and the Azerbaidzhanis.[38]

The Abkhazians have reacted against what they contend is Georgian interference in their national life and Tbilisi's failure to foster Abkhaz cultural and economic progress. In December 1977 one hundred thirty Abkhaz intellectuals signed a letter of collective protest and circulated it widely. In May 1978 twelve thousand people gathered in the village of Lichny to support the signers of the letter and to demand that Abkhazia be allowed to secede from Georgia and join the Russian republic. After being deluged with letters and telegrams in favor of secession, Moscow dispatched Ivan Kapitonov, a secretary of the Central Committee, to Sukhumi, the Abkhaz capital. Kapitonov told the local party organization that secession was impermissible and had the party leader, Boris Adleiba, dismissed. The central government acknowledged the seriousness of Abkhaz complaints soon after, however, by decreeing a costly plan "for further development of the economy and culture of the Abkhaz ASSR."[39] A decade later Gorbachev's new tolerance for dissent encouraged the Abkhazians to call once again for separation from Georgia. This time, however, Georgian nationalists reacted with counter-demonstrations, and in the summer of 1989 Georgians and Abkhazians used firearms in violent confrontations.

An autonomous oblast lying entirely within Azerbaidzhan, Nagorno-Karabakh as late as 1959 was almost 85% Armenian in population, but by 1979 that proportion had fallen to 75%. Local Armenians, supported by their compatriots in the Armenian republic, claimed that the region was being kept backward by the Azerbaidzhani government and that Armenians were being encouraged to emigrate. Both in Karabakh and Armenia proper, activists had begun to agitate for the incorporation of Karabakh into Armenia in the 1960s. The novelist Sero Khanzadian, a party member originally sent by the authorities in Armenia to investigate the grievances of the local Armenians, later wrote to Brezhnev about this "instance of injustice which calls for liquidation." Although a series of protests were made, the central Soviet government repeatedly affirmed that Karabakh would remain part of Azerbaidzhan. But the issue continued to stir emotions into the Gorbachev years, and in August 1987 hundreds of thousands of signatures were gathered on a petition to incorporate Karabakh into Armenia. Two months later there were reports of violence against Armenians in Karabakh. In October Geidar Aliev, the former first secretary of Azerbaidzhan and highest ranking Muslim in the party, was removed from his seat on the Politburo, and the Gorbachev forces increased their pressure on the Armenians to dismiss Demirchian as their party leader. Tensions rose in Armenia, as a severe environmental crisis—air pollution, chemical poisons, and a feared nuclear plant—contributed to a national sense of danger to Armenian survival. The political opening provided by *glasnost'* and *perestroika* was seized by protesters who gathered in Erevan to demand that ecological problems be confronted and, more pointedly, that both Karabakh and the historically Armenian region of Nakhichevan, now an autonomous republic within the Azerbaidzhani SSR and largely Muslim in population, be brought into the Armenian republic.

Suddenly, unpredictably, on 13 February 1988 the Karabakh Armenians themselves began a series of demonstrations in favor of incorporation into Armenia.[40] Five days later Gorbachev tried to placate them by offering to hold a special session of the Central Committee to discuss state policy toward the nationalities. The very next day thousands marched in Erevan in support of Karabakh, and an unprecedented ethnopolitical crisis faced the Kremlin. In a historic move the Karabakh soviet, usually nothing more than a transmitter of party policy, voted, 110 to 17, to intercede with the Supreme Soviet of the USSR for the transfer of Karabakh to Armenia.

The authorities in Moscow hesitated to act and seemed at times confused. Some spokesmen condemned the demonstrations, while others sympathetically explained the roots of the protests. By the last week of February hundreds of thousands were marching in Erevan in continuous demonstrations. The Karabakh party boss, Boris Kevorkov, who had supervised the region while Armenian cultural institutions atrophied, was replaced by Genrikh Pogosian (*Arm.* Henrik Poghosian). Soviet troops were sent to Erevan, and with the report of four Armenians killed in Karabakh Gorbachev intervened directly, meeting with two prominent Armenian writers, the poet Silva Kaputikian and the journalist Zori Balayan. He called for calm and asked for a moratorium on demonstrations for one month while the leadership considered the issue. The writers returned to Erevan and convinced the protestors to agree to Gorbachev's request. Erevan quieted down, but Stepanakert, the capital of Karabakh, continued to demonstrate.

Azerbaidzhani refugees, fearing attack, fled from Armenia to Azerbaidzhan, and there rumors spread about Armenian violence against Muslims. For two days, 28–29 February, rioters in the Azerbaidzhani industrial town of Sumgait rampaged through the streets in search of Armenian victims. Busses were stopped and searched; hospitals were invaded. Before military forces could quell the riots, thirty-one were dead and hundreds beaten. Azerbaidzhani intellectuals and officials condemned the riots but maintained that Karabakh was historically a part of their homeland. The Gorbachev government was faced with an impossible task for which neither the Soviet constitution nor political precedent provided much guidance—to settle a violently contested territorial conflict between two union republics.

In late March 1988 *Pravda* attacked the Armenian demonstrations as "anti-socialist," thus signaling that the government would not concede Karabakh to Armenia. Instead a compromise seven-year plan of economic and cultural development, along the lines offered Abkhazia a decade earlier, was outlined. Azerbaidzhani discrimination against Armenians in Karabakh was tacitly admitted, but a final political solution was precluded. With new leaderships installed in both Azerbaidzhan and Armenia in May, the republican Supreme Soviets took up the issue. The Armenian body, predictably, voted to incorporate Karabakh into its republic, the Azerbaidzhani—vetoed the suggestion. The Soviet constitution made no specific allowance for such an impasse, and the decision again lay with Moscow.

Though the demonstrations in Erevan temporarily abated, the Karabakh Armenians continued their protests, even occasionally organizing a general strike. Hopes were placed on the June party conference in Moscow, but when no fundamental consideration of the national question was broached by the conference, the Armenians returned to the streets in force. In early July a general strike was called in Erevan and protestors closed down the airport. Soviet troops were called in, and at least one person was killed. Hundreds of thousands marched in his funeral-demonstration.

Nothing the central government did seemed to work, and support for the Armenians among other nationalities grew. A demonstration of one hundred thousand Lithuanians in Vilnius voted to support the incorporation of Karabakh into Armenia. The commitment to national self-determination, as much a Leninist as a Wilsonian principle, brought diverse and distant peoples together in a unique internationalist political embrace. Finally, after nearly six months, the government acted. On 18 July the Presidium of the Supreme Soviet met to discuss the Karabakh question, and for a full day Gorbachev presided over the emotional and divisive debate, much of which was televised to the country. Tension was evident between Gorbachev, who pressed for a compromise solution, and the Armenians, for whom anything short of incorporation of Karabakh into their republic represented an in- fringement of their rights. The decision was taken not to change the status of Karabakh, and the Armenian demonstrations, which had begun as loyalist manifestations, acts of optimism and commitment to reform along the lines suggested by Gorbachev's program of democratization, turned ever more hostile to the central government.

Though Armenians had not realized their goal of unification with Kar- abakh, the disputed region was placed under a special commission headed by a Moscow appointee, Arkadii Volsky. A real result of Armenian political protest, thus, was the de facto removal of Azerbaidzhani sovereignty over Karabakh. As reforms were implemented and the future status of Karabakh remained unclear, new clashes between Armenians and Azerbaidzhanis were reported in September. Soviet troops moved once again into Erevan. Renewed eruptions of Azerbaidzhani violence against Armenians broke out at the end of November in Kirovabad and Nakhichevan, areas where Armenians were a minority. Crowds killed three Soviet soldiers, and 126 people were injured. The complete breakdown of the interethnic symbiosis in Azerbai- dzhan and Armenia, compounded by the simultaneous demands for greater autonomy in the Baltic region, led Gorbachev to warn the non-Russians that the future of *perestroika* was at stake. "We are one family," he pleaded, "we have one common home."[41] But anger and fear in both Armenia and Azerbaidzhan could not be overcome with pleas or postponements. Tens of thousands of Armenian refugees began leaving Azerbaidzhan for Armenia, and Azerbaidzhanis, fearing reprisals, migrated from Armenia. Many of the now homeless Armenians settled in Leninakan and Kirovakan, just days before the massive earthquake of 7 December demolished the second and third largest cities of the republic. As 1988 came to an end, Armenians, stunned by the double tragedy imposed by nature and neighbors, tried to sort out the dismal results of a year of political promises and frustrated hopes. At the same time Gorbachev and his comrades, who had seen their triumphal visit to the United States cut short by the devastation in Armenia, were forced to face the most fundamental of Soviet dilemmas—how to democratize and modernize the largest country on the globe while maintaining the last multinational empire.

Rather than diminishing, national unrest increased in 1989. The official decision, announced in January, to place Karabakh directly under Moscow's supervision satisfied neither side. A state of civil war became the norm in and around Karabakh. In late summer the recently formed Azerbaidzhani Popular Front declared a general strike and a boycott of Armenia. The rail lines were blockaded, and Armenia, still devasted by the earthquake, lived with little fuel and food for weeks. For the first time in Soviet history one republic was in a de facto state of war with another. In November, Moscow ceded direct control over Karabakh back to the Azerbaidzhani republic. Ethnic hostilities and violence intensified yet again, and a widespread demoralization, even despair, seemed to call into question the future of *perestroika* in the region.

Conclusion

In the Western scholarly discussion of the aims and the results of Soviet nationalities policy, the same legislation or policy pronouncements, whether it was Khrushchev's educational reform of 1959 (which gave parents the right to choose the language of instruction of their children) or the Party Program of 1961 (which spoke of the eventual disappearance of ethnic distinctions and the adoption of a single lingua franca) or the Brezhnev constitution of 1977 (which announced the arrival of a new "Soviet people"), have been subjected to the most diverse interpretations. The government's promotion of bilingualism has been seen by many in the West (and, incidentally, by some members of national intelligentsias in the USSR) as an attempt to eliminate over time the non-Russian languages. Because the experience of different nationalities in language retention and assimilation varies tremendously, generalization from one to another is often misleading. The Transcaucasian case illustrates two processes that appear to be going on simultaneously in the Soviet Union: the ethnic consolidation of the larger nationalities, those with national political units, and the uneven adaptation of distinct ethnic groups to the common aspects of Soviet society and culture.

In contrast to the prediction of many social scientists, rather than assimilation or acculturation the Transcaucasian experience has been one of ethnic consolidation, a decisive decline in ethnic heterogeneity in all three republics, and effective resistance to attempts by the central party leaders to limit the renationalization of the region. Russification is simply not evident in Transcaucasia, either in the objective demographic and cultural trends or in the policies of the local Communist parties. In this way the experience of Transcaucasia may contrast with those of the more western nationalities, the Ukrainians, Belorussians, and the Baltic peoples. What is evident is the strengthening of the local ethnic groups as self-conscious nationalities even as they are educated in Soviet schools, find jobs in Soviet enterprises, and live lives increasingly like those of other Soviet peoples. Adaptation to Soviet social norms has gone hand in hand with the development of national cultures, but in the process those cultures have changed significantly. Religion has become more a form of cultural identification and has been relegated to a less dominant place in the lives of most Transcaucasians than it had been a half century earlier when the church and the mosque represented institutional and spiritual alternatives to the Soviet system. Inroads have been made in the traditional male dominance of women, though women remain far from equal to men. Customs, traditional holidays, costumes, and games have all been lost in the last half century, so that folk arts are difficult to find outside of museums, and village dances are more likely to be performed by professional companies. The national cultures of Transcaucasia today are a hybrid of traditional forms and practices heavily overlaid with new forms of behavior and invented "traditions" of the Soviet period.

Within the framework of the possible, the Soviet state and its ethnic societies struggle on the limits of national expression. For reasons of economic and bureaucratic efficiency, the state promoted the development of the Russian language. For political and ideological reasons, concessions were made to the national cultural elites. Instead of a one-sided repression or systematic Russification, which many in the West believed to be the norm in the USSR, the nationalities policy in Transcaucasia was characterized by political maneuvering by a state attempting to shape the forms of national discourse while promoting bilingualism and a popular commitment to the Soviet project. From the other side, an increasingly articulate civil society, more confident of the legitimacy of its claims, worked in its own way, using the cultural and institutional tools at its disposal, to expand its area of competence and protect the social and ethnic gains it has made. It may be that the eruptions in Transcaucasia are a warning to Soviet leaders that the dual revolutions they have promoted, modernization and ethnic cultural consolidation, can only be reconciled if the full meaning of Gorbachev's revolution for democracy and socialism is realized.

Notes

1. From 1954 to 1973 Armenia's Communist party had both first and second secretaries who were Armenian. Of the union republics, only Ukraine, Belorussia, and Estonia (to 1971) also enjoyed this privilege. All other republics had a native first secretary and a Russian or other Slav as second secretary. Georgia lost its native second secretary in 1956, Azerbaidzhan in 1957. "The dyarchy of native first secretary and Russian second secretary in charge of cadres is now the norm," wrote John H. Miller in 1977. "This is not the same as a strengthening of Russian control, but represents rather the strengthening of institutional procedures, in an area, where, before 1953, equivalent functions would have been performed by the security police." "Cadres Policy in Nationality Areas—Recruitment of CPSU First and Second Secretaries in Non-Russian Republics of the USSR," *Soviet Studies*, vol. 39, no. 1 (January 1977), p. 35.

2. *Narodnoe khoziaistvo SSSR v 1967 g.* (Moscow: Statistika, 1968), pp. 211–12; . . . *v 1968 g.* (1969), pp. 149, 558.

3. For an excellent discussion of the creation and functioning of the Aliev network, see John Patton Willerton, *Patronage and Politics in the Soviet Union* (Ph.D. diss., University of Michigan, 1985), chap. 4.

4. *Zaria vostoka*, 28 February 1973, translated in *Current Digest of the Soviet Press* (henceforth *CDSP*), vol. 25, no. 13 (25 April 1973), pp. 1–8.

5. *Zaria vostoka,* 3 November 1973, in *CDSP,* vol. 25, no. 44 (28 November 1973), p. 4; Konstantin Simis, *USSR—The Corrupt Society: The Secret World of Soviet Capitalism* (New York: Simon and Schuster, 1982), pp. 237–38.

6. *Pravda,* 14 May 1983, in *CDSP,* vol. 35, no. 19 (8 June 1983), pp. 6–7.

7. For the most detailed treatment of events and political shifts in the Armenian republic since the death of Stalin, see Claire Mouradian, *L'Arménie soviétique depuis la mort de Staline* (Thèse de Doctorat de 3ème cycle, École des Hautes Études en Sciences Sociales, 1982).

8. Gerald Mars and Yochanan Altman, "The Cultural Bases of Soviet Georgia's Second Economy," *Soviet Studies,* vol. 25, no. 4 (October 1983), p. 549.

9. *Narodnoe khoziaistvo SSSR v 1973 g.* (Moscow: Statistika, 1974), pp. 181–94, 574.

10. Gertrude E. Schroeder, "Transcaucasia since Stalin: The Economic Dimension," in Ronald Grigor Suny, ed., *Transcaucasia: Nationalism and Social Change. Essays in the History of Armenia, Azerbaijan, and Georgia* (Ann Arbor: Michigan Slavic Publications, 1983), p. 405.

11. *Ekonomicheskaia gazeta,* 1982, no. 21 (May), pp. 7–8, in *CDSP,* vol. 34, no. 20 (16 June 1982), pp. 8–10; interview with E. A. Shevardnadze, *Pravda,* 14 May 1983, in *CDSP,* vol. 35, no. 19 (8 June 1983), pp. 6–7; *Zaria vostoka,* 20 January 1984. For a review of Shevardnadze's career, see Elizabeth Fuller, "A Portrait of Eduard Shevardnadze," *Radio Liberty Research Bulletin,* RL 219/85 (3 July 1985), pp. 1–11.

12. *Sunday Times* (London), 11 September 1983.

13. For more on Georgia's Jews, see Mordechai Altshuler, "Georgian Jewish Culture under the Soviet Regime," *Soviet Jewish Affairs,* vol. 5, no. 2 (1975), pp. 21–39; and David M. Lang, "Religion and Nationalism—A Case Study: The Caucasus," in Max Hayward and William C. Fletcher, eds., *Religion and the Soviet State: A Dilemma of Power* (New York: Praeger, 1969), pp. 169–86.

14. *Pravda,* 23 November 1978; *Radio Liberty Research Bulletin,* RL 269/78 (1 December 1978).

15. A. M. Pogosian, *Karskaia oblast' v sostave Rossii* (Erevan: Haiastan, 1983).

16. *Kommunisticheskaia partiia Gruzii v tsifrakh (1921–1970 gg.): Sbornik statisticheskikh materialov* (Tbilisi, 1971), p. 265; J. A. Newth, "The 1970 Soviet Census," *Soviet Studies,* vol. 24, no. 2 (October 1972), p. 215.

17. Richard B. Dobson, "Georgia and the Georgians," in Zev Katz, Rosemarie Rogers, and Frederic Harned, eds., *Handbook of Major Soviet Nationalities* (New York: The Free Press, 1975), p. 177.

18. *Zaria vostoka,* 22 November 1983, in *CDSP,* vol. 35, no. 49 (4 January 1984), pp. 1–6.

19. Brian D. Silver, "Population Redistribution and the Ethnic Balance in Transcaucasia," in Suny, *Transcaucasia,* p. 384. Of the Armenian specialists working outside the republic in 1960, 29% were in Azerbaidzhan, 21% in Georgia, and 34% in the RSFSR. *Vysshee obrazovanie v SSSR: Statisticheskii sbornik* (Moscow: Gosstatizdat TsSU SSSR, 1961), pp. 70–71.

20. Silver, "Population Redistribution," p. 382. For a full discussion of labor resources in Armenia, see V. E. Khojabekian, *Haikakan SSH Bnakchutyune ev Ashkhatankayin Resursneri Verartadrutyan Ardi Problemnere* (Erevan: Haikakan SSH GA Hratarakchutyun, 1976).

21. Silver, "Population Redistribution," pp. 386–87. Citing two Soviet studies, Silver notes that they contradict one another but supply interesting data on Armenian marriage preferences. L. V. Chuiko (*Braki i razvody* [Moscow: Statistika, 1975]) makes the argument that Armenians, more than any other major nationality in the USSR,

were willing to consider intermarriage, but an Armenian study by A. E. Ter-Sarkisiants ("O natsional'nom aspekte brakov v Armianskoi SSR," *Sovetskaia etnografiia*, 1973, no. 4) claims that in the years 1967, 1969, and 1970 Armenians married other Armenians in the Armenian republic between 93% and 98% of the time.

22. Wesley A. Fisher, "Ethnic Consciousness and Intermarriage: Correlates of Endogamy among the Major Soviet Nationalities," *Soviet Studies*, vol. 29, no. 3 (July 1977), p. 398. These figures are for marriages within the Georgian republic.

23. R. K. Grdzelidze, *Mezhnatsional'noe obshchenie v razvitom sotsialisticheskom obshchestve: Na primere Gruzinskoi SSR* (Tbilisi: Izdatel'stvo Tbilisskogo universiteta, 1980), p. 126. See also Darrell Slider, "A Note on the Class Structure of Soviet Nationalities," *Soviet Studies*, vol. 37, no. 4 (October 1985), pp. 535–40.

24. Silver, "Population Redistribution," p. 379.

25. Brian D. Silver, "Methods of Deriving Data on Bilingualism from the 1970 Soviet Census," *Soviet Studies*, vol. 27, no. 4 (October 1975), pp. 574–97.

26. Whereas in 1940/41 12% of the school population in Azerbaidzhan was taught in Armenian, by 1963/64 that figure had fallen to 5.4%. The percentage of children taught in Russian grew over the same period from 18.8% to 23.4%, as did the proportion of those taught in Azerbaidzhani—from 68.9% to 71.0%, just above the proportion of Azerbaidzhanis in the population (67.5%). Since Azerbaidzhanis are probably more highly represented in the school-age population than the population overall, caution should be used with these figures. *Azerbaidzhan v tsifrakh: Kratkii statisticheskii sbornik* (Baku: Azerbaidzhanskoe gosudarstvennoe izdatel'stvo, 1964), pp. 192–93; Yaroslav Bilinsky, "Education of the Non-Russian Peoples in the USSR, 1917–1967: An Essay," *Slavic Review*, vol. 27, no. 3 (September 1968), pp. 420–21.

27. *Zaria vostoka*, 27 April 1973, in *CDSP*, vol. 25, no. 16 (16 May 1973), pp. 5–6.

28. *Sotsiologicheskie issledovaniia*, 1984, no. 4, pp. 104–7.

29. *Pravda*, 21 October 1984, in *CDSP*, vol. 36, no. 42 (14 November 1984), pp. 5–6.

30. *Zaria vostoka*, 8 February 1974, in *CDSP*, vol. 36, no. 8 (20 March 1974), p. 3.

31. *Voprosy istorii KPSS*, 1972, no. 8; *Istoriia SSSR*, 1972, no. 3; *Literaturnaia gazeta*, 15 November 1972.

32. U.S. Department of State, Bureau of Intelligence and Research, *Soviet Nationalities Survey*, no. 2 (1 April–30 June 1983), pp. 11–12.

33. Azade-Ayşe Rorlich, "Not by History Alone: The Retrieval of the Past among the Tatars and the Azeris," *Central Asian Survey*, vol. 3, no. 2 (1984), pp. 91–97.

34. *Arkhiv samizdata*, AS 2583, in *Materialy samizdata*, no. 23/76 (14 July 1976).

35. The new article in the constitution was to have read: "The Georgian Republic ensures the use of the Georgian language in state and public agencies and in cultural and other institutions and . . . , on the basis of equality, ensures the free use in all these agencies and institutions of Russian, as well as other languages used by the population." *Zaria vostoka*, 24 March 1978, in *CDSP*, vol. 30, no. 17 (24 May 1978), p. 12.

36. For a brief discussion of Armenian nationalism in the USSR, see Ronald Grigor Suny, *Armenia in the Twentieth Century* (Chico, CA: Scholars Press, 1983), pp. 69–83.

37. A full treatment of the Helsinki Watch Committees in Transcaucasia can be found in Yaroslav Bilinsky and Tönu Parming, *Helsinki Watch Committees in the Soviet Republics: Implications for the Soviet Nationality Question* (Final Report to the National Council for Soviet and East European Research, 1980). See also Ludmilla Alexeyeva,

Soviet Dissent: Contemporary Movements for National, Religious, and Human Rights (Middletown, CT: Wesleyan University Press, 1985), pp. 106–33.

38. On the conflicts between Azerbaidzhanis and Georgians, see Elizabeth Fuller, "The Azeris in Georgia and the Ingilos: Ethnic Minorities in the Limelight," *Central Asian Survey*, vol. 3, no. 2 (1984), pp. 75–85.

39. *Zaria vostoka*, 26 May and 7 June 1978; *New York Times*, 5 June 1978. For more on the conflict in Abkhazia, see Roman Solchanyk and Ann Sheehy, "Kapitonov on Nationality Relations in Georgia," *Radio Liberty Research Bulletin*, RL 125/78 (1 June 1978); Ann Sheehy, "Recent Events in Abkhazia Mirror the Complexities of National Relations in the USSR," ibid., RL 141/78 (26 June 1978).

40. For information on the events in Armenia, Azerbaidzhan, and Karabakh, see *CDSP*, vol. 40 (1988), nos. 3, 8–17, 21, et seq.; Gerard J. Libaridian, ed., *The Karabagh File: Documents and Facts on the Question of Mountainous Karabagh, 1918–1988* (Cambridge, MA-Toronto: The Zoryan Institute, 1988); Ronald G. Suny, "What Happened in Soviet Armenia?" *Middle East Report*, vol. 18, no. 4 (July–August 1988), pp. 37–40.

41. *New York Times*, 28 November 1988; Ronald G. Suny, "Nationalism and Democracy in Gorbachev's Soviet Union: The Case of Karabagh," *Michigan Quarterly Review*, vol. 28, no. 4 (Fall 1989), pp. 481–506.

CHAPTER 11

Central Asia:
The Reformers Challenge
a Traditional Society

Martha Brill Olcott

Although the Soviet regime claims to have created a political order based on the equality of all its numerous and various peoples, in reality the USSR is, if not a Russian, then at least a Slavic-dominated state. This is particularly evident in Central Asia, the last area to be incorporated into the Russian Empire, where the indigenous Turkic and Iranian peoples have had to respond to Russian-dominated development schemes since the middle of the nineteenth century. First the Imperial and then the Soviet bureaucracies have sought to integrate the area politically, economically, and culturally with the Russian heartland. It is undoubtedly true that the over one hundred years of combined Imperial Russian and Soviet rule have left an indelible mark on the lives of the Central Asians and led to the partial integration of this region with the center. However, the traditional culture of Central Asian society has proven quite resilient, and the society has managed to transform the goals of the colonizers as well as being transformed by them.

Probably the greatest single source of cultural vitality in Central Asia has been the Islamic heritage of its population. While seventy years of rule by an atheistic party have severely reduced the sway of institutional religion, Islamic values, rituals, and practices continue to dominate life in Central Asia. Indeed, all Central Asians consider themselves to be Muslims, even if they may differ among themselves as to what is meant by the designation.

Nonetheless, the common Islamic heritage of Central Asia has never served as a basis of unity. For centuries the area has been home to a number of ethnically distinct communities. The Turko-Mongol Kazakh pastoral nomads of the northern steppe were quite similar to the Kirghiz, herdsmen in the mountains to the southeast. But even though their languages were mutually intelligible and intermarriage common, the Kazakhs and Kirghiz maintained distinct tribal structures, and their sense of ethnic uniqueness was strengthened over time as each group created its own relations with the various and ever-changing neighboring powers. The third nomadic people, the Turkmen, lived in the isolated desert area of western Central Asia, and their language was far closer to the Turkic spoken on the other side of the Caspian Sea in present-day Azerbaidzhan than to Kazakh and Kirghiz. They, too, had their own tribal system and rarely intermarried with others. The patrilineal tribal systems of these three nomadic ethnic communities survived the Revolution virtually intact and have persisted in attenuated forms in the countryside to the present.

The Uzbeks represent a more complex case of ethnic development. Many are descendants of Turkic nomads whose lives were little different from those of the Kazakhs. Indeed, the separation of the two peoples occurred in the fifteenth century, when the ancestors of the Kazakhs broke from the Uzbek tribesmen and moved to territories further north. Ethnic differentiation between the two continued as Uzbek lands came under the rule and cultural sway of medieval Islamic city-states. Uzbeks increasingly became sedentary or semi-sedentary farmers, and their tribal structure was breaking down well before the Russian conquest. Over time their language also underwent considerable change under the strong influence of the Iranian speakers of the oasis cities with whom they frequently intermingled and intermarried.

The Tadzhiks are speakers of Iranian, descendants of the indigenous Indo-European population present in Central Asia throughout recorded history. The original Iranian stock, however, has been much diluted by the admixture of Turkic blood. Indeed, with intermarriage and bilingualism common, the choice between Tadzhik or Uzbek nationality that the native peoples were called on to make in the 1920s was often the product of such considerations as to which republic one's village was assigned, or which of the two languages was more frequently used at home, rather than notions of ethnic descent.

Centripetal forces have always been at work in Central Asia. Tribal or clan identification has created consistent ethnic differentiation in the area. Respect for one's ancestors is as strong among the Uzbeks and Tadzhiks as it is among the Turkmen, Kazakhs, or Kirghiz. In some cases it is linked to clan; in others it is a product of place, of having lived in the same village or area for several generations. Moreover, the scarceness of natural resources necessary for survival in a subsistence economy, especially shortages of grazing land and water, have always intensified natural competition.

The history of Central Asia is the history of rival indigenous states and of foreign powers competing for control over the territory. The Silk Road brought traders through the area; khanates, based more or less on rule by Islamic law, grew up around the cities near sources of irrigation on the Amu Darya or Syr Darya (the Jaxartes and Oxus of antiquity); empires centered in Khorezm and Samarkand rose and fell, as rival armies successfully challenged them; and new states eventually emerged in Kokand, Khiva, and Bukhara. Islam played a less direct role in the lives of the Central Asian nomads, and their tribal-based confederations were less successful at withstanding external pressure. In the context of the times, the mid-eighteenth century, swearing fealty to the Russian Tsar seemed the lesser evil to most Kazakh leaders, who feared extinction at the hands of the Mongol Kalmyks, while the Kirghiz lands came under the control first of the Manchus and then of the Central Asian khanates.

The imposition of Russian colonial rule in the 1870s, after four decades of encroachment, introduced further ethnic tensions and economic and cultural pressures in the area. Administrative subdivisions often did not correspond to ethnic ones, and in most cases the colonial administrators never knew precisely whom they ruled. The Turkmen were known by their proper name, but the Kazakhs were termed "Kirghiz," and the Kirghiz—"Kara-Kirghiz" ("black Kirghiz"), while all the rest were divided into Turkestanis or Sarts, distinctions that were not ethnically based. Moreover, colonial rule further upset the economic balance of the region. The subsistence-based agricultural economy was disturbed by the introduction of large-scale cotton growing; pastoral nomadism was deemed "irrational" and many Kazakhs were forced off their land to make way for Russian settlement. World War I and the introduction of a war-time economy increased the local sense of grievance, and violent protest (by the Kirghiz and Kazakhs) accompanied the drafting of Central Asians to serve in forced labor battalions for the Russian Imperial Army.

Hence there were few who mourned the passing of Tsarist rule in February 1917, though the first Russian Revolution left many Central Asian leaders unsure of how to proceed. Some, especially those from the traditional elite, saw this as an opportunity for reinstituting khan-based rule (the Khanates of Khiva and Bukhara were still intact, as Russian protectorates); others were committed to reform programs, either in concert with Pan-Islamic elements, or, in the case of some Kazakh intellectuals, in accordance with a secular model of national development. Only few indigenous Central Asians saw much in the Bolshevik program to recommend it, and after the Bolsheviks seized power popular antagonism toward them grew. The Tashkent Soviet, exclusively Russian in makeup, which ruled in Moscow's name, called for the nationalization of all land, both privately and clerically held, sparking the Basmachi revolt, which took six years for the Red Army to put down.

Once peace was restored, the Bolsheviks showed greater sensitivity to popular feelings and tried to enlist local support through policies designed to demonstrate tolerance for traditional practices, including religious ones. Nonetheless, Moscow decided to use the structure of the new Soviet state to increase ethnic differentiation. In 1924 five separate national units were established in Central Asia.[1] While this certainly suited some ethnic groups, like the Kazakhs and Turkmen, whose elites viewed themselves as belonging to a distinct national community, it certainly dealt a death blow to the goals of the Pan-Turkic and Pan-Islamic reformers who dreamed of a single independent Central Asian state.

Since the "national delimitation" of 1924 Soviet officials have worked hard to increase the distinctiveness of the Central Asian nationalities. Separate literary languages were created, which have grown more and more distinct through waves of language and alphabet reform.[2] New histories were written, in ways that emphasized "national" uniqueness. National literatures were developed, which, as censorship became more severe, drew more on folklore than on the largely religious prerevolutionary written legacy of the people. Many national reformist intellectuals went to work for the Bolshevik regime. But by the mid-1930s only the obsequious members of the indigenous nationalities survived in the employ of the state and party, and policy goals in all areas of economic, social, and political life were being set by Moscow.

The introduction of a planned economy and the collectivization of agriculture served to dislocate the traditional economy everywhere in Central Asia. It increased the dominant role of cotton in the irrigated areas and left the local populations in these regions no longer able to feed themselves. However, the ugliest toll of Stalinism was felt in Kazakhstan, where informal estimates hold that one in every three people died as a result of the forced settlement of the nomads that accompanied collectivization. Kazakhstan again became a special target for Moscow's economic planners in the 1950s; the northern half of the republic was claimed as Virgin Lands, destined as the new bread-basket of the Soviet Union, and Kazakh animal husbandry was once again dislocated. Although Central Asia remained the least industrialized region of the country, local agriculture still had to make way for growing more cotton. Energy, mineral extractive, and chemical industries first came to occupy a significant place in the local economies during the evacuation of factories in World War II, continuing to grow thereafter. But these branches of the economy have always been Russian-managed and Russian-dominated.

Through Stalin's lifetime the local Communist parties were also Russian-dominated, although the cadres in the countryside were always drawn heavily from the indigenous population and, once the purges were complete, could often screen their co-nationals from the intended effects of Moscow's social and cultural policies. Thus, traditional Central Asian society, with the exception of northern Kazakhstan and the Russian-dominated republican capitals, was never destroyed, but only altered and camouflaged to avoid detection by prying Russian eyes.

Political Developments

With the exception of Kazakhstan, which was the site of the Virgin Lands drive launched in 1954 and sustained through the early 1960s, Central Asia remained a political backwater during the Khrushchev and Brezhnev years. The great political waves produced by de-Stalinization in other parts of the USSR largely passed Central Asia by. The Stalin-era party leaderships were ultimately all dismissed after Khrushchev came to power,[3] but their replacements were generally chosen through the playing out of old political and sometimes even clan rivalries rather than any systematic review designed to find reform-minded elites. This is certainly true of Uzbekistan, about whose party politics we know the most and which sent the only Central Asian to the Presidium (as the Politburo was then called) during the Khrushchev years.[4]

In the area as a whole, the patterns established in the late Stalin years continued to predominate: first secretaries came from the indigenous nationality and second secretaries, generally charged with supervising personnel, were Russians with few direct ties to the areas of their assignment. Russians also played a key role in the state apparatus, as deputies in those ministries headed by local nationals and as heads of most of the principal economic ministries. In comparison to their percentage in the local population, the Russians were generally overrepresented in the party and state bureaucracies.

Russians played an even more prominent role in the administration of Kazakhstan. The decision to turn northern Kazakhstan into a major grain-producing area meant that Moscow had to have reliable cadres in place. Thus, from 1954 through 1959 Khrushchev dispatched a series of senior Russian party officials, most of them with extensive background in agriculture, as first and second secretaries of Kazakhstan's Communist party, including Leonid Brezhnev, who served in Kazakhstan in 1954–56. Only in 1960 was a Kazakh again appointed to either of these two positions. This was a protégé of Brezhnev—Dinmukhamed Kunaev, who served as first secretary until 1962, when he was replaced by Ismail Yusupov. Russians also staffed virtually all of the key economic ministries in this period.[5]

With the accession of Brezhnev, the party elites of the local nationalities came to dominate the political lives of their respective republics. This was true even of Kazakhstan, where Kunaev was reappointed first secretary in December 1964. Kunaev, promoted to the Politburo in 1971, established a republic-wide party network that eventually encompassed both Russians and Kazakhs. While the pattern of appointing Russians as second secretaries persisted, by the mid-1970s these men were more Kunaev's creatures than Moscow's.[6]

The Brezhnev years (1964–82) were a period of remarkable political stability throughout Central Asia. The tenures of the republican first secretaries were marked by unprecedented longevity. Only in Turkmenia was the party leader, Balysh Ovezov, dismissed; in 1969 he was replaced by Mukhamednazar Gapurov. Dzhabar Rasulov of Tadzhikistan, appointed in 1961, died in office in 1982, a few months before Brezhnev, and was succeeded by Rakhman Nabiev. The rest survived Brezhnev's death still in office, having served almost a quarter century each: Sharaf Rashidov in Uzbekistan (appointed in 1959), Turdakun Usubaliev in Kirghizia (appointed in 1961), and Kunaev in Kazakhstan (reappointed in 1964, two months after Brezhnev's accession to power in Moscow). Apart from Kunaev, only Rashidov was able to parlay his influence to Moscow, and even he, named candidate member of the Politburo in 1966, never became a full Politburo member. In general, Central Asians did not fare too well in the all-union party bureaucracy; at the time of Brezhnev's death, less than ten percent of the CPSU Central Committee members were from the Communist parties of Central Asia, and the majority of these came from Kazakhstan. However, all of the republican first secretaries became very powerful locally; they controlled and appointed numerous protégés to positions of importance in their republics, so that not only were there fewer Russians in positions of responsibility than previously, but many of these Russians were local and not dispatched as Moscow's eyes and ears.[7]

The system that developed was efficient after a fashion. The Central Asian party leaders amassed sufficient power both systematically to reward and punish. But the criteria that they used in distributing their favors rarely coincided with those of official policies, and were a far cry from those applied by modern Western-style managers. Thus, it was almost predictable that the Central Asian elites would come under attack by the reformers who came to power after Brezhnev's death.

Almost immediately on his election as general secretary in 1982, Yurii Andropov and his supporters initiated a campaign to force both party and state officials to take seriously their responsibility for supervising a working economy, and not simply use their jobs as sinecures to assure their personal well-being and the well-being of their friends and relatives. The national republics were singled out for particular scrutiny, and the levels of performance of several republican party organizations were found wanting. Even after Andropov's death in 1984, the party continued its drive to weed out weak, corrupt, and inefficient cadres. All five Central Asian republics experienced large turnovers of personnel, especially in the state sector.[8]

Kunaev, the long-time intimate of Brezhnev, found the Kazakh party organization pulled out of his grasp; several oblast party committee first secretaries were retired, the chairman of the Council of Ministers was replaced (as were several influential ministers), and the chairman of the Presidium of the Supreme Soviet died.

The most dramatic turnover of personnel occurred in Uzbekistan, where Inamzhon Usmankhodzhaev, chairman of Uzbekistan's Supreme Soviet, was named first secretary of the party after the death of Rashidov in 1983. In the year and a half that followed, five oblast first secretaries were replaced, as was the first secretary of the Karakalpak ASSR, the chairman of the Presidium of the Supreme Soviet, the heads of most economic ministries, as well as many other influential public figures.

After Mikhail Gorbachev assumed the position of general secretary in 1985, an even more concerted attempt was made to clean up the Central Asian party and state organs. In an effort to undermine Kunaev's position on the Politburo, the leadership of the Kazakh republic was quickly subjected to open ridicule through the public manner in which a large number of senior party and government officials were dismissed.[9]

The corrupt and inefficient management of the Central Asian Communist parties was discussed at some length at the Twenty-seventh Party Congress of the CPSU. Mikhail Gorbachev described the legacy of party corruption in Uzbekistan, the scandals in both the Kazakh and Kirghiz party organizations, and the economic stagnation of the Turkmen republic.[10] The key element of Gorbachev's cadres policy in his early years in office was his commitment to the idea of an interrepublican exchange of cadres, as became clear at the party congress and in subsequent developments. Republican parties would not be permitted to exist in a vacuum: the leading members of these parties must be trained in the center; local self-management of republican parties must be seen as a privilege and not a right; and errant parties would receive "transfusions" of cadres from the center.

The application of this policy preceded its formal adoption. The Communist parties of Kirghizia, Turkmenia, and Tadzhikistan all had new first secretaries appointed during November and December 1985. Absamat Masaliev, who before a six-month stint at the Central Committee in Moscow had been first secretary of Issyk Kul oblast party committee, became first secretary of the Kirghiz party. Like Masaliev, the new first secretary of Turkmenia, Saparmurad Niyazov, also had served for six months in the Central Committee, returning to Turkmenia as chairman of the republican Council of Ministers only days after Gorbachev came to power. Only the Tadzhiks were spared rule by a relative outsider. Before his appointment as first secretary of Tadzhikistan, Kakhar Makhkamov had been chairman of the republican Council of Ministers (since 1981), and before that a deputy chairman of the Council of Ministers and head of Tadzhikistan's Gosplan.

The new leaderships of the three republics repudiated the work of their predecessors, who have all been personally vilified but allowed to live in retirement. Nonetheless, the purges of cadres in Kirghizia, Tadzhikistan, and Turkmenia have proceeded more slowly than elsewhere in Central Asia. While literally hundreds of local and republic-level cadres have been replaced, the sensationalism that accompanied the process both in Uzbekistan and Kazakhstan has been largely absent. Although, despite the political reforms, increases in the rates of economic development remained disappointing, all three first secretaries appeared to be secure in their positions.

Given the greater economic potential of both Uzbekistan and Kazakhstan, and the fact that their former leaders were part of the Brezhnev coterie in Moscow, it was perhaps inevitable that the course of the purge in these republics would be more dramatic than in the other three. Nonetheless, the process of purging the party apparatuses of these two populous republics has defied Moscow's careful orchestration.

In the first months of Gorbachev's rule several additional oblast first secretaries were dismissed in Uzbekistan, as were a number of other prominent republican officials. Moreover, public condemnation of the deceased Sharaf Rashidov soon followed. The late leader was attacked for the first time at the Uzbek party congress in 1986.[11] Several months later the Central Committee of the CPSU and the Council of Ministers of the USSR rescinded all the orders with which Rashidov had been honored, and shortly thereafter the Uzbek party revoked the party membership of Narmakhonmadi Khudaiberdiev, the long-time chairman of the Council of Ministers of the Uzbek SSR.

Purges of Uzbekistan's party officials continued as investigations revealed the existence of republic-wide fraud in the production and sale of cotton. Initial investigations implicated four oblast first secretaries,[12] and a prosecutor was appointed by Moscow to investigate the entire Uzbek party organization. Over the next three years this investigation eventually led to the implication of the entire Uzbek party apparatus, the arrest of a former second secretary (Timofei Osetrov, a Russian) and Khudaiberdiev, and finally in January 1988 the dismissal of Usmankhodzhaev, who soon found himself under house arrest.[13]

Many Uzbeks had criticized the investigation, designed to demonstrate the criminality of Brezhnev's son-in-law and former Ministry of Internal Affairs official, Yurii Churbanov, for falsely slandering the entire Uzbek nation. In May 1989 they received partial vindication when the prosecutors themselves were publicly charged with having forced confessions in order to lay a false trail to the senior leaders of the republic. The web of lies and true accusations may never be fully untangled and the degree of complicity of the top leadership of the Uzbek party apparatus will probably remain unknown. Usmankhodzhaev's replacement as first secretary, Rafik Nishanov, who had spent most of his career in Moscow or in diplomatic service, managed to discharge his responsibilities without being tarnished. He was elected chairman of the Soviet of Nationalities of the reformed Supreme Soviet in Moscow in June 1989, and replaced by Islam Karimov, a former Uzbek oblast first secretary and Gosplan official.

The dismantling of Kunaev's party organization in Kazakhstan has provided less consistent drama than the events in Uzbekistan, but the forces that it unleashed continue to have implications for nationality politics in the Soviet Union as a whole. Dinmukhamed Kunaev managed to obtain reelection at Kazakhstan's party congress in 1986. His power, however, was severely reduced by a divided party which, with Moscow's clear encouragement, had turned against him and blamed him for the economic decline of recent years.[14] He remained on the Politburo until December 1986, when his "retirement" was announced, as was his replacement in the post of first secretary of Kazakhstan by Gennadii Kolbin, at the time first secretary of Ulyanovsk oblast, a Russian with no career or personal ties to the republic. While this was Kolbin's attraction to Moscow, it was also his greatest liability, for his appointment led to three days of rioting in Alma-Ata. These riots have been described officially as the isolated work of nationalists and opponents of *perestroika* within the republic, but as Kazakh officials now admit, they were both larger, more widely supported, and more violently suppressed than was officially reported at the time.

The Alma-Ata riots clearly taught the authorities a lesson on the limits of a policy of interrepublican exchange of cadres in Kazakhstan and elsewhere. This violent expression of popular dissatisfaction with Moscow's policies was but a harbinger of more national unrest to come. Ironically, even though more sustained protest elsewhere followed the Kazakh riots, the riots themselves seem to have sensitized Gorbachev to the feelings of the non-Russian nationalities. Kolbin, too, showed sensitivity toward the Kazakhs throughout his nearly three-year tenure in the republic.[15] He was responsible for legislation mandating that Kazakh become one of the two official languages of the republic, and he himself learned some Kazakh and used it publicly. More importantly, Moscow, while maintaining its right to appoint cadres of any nationality to any position, nonetheless subsequently refrained from naming first secretaries who were not from the titular nationality of the republic in which they were to serve.

Moscow seems to have decided that the transformation of the party apparatuses of Central Asia should proceed gradually. The makeup of the Kazakh party apparatus is quite different today than at the time of Brezhnev's death, but it is hard to tell if this represents the promotion of a new reformist elite or simply the generational change that Kunaev's longevity had long put off. The appointment in June 1989 of Nursultan Nazarbaev as first secretary of Kazakhstan seems a case in point. Nazarbaev, the former chairman of the Council of Ministers of Kazakhstan, came to prominence through the Kunaev organization, but he has consistently supported Moscow's agenda of reform. The same is true in the other Central Asian republics. The wave of Russians sent from the center, deployed most prominently in Uzbekistan, is tapering off and the balance between Russians and indigenous nationals in leadership positions is slowly moving toward what it was in the past.[16] Moscow is watching more carefully to make sure that new political dynasties do not emerge, and cadres are moved around more frequently than in the past to help forestall such a development. But only time will tell whether the age-old patterns of ethnically based cronyism in Central Asia will manage yet again to find ways to reappear.

Demographic, Social, and Economic Trends

One of the greatest challenges facing Soviet planners in the realm of social and economic policy in Central Asia is the high rate of population growth among the indigenous nationalities. The increase in population has been especially rapid in rural areas, where education facilities are inadequate and youths, often unable to speak Russian, find it difficult to obtain employment. This underutilized population, moreover, will continue to pose problems for the employment and social service network for the rest of their lives.[17]

As may be seen from Table 1A, between 1959 and 1989 the Central Asian nationalities registered population increases that ranged from a high of 201.9% among the Tadzhiks to a "low" of 124.7% among the Kazakhs. By contrast, the Russian population increased by 27.1% and the population of the USSR as a whole by 36.8% in the same period.

These rates have made Central Asia the fastest growing region of the country. Preliminary data from the 1989 census show convincingly that the trends observed in the 1960s and 1970s have continued. Population growth in Central Asia during the 1980s exceeded by far that of any other region, as well as the USSR average.[18] Thus, for example, the RSFSR, with a total population more than seven times that of Uzbekistan, registered an absolute numerical increase only twice as high as this single Central Asian republic. But even more significantly, the ethnic balance in each Central Asian republic continued to shift rapidly in favor of the titular nationality. In their respective republics, the share of Uzbeks and Turkmen is fast approaching three-

TABLE 1A. Demographic Trends among the Central Asian Nationalities in the USSR, 1959-1989

	Total Population (in thousands)				Population Increase
	1959	1970	1979	1989	1959-89
USSR	208,827	241,720	262,085	285,689	76,862
Russians	114,114	129,105	137,397	145,072	30,958
Kazakhs	3,622	5,299	6,556	8,138	4,516
Kirghiz	969	1,452	1,906	2,531	1,562
Turkmen	1,002	1,525	2,028	2,718	1,716
Uzbeks	6,015	9,195	12,456	16,686	10,671
Tadzhiks	1,397	2,136	2,898	4,217	2,820

	Percent Increase				Percent of Population			
	1959-70	1970-79	1979-89	1959-89	1959	1970	1979	1989
USSR	15.7	8.4	9.0	36.8	100	100	100	100
Russians	13.1	6.5	5.6	27.1	54.65	53.37	52.42	50.78
Kazakhs	46.3	23.7	24.1	124.7	1.73	2.19	2.50	2.85
Kirghiz	49.9	31.3	32.8	161.2	0.46	0.60	0.73	0.89
Turkmen	52.3	33.0	34.0	171.3	0.48	0.63	0.77	0.95
Uzbeks	52.9	35.5	34.0	177.4	2.88	3.80	4.75	5.84
Tadzhiks	52.9	35.7	45.5	201.9	0.67	0.88	1.11	1.48

TABLE 1B. Percentage Concentration Rates of Nationalities in Their Titular Republics, 1959-1989

	1959	1970	1979	1989	Change 1959-89
Russians	85.8	83.5	82.6	82.6	- 3.2
Kazakhs	77.2	79.9	80.7	80.3	+ 3.1
Kirghiz	86.4	88.5	88.5	88.0	+ 1.6
Turkmen	92.2	92.9	93.3	92.9	+ 0.7
Uzbeks	83.8	84.0	84.9	84.6	+ 0.8
Tadzhiks	75.2	76.3	77.2	75.1	- 0.1

TABLE 1C. Ethnodemographic Trends in the Central Asian Republics, 1959-1989

	Total Population (in thousands)				Population Increase
	1959	1970	1979	1989	1959-89
Kazakhstan	9,310	13,009	14,684	16,463	7,153
Kazakhs	2,787	4,234	5,289	6,532	3,745
Russians	3,972	5,522	5,991	6,226	2,254
Germans	NA	858	900	956	NA
Ukrainians	762	933	898	896	134
Kirghizia	2,065	2,933	3,523	4,258	2,193
Kirghiz	837	1,285	1,687	2,228	1,391
Russians	624	856	912	917	293
Uzbeks	219	333	426	550	331
Turkmenia	1,516	2,159	2,765	3,512	1,996
Turkmen	924	1,417	1,892	2,524	1,600
Russians	263	313	349	334	71
Uzbeks	125	179	234	317	192
Uzbekistan	8,106	11,799	15,389	19,808	11,702
Uzbeks	5,038	7,725	10,569	14,124	9,086
Russians	1,092	1,473	1,666	1,652	560
Tadzhiks	311	449	595	932	621
Tadzhikistan	1,980	2,900	3,806	5,090	3,110
Tadzhiks	1,051	1,630	2,237	3,168	2,117
Uzbeks	455	666	873	1,197	742
Russians	263	344	395	387	124

	Percent Increase				Percent of Population			
	1959-70	1970-79	1979-89	1959-89	1959	1970	1979	1989
Kazakhstan	39.7	12.9	12.1	76.8	100	100	100	100
Kazakhs	51.9	24.9	23.5	134.4	29.99	32.55	36.02	39.68
Russians	39.0	8.5	3.9	56.7	42.73	42.45	40.80	37.82
Germans	NA	4.9	6.2	NA	NA	6.60	6.13	5.81
Ukrainians	22.5	- 3.8	- 0.2	17.6	8.19	7.18	6.12	5.44
Kirghizia	42.0	20.1	20.9	106.2	100	100	100	100
Kirghiz	53.5	31.3	32.1	166.2	40.51	43.81	47.89	52.34
Russians	37.3	6.5	0.5	47.0	30.18	29.18	25.89	21.53
Uzbeks	52.1	28.1	29.1	151.1	10.58	11.34	12.10	12.92
Turkmenia	42.4	28.1	27.0	131.7	100	100	100	100
Turkmen	53.4	33.5	33.4	173.2	60.92	65.62	68.43	71.87
Russians	19.2	11.5	- 4.2	27.0	17.32	14.50	12.62	9.52
Uzbeks	43.3	30.2	35.7	153.6	8.26	8.31	8.45	9.03
Uzbekistan	45.6	30.4	28.7	144.4	100	100	100	100
Uzbeks	53.3	36.8	33.6	180.3	62.05	65.47	68.68	71.32
Russians	34.9	13.1	- 0.8	51.3	13.46	12.49	10.83	8.34
Tadzhiks	44.4	32.5	56.7	199.7	3.84	3.80	3.86	4.71
Tadzhikistan	46.5	31.3	33.7	157.1	100	100	100	100
Tadzhiks	55.1	37.2	41.6	201.4	53.07	56.21	58.78	62.25
Uzbeks	46.3	31.1	37.1	163.1	22.98	22.96	22.94	23.52
Russians	31.0	14.8	- 2.1	47.1	13.26	11.87	10.38	7.60

Sources: Derived from 1959, 1970, 1979, and 1989 Soviet census data. Itogi Vsesoiuznoi perepisi naseleniia 1959 goda: SSSR; ... Kazakhskaia SSR; ... Kirgizskaia SSR; ... Turkmenskaia SSR; Uzbekskaia SSR; ... Tadzhikskaia SSR (Moscow: Gosstatizdat, 1962). Itogi Vsesoiuznoi perepisi naseleniia 1970 goda, vol. 4 (Moscow: Statistika, 1974). Chislennost' i sostav naseleniia SSSR: Po dannym Vsesoiuznoi perepisi naseleniia 1979 goda (Moscow: Finansy i statistika, 1984). Data for 1989 are from preliminary unpublished results of the 1989 census, and are subject to correction.

fourths, and that of the Tadzhiks two-thirds, of the total population. The Kirghiz, who formed only 40.5% of the population of Kirghizia in 1959, have already regained their majority. And the proportion of Kazakhs in Kazakhstan, down to below 30% in 1959, has rebounded to almost 40%, making the Kazakhs a plurality in their republic's population for the first time since the Virgin Lands campaign.[19] Concurrently, the weight of Russians decreased in all five republics, as did, for the first time, their absolute number in three of them: Turkmenia, Uzbekistan, and Tadzhikistan. Not only do the Russians have a lower birth rate, but there has clearly been net out-migration of Russians from the region.

The demographic "bulge" which developed in Central Asia since the 1960s will continue to have serious consequences, as the Central Asian "baby boomers" can be expected to have larger families than their Slavic counterparts. According to the 1979 census, the average family size of the Central Asian nationalities ranged from a high of 6.5 members for the Tadzhiks to a low of 5.5 for the Kazakhs, compared to an average family size of 3.2 among the Russians and 3.5 members for the USSR as a whole.[20] There is strong reason to believe that these differentials in birth rates will persist for at least another generation or two. An all-union survey of married women between the ages of eighteen and fifty-nine, conducted in 1978, provides some information on expectations of family size by nationality. The study found that Russian women hoped for an average of 2.02 children, while their Central Asian counterparts' expectations varied from an average of 4.85 children among the Kazakhs to 6.09 for the Tadzhiks, with the Uzbeks, Kirghiz, and Turkmen ranged in between, with family expectations of 5.42, 5.44, and 5.86 children, respectively.[21] A survey conducted seven years later showed that only among Kazakh women was there an expectation of smaller families, but even they still hoped for 4.28 children on average. The number of expected children dropped insignificantly among the Tadzhiks, to 5.94, and increased among the other three nationalities—to 5.58 for the Uzbeks, 5.56 for the Kirghiz, and 6.31 for the Turkmen.[22]

The growth in population continues to be disproportionately higher in the countryside. While the percentage of the population living in rural areas in 1989 as compared to 1979 declined union-wide from 38% to 34% and in the RSFSR from 31% to 26%, in Central Asia the share of the rural population, well above the USSR average to begin with, actually increased in three of the republics. Only in Kazakhstan, which has the largest percentage of Russians and other European nationalities in the region, did the proportion of the rural population drop, from 46% to 43%. In Uzbekistan it remained stable, but still at a high 59%. In Turkmenia the share of the rural population increased from 52% to 55%, in Kirghizia from 61% to 62%, and in Tadzhikistan from 65% to 67%, giving that republic an urban-rural balance that is exactly the opposite of the country as a whole.[23]

The increase in both the absolute number and relative weight of Central Asians in the Soviet population poses numerous problems for the party leadership in Moscow and in the republican capitals as well, with ramifications for every sphere of life. Absorbing such large numbers of non-Russians into the economic, cultural, and political life of the country is an enormous and complex task. And it is already changing the character of the republics themselves. As the indigenous population grows, the local Russian residents feel more beleaguered, and the observed outflow of Russians is sure to increase in the current atmosphere of interethnic tension.

The increasing numerical preponderance of the Central Asians in their own republics undoubtedly will serve to legitimate their calls for greater control of their republics, and Moscow will have to find ways to meet at least some of their expectations in order to ensure the orderly economic development of the region. For the moment, however, the more pragmatic concerns of raising economic productivity and ensuring the social integration of the population seem the more serious.

A whole set of obvious problems stems from the fact that not all Central Asians speak, understand, and read Russian. As shown in Table 2, at times spectacular increases in the percentage of Central Asians claiming Russian-language fluency have been reported in the USSR. However, it is hard to determine the level of linguistic proficiency claimed, or the actual accuracy of the census data. Some of the increases seem implausible, to say the least. The 1979 data for the Uzbeks, which reported 49.3% of the population to be fluent in Russian, an increase from 14.5% in nine years, were called into question even by some Soviet scholars;[24] the 1989 census shows a more

TABLE 2. Language Patterns among the Central Asian Nationalities in the USSR, 1959-1989 (in percent)

Nationality	National Language as Native Language				Russian as Native Language				Russian as Second Language			
	1959	1970	1979	1989	1959	1970	1979	1989	1959	1970	1979	1989
Kazakhs	98.4	98.0	97.5	97.0	1.2	1.6	2.0	NA	NA	41.8	52.3	60.4
Kirghiz	98.7	98.8	97.9	97.8	0.3	0.3	0.5	NA	NA	19.1	29.4	35.2
Turkmen	98.9	98.9	98.7	98.5	0.7	0.8	1.0	NA	NA	15.4	25.4	27.8
Uzbeks	98.4	98.6	98.5	98.3	0.5	0.5	0.6	NA	NA	14.5	49.3	23.8
Tadzhiks	98.1	98.5	97.8	97.7	0.5	0.6	0.8	NA	NA	15.4	29.6	27.7

Sources: Calculations for 1959, 1970, and 1979 derived from published Soviet census data, as given in Table 1. Partial language data from the 1989 census were published in Rahva Hääl (Tallinn), 19 September 1989, and reported in Ann Sheehy, "Russian Share of Soviet Population Down to 50.8 Percent," Radio Liberty, Report on the USSR, vol. 1, no. 42 (20 October 1989), pp. 3-4.

reasonable 23.8%. Over half of the Kazakhs reported fluent knowledge of Russian; but only some thirty percent or less of the Kirghiz, Tadzhiks, and Turkmen claimed Russian language fluency. Even assuming, reasonably, that Russian-language proficiency among the school-age population is higher than for the population as a whole, the available statistics still suggest that the Central Asians do not have the language skills necessary for their complete integration into the economic and political life of the USSR, or to serve successfully in combat positions in the military. Indeed, growing complaints by military officials that up to half of the Central Asian draftees have severe language deficiencies attest that the situation has not improved over time.

Given the large numbers of Central Asians that must be absorbed into the work force and the military, their linguistic limitations are a serious liability. Ten or fifteen years ago the management of the Central Asian republics and the maximum utilization of their manpower was certainly of interest to Moscow, but not an issue of critical importance to the direct or immediate functioning of the Soviet system. However, today's leadership cannot regard the proper management of the Muslim regions or the socialization of Muslim youth as an abstract concern, particularly given the social costs their growing sense of dislocation entails. The economic potential of these regions has yet to be adequately tapped. Natural resources lie untouched and manpower underutilized. Approximately half of the Muslim population is under sixteen years of age.[25] At a time when the labor force in the traditional industrial centers of the European USSR is contracting, this population becomes more valuable. And Moscow clearly is reluctant to entrust the responsibility for managing this population to a local leadership which it feels is undependable.

The past failures of the old Central Asian leadership are everywhere apparent. Nowhere is this more true than in education. The diversion of construction materials to party-supported private construction projects, for example, exacerbated the already severe shortage of schools, leaving virtually all schools with double sessions, and some with triple and even quadruple sessions. At the same time that the economic development of the region demands rising educational levels among the Central Asians, a study drawn on unpublished 1979 census data confirms that the differences in educational attainment by ethnic groups reported in the 1970 census continue to persist. Whereas 661 Russians over the age of ten per thousand reported some secondary or higher education in 1979, the figures for the Central Asian nationalities varied from 615 for the Uzbeks to 565 for the Tadzhiks.[26]

The quality of the education that the Central Asians receive lags behind all-union standards. Rural schools are notoriously worse than urban ones in terms of overcrowding, quality of instruction, and availability of instructional materials—and the overwhelming number of Central Asian youths still live in the countryside.[27] The difference appears most striking in the area of scientific and technical education, as recently published statistics demonstrate quite convincingly. While only 9% of rural secondary schools for the USSR as a whole lacked departments of biology, 30% of the rural secondary schools in Tadzhikistan, and 24% in Turkmenia, were without such facilities. The same pattern was observed for all other scientific and technical subjects.[28]

In recent years Soviet officials have begun to pay closer attention to the problem of improving general as well as scientific and technical education in the Soviet Union as a whole, notably through the 1984 general school reform and subsequent reforms in higher and specialized technical education. More schools, better trained teachers, and improved curriculums with texts in the necessary languages have all been mandated for development, but schools in the Muslim republics remain understaffed and overcrowded, and more often than not served by outdated texts and poorly trained teachers.[29] Even the technical subjects in which young Central Asians are trained often do not correspond to the fields in which there is local demand. Nonetheless, in republics like Turkmenia there are still more places in the science faculties at institutions of higher education than applicants, and efforts to encourage Muslim youth to accept places at PTUs (technical high schools) in the RSFSR or Ukraine have been only partially successful. Recruitment has proved difficult, and many who do go to the center stay to find jobs there rather than return to fill skilled posts in their home regions.[30]

Unemployed rural youths constitute another growing problem in Central Asia. Precise estimates of their numbers are difficult to obtain, but there appear to be at least hundreds of thousands, if not a few million, idle youth in the region. Their numbers are likely to grow, as the mechanization of the cotton industry continues and young people refuse to leave their home regions to take unskilled or semi-skilled jobs in the cities, or to pursue the necessary education to fill the available skilled jobs in either the rural or urban areas. The growing alienation of these Central Asian youths has created a number of social problems, ranging from drug addiction, alcoholism, and the development of youth gangs, to outbursts of anomic ethnic violence. Their presence further exacerbates the economic problems of the region as well, as the goals of the current economic plan have been predicated on the redeployment of underutilized manpower resources.

The goals of the Twelfth Five-Year Plan, the economic program for 1986–90, included some major developmental projects in Central Asia, such as the construction or expansion of large regional production complexes in Kazakhstan, Tadzhikistan, and Turkmenia, and the expansion of the petroleum and coal industries of Kazakhstan.[31] Large increases in industrial production were called for in all five republics, averaging about 25%, and agricultural output was to increase by nearly 15%. For the various republican organizations to go from their past rates of growth to these doubled rates of growth would, under current conditions, be nothing less than miraculous.

Projected growth rates for industry will certainly be difficult to achieve, as shortages of materials and machinery are compounded by a shortage of trained cadres in all the Central Asian republics, probably most acute in the smaller cities and more rural areas. These manpower constraints are further exacerbated by the quotas that each republic has received for the out-migration of trained labor, for in addition to the demands from their own factories, the Central Asian and Transcaucasian republics have also been "asked" to provide thousands of trained "volunteers" to work in the new regions of Siberia.[32]

Agriculture has always been problematic in Central Asia, with the ill effects of corrupt party leadership magnified by bad weather and shortages of trained manpower, equipment, fertilizer, and water. For the local elites the most disturbing aspect of the Twelfth Five-Year Plan was the decision not to proceed with the diversion of Siberian rivers, as the severe water shortage is undoubtedly the most serious problem facing agriculture in the region.[33]

The planned diversion of the Siberian rivers (the Ob and lower Irtysh) was controversial since its first mention. Its critics variously argued that the scheme would lead to the destruction of the ecological balance both in the North and in Central Asia, that the architectural heritage of the northern towns and villages would be destroyed, and, probably most importantly, that the project would be ruinously expensive, even in its initial stages.

Instead of the proposed river diversion, in 1986 Moscow decided that the water shortage in Central Asia could be remedied by the more effective use of existing irrigation networks, their expansion using local water sources, and the application of water-collection irrigation techniques. Some experts disagreed with this decision at the time. Specialists in Uzbekistan have argued that current sources can meet the republic's irrigation needs only through the early 1990s, and even with the application of what was termed prohibitively expensive technology—only until sometime into the Fourteenth Five-Year Plan (i.e., through the end of the century).[34] Over time it has become clear that the water shortage in Central Asia is even more serious than was originally projected. There is some talk that the river diversion project may be revived, but for now attention remains focused on maximum utilization of existing water resources.

The most serious ecological disaster in Central Asia is the death of the Aral Sea. It has lost a third of its water since the 1960s, and the dispersion of salts from its dry sea bed is poisoning surrounding crops and sources of drinking water. Water pollution more generally has become a matter of great public concern, as has the use of chemicals to increase agricultural yields. Both are said to pose serious danger to the health of agricultural workers and to account for the rising rates of infant mortality throughout the cotton-growing regions in particular.

While policy makers in Moscow have concentrated their efforts on the fulfillment of centrally mandated economic plans by the various republics, many Central Asians have come to question Moscow's right to determine the economic priorities for their region. Since 1987 there have been more frequent calls for reducing the dominant role of cotton in the economies of Uzbekistan and Turkmenia and for increasing subsistence-based agriculture in all of the republics. There have also been calls to cut back on proposed hydroelectric plants and other heavy industrial projects, and to invest instead in factories to process local products for sale within the republics. Central Asians are also disturbed by their increased responsibility for plan fulfillment under the projected reforms. Whereas many Balts support regional economic autonomy and criticize Moscow's reform program for not going far enough in this direction, Central Asians argue that their economies are bound to suffer from the new arrangements. They attribute the current economic crisis of the region more to Moscow's unjust and poorly conceived policies than to the past corruption of Central Asian officials themselves. Thus, most Central Asian leaders and intellectuals alike conclude that Moscow should fund the reconstruction of the region.

Many of these ideas directly contradict the basic principles of economic reform projected by Moscow, which still preserve the notion that economic priorities will be decided at the center, albeit now in some consultation with the periphery, and that these priorities will be determined with the good of the whole country taking precedence over local perceptions of the welfare of the region or nationality involved.

Thus, there is a real clash in vision between economic planners in Moscow and those who must execute their decisions in Central Asia and live with the consequences. Nevertheless, economic policy makers in Moscow and Central Asia alike believe that no model of economic reform will succeed unless the traditional society of rural Central Asia becomes more susceptible to change. Economic change cannot occur in the region until the vast numbers of rural Central Asians themselves become willing to have their lives transformed. But although much is written about the need to introduce a major change in the psychological disposition of this population,[35] no one seems to have a very precise idea of how this can be achieved.

Cultural and Religious Trends

The success of Moscow's economic policies depends on the support of the Central Asian elites, as well as the cooperation of the masses. While Moscow may ultimately find competent native cadres to do its bidding and satisfactorily fill positions of leadership in their republics, there is little reason to assume that the masses will be sufficiently malleable to allow current economic and political goals to be met. The social and cultural values of the Central Asian population are still imbued with much that may be considered "Islamic." Central Asians are tied to the perpetuation of a traditional family structure. This means that women spend much of their maturity in child-rearing and consequently contribute to the unemployment or underemployment problem in the region. Moreover, the families are close-knit, and extended families often reside in common. The strong role accorded to the family and preference for living among kin sharply limit any desire on the part of most Central Asians to migrate outside their republic, or even to regions within their republic in which they have no kin.

Islam is omnipresent in Central Asia, if religion is defined in strictly cultural terms. Soviet antireligious policy unquestionably succeeded in destroying the dominance of the traditional prerevolutionary Islamic religion. However, it has been far less successful in eliminating the more unstructured and informal religion as practiced in the countryside, and even in the cities. The type of religious practice that has been preserved is based more on ritual than on doctrine. Religious practices have become more syncretic, often infused with local pre-Islamic rituals, and thus with some jusitification may be viewed as ethnic or national traditions as much as religious ones. Variations in local customs notwithstanding, the religious identity of Soviet Muslims still provides some basis for a common bond. Islam is predicated on the existence of a community of believers, even though today's Soviet Muslims are conscious of belonging to a national community as well as a religious one.

Soviet antireligious propagandists (who are generally trained as sociologists of religion as well as propagandists) admit that Islam has proved itself a pervasive social force and that religion still plays an important role in contemporary Central Asian society. The authors of the 1983 collective work *Islam in the USSR* [Islam v SSSR] argue that this pervasiveness is a result of Islam's uniqueness: Islam is a form of national consciousness in which doctrine is subsumed by ritual and ritual itself is able to adapt to earlier cultural forms.[36] Moreover, Soviet analysts are no longer optimistic that the influence of religion will die out in the Muslim areas even after industrialization and economic modernization have become more deeply entrenched. Most Soviet students of Islam also admit that religion is still viewed as "morally uplifting" by the majority of Central Asians.

Although Islam—or, more properly, the heritage of Islam—plays some part in the lives of all Soviet Central Asians, it is nonetheless useful to distinguish three distinct types of Muslims, for from each group stem different consequences for the system. The first group comprises "ethnic Muslims." Their identification with Islam is almost entirely passive, an expression of their ethnic or national identity. They are "Muslims" because they are members of an ethnic or national group that has historically been Muslim. Such people may practice certain rituals, particularly those viewed as signs of communal membership, but they do not support the perpetuation of religion for its own sake. Some in this group may even consider themselves to be atheists, though "Muslims" as well. Thus, a traditional Islamic ritual like male circumcision, *sunnat*, appears to be universally practiced across all sectors of society, including the children of party members.[37]

The second group are "cultural Muslims"—those who adhere to religious practices, but have little or no awareness of the doctrinal teachings of Islam. This, the largest, category includes people who commemorate all the key events of human life—birth, the onset of manhood, marriage, and death—with religious observances. Many of them try to observe the major Muslim holidays. These individuals follow customary funeral practices—which have become more elaborate, expensive, and widespread in recent years as portions of the secularized population have come to consider them as national customs—and often traditional marriage practices as well. Numbers of studies report the continued popular observance of the *nikah*, an Islamic wedding ceremony performed by a mullah, but evidence on the prevalence of such practices is contradictory.[38] More invidious, at least from the point of view of Moscow, is the perpetuation of customs such as the *kalym* (bride price), which not only symbolize the continued hold of Islam, but also represent practical impediments to the complete integration of women into the economy. In the countryside, particularly, the payment of the *kalym* is a vital part of the local culture, and is often accompanied by such practices as forced marriage and marriage of minors.

The third, and by far the smallest, group consists of "doctrinal Muslims"— people who have at least some knowledge of Islamic doctrine and attempt to work their faith into their daily life. Most try to attend weekly prayers, many pray daily, and all believe that the teachings of the faith must be perpetuated. Evidence suggests that while "doctrinal believers" are relatively few and the number of people with religious education has declined since World War II, the pull toward religion continues to be felt within each successive generation, and "doctrinal Muslims" are to be found in almost all walks of life. Moreover, it seems that the linkage of religion with national consciousness has created a new and powerful tool for spreading religious ideas among a secularized population; more young people among the postwar generation are turning to religion than was true of their parents' generation. Children of believers are more likely to become believers themselves, but not all new "doctrinal believers" come from religious homes.[39] Soviet experts themselves admit that the practice of religion has increased in recent years.

For almost all Soviet citizens of Turko-Iranian stock there is a definitional link between national and religious identity. Virtually everyone who calls himself a Kazakh, Kirghiz, Tadzhik, Turkmen, or Uzbek is likely to call himself a Muslim as well, although a party member might hastily and with embarrassment explain to a foreigner that Islam is his "former faith." To claim to be a Muslim expresses pride in one's ancestry and need not be an assertion of faith in God or in the teachings of Muhammad. Moreover, few Soviet Muslims, no matter how attenuated the tie to their former faith, feel comfortable enforcing restrictions against the observance of religious rituals, and many are reluctant to stop those who proselytize the faith.

Some Soviet scholars argue that, while not desirable, the linkage between Islam and nationalism is inevitable in Muslim societies.

> Islam not only compensates man's weakness, but can also satisfy his needs unconnected with religion: it can help man express himself, to 'find' himself among people, to develop a sense of identification with a nation and its history, to satisfy his needs in social intercourse, and so forth.[40]

Soviet analysts maintain that this fusion between religious and national consciousness is a stage to be endured as an internationalist community takes form. While this process unfolds, the state must make sure that the assertion of national identity not take on explicitly anti-Soviet political overtones or turn into national chauvinism. Most Soviet analysts aver that, despite their ties to the faith, Islamic believers, generally speaking, can and do make loyal Soviet citizens.

> The vast majority of believers are honest people, patriots to their motherland. Raised in conditions of a socialist society, they, under the influence of the Soviet way of life, deeply perceive and value the ideas of friendship of peoples, mutual assistance, and internationalism, whimsically linking them with their belief in God, but in practical life rejecting notions of religious particularism.[41]

Gorbachev and his circle have demonstrated very contradictory impulses regarding Islam. Initially Gorbachev identified religion as an impediment to the success of his economic and political goals in Central Asia. The linkage of religion with nationalism was seen to pose a serious threat to his drive to achieve an accelerated rate of economic growth, as well as to hopes of obtaining ideological conformity. Thus, Moscow urged the party leadership in the various Muslim regions to attack religious "excesses," while simultaneously defining as excessive what most Central Asian leaders saw as normal.

Throughout 1985 and 1986 antireligious propaganda increased in intensity in Central Asia,[42] and the "invidious" role played by Islam was highlighted at a number of republican party congresses.[43] Moreover, the dismissal of a local party official in Uzbekistan in July 1986 for failing to enforce state laws against religion testified to Moscow's commitment to hold party officials responsible for executing the official antireligious policy.[44]

In 1987, however, Moscow began to reevaluate its antireligious policy. Since that time a more tolerant public attitude has emerged toward religion. Most striking is the reversal in official attitude toward the Russian Orthodox Church, whose hierarchy has been asked to become a partner in the reconstruction of Russian society. The concessions made toward Islam are inconsequential by comparison. A new religious school in Bukhara and over twenty new or rebuilt mosques have been opened, with several others planned. These changes hardly meet the demand for state-sanctioned religious establishments. Moscow remains reluctant to allow the full-scale restoration of Islam and continues to reject calls for recognition of unsanctioned clerics and unofficial mosques and religious schools. Still, the new policy toward Islam is a more pragmatic one. Gorbachev has come to understand the depth of Islam's penetration of Central Asian society and the reluctance of local officials to combat the practice of Islamic rituals because they, too, still identify with them.[45] While Moscow continues to call for the elimination of the negative manifestations of Islam, which are said to retard economic development and social change in the countryside, the potentially good sides of Islam are recognized.

Thus Islam, like Russian Orthodoxy, is seen as a potential source of morality, and Islamic religious leaders are now expected to help prevent manifestations of antisocial and, more importantly, anti-Soviet behavior. While the authorities in Moscow still hope that antireligious propaganda can promote, among young people in particular, a secular, if not socialist, world view, they concede that the types of propaganda that prevailed in the past were wholly inappropriate and, consequently, completely ineffectual. Thus, much of the current toleration of Islam simply reflects Moscow's effort to make the best of a bad situation in the hope that a future generation can be raised in a manner that will better serve the regime's goals.

However, much of recent Soviet social policy would seem to militate against this. Since the Alma-Ata riots of December 1986, Moscow has shown greater sensitivity to the cultural demands of the national minorities. Concessions made so far have hardly appeased the Central Asians, however, and their demands have escalated—in part because of their perception of trends in the USSR more generally. Today all of the nationalities of Central Asia are striving to protect their national cultures, to save them from the extinction which, it is claimed, Stalinist policies had charted for them.

Some of the nationalities have been more outspoken about this than others, with writers and poets taking the lead in putting forward the national position. The Kazakhs and Kirghiz have eloquent spokesmen in the persons of Olzhas Suleimenov and Chingiz Aitmatov, respectively, who have advanced their cause before all-union audiences. The Uzbeks also have a group of articulate young writers, prominent among whom is Mukhammad Salikh, who have promoted the national position within Uzbekistan but have not yet received much attention outside their republic. The Tadzhiks and Turkmen are still trying to find their public voice.

The demands are similar in each case: official status for the language of the indigenous nationality and mandatory teaching of that language to all pupils and students in the republic's schools. The Central Asians are also asking for the rehabilitation of their national heroes, both those purged by Stalin and those who form the "blank spots" in their national histories for the roles they played in resisting either Russian colonization or Soviet rule. In general, they want an open and honest account of their past and the right to develop their cultures freely, without the intervention of Moscow or the local Communist party. Their national cultures are still not fully formed, they maintain, and the balance between disparate cultural elements— religion, ethnic or tribal heritage, language, and the pre- and postrevolutionary histories—must be worked out in an unhampered fashion if these nations are to survive and prosper.

Moscow has been willing to accede to some of these demands, and has tried to shelve others. All five Central Asian republics have drafted legislation giving official status to the language of the titular nationality, to be used anywhere in the republic, in official and in private life. But the difficulties in realizing these rights are legion, as none of the republics have the facilities necessary to ensure the training of translators, or the supply of books and teachers necessary to introduce courses in the language of the titular nationality throughout the republican school system.

Every republic has begun the process of filling in the "blank pages" of its national history. Rehabilitations are being announced at a steady pace, and the rewriting of the period of collectivization is everywhere under way.

But little has yet been done to rewrite the histories of the prerevolutionary period in any systematic fashion, although a few tentative steps have been taken in the celebration of landmark birthdays of previously suppressed figures, such as the Kazakh poet Shakarim.

In general, cultural policies of *glasnost'* have been introduced more slowly in Central Asia than elsewhere in the USSR. Most of the old cultural bureaucracies remain largely intact. Some symbolic dismissals have been made, particularly in Kirghizia, where Chingiz Aitmatov's works were considered nationalistic at the very time that they were winning awards in Moscow. The mechanisms of censorship in the republican publishing houses seem firmly in place, however, although the standards of censorship have certainly been loosened to some degree. But what seems more significant is that the expectations of the nationalists have risen faster than the regime's capacity to meet their demands.

Discontent and Opposition in Central Asia

Since 1986 there have been numerous indications of growing popular discontent over Moscow's policies toward Central Asia. This discontent has been reflected both in outbursts of anomic violence and in the organization of elite-dominated reform or protest movements, of both sanctioned and unsanctioned groups. Organized peaceful mass protest has been slower in coming than in the Baltic and other European republics.

The Alma-Ata riots in December 1986 were the first nationalist-inspired upheaval in the USSR to occur during Gorbachev's rule. Their full story has yet to be revealed. Eyewitnesses claim that the protests were far more extensive and better organized than official accounts allow. Moscow maintains that they were the work of isolated, disgruntled Kazakh nationalists, the children of the enemies of *perestroika*.[46]

It now appears that thousands of students came into the city from all over southern Kazakhstan, and not hundreds as originally reported, with the support of local authorities. While Moscow has depicted the protesters as hooligans, other observers claim that the demonstrations began peacefully, to protest the national affront delivered by the appointment of the Russian, Genadii Kolbin, as first secretary and to express popular fears that further punishments were to be visited on the Kazakh people. The Kazakhs seem to have felt that they were punished, but did not appear to know why, as Kunaev was viewed as a far more benevolent figure in the republic than Moscow subsequently charged. As one young demonstrator put it, "at least we often got meat." Eyewitnesses report that the crowd was broken up by force and that the rampage through the city followed, as young people were chased by the troops. They also claim that scores were killed and hundreds injured. Olzhas Suleimenov's demand that the new Congress of People's Deputies in Moscow investigate the Alma-Ata events because they were a national tragedy, as great as the 9 April 1989 attack in Tbilisi, adds real credence to these reports.[47] While these events certainly influenced Moscow's thinking about its nationality policies, it is hard to know the impact of the riots on the subsequent course of protest in Central Asia. The use of the military seemed to scare the Kazakhs into submission. At the same time, the policy line that the new first secretary, Kolbin, pursued—increased cultural autonomy for the Kazakhs (as well as other national minorities within the republic) and a gradual overhaul of the party apparatus—was far more supportive of Kazakh interests than what his appointment seemed to portend.

Probably more important from the point of view of mobilizing nationalist protest union-wide were the public demonstrations by the Crimean Tatars of Central Asia, held in Tashkent and Moscow throughout spring and summer 1987. These protests, which occasioned a great deal of sympathy from the European nationalities throughout the USSR, ceased only after a Supreme Soviet commission was formed to examine the Tatar demands. The report of the commission, issued after nearly a year, agreed that the Crimean Tatars had been unjustly treated and were entitled to receive the support necessary for their culture to be preserved—but in the places of their current residence. The report rejected Crimean Tatar demands that the Crimea be returned to their control on the grounds, as commission chairman Andrei Gromyko maintained, that the wrongs done to one people cannot be rectified at the expense of another.[48]

While the protests of the Crimean Tatars have led to the satisfaction of only the simplest of their demands, the resultant publicity made the injustices of Stalin's nationality policies a topic of official discussion for the first time, encouraging other nationalities to make their grievances public. This, however, also shifted the focus of nationalist protest first to the Baltic republics, and then to Transcaucasia. Eventually, events in these two areas had their own impact on Central Asia.

The creation of unofficial, and especially mass, organizations in Central Asia has proceeded more slowly than in any other part of the country. In such efforts the Central Asian nationalities face serious problems. They lack the organizational skills and political sophistication of the local Russian population. At the same time, except in Kazakhstan where the long tradition of living together makes it possible for some of the intellectuals to work in concert, the agendas of the Russians and Central Asians are almost entirely in conflict. Thus, the political potential of informal organizations has not yet been reached in the area. Still, Central Asian nationalists are making increasing use of informal groups to gain recognition of their demands.

Concern with serious environmental problems in the region has led to the formation of several ecology groups. Most prominent of these is "Nevada–Semipalatinsk," organized in Kazakhstan by the prominent writer Olzhas Suleimenov—the only bi-national unofficial group in Central Asia. Formed originally to protest nuclear testing, the group has added other ecological and political issues to its agenda.

In both Tadzhikistan and Uzbekistan, a series of demonstrations have been held by an umbrella of organizations, designed to have the local language declared official in its republic. Legislation to this effect—though hedged with various provisions to safeguard Russian and minority languages—was passed or under consideration in all five republics in 1989. A largely Uzbek group, though founded and centered in Alma-Ata, "Islam and Democracy," succeeded in gaining the dismissal of the head of the Muslim ecclesiastical administration for Central Asia in 1989; however, it apparently had no voice in the appointment of his successor and seems to have faded in importance.

Perhaps most importantly in the long term, despite numerous difficulties, popular fronts based on the Baltic model were in various stages of organization in all Central Asian republics in 1989. The most promising starts were in Tadzhikistan and Uzbekistan. The Uzbek group in Tashkent, known as *Birlik* [Unity], was already a growing political force, with an agenda that was both nationalist and strongly influenced by Islam.[49]

Islam is both a unifying force and a source of disunity among the Central Asians. All Central Asians are proud of their Islamic heritage and oppose restriction on the faith. Many intellectuals are seeking to embrace their Islamic heritage by providing for the religious instruction of their children and calling for increased Arabic-language instruction and even a return to the old Arabic script in writing their native languages. But most urban secularized intellectuals have little in common with the Islamic fringe groups that are springing up in the rural areas of Central Asia, groups whose agendas are explicitly influenced by religious broadcasts from Iran or religious materials smuggled in from Afghanistan. Their activities are the most difficult of all for Western analysts to track. It is clear that they have had a role in political protests in the recent past, both in Tadzhikistan and in Uzbekistan, but what role they will play in the future still remains to be seen.

The growth of anomic violence in mid-1989 in Uzbekistan and Kazakhstan is sure to work to their advantage. The rampage of thousands of unemployed youths in the Fergana, Kokand, and Namangan regions took on religious coloration at times, even though the target of the violence, the Meskhetian Turks (deported to the area in 1944), are also Sunni Muslims. The riots in Uzbekistan were an ominous portent for the region as a whole because of the deep-set frustration of rural youth that they revealed. Conditions in the Fergana valley are replicated everywhere in Central Asia. Population density may vary and local hardships may be more or less severe, but everywhere there are thousands of unemployed or underemployed Central Asians, with little or no Russian-language or technical skills. Riots broke out in western Kazakhstan even while the riots were still being put down in Uzbekistan. Here the problem was simply the hardships of life for the unemployed Kazakh youths who thought that migrant workers from Daghestan enjoyed better living conditions than they—and tore up the city of Novyi Uzen in protest. Violence begets violence, and protests will continue until conditions improve. Interethnic rivalries, in which the area abounds, will likely become a growing source of conflict, conflict which whenever possible will be validated on national and even religious grounds.

Conclusion

The death of Stalin left Central Asia under the firm central control of Moscow. Under Khrushchev the local nationalities gained more discretionary authority in the management of the day-to-day lives of their republics. The discretionary power of national elites was further strengthened under Brezhnev, in part by design, and then because the distance between Moscow and the republican capitals grew greater and greater as Brezhnev's grasp of events grew more and more tenuous. Decisions about the direction of the economy rested firmly in Moscow, as did the right to make, or at least authorize, all senior party and government appointments. But the party leaders from Central Asia occupied their positions for decades at a time, and had accumulated enormous reserves of personal authority. Two were in the Politburo—Kunaev of Kazakhstan as full member and Rashidov of Uzbekistan as candidate member—and even the others were forces to be reckoned with, controlling as they did vast personal networks in the party and throughout the various branches of the legal and illegal economies. Their power was great enough to block economic change and to shape the course of nationalist revival or protest. It was this structure that Gorbachev decided he must dismantle for his reform program to succeed in Central Asia.

Moscow, however, certainly faces a rough road ahead in Central Asia, particularly given its commitment to integrate the area with the center both economically and politically. The policies of reform initiated by Gorbachev appear to make these goals more distant. Nationalist sentiments are on the rise throughout Central Asia, making cultural and political integration more problematic. Moreover, the economic reforms planned by the center seem, both to the Central Asians and to many outside observers, to be a retreat from the kind of large-scale commitment of resources that the region needs to revitalize its economy. Even in the unlikely event that such resources become available, Moscow and the Central Asian elites are sure to differ on how they should be deployed.

The national and cultural differences that distinguish Central Asians from the center cannot simply be wished away. The Central Asian party elites' own commitment to Gorbachev's reform program is weak, and it is proving difficult to identify and recruit cadres from the indigenous nationalities who more closely share Moscow's vision. Even if Moscow recruits a satisfactory leadership in Central Asia, this leadership will still have to obtain mass support. Widespread mass support, on the other hand, can be achieved only if there is some sort of major social transformation. There are substantial material problems that must be solved before the mandated social transformation can occur, however. Schools have to be built and staffed, and new curriculums have to be designed with texts to match. All this costs money and demands trained manpower—two things that are in very short supply.

Even in the unlikely event that Moscow can allocate sufficient resources to fund adequately the social and economic policies it desires, success would still be far from assured. Many of the most difficult barriers these policies confront are cultural. The perpetuation of Islamic values impedes the kind of social and economic development that Moscow is striving hard for these national regions to attain. Better Russian-language training and improved technical education will not by themselves make the Muslim population as mobile as Moscow desires.

A social revolution of some kind is necessary for the Central Asian populations to accept the values that are implicit in the economic and political features of Gorbachev's nationalities policy. Their Islamic heritage—or, viewed more precisely, their traditional cultural values which stem in part from their religion—has not been wholly altered by seventy years of Soviet rule. Given the direction of cultural reform to which Moscow currently seems committed, the social distance between the Central Asians and the rest of the Soviet nationalities seems likely to grow.

Notes

1. The status of these new national units in the federal state structure initially varied. Turkmenia and Uzbekistan were created union republics in 1924, the latter including Tadzhikistan as an autonomous republic until 1929, when it achieved separate union republic status. Kazakhstan, formed in 1920 as the "Kirghiz" (renamed "Kazakh" in 1925) ASSR within the Russian SFSR, became a union republic in 1936, as did Kirghizia, which was established in 1924 as the "Kara-Kirghiz" (in 1925 renamed "Kirghiz") Autonomous Oblast and elevated to an autonomous republic in 1926. The Karakalpak territory was formed into an autonomous oblast in 1925, first within the Kazakh ASSR and in 1930 directly under the RSFSR; raised to ASSR status in 1932, it was transferred from the RSFSR to the jurisdiction of the Uzbek SSR in 1936.

2. The Arabic script traditionally used in Central Asia was abandoned in the late 1920s in favor of the Latin alphabet; this was in turn replaced by the Cyrillic a decade later, with variant orthographies developed for each language.

3. Brought into office as first secretaries were: in Uzbekistan in 1955—Nuritdin Mukhitdinov, and after his transfer to Moscow in 1957—Sabir Kamalov; in Tadzhikistan in 1956—Tursunbai Uldzhabaev, replaced in 1961 by Dzhabar Rasulov; in Turkmenia in 1958—Dzhuma Karaev, succeeded on his death in 1960 by Balysh Ovezov; and in Kirghizia in 1961—Turdakun Usubaliev.

4. See Donald S. Carlisle, "The Uzbek Power Elite: Politburo and Secretariat (1938–83)," *Central Asian Survey,* vol. 5, no. 3–4 (1986), pp. 91–132.

5. For details on the post-Stalin period in Kazakhstan, see Martha Brill Olcott, *The Kazakhs* (Stanford, CA: Hoover Institution Press, 1987), chap. 10.

6. There was, in any case, no real potential for a conflict of interests between Moscow and Kazakhstan during these years, as Brezhnev had de facto ceded a great deal of control over affairs in the republic to Kunaev.

7. For a discussion of leadership appointments by nationality for the period 1955–72, see Grey Hodnett, *Leadership in the Soviet National Republics: A Quantitative Study of Recruitment Policy* (Oakville, Ont.: Mosaic Press, 1978).

8. For a more complete account of party politics in Central Asia, see Martha Brill Olcott, "Gorbachev's Nationalities Policy and Soviet Central Asia," in Rajan Menon

and Daniel N. Nelson, eds., *Limits to Soviet Power* (Lexington, KY: Lexington Books, 1989), pp. 69–93.

9. See, for example, the critical editorial in *Partiinaia zhizn' Kazakhstana*, 1985, no. 8, pp. 14–19, which was immediately followed by a series of negative articles about Kazakhstan in *Pravda*.

10. *Pravda*, 26 February 1986.

11. *Pravda vostoka*, 1 February 1986.

12. These were the first secretaries of Dzhizak, Khorezm, Kashka Darya, and Bukhara oblasts, all later arrested and convicted of the theft of state property and bribery.

13. *Pravda vostoka*, 23 January 1988.

14. *Pravda*, 9 February 1986, and *Kazakhstanskaia pravda*, 8–11 February 1986.

15. Kolbin was appointed head of the revamped Peoples' Control Commission in Moscow in June 1989.

16. For a detailed discussion of the reassertion of Uzbek control in Uzbekistan, see James Critchlow, "Obduracy of Uzbek Cadres Casting Shadow on Nationalities Plenum," Radio Liberty, *Report on the USSR*, vol. 1, no. 12 (24 March 1989), pp. 20–22.

17. *Kazakhstanskaia pravda*, 30 April 1989.

18. See the data published in *Pravda*, 29 April 1989.

19. For some details on demographic trends in Kazakhstan, see Ann Sheehy, "Do Kazakhs Now Outnumber Russians in Kazakhstan?" *Radio Liberty Research Bulletin*, RL 65/87 (19 February 1987).

20. The average Kirghiz family comprised 5.7, the Uzbek—6.2, and the Turkmen—6.3 members. *Chislennost' i sostav naseleniia SSSR: Po dannym Vsesoiuznoi perepisi naseleniia 1979 goda* (Moscow: Finansy i statistika, 1984), pp. 284–86.

21. See G. A. Bondarskaia, "Rozhdaemost' u narodov SSSR," in *Sto natsii i narodnostei: Etnodemograficheskoe razvitie SSSR*, ed. E. K. Vasil'eva et al. (Moscow: Mysl', 1985), p. 26.

22. See *Vestnik statistiki*, 1986, no. 9, pp. 77–78. Without more knowledge about the sampling techniques used in the two surveys, it is hard to conclude anything about the significance of these changes.

23. *Kazakhstanskaia pravda*, 30 April 1989.

24. U.S. Joint Publications Research Service [henceforth JPRS], *USSR: Political and Social Report*, UPS 85–043 (17 May 1985), p. 51.

25. Murray Feshbach, "Trends in the Soviet Muslim Population," in Yaacov Ro'i, ed., *The USSR and the Muslim World* (London: George Allen & Unwin, 1984), p. 67.

26. The comparable figure for the Turkmen was 597, the Kazakhs—592, and the Kirghiz—590. In 1970 the Russians reported 508 per thousand with some secondary education or higher, while the Turkmen reported 430, the Uzbeks—412, the Kirghiz—400, and the Kazakhs and Tadzhiks—390. See I. P. Zinchenko, "Natsional'nyi sostav naseleniia SSSR," in A. A. Isupov and N. Z. Shvartser, eds., *Vsesoiuznaia perepis' naseleniia 1979 goda: Sbornik statei* (Moscow: Finansy i statistika, 1984), p. 160.

27. According to the 1979 census, 83.0% of all Kirghiz families in their titular republic lived in rural areas; for the other nationalities the analogous figures were: Tadzhiks—75.8%, Uzbeks—72.7%, Kazakhs—69.3%, and Turkmen—67.7%. *Chislennost' i sostav naseleniia*, pp. 284–321.

28. *Vestnik statistiki*, 1986, no. 5, p. 79.

29. *Kazakhstanskaia pravda*, 8 February 1986.

30. *Pravda*, 1 March 1986.

31. *Pravda*, 9 March 1986.

32. For an excellent consideration of this problem in the early 1980s, see Nancy Lubin, *Labour and Nationality in Soviet Central Asia: An Uneasy Compromise* (Princeton: Princeton University Press, 1984).

33. Moscow announced the cancellation of preparatory work on the diversion of the Siberian rivers on 19 August 1986. See U.S. Foreign Broadcast Information Service, *Daily Report: Soviet Union*, 19 August 1986, p. R1.

34. Viktor Dukhovnyi, "Voda dlia regiona," *Zvezda vostoka*, 1986, no. 2, pp. 107–15.

35. For a good example of this literature, see *Kommunist Uzbekistana*, 1985, no. 3, pp. 43–48, as translated in JPRS, *USSR: Political and Social Report*, UPS 85-1985, pp. 62–68.

36. A. I. Abdusamedov et al., *Islam v SSSR: Osobennosti protsessa sekuliarizatsii v respublikakh sovetskogo Vostoka* (Moscow: Mysl', 1983), p. 68.

37. T. Dzh. Baialieva, *Religioznye perezhitki u kirgizov i ikh preodolenie* (Frunze: Ilim, 1984).

38. For a summary of Soviet survey data on religion, see T. S. Saidbaev, *Islam i obshchestvo: Opyt istoriko-sotsiologicheskogo issledovaniia* (Moscow: Nauka, 1978); 2d ed., rev. and enl. (Moscow: Nauka, 1984).

39. *Voprosy teorii i praktiki ateisticheskogo vospitaniia* (Tashkent: Uzbekistan, 1979), p. 175.

40. Saidbaev, *Islam i obshchestvo* (1978), p. 191.

41. *Islam v SSSR*, p. 80.

42. For some examples, see *Kommunist Tadzhikistana*, 8 July 1986; *Komsomol'skaia pravda*, 4 June 1986; *Leninskaia smena*, 11 July 1986; and *Pravda vostoka*, 28 June 1986.

43. *Pravda vostoka*, 31 January 1986.

44. *Sovet Özbekistani*, 6 August 1986.

45. For some discussion of this issue, see *Pravda*, 18 December 1985, and *Kazakhstanskaia pravda*, 21 January 1986.

46. See *Kazakhstanskaia pravda*, 18–21 December 1986.

47. *Kazakhstanskaia pravda*, 10 June 1989.

48. *Pravda*, 9 June 1988.

49. See Timur Kocaoglu, "Demonstrations by Uzbek Popular Front," Radio Liberty, *Report on the USSR*, vol. 1, no. 17 (28 April 1989), pp. 13–16.

CHAPTER 12

Russian Nationalism
and Soviet Politics

Dina Rome Spechler

The past quarter century has witnessed an extraordinary resurgence of Russian nationalism in the USSR. Expressed first in literary, artistic, and scholarly works and in the dissent of intellectuals, it soon became a mass phenomenon—both welcomed and encouraged, and at the same time carefully monitored and curbed, by portions of the political establishment. Unlike the previous upsurge of Russian nationalism which occurred during World War II and the immediate postwar years, this one was not initiated from above, by the top leader or leadership, but from below, by discontented citizens and concerned elites. Also unlike the Russian nationalism of Stalin's day, the contemporary movement has to a significant extent been aimed at fundamentally altering official policies and values. This widespread and sustained expression of intense Russian nationalism, the orientation of much of this sentiment against the political and ideological status quo, and the high-level support which its manifestations have received hold major implications for the stability of the Soviet political system. The destabilizing potential of Russian nationalism lies, above all, in its capacity to upset the fragile modus vivendi between Russians and non-Russians in Soviet society.

The Concept of Political Stability

A stable political system is one whose basic character or "critical components" persist for long periods of time without fundamental alteration or are altered gradually, without marked discontinuities. These components include the principal political institutions, the dominant political values or ideology, and the distribution of power among the major political institutions and groups.[1] A stable system has the capacity to absorb shocks and overcome

---

I would like to thank Peter Sugar, Zvi Gitelman, Roman Szporluk, and Darrell Hammer for their comments and suggestions regarding the research and arguments presented in this article. I would also like to acknowledge with thanks the able research assistance of Ida Isaac and Paul Richardson.

crises without a breakdown in the regime's capacity to govern or maintain order, and without a major alteration in the character of the system resulting from such a breakdown. It is, therefore, of necessity a system in which the regime is regarded as legitimate by all politically significant groups—especially by elites, on whose support the regime depends. In a stable system pressures for change are expressed in an orderly fashion, legally and peacefully, through institutional structures, rather than violently, in violation of the law.[2] Demands for non-incremental or fundamental change are rare, and made only by politically insignificant social forces or groups.[3] Destabilizing factors or forces in a political system are those that are likely to move the system in the direction of instability, i.e., factors or forces which tend to incite large-scale or frequent disorder, encourage expression of radical demands for change on the part of significant social groups, or in some other way lead to major, discontinuous systemic change.

In light of this concept of political stability and those forces which disrupt it, we may analyze the rise of contemporary Russian nationalism and its implications for Soviet politics and society.

The Resurgence of Russian Nationalism

The resurgence of Russian nationalism began in the mid-1960s and was manifested almost immediately on four different levels: (1) underground; (2) in legally published literature and scholarship; (3) among political elites; and (4) in organizations with official patronage. In 1964 a secret nationalist revolutionary organization, the All-Russian Social-Christian Union for the Liberation of the People (VSKhSON), was founded.[4] In 1965 the art historian and novelist Vladimir Soloukhin began to publish a series of literary works glorifying religious and cultural aspects of the prerevolutionary Russian past.[5] Soloukhin's most influential work, "Letters from the Russian Museum," was published in 1966 in the literary journal *Molodaia gvardiia*, which soon became the principal mouthpiece of Russian nationalism.[6] There followed a proliferation of scholarly treatises on Russian architecture, sculpture, art, and iconography, as well as works designed to popularize and arouse interest in Russia's cultural and religious heritage.[7] A high official in the Moscow Komsomol organization, Valerii Skurlatov, distributed a document entitled "Rules of Morality" among Komsomol activists which glorified "the Russian race" and spoke of "the cosmic mission of the Russian people" and their "duty to [their] ancestors" to preserve racial purity.[8] The nascent Russian nationalist movement was greatly abetted by the formation, in 1966, of the All-Russian Society for the Preservation of Historical and Cultural Monuments (VOOPIK), an officially sponsored, voluntary organization led by self-styled establishment "Russites."[9] The All-Russian Society for the Preservation of Nature and the "Rossiia" Literary Club, founded soon after, were likewise officially approved and controlled by establishment Russian nationalists.[10]

For a short while the movement was allowed to flourish without hindrance, the leadership uncertain or in disagreement on whether to restrain it. Soon, however, curbs began to be imposed—first on underground activities, then on the most extreme expressions of Russian nationalism in open publications. The founder and leader of VSKhSON was arrested in 1967 and his organization disbanded.[11] The Fetisov group, authors of a blatantly chauvinistic, anti-Semitic program glorifying the Slavic race, were arrested the following year.[12] *Molodaia gvardiia* was censured in 1970 and its chief editor dismissed in 1971.[13]

After these restrictive moves, legal expressions of Russian nationalism became more moderate. Individuals whose ideas were overtly in conflict with official ideology were forced to publish in *samizdat* and eventually silenced or sent abroad. Thus, an essay entitled "A Word to the Nation," whose plea to safeguard the purity of the Russian race was very much in the spirit of Skurlatov's "Rules of Morality," could not be circulated openly by 1971; it appeared in that year in *samizdat*, signed anonymously by "Russian patriots."[14] In the same year, a former VSKhSON member, Vladimir Osipov, created a *samizdat* publication entitled *Veche*. Devoted to an ethical-religious brand of Russian nationalism, *Veche* was suppressed three years later.[15] Solzhenitsyn's 1974 "Letter to the Soviet Leaders," which expressed grave concern for the fate of the Russian people and urged that minority groups be allowed to secede from the USSR, was probably a primary cause of the author's expulsion from the country in that year.[16]

What is most remarkable about these curbs on Russian nationalism, however, is how limited their effect was. The movement continued to gain momentum and acquire new supporters. Membership in VOOPIK reached one million a year after it was founded and by 1982 exceeded fourteen million.[17] Moreover, suppression of unofficial groups and periodicals resulted only in the appearance of new ones. When *Veche* was closed down, Osipov published a new, more religiously oriented journal, *Zemlia*, and after his arrest still another *samizdat* publication with a similar outlook, *Moskovskii sbornik*, appeared. Religio-philosophical study groups with a Russian nationalist orientation began to be organized in 1974 in Moscow and soon afterward in Leningrad and Kiev. The Christian Committee for the Defense of Believers' Rights in the USSR was formed in 1976 with the aim of improving the status of Russian Orthodoxy. A wave of arrests of Russian nationalists in 1979–80, including the leaders of the Moscow Religio-Philosophical Seminar and the Christian Committee, was followed by the organization of a Russian nationalist Christian women's group, the Maria Club, in 1980.[18]

Most importantly, Russian nationalist ideas are now expressed openly and frequently, if more circumspectly and less stridently than earlier, in official journals.[19] At least one mass circulation newspaper, *Sovetskaia Rossiia*, can be characterized as a mouthpiece of the movement. All-union newspapers such as *Pravda* and *Literaturnaia gazeta* sometimes open their pages to nationalist contributors, and several large publishing houses (Sovetskaia Rossiia, Molodaia gvardiia, and Sovremennik) are known for their Russian nationalist orientation. A "ruralist" trend in literature exalts traditional

Russian values and increasingly concentrates on the issue of the physical and spiritual survival of the Russian people.[20] Russian nationalist art, best represented by the works of Il'ia Glazunov, has been exhibited to millions of viewers in public galleries.[21]

With the advent of *glasnost'*, even extreme manifestations of Russian nationalism have been tolerated. An unofficial group which calls itself *Pamiat'* (Memory) has held public meetings and demonstrations in Moscow, Leningrad, Novosibirsk, and many other major cities. The group's principal objective is to protect Russia from an alleged Jewish conspiracy to destroy it, and meetings are devoted to "demonstrations" of the pernicious influence of Jews on Russian politics, culture, and society.[22]

Russian Nationalism and the Soviet Regime

The Russian nationalist movement may be usefully depicted in terms of the relationship between each of its components and the Soviet regime. The various groups in the movement can be represented schematically along a continuum, with those most opposed to the regime and its values on one end and those with the closest links to the political establishment on the other.

As can be seen from the diagram, there are two principal tendencies within the Russian nationalist movement. One is primarily concerned with the spiritual well-being and physical survival of the Russian people as a distinct ethnic group. It sees the Russian people as undergoing a profound spiritual and demographic crisis because its values, culture, and traditions are disappearing. It therefore seeks a revival of Russian Orthodox religious values, Russian culture, and/or the traditional, preindustrial Russian way of life. As a result, it is drawn toward the pole of opposition to the regime. The second tendency is primarily concerned with preserving or enhancing the political and/or military power of the Russian nation, vis-à-vis both other national groups within the USSR and the rest of the world. It generally regards the Soviet regime as the actual or potential representative and protector of the Russian people and thus favors strengthening Soviet state power, both internally and externally. However, it is important to note that there is by no means an absolute dichotomy between the two tendencies: ideas characteristic of one are often articulated by adherents of the other. Thus, individuals and groups located near opposite ends of the continuum have sometimes expressed very similar sentiments.

It is significant that among those nationalists closest to the pole of opposition, only one group, VSKhSON, was from the outset militantly opposed to the regime and dedicated to its overthrow.[23] Nearly all other groups were at least initially interested in a modus vivendi with the authorities. More importantly, nearly all initially believed that their ideas could be acceptable, even appealing, to at least some portions of the political establishment.

Solzhenitsyn's first work with a clearly nationalist message was addressed not to opponents of the regime, but to the Soviet leadership itself, and his

RUSSIAN NATIONALISTS AND THE SOVIET REGIME

GROUP

Chief Concern   Relation to the Regime

Dissident Nationalists

	All-Russian Social-Christian Union for the Liberation of the People (1964-1967)	Absolute Antagonists
Russian religious and cultural revival	Solzhenitsyn & his circle: Letter to the Soviet Leaders; From under the Rubble (1974-1975) Osipov; contributors to Veche (1971-1974); Zemlia (1974) Religio-Philosophical Seminars: Obshchina (Moscow); 37 (Leningrad); Kiev (1974- ?) Maria Club (1980- ?) Christian Committee for the Defense of Believers' Rights in the USSR (1976-1980?)	Tried and failed to achieve modus vivendi
Russian political and military power	Ruralists: Nash sovremennik (1965-) Glazunov & his circle National Bolsheviks: Molodaia gvardiia (1966-)	Achieved modus vivendi
	Chauvinists, anti-Semites, fascists (1965-)	Part of political establishment
	Russian patriots: All-Russian Society for the Preservation of Historical and Cultural Monuments (1966-)	

Establishment Nationalists

plea for more investment in the areas settled by Russians may, in fact, have had an impact on official policy.[24] Only after his expulsion from the USSR, when he edited the volume *From under the Rubble*, did Solzhenitsyn begin to express absolute, principled opposition to Marxism-Leninism because of its godlessness.[25]

Veche also initially proclaimed loyalty and support for the "great Soviet power" and opposition to the "cosmopolitan" human rights movement. It defended the regime's foreign and nationalities policies and insisted on the maintenance of Russian rule over the non-Russian areas of the USSR, even though they had been conquered by force.[26] Only when Osipov and his journal were increasingly harassed was he persuaded that a Russian cultural and religious renaissance would require substantial liberalization of Soviet political life, including guarantees of constitutional rights and freedoms. It was only then that he established links with the human rights movement and became part of the illegal opposition.[27]

The various Russian Orthodox study groups and clubs which have been organized outside the framework of the officially sanctioned Church have also found it necessary to operate clandestinely. Dedicated to a reintroduction of religious values into the lives of the Russian people, they have been regarded with considerable suspicion by the guardians of Marxist-Leninist orthodoxy. However, these groups have generally refrained from adopting positions on political and ideological issues. This is particularly true of the Christian Committee for the Defense of Believers' Rights, which has made every effort to work within the system, using exclusively legal methods and channels to assist believers.

More successful in finding a modus vivendi with the regime are the "ruralist" prose writers. Their primary concern is the fate of the disappearing Russian village, which they regard as the repository of the finest values and traditions of the Russian people, the source of its spiritual strength and the key to its physical survival.[28] This concern appears to be either shared by or highly useful to persons well-placed in the political establishment, and consequently ruralist authors have had few difficulties in publishing their works. Some, like Vladimir Soloukhin, may have close ties to the establishment. Soloukhin and the outspokenly nationalist artist Il'ia Glazunov are believed to have influenced the authorities to agree to the formation of the Society for the Preservation of Historical and Cultural Monuments.[29]

Closer to the regime is a group of writers and publicists who, while still holding controversial views, have made even more strenuous efforts to achieve a modus vivendi with the authorities. They have, in varying degrees, either justified Russian nationalism in Communist terms or Communist power in Russian nationalist terms—i.e., in terms of what the Soviet regime has accomplished or can accomplish for the Russian people. For this reason they have been described as "National Bolsheviks." They include the authors of the stridently nationalistic essays published in *Molodaia gvardiia*, for which the journal was reprimanded in 1970, and others who have written in the same vein.[30]

Very close to the political establishment, and in many cases well inside it, is a large assortment of writers, publicists, and officials whose Russian nationalism expresses itself in such forms as extreme chauvinism, anti-Semitism, general xenophobia, and fascism (a combination of racism with either traditional authoritarianism or neo-Stalinism). The "Rules of Morality" circulated by Skurlatov represents this tendency, as do the writings of the Russian nationalist theoretician Petr Palievsky and the anti-Semitic diatribes of Central Committee researcher Yurii Ivanov, official propagandists Vladimir Vagon and Evgenii Evseev, and literary critic Vadim Kozhinov. *Pamiat'*, whose orators proclaim the authenticity of the notorious Okhrana forgery, *The Protocols of the Elders of Zion*, reflects this current within Russian nationalism. However, the public demonstrations held by *Pamiat'*, which have attracted hundreds of people, and the group's ability to win supporters throughout the Soviet Union have aroused concern within the establishment. The organization's official status has thus been revoked.[31]

Within the political establishment there are also numerous relatively moderate Russian nationalists in whom Russian and Soviet patriotisms often tend to merge. Most of them subscribe to no coherent doctrine. However, they provide patronage, support, and official protection to Russian nationalists of all kinds, particularly those who would enhance Russia's political and military might.

Russian Nationalism and Political Stability

Russian Nationalism and Marxism-Leninism

In some sense the very existence of a Russian nationalist movement that has found widespread sympathy among the Russian masses (chiefly urban youth), the intelligentsia, and the political elite is itself an indicator of instability in the Soviet political system. For however close the ties between certain nationalists and the political establishment, however hard they may try to achieve an ideological and political modus vivendi with the regime,[32] there is an inescapable contradiction between Russian (indeed, any) nationalism and some basic tenets of Marxism-Leninism. The essence of nationalism—concern for the preservation and well-being of a single nation—places it in opposition to the internationalist or supranational orientation of Marxism-Leninism. Whatever their private sentiments, Soviet leaders have repeatedly affirmed their commitment to internationalism—i.e., to the well-being of all working people on an equal basis, regardless of nationality, and to the eradication of national differences.[33] This commitment and progress toward its attainment provide one of the most important legitimations for the existence of the Soviet system and, even more, for Russian rule over non-Russians. That there is widespread sentiment which rejects internationalism and posits the interests of one nation as its central concern is a sign that a basic, system-legitimizing value in Soviet political life is widely rejected, and hence that the system contains a significant element of instability.[34]

Political stability in the USSR is to a significant degree contingent upon a community of assumptions, or a world view, among political and other elites. This community or unity has been essential in insulating the party from political opposition, ensuring continuity of doctrine and policy direction, and sustaining popular acceptance of party rule.[35] The spontaneous resurgence of Russian nationalism among some elements of the political elite, while other elements remain strongly internationalist in orientation, has already helped to undermine this unity and hence to destroy one of the main sources of political stability.

A substantial portion of the Russian nationalist movement explicitly denounces Marxism-Leninism, exemplifying the challenge that Russian nationalism presents to official political values, and hence to systemic stability. Of course this rejection is more characteristic of those whom the regime has persecuted: VSKhSON, Solzhenitsyn and his circle, and some contributors to *Veche*. However, even many of the "legal" Russian nationalists view Marxism-Leninism as an alien import which has done more harm than good to the Russian people. Many—both dissidents and "legals"—seek an alternative source of values, which they often find in the prerevolutionary, preindustrial past and in religion. Rejecting the official doctrine that the October Revolution and the radical transformation it accomplished brought salvation to an oppressed Russia, they emphasize the Russian people's historical and cultural continuity. Some openly praise the Tsarist regime; others denigrate the notion of class struggle and laud the so-called "reactionary elements" of prerevolutionary Russia; still others denounce collectivization and the destruction of the Russian peasantry that accompanied it.[36] Many explicitly oppose both industrialization and scientific-technical progress, which, they claim, destroyed the Russian village and left a spiritual vacuum, unfilled by ideology.[37] Modernization, in their view, has had a devastating effect on Russian fertility, purportedly threatening the very existence of the Russian people.[38] Above all, many Russian nationalists, even those closely linked with the establishment, seek to return the Russian people to their traditional religion, which they see as the spiritual foundation of the nation.[39] This is indeed quite fundamental dissent, reflecting the existence of forces which are not reconciled to basic values of the system.

Russian Nationalism and the Non-Russians

In the USSR, by contemporary international standards, until recently there had been relatively little minority protest, especially violent protest, directed against the ethnic majority and the system imposed and dominated by it. It may be argued that the official nationalities policy, although unable to "solve" the nationality problem, nonetheless constituted a stabilizing force in the Soviet political system. Official commitment to the equality of all national groups has been one important component of that policy. Another has been the care taken by the regime throughout most of its history—the period of World War II is one notable exception—to restrain Russian nationalism. Soviet leaders have been extremely sensitive to the danger posed by Russian chauvinism and its potential for disrupting the frangible multinational edifice on which the Soviet system rests, and have at times denounced excessive Russian nationalism. Indeed, Russian nationalists claim that Russians have been denied some of the official recognition and opportunities for national self-expression extended to other ethnic groups in the USSR.[40] Most importantly, the Soviet regime traditionally carefully pursued what might be described as a concessionary and compensatory nationalities policy. Allowing the non-Russians little autonomy in political and economic affairs and vigorously suppressing overt expressions of nationalism, it granted the minority nationalities, to varying degrees, considerable administrative autonomy and opportunities to develop their own cultures and employ their own languages. Although most non-Russian nationalities are underrepresented in the all-union government, some groups—such as the Ukrainians or, more recently, the Belorussians—have at times played a significant role in ruling and administering the country.[41] The non-Russians generally were given substantial symbolic representation at all levels of government. In compensation for their lack of real political power or political autonomy, many non-Russian groups received substantial economic benefits from the Soviet state.[42]

The rise of Russian nationalism may alter this carefully devised and balanced policy, becoming a significant threat to political stability. Should the regime appear to endorse the extreme racist and chauvinist views of some Russian nationalists, for example, this would constitute a major deviation from previous policy and would, in and of itself, be highly provocative to the non-Russian peoples. The most blatant expression of Russian nationalist racism to date—a denunciation of "random hybridization" of races in the USSR on the grounds that it would lead to the biological degeneration of the Russian nation—was published illegally in *samizdat*.[43] The official press, however, has echoed such sentiments: the journal *Voprosy istorii* approvingly discussed the views of Lev Gumilev that since ethnically mixed marriages result in genetically inferior offspring, and hence in inferior states and social institutions, intermarriage between Russians and others would lead to national self-destruction.[44] And it was a high Komsomol official who circulated a manifesto demanding sterilization of Russian women who "give themselves to foreigners."[45]

Equally provocative to the non-Russian nationalities of the USSR have been paeans to the greatness of the Russian people, their "healthy" civilization, and their superior national spirit or soul.[46] In the 1970s and early 1980s references to Russia as the "first among equals" among the nations of the USSR became more frequent in the mass media.[47] History lessons in non-Russian schools increasingly stressed the contributions of Russians to the development of the USSR and by their silence belittled those of non-Russians. Non-Russian historians were publicly excoriated for failing to emphasize the "massive aid" which their peoples received from the Russians and which made their cultural achievements possible.[48] Expressions of such views had significant political consequences. They helped to trigger and intensify outbursts of minority nationalism,[49] and apparently generated considerable interethnic tension in the armed forces.[50] If such sentiments come to be articulated more often in official forums and, in so doing, become increasingly identified with Russian nationalism, minority resentment, traditionally directed primarily against Russians, will turn sharply against the regime and the system.

The more the regime gives free rein to the cultural, religious, and historical quest of the Russian nationalists, the more it will find itself pressed to be equally tolerant of minority nationalisms expressed in similar quests. The dissemination of Russian culture has been highly useful as a means of political integration and domination. Efforts to revive and promote that culture, while contrary to the internationalism of official ideology, are not necessarily inconsistent with the objectives and policies of the regime. Russian Orthodoxy was the cradle of the dominant culture, and its representatives have actively cooperated with and supported the Soviet state. By contrast, efforts to revive and develop minority cultures and religions have always been directed against the Russifying thrusts of official policy. Similarly, celebration of the deeds of Russian heroes—explorers and generals who, however reactionary the regime they served, helped the Russian Empire expand—has implied approval of the perpetuation of that empire. Praise for non-Russian military and political figures, on the other hand, has implied approval of resistance to Russian domination and advocacy of a major change in the political status quo. Such praise, therefore, was traditionally regarded as politically subversive and unacceptable. Thus, the more the regime indulged Russian nationalism in its search for spiritual roots and historical continuity, the more it created a double standard, tending to arouse intense resentment.

Still more potentially inimical to political stability is the possibility that the regime might abandon its concessionary and compensatory nationalities policy in response to Russian nationalist pressure. The political strength of Russians would significantly increase, and symbolic non-Russian presence at the center of the political system would be noticeably reduced. Russian nationalist influence on policy would likely result in a major reduction in the economic benefits enjoyed by non-Russians.

One current of thought within the Russian nationalist movement favors a drastic decrease in the pace of economic growth in the USSR. Those who take this position argue that a high level of economic growth has been sustained at the expense of Russian interests. They contend that Russians constitute the bulk of the labor force with the skills necessary for industrial development, and that it is mainly Russians who have been taken from their native villages and resettled in large industrial centers—with a drastic effect on their culture, their values, and their fertility.[51] Growth must be slowed, these Russian nationalists aver, to halt this pernicious process. Were the regime to comply with these demands, the result might be stagnation or decline in the living standards of all Soviet citizens.

Another school of Russian nationalist thought favors a major increase in Soviet military might, accompanied by a more forceful and expansionist foreign policy, as redounding to the glory of the Russian people.[52] Their program would require a major shift of resources away from consumption into the military sector. As with the case of a low-growth policy, the living standards of all citizens would suffer. But most significantly, if some Russian nationalists had their way, there would be a substantial transfer of resources from non-Russians to Russians. A higher proportion of well-paying jobs in the republics would be reserved for Russians, and there would be a major shift in the allocation of investment and consumption resources from non-Russian to Russian areas.[53] Official efforts to reduce economic disparities among national groups and republics would be ended, and special efforts would be made to develop Russian agriculture and improve the living conditions of Russian peasants.[54]

There could be no better recipe for exacerbating tensions between Russians and non-Russians than a political and economic program of this sort. The significant number of positions closed to non-Russians in the party and state bureaucracies is already an important grievance of minority elites.[55] The perceived prosperity of Russians is likewise widely resented by many non-Russians, who believe that the Russians are exploiting them. Ukrainians, Georgians, Estonians, Latvians, and Lithuanians have complained that their republics contribute more to the central budget than they receive.[56] Central Asians have demanded large transfers of resources, particularly water, from the RSFSR to their region.[57] There are increasing signs of conflict between Russians and other groups over economic development funds.[58] Such conflicts are likely to intensify even if there is no change in current allocation policy, since both the need and expectation of resources by many non-Russian populations have been growing rapidly. At present the struggle for consumption and investment funds is waged more among republics than against the center.[59] Should the influence of the Russian nationalist movement result in a policy blatantly favoring Russians over other ethnic groups, and the RSFSR over other national areas, this could unite non-Russians against the regime. The tensions that would be generated by abandoning the compensatory policies now pursued would have most serious, destabilizing consequences for the regime and the system.

Also destabilizing would be a move on the part of the regime to withdraw or substantially reduce the concessions it now makes to minority aspirations for autonomy. A strong tendency within the Russian nationalist movement favors a more repressive approach to non-Russian peoples. Adherents of this view desire a more powerful, centralized state to facilitate greater Russian control over non-Russian areas. They admire the expansionist, imperialist policy of the Tsarist state and urge its Soviet successor to impose similarly "undiluted" Russian rule.[60] Some are even critical of Soviet federalism, which they would replace with a unitary state dominated by Russians.[61] Others call for the incorporation of republics with large Russian populations (Kazakhstan, Ukraine) into the RSFSR and ending the administrative autonomy of minorities within the Russian republic (Tatars, Bashkirs, Karelians, etc.).[62] At the very least, these Russian nationalists are determined to preserve the Russian empire and would firmly repress what one of them calls the "zoological nationalisms of the borderlands" that endanger the unity of the country.[63] Nationalists of this ilk are enthusiastic about Russian colonization of non-Russian areas,[64] and some are eager to see the non-Russian peoples thoroughly Russified, although they do not generally favor intermarriage.[65] Most of the nationalists who favor expansion of Russian control over non-Russians are also neo-Stalinists who favor the use of force to repress minority resistance to their program.[66]

The Russian nationalist movement has arisen in what is already a highly charged ethnic political situation. Even now the compensatory aspects of Soviet nationalities policy are deemed inadequate by many non-Russians. This is even more true of the concessions granted to minority aspirations for self-determination. Centralization of political and economic decision making is already a major grievance of non-Russian elites, who feel that their interests are inadequately represented. Measures that reduce autonomy have already led to demonstrations and even outbreaks of rioting, arson, and assaults on Russians.[67] Efforts by the regime to expand Russian language instruction and somewhat curtail the use of local languages have caused thousands to sign petitions and take to the streets in angry protest.[68]

Should official policy come to be guided by Russian nationalist views, one could expect that protest of this sort would be very greatly intensified. Demands for major systemic change would surely be voiced with greater frequency, as the non-Russian peoples became convinced that a one-party state with a highly centralized economy and administrative structure dominated by Russians could never meet their needs or serve their interests.

Russian Nationalism and the Russians

The destabilizing effects of Russian nationalism are likely to be felt primarily through its impact on official policy and non-Russian reactions to that policy. But it could also have an impact on the stability of the Soviet political system through its influence on the thoughts, feelings, and behavior of the Russian population itself. For instance, increasingly forceful demands by non-Russians for linguistic, cultural, economic, and political autonomy, as well as efforts to restrict Russian in-migration have had the effect of fanning nationalism among Russians residing in the non-Russian republics. The rise of so-called internationalist movements in the Baltic republics and Moldavia, and the disruptive strikes in these areas by Russian workers in the summer and fall of 1989, were responses by Russians to the threat that their favored status within the system was being undermined.[69]

It is important to remember that many Russian nationalists are highly critical of the Soviet system for having destroyed the basis of Russian identity and sacrificed the Russian nation in its drive for economic and military power and societal reconstruction. If it gained currency, such criticism could undermine the legitimacy of the system in the eyes of Russians. This would be of enormous political significance, since the Russians' support for the system has constituted perhaps the most important stabilizing factor in

Soviet political life. A weakening of the regime's legitimacy among Russians is more likely to occur if the Russian nationalist movement were frustrated in its efforts to influence policy or Russians came to see the regime as unresponsive to their interests. Hence, even if the movement were a political failure, it might, paradoxically, still become a significant destabilizing force.

The rise of Russian nationalism has not only increased Russian self-awareness, but has also, to a certain extent, encouraged Russian arrogance, chauvinism, and hostility toward non-Russians. High-handedness on the part of Russian officials toward non-Russians has been a widespread and deeply resented phenomenon. Incidents of Russian violence against non-Russians are likewise not infrequent.[70] The spread of nationalist ideas about Russian superiority and entitlement to greater economic benefits could further incite such behavior. The probable results would again be radical political protest and large-scale ethnic violence. In the coming decades modernization, urbanization, and increased economic integration will likely lead to significantly more contact between Russians and non-Russians. This will render the potentially destabilizing impact of Russian nationalism all the greater.

Not all facets of Russian nationalism should be considered destabilizing. Indeed, the movement is by no means united on all important issues. If the ideas voiced by certain Russian nationalists were to become the basis of policy, they would probably increase support for the regime among minority groups. Some nationalists, for example, oppose Russian settlement outside the RSFSR on the grounds that the dispersion of the Russian people will lead to its disintegration and ultimate extinction as a distinct ethnic group. Russians, they argue, should reconverge on the Russian republic, consolidate demographically, and develop greater self-consciousness as a nation.[71] There are also Russian nationalists who advocate complete political and economic decentralization,[72] and others who favor removal of all restrictions on freedom of expression and religious worship.[73] Some explicitly stress that every ethnic group should have the right to cultivate and express its unique values and identity.[74] There are even Russian nationalists who believe that Russian rule over non-Russians is imprudent or immoral and gravely threatens Russian cohesion and self-preservation. They would allow most minority groups to secede from the USSR so that a truly Russian state, ruled exclusively by and for Russians, could be established.[75]

These views, however, are expressed by only a tiny handful, most of whom are now in exile and none of whom are close to the political establishment. Their ideas constitute a direct challenge to the three most central principles of Soviet political practice: party rule, Russian political dominance, and the power of the Soviet state. At most, these nationalists—former VSKhSON members, Solzhenitsyn and his circle, and Osipov and some *Veche* contributors—could have an impact on the thought and behavior of Russians themselves. At least one representative of this "coexistential" trend in Russian nationalism has indeed exerted considerable influence on certain segments of the Russian intelligentsia—Solzhenitsyn. However, there is little indication that Solzhenitsyn's ideas appeal to the Russian masses, and it is by and large his interest in reviving Russian culture, religion, and village life—not his political views or attitudes toward non-Russians—that have gained currency among Russian intellectuals. Thus, although in theory the "coexistentialists" could have a stabilizing impact on Soviet political life, in fact it is unlikely they will do so.

Russian Nationalism and Soviet Politics

The dominant trend in Russian nationalism constitutes a destabilizing force primarily because of its potential for rousing the non-Russian population against the regime, should that trend succeed in influencing official policy. The importance of this force thus depends to a significant extent on the likelihood that it will indeed have an impact on policy. One way to gauge that likelihood is to examine the regime's response to the resurgence of Russian nationalism. What indications are there that the movement has found sympathy at the top? What has been the stance of the party leadership toward those Russian nationalist ideas and demands which have provoked and are likely to provoke non-Russian discontent?

Overall, the regime's response to the resurgence of Russian nationalism in the last two decades has been ambivalent.[76] Leonid Brezhnev took strong measures to suppress overt attacks on party rule and attempts by members of the movement to evade party control. He likewise made it clear that exceptionally strident or chauvinistic declarations of Russian superiority and blatant advocacy of neo-Stalinist methods were unacceptable.[77] Moreover, he took steps to insure that even moderate formulations of Russian nationalist ideas were not represented as the dominant line or policy of the regime, personally condemning such ideas on at least one major occasion.[78] During his tenure, two full members of the Politburo, Dmitrii Poliansky and Aleksandr Shelepin, were dismissed for, allegedly, too openly patronizing Russian nationalists and promoting Russian national interests, among other reasons.[79] However, overly zealous criticism of the nationalists was proscribed, along with overly zealous nationalism.[80] Moreover, no thoroughgoing effort to halt or even discourage the expression of Russian nationalist ideas through legal channels was made. On the contrary, adherents of the movement were given many opportunities to pursue their interests and present their views under official auspices. The Voluntary Society for the Preservation of Historical Monuments was officially recognized, extensive government funds were allocated for the repair of churches, and prestigious facilities were provided for the performance of drama and exhibition of art with Russian nationalist themes.[81] Brezhnev himself paid tribute to the "great Russian people," stressing their "special historical role" and describing the RSFSR as the "first among equals" among union republics.[82] The general secretary thus not only tolerated, but actually promoted the growth of Russian national self-awareness and the expression of Russian ethnocentrism.

The situation did not change greatly under Brezhnev's two immediate successors. There is some evidence that Yurii Andropov and Konstantin

Chernenko were more sensitive to feelings of non-Russians, more concerned by the growing interest in religion among young Russians, and possibly more hostile to Russian nationalist ideas.[83] Persecution of Russian nationalists who attempted to organize independently, without official supervision, was intensified, as were attacks on Russian nationalism—particularly its religious manifestations—in the official media.[84] At the same time, however, literary journals continued to open their pages to works proclaiming a spiritual crisis in Russian society brought on by the neglect of tradition and the destruction of religion.

Under Gorbachev the dualism of official policy was sustained. However, initially there appeared to be more tolerance of and greater receptivity to Russian nationalist ideas on the part of the regime than at any time in the post-Stalin era. True, Russian writers and party cadres who "flirt with religion" continued to be criticized, and diatribes against prominent Russian nationalists occasionally appeared in the official press.[85] Gorbachev's report to the Twenty-seventh Party Congress contained a condemnation of "reactionary nationalist and religious survivals" that was probably aimed at Russian—as well as non-Russian—literary, artistic, and scholarly works.[86] Aleksandr Yakovlev, one of the most zealous establishment critics of the Russian nationalist movement, was promoted to Politburo membership and has been a close adviser to Gorbachev. A frequent target of attack by *Pamiat'* extremists, Yakovlev may be responsible for a prolonged media campaign against the organization in the summer of 1987 and again in August 1988, as well as for the earlier decision (at the end of 1985) to revoke the organization's official status.[87] On the other hand, Yakovlev was by no means given a free hand to clamp down on Russian nationalism, even its most extreme manifestations. Ejected from its original home in the Ministry of the Aviation Industry, *Pamiat'* was provided facilities for its meetings by a series of party and state organizations.[88] Although one of its demonstrations (in Leningrad in August 1988) was dispersed, the participants were not arrested or harassed. In the new climate of political tolerance, Soviet observers expect the group to remain active.[89]

More moderate exponents of Russian nationalism have likewise benefited from the regime's willingness to permit a wider range of literary and artistic expression. At the Eighth Congress of Soviet Writers in June 1986, notable for the assault on the literary establishment staged there, a group of ruralist writers presented what amounted to a Russian nationalist political-literary action program.[90] Soon after, the nationalist artist Il'ia Glazunov was allowed to mount a major exhibit at the country's main exhibition hall, the Manege, in Moscow. When this exhibit was criticized for its repetitive images of Russia and "inordinate fascination with the icon," it was strongly defended in *Pravda*.[91] This immensely popular artist was permitted to stage still another Moscow exhibit in the summer of 1988. Former dissidents are also being given an opportunity to express themselves. VSKhSON leader Leonid Borodin was released from prison in 1987 and allowed to publish in the official media, and Vladimir Osipov has revived the publication of *Zemlia*.[92]

Gorbachev's policy is not merely one of tolerance. The regime again seems to be actively promoting Russian patriotism, seizing on occasions such as the 800th anniversary of *The Lay of the Host of Igor*, the literary masterpiece of Kievan Rus', and the fortieth anniversary of V-E Day to laud the special contributions and virtues of the Russian people.[93] For the first time in the post-Stalin period, the regime has begun to reach out to the Russian Orthodox Church, giving official blessing to its lavish celebration in 1988 of the millenium of Christianity in Kievan Rus'—or simply Russia, as it was represented. Gorbachev even met with Church leaders to congratulate them and ask for their support for his program of social and economic reconstruction.

Of perhaps greater political significance is the striking coincidence between some of the principal policies advocated by Russian nationalists and those at one time or another adopted or proposed by the general secretary. While a similar coincidence was observable in the past, most notably under Brezhnev, Gorbachev moved with unprecedented speed and thoroughness in a direction desired by many Russian nationalists. He drastically reduced the symbolic representation of national minorities at the center of the political system, retaining only one non-Slav (Eduard Shevardnadze) as a full member of the Politburo as of 1989. He conducted a major purge of republican party organizations, and in at least three critical cases (Turkmenia, Uzbekistan, and Kazakhstan) gave Slavs a much larger role. He rejected the pleas of the Central Asians for additional water resources, arguing that it is economically more rational to allocate the huge investment funds required to projects in the Russian republic. Initially, at least, he demonstrated marked enthusiasm for intensification of linguistic Russification, for example, approving (on an experimental basis in the Estonian city of Tartu) the compulsory extension of Russian language instruction to day-care centers.[94] More recently, he has used the "internationalist movements" that have arisen among Russian residents of some non-Russian republics to bring pressure to bear on non-Russian elites not to go too far in their demands for independence from Moscow.

Conclusion

The record of regime behavior in the post-Khrushchev years suggests that the Soviet leaders are highly cognizant of the potential threat that Russian nationalism poses to political stability. They are quite aware that it presents a challenge to the legitimacy of party rule, to the critical unity of elites in Soviet society, and, most of all, to the modus vivendi between Russians and non-Russians that is essential to the functioning—indeed, the persistence—of the system. Hence, political calculation (and sometimes, perhaps, also personal conviction) has rendered successive party chiefs extremely wary of acceding to most Russian nationalist demands or even appearing to endorse them.

On the other hand, the Soviet leaders have found it expedient, in some cases actually congenial, to make concessions to Russian nationalism. They have attempted to contain and channel it in order to prevent the movement from becoming a frustrated, alienated opposition. More than one general secretary has perceived some utility in a limited identification with the movement, perhaps believing that this could win the regime a degree of legitimacy in Russian eyes that its internationalist ideology has not. Similarly, at least some leaders have recognized the mobilizing potential of Russian patriotism and at times have been eager to exploit it.

These conflicting considerations are all apparent in the policies of the present leadership. Yet at the same time Gorbachev's radically new political and economic agenda and his strategy for realizing that agenda have introduced some important new elements into the political calculus of the regime. For Gorbachev, Russian nationalist extremism represents a particularly grave threat, because it provides ammunition to conservative opponents of *glasnost'*, eager to seize on anything that might discredit the general secretary's program of far-reaching change.[95] But Gorbachev cannot move forcefully to suppress the articulation of extremist views because those views have considerable support in the political establishment. He cannot afford to expend his scarce political capital, which he so badly needs to carry out his reforms, on a confrontation with Russian nationalist sympathizers in the party apparatus. Nor can he apply *glasnost'* selectively, extending it only to those ideas he wants expressed. Tolerance can have the effect he desires— stimulating original thought, critical scrutiny, and personal initiative—only if it is universal in scope.

Because his program of *perestroika* is so controversial, both among the political elites and among the population as a whole, Gorbachev has an acute need to cultivate allies, especially molders of opinion. For this reason he has sought support from the intelligentsia, among whom all of the diverse currents of Russian nationalism have wide appeal. His need for allies has likewise led him to the Russian Orthodox Church, with its estimated seventy million members and perhaps equal number of sympathizers.[96]

Finally, during the period of Gorbachev's tenure, a close relationship, although by no means complete identity, has developed between the goals of establishment Russian nationalists and the objectives of the regime. If there are similarities between the policies advocated by nationalists and those promoted by Gorbachev, it is because some measures required to achieve the powerful state desired by Russian nationalists are regarded by the party chief as necessary to create an efficient economy. As Gorbachev appears to see it, at least some of the aspirations of non-Russians for greater political autonomy, material prosperity, and cultural differentiation must be repressed or ignored in order to enhance the capabilities of a Russian-dominated system.[97]

Gorbachev's assessment of the situation may change if minority unrest intensifies, spreads, or even continues at the levels it reached in Kazakhstan in 1986, in Transcaucasia and the Baltic republics since 1988, and in Moldavia in 1989. But unless the general secretary changes his strategy or priorities, while he remains in power one can expect that Russian nationalist ideas will not only be widely articulated in public forums, but will also gain a sympathetic hearing and will be reflected in official policy. This will almost certainly continue to generate considerable discontent on the part of non-Russians. Coping with the instability arising from the clash between majority and minority nationalisms will be one of the greatest challenges confronting the regime in the years to come.

Notes

1. On political stability, see Ted Robert Gurr, "Persistence and Change in Political Systems, 1800–1971," *American Political Science Review*, vol. 68, no. 4 (December 1974), pp. 1482–85; Leon Hurwitz, "Contemporary Approaches to Political Stability," *Comparative Politics*, vol. 5, no. 3 (April 1973), pp. 449–63; and Fred I. Greenstein, ed., *Handbook of Political Science*, vol. 3, *Macropolitical Theory* (Reading, MA: Addison-Wesley, 1975), pp. 6–11.

2. Commonly accepted indicators of political stability include low levels of deaths from political violence and the absence of assassinations, insurrections, riots, and/or intergroup violence. Greenstein, *Handbook*, vol. 3, p. 7.

3. Ibid., and Arend Lijphart, *The Politics of Accommodation: Pluralism and Democracy in the Netherlands* (Berkeley: University of California Press, 1968), pp. 71–77.

4. See John B. Dunlop, *The New Russian Revolutionaries* (Belmont, MA: Nordland, 1976).

5. *S liricheskikh pozitsii* (Moscow: Sovetskii pisatel', 1965). Soloukhin is widely recognized as one of the "founding fathers" of the Russian nationalist movement. Some even feel that his *Vladimirskie proselki* (1957), which extolled the beauty of the Russian countryside, helped spark the movement. John B. Dunlop, "The Many Faces of Contemporary Russian Nationalism," *Survey*, vol. 24, no. 3 (Summer 1979), p. 28.

6. "Pis'ma iz Russkogo muzeia," *Molodaia gvardiia*, 1966, nos. 9 and 10.

7. See Jack Haney, "The Revival of Interest in the Russian Past in the Soviet Union," *Slavic Review*, vol. 32, no. 1 (March 1973), pp. 1–3.

8. See Roy Medvedev, *On Socialist Democracy* (New York: Knopf, 1975), p. 88.

9. Alexander Yanov, *The Russian New Right: Right-Wing Ideologies in the Contemporary USSR* (Berkeley: Institute of International Relations, University of California, 1978), p. 113.

10. On these organizations, see John B. Dunlop, "Ruralist Prose Writers in the Russian Ethnic Movement," in Edward Allworth, ed., *Ethnic Russia in the USSR: The Dilemma of Dominance* (New York: Pergamon, 1980), p. 85; Medvedev, *On Socialist Democracy*, p. 88; Peter Reddaway, *Uncensored Russia* (New York: American Heritage Press, 1972), pp. 430–31.

11. Dunlop, "Many Faces," p. 20.

12. Reddaway, *Uncensored Russia*, pp. 431–32.

13. *Politicheskii dnevnik*, vol. 2 (Amsterdam: Alexander Herzen Foundation, 1975), p. 702; *Kommunist*, 1970, no. 17, pp. 89–100.

14. "A Word to the Nation" was published in translation in *Survey*, vol. 17, no. 3 (Summer 1971), pp. 191–99.

15. See Darrell P. Hammer, "Vladimir Osipov and the Veche Group (1971–1974): A Page from the History of Political Dissent," *Russian Review*, vol. 43, no. 4 (October 1984), pp. 355–75. The nine issues of *Veche* are reproduced in *Arkhiv samizdata*, in *Sobranie dokumentov samizdata*, vols. 21, 21A, and 21B.

16. Alexander Solzhenitsyn, *Letter to the Soviet Leaders* (New York: Harper & Row, 1974).

17. *Izvestiia*, 11 December 1982.

18. The Moscow Religio-Philosophical Seminar was organized by Fr. Aleksandr Ogorodnikov; its *samizdat* journal, *Obshchina*, was suppressed almost as soon as it appeared (1974). The Leningrad seminar was founded in 1975, and at least until 1979–80 published another *samizdat* journal, 37. One of the organizers of the Leningrad seminar, Tat'iana Goricheva, subsequently helped to create the Maria Club. The Christian Committee was founded by Fr. Gleb Yakunin, Deacon Varsonofii Khaibulin, and Viktor Kapitanchuk; Khaibulin and Kapitanchuk were previously linked to *Veche*. On all these groups, see John B. Dunlop, "The Russian Nationalist Spectrum Today: Trends and Movements," *Canadian Review of Studies in Nationalism*, vol. 11, no. 1 (Spring 1984), pp. 63–64, and idem, *The Faces of Contemporary Russian Nationalism* (Princeton: Princeton University Press, 1983), pp. 51–56, 292–93.

19. The journal which, even more than *Molodaia gvardiia*, is now most closely identified with the movement is *Nash sovremennik*. On journals which frequently contain Russian nationalist writing, see Mikhail Agursky, *The New Russian Literature*, Research Paper No. 40 (Jerusalem: The Soviet and East European Research Centre, Hebrew University, July 1980), pp. 20–21.

20. See Dunlop, "Ruralist Prose Writers"; Agursky, *New Russian Literature*; and Catherine Theimer Nepomnyashchy, "The Search for Russian Identity in Contemporary Soviet Russian Literature," in Allworth, *Ethnic Russia*, pp. 88–97.

21. Craig Whitney, "Unbridled Artist Proves Popular at Soviet Show," *New York Times*, 17 June 1978.

22. *Pamiat'* has spawned a sister society in Sverdlovsk which calls itself *Otechestvo* (Fatherland). See Julia Wishnevsky, "The Emergence of *Pamyat'* and *Otechestvo*," *Radio Liberty Research Bulletin*, RL 342/87 (26 August 1987).

23. Its program called for "the overthrow of the Communist dictatorship" and the establishment of a theocratic regime headed by a Church council or synod. See *Vserossiiskii sotsial'no-khristianskii soiuz osvobozhdeniia naroda* (Paris: YMCA Press, 1975), pp. 61, 73–74.

24. S. Enders Wimbush, "The Russian Nationalist Backlash," *Survey*, vol. 14, no. 3 (Summer 1979), pp. 43–44; Roman Szporluk, "History and Russian Nationalism," ibid., p. 17.

25. Alexander Solzhenitsyn et al., *From under the Rubble* (London: Collins and Harvill, 1975).

26. "Bor'ba s tak nazyvaemym 'russofil'stvom' ili put' gosudarstvennogo samoubiistva," *Veche*, no. 7, pp. 4–9. Also see Vladimir Osipov, *Tri otnosheniia k rodine* (Frankfurt: Posev, 1978), pp. 112–47; "Russkoe reshenie natsional'nogo voprosa," *Veche*, no. 6, pp. 7–8.

27. Michael Meerson-Aksenov and Boris Shragin, eds., *The Political, Social, and Religious Thought of Russian "Samizdat": An Anthology* (Belmont, MA: Nordland, 1977), p. 350.

28. See, for example, Fedor Abramov, "O khlebe nasushchnom i khlebe dukhovnom: Vystuplenie na VI s"ezde pisatelei SSSR," *Nash sovremennik*, 1976, no. 9, p. 172. The best known of numerous "ruralist" writers include—in addition to Soloukhin and Abramov—Valentin Rasputin, Viktor Astaf'ev, Sergei Zalygin, Vasilii Belov, Vasilii Shukshin, Evgenii Nosov, and Boris Mozhaev.

29. Dunlop, "Many Faces," pp. 28, 30.

30. The offending essays were Viktor Chalmaev, "Velikie iskaniia," *Molodaia gvardiia*, 1968, no. 3, pp. 270–95; Mikhail Lobanov, "Prosveshchennoe meshchanstvo,"

ibid., 1968, no. 4, pp. 294–306; Viktor Chalmaev, "Neizbezhnost'," ibid., 1968, no. 9, pp. 259–89; and Sergei Semanov, "O tsennostiakh otnositel'nykh i vechnykh," ibid., 1970, no. 8, pp. 308–20. The literary critic Anatolii Lanshchikov, who vigorously defended these articles; the editor responsible for their publication, Anatolii Nikonov; and the like-minded editor who replaced him, Anatolii Ivanov—are likewise members of this group, as are many other contributors to the journal. Those writers and publicists who might be described as "National Bolsheviks" include Petr Proskurin, Nikolai Yakovlev, and Valentin Pikul'.

31. Wishnevsky, "Emergence of *Pamyat'* and *Otechestvo*."

32. On the extensive support for the movement within the political establishment see, for example, Elena Klepikova and Vladimir Solovyev, "The Secret Russian Party," *Midstream*, October 1980, pp. 12–19; Mikhail Agursky, "Ha-golem ha-tasiati kam al yotzro" (The Industrial Golem Turns on Its Creator), *Ha'aretz*, 5 February 1982; Yanov, *Russian New Right*, p. 13; Medvedev, *On Socialist Democracy*, p. 90; Dunlop, *Faces*, pp. 270–72.

33. See, especially, the Central Committee resolution on the sixtieth anniversary of the formation of the USSR (*Pravda*, 21 February 1982), and the speech by Andropov devoted to the same occasion (*Pravda*, 22 December 1982). Also see Konstantin Chernenko, *Human Rights in Soviet Society* (New York: International Publishers, 1981), pp. 46–51, and Gorbachev's speech to the Twenty-seventh Party Congress (*Pravda*, 26 February 1986).

34. For recognition by a Soviet critic, writing in the official press, of the incompatibility of Russian nationalism and proletarian internationalism, see A. Dement'ev, "O traditsiiakh i narodnosti," *Novyi mir*, 1969, no. 4, pp. 221–22.

35. Seweryn Bialer, *Stalin's Successors* (Cambridge: Cambridge University Press, 1980), p. 140.

36. See, for example, Viktor Astaf'ev, "Krazha," in his *Povesti* (Moscow: Sovetskaia Rossiia, 1969), pp. 224, 236; Mikhail Alekseev, "Seiatel' i khranitel'," *Nash sovremennik*, 1972, no. 9, p. 96; Mikhail Lobanov, "Osvobozhdenie," *Volga*, 1982, no. 10.

37. See, for example, Abramov, "O khlebe nasushchnom," p. 172. On the moral superiority of the Russian peasantry over the ideologically well-versed party cadres sent out to destroy their way of life, see the discussion of the works of Vasilii Belov by Mikhail Lobanov in *Oktiabr'*, 1982, no. 10, pp. 179–86.

38. Agursky, *New Russian Literature*, p. 16; idem, "Ha-golem."

39. "About religion," declared *Molodaia gvardiia* contributor Anatolii Lanshchikov at a meeting of literary critics in Moscow in 1969, "I say openly: if we would deny the role of Orthodoxy, I do not know what would remain in Russia." ("Iz literaturnoi zhizni: Na seminare literaturnykh kritikov," *Politicheskii dnevnik*, vol. 1 [1972], p. 505.) A *Veche* contributor wrote that "the Russian people, if they wish to regenerate as a great nation, must . . . return to the sources of greatness, to the Orthodox Church and their national culture." (N. V., "Otryvki iz dnevnika," *Veche*, no. 4, p. 43.) And Viktor Astaf'ev asks rhetorically, "Who has extinguished the light of goodness in our soul" and "hurled us into the depths of evil and misfortune?" That light "has been stolen from us and nothing has been given us in its place." Marxism-Leninism is clearly no substitute for religion: "What use do we have for the light that leads to the fires of hell?" ("Slepoi rybak," *Nash sovremennik*, 1986, no. 5, p. 118.) In another Astaf'ev story the narrator calls for "a final, chastising rain" to be "brought down on the heads of present-day desecrators of temples [and] blasphemers." ("Lovlia peskarei v Gruzii," *Nash sovremennik*, 1986, no. 5, p. 133.)

40. Russian nationalists have pointed out that there is no Russian branch of the CPSU, no separate republican capital for the RSFSR, and no strictly Russian Academy

of Sciences. They also stress that Russian culture began to be suppressed at a time when official encouragement was given to the development of other national cultures, and the Russian Orthodox Church was attacked long before Islam and the religions of other nationalities. See, for example, Igor Shafarevich, "Separation or Reconciliation: The Nationalities Question in the USSR," in Solzhenitsyn et al., *From under the Rubble,* pp. 94–97.

41. See Bialer, *Stalin's Successors,* pp. 219–20, 222–24.

42. On the "welfare colonialism" of the Brezhnev regime, see Martin C. Spechler, "Regional Developments in the USSR, 1958–1978," in U.S. Congress, Joint Economic Committee, *Soviet Economy in a Time of Change* (Washington: U.S. Government Printing Office, 1979), vol. 1, pp. 161–62. On the priority often given to natives in filling jobs in the non-Russian republics, see Michael Rywkin, "Religion, Modern Nationalism, and Political Power in Soviet Central Asia," *Canadian Slavonic Papers,* vol. 17, nos. 2–3 (Summer–Fall 1975), pp. 278–79.

43. "Word to the Nation," pp. 198–99.

44. V. I. Kozlov, "O biologo-geograficheskoi kontseptsii etnicheskoi istorii," *Voprosy istorii,* 1974, no. 12, pp. 72–85.

45. See Medvedev, *On Socialist Democracy,* p. 88.

46. Among the most notable of these is Chalmaev, "Neizbezhnost'," pp. 264, 266–68. Also see the discussion of the novels of Vsevolod Ivanov in Valentin Oskotskii, *Roman i istoriia: Traditsii i novatorstvo sovetskogo istoricheskogo romana* (Moscow: Khudozhestvennaia literatura, 1980).

47. Medvedev, *On Socialist Democracy,* pp. 87–88.

48. See, for example, "Open Letter from the Estonian SSR" (Tallinn-Tartu, 28 October 1980), quoted in Jüri Estam and Jaan Pennar, "Estonian Intellectuals Express Their Views on Causes of Recent Demonstrations in Open Letter," *Radio Liberty Research Bulletin,* RL 477/80 (15 December 1980), p. 3; S. L. Tykhvins'kyi, "Aktual'ni problemy radians'koi istorychnoi nauky i deiaki pytannia vdoskonalennia pidhotovky i atestatsii naukovykh kadriv," *Ukrains'kyi istorychnyi zhurnal,* 1985, no. 2, p. 8, cited in Roman Solchanyk, "Guidelines for Soviet Historians on the National Question— Russian and Non-Russian," *Radio Liberty Research Bulletin,* RL 165/85 (20 May 1985), p. 3.

49. See, for example, Medvedev, *On Socialist Democracy,* p. 362.

50. S. Enders Wimbush and Alex Alexiev, *The Ethnic Factor in the Soviet Armed Forces: Preliminary Findings,* N-1486-NA (Santa Monica, CA: Rand Corporation, May 1980), pp. 50–51.

51. On the views of these Russian nationalists, see Mikhail Agurskii, "Kloko-chushchii vulkan," *Russkaia mysl',* 18 September 1980, p. 13, and idem, *New Russian Literature,* pp. 12, 16, 18, 23–25, 60–61.

52. See Mikhail Agursky, "Le'umanim v'kivunim shonim" (Nationalists and Different Directions), *Ha'aretz,* 3 March 1982.

53. Siberia and the Russian North are cited by some nationalists as areas to which more investment funds should urgently be allocated. (Solzhenitsyn, *Letter to the Soviet Leaders,* p. 27.) Others stress the need to devote more funds to Central Russia. (Petr Proskurin, "Imia tvoe," *Roman-gazeta,* 1978, nos. 13–16.)

54. Proskurin, "Imia tvoe."

55. Bennigsen, "Several Nations or One People: Ethnic Consciousness among Soviet Central Asian Moslems," *Survey,* vol. 24, no. 3 (Summer 1979), p. 63.

56. Medvedev, *On Socialist Democracy,* p. 357.

57. See, for example, B. Korzhavin, A. Bostandzhoglo, and A. Pugachev (Uzbek Republic Honored Irrigation Workers), and E. Rakhimov (Candidate of Economic

Sciences), "Eshche raz o vodnykh resursakh i iuzhnom zemledelii," *Ekonomicheskaia gazeta*, 1981, no. 45. Dinmukhamed Kunaev, at that time the head of the Kazakhstan party organization, made a particularly strong plea in this regard at the Twenty-seventh Party Congress. (*Pravda*, 27 February 1986.)

58. See Matthews Pavlovich, "Ethnic Impact of Russian Dispersion in and beyond the RSFSR," in Allworth, *Ethnic Russia*, p. 301.

59. Bialer, *Stalin's Successors*, p. 218.

60. For example, "Word to the Nation," pp. 193, 195–99; Semanov, "O tsennostiakh," pp. 316–17; Chalmaev, "Neizbezhnost'," p. 269.

61. "Word to the Nation," p. 199.

62. See Wimbush, "Russian Nationalist Backlash," pp. 44–45.

63. *Veche*, no. 7, p. 2.

64. *Veche*, no. 6, pp. 9–10.

65. Michael Aksenov Meerson, "The Influence of the Orthodox Church on Russian Ethnic Identity," in Allworth, *Ethnic Russia*, p. 112.

66. Semanov, for example, praises the purges and terror of the thirties as a turning point in the struggle with the "wreckers and nihilists"; he goes on to emphasize that nihilism is still present in the USSR and must be fought. ("O tsennostiakh," pp. 319–20.) Chalmaev praises Russian generals who conquered the borderlands by force and used the most brutal of methods to attain their goals. ("Neizhbezhnost'," p. 269.)

67. Such was the reaction in Alma-Ata, for example, when the Kazakh Dinmukhamed Kunaev was replaced as the head of his republic's party organization by the Russian Gennadii Kolbin. (*New York Times*, 19 and 20 December 1986.) Demonstrators in the Baltic republics have increasingly demanded greater local control over economic and political decisions since 1988.

68. For numerous examples, see Ludmilla Alexeyeva, *Soviet Dissent: Contemporary Movements for National, Religious, and Human Rights* (Middletown, CT: Wesleyan University Press, 1985).

69. For extensive and especially sympathetic accounts of strikes and demonstrations by Russians in Estonia and Moldavia, see, for example, *Sotsialisticheskaia industriia*, 20 August 1989, and *Krasnaia zvezda*, 31 August 1989, respectively.

70. Wimbush and Alexiev, *Ethnic Factor*, pp. 57–58.

71. See Solzhenitsyn, *Letter to the Soviet Leaders*.

72. Solzhenitsyn, "Repentance and Self-Limitation," in Solzhenitsyn et al., *From under the Rubble*, pp. 135–43; *Vserossiiskii sotsial'no-khristianskii soiuz*, pp. 64, 73–74.

73. *Zemlia*, no. 1 (1 August 1974), published in *Vol'noe slovo*, 1975, no. 20, pp. 5–6; *Vserossiiskii sotsial'no-khristianskii soiuz*, pp. 76–77.

74. Solzhenitsyn, *Letter to the Soviet Leaders*; Vadim Borisov, "Personality and National Awareness," in Solzhenitsyn et al., *From under the Rubble*, pp. 194–228.

75. Solzhenitsyn, *Letter to the Soviet Leaders*; Theodore Shabad, "Solzhenitsyn Asks Kremlin to Abandon Communism and Split up Soviet Union," *New York Times*, 3 March 1974. One might argue that such a program would be destabilizing in the extreme. Its advocates would probably respond that, on the contrary, it would create a Russian state that would meet the most important condition for stability, i.e., full legitimacy in the eyes of the entire population over which it ruled.

76. For a more extensive treatment, see Dina Rome Spechler, *Russian Nationalism and Political Stability in the USSR* (Cambridge, MA: Center for International Affairs, Harvard University, and Center for International Studies, MIT, 1983), pp. 31–54.

77. It was apparently these features which led him to condemn the articles published in *Molodaia gvardiia* in 1968–70. (*Politicheskii dnevnik*, vol. 2, p. 702.) Also

see V. Ivanov, "Sotsializm i kul'turnoe nasledie," *Kommunist*, 1970, no. 17, pp. 96–99.

78. See his speech to the Twenty-fifth Party Congress, in *XXV s"ezd Kommunisticheskoi partii Sovetskogo soiuza: Stenograficheskii otchet* (Moscow: Izdatel'stvo politicheskoi literatury, 1976), vol. 1, p. 101.

79. See Yanov, *Russian New Right*, pp. 15, 60; Wimbush, "Russian Nationalist Backlash," pp. 43–44, 46.

80. Thus, when the then acting head of the Propaganda Department of the Central Committee, Aleksandr Yakovlev, followed up the authoritative critique of *Molodaia gvardiia* published in *Kommunist* (see n. 75 above) with a far stronger and more thoroughgoing condemnation of the offending articles and their like, he had great difficulty publishing this piece. When, after almost a year, it finally appeared, Yakovlev was dismissed from his post and sent to Canada as ambassador. See Aleksandr Iakovlev, "Protiv antiistorizma," *Literaturnaia gazeta*, 15 November 1972, pp. 4–5; and Robert G. Kaiser, *Russia: The People and the Power* (Harmondsworth, England: Penguin Books, 1976), p. 167.

81. Official reports on the activities of VOOPIK indicate that the Brezhnev regime invested "massive resources" in the restoration projects sponsored by that organization. (Frederick C. Barghoorn, "Russian Nationalism and Soviet Politics: Official and Unofficial Perspectives," in Robert Conquest, ed., *The Last Empire: Nationality and the Soviet Future*, [Stanford: Hoover Institution Press, 1986], p. 67.) Konstantin Simonov's *Russkie liudi*, for example, was performed at the Malyi Theater in Moscow in 1975–76. Four hundred of the intensely religious and nationalistic paintings—described as "mystical panoramas of icon-like figures from the Russian past"—of Il'ia Glazunov were displayed at Moscow's Manege Exhibition Hall in 1978 and subsequently in a travelling exhibition viewed by millions. (*New York Times*, 12 October 1980.) Brezhnev himself reportedly intervened to authorize the showing of Vasilii Shukshin's nationalistic film *Kalina krasnaia* in a major Moscow movie house in 1974. (Hedrick Smith, *The Russians* [London: Sphere Books, 1976], pp. 463–64.)

82. *Kommunist*, 1971, no. 5, p. 60; 1972, no. 18, p. 13. Brezhnev's speech to the Twenty-sixth Party Congress in 1981 not only praised the "unselfish assistance of the Russian people" to the development of non-Russian areas, but also unflatteringly described those areas as the former "national hinterlands" of Russia. *Pravda*, 24 February 1981.

83. Andropov's most important speech on nationality issues emphasized the need for "proper" ethnic representation at all levels of the party and state bureaucracies, condemned national arrogance and exclusiveness, and stressed the importance of eliminating mutual distrust among the nationalities of the USSR. At the same time, however, it called on non-Russians to "address special words of gratitude" to the Russian people, without whose assistance their present achievements would not have been possible. (*Pravda*, 22 December 1982.) Chernenko opposed the promotion of religion and the idealization of patriarchal society characteristic of Russian nationalist writers in his speech to the Central Committee Plenum of June 1983. (*Pravda*, 15 June 1983.) See also Chernenko's attack on Russian nationalism in his essay, "Friendship and Fraternity of Peoples" (in Chernenko, *Human Rights*, p. 49).

84. Persecution of Russian nationalists increased noticeably in the spring and summer of 1982, a fact Dunlop attributes to Andropov's growing influence. (*Faces*, pp. 292–94.) The trial of the prominent former VSKhSON member Leonid Borodin in May 1983 and his severe fifteen-year sentence may have been intended as a warning to other dissident nationalists. (See the comments of Georgii Vladimov in *Russkaia mysl'*, 7 July 1983, cited in Darrell P. Hammer, "Russian Nationalism and

Soviet Politics," in Joseph Nogee, ed., *Soviet Politics: Russia after Brezhnev* [New York: Praeger, 1985], pp. 141–42.)

85. A particularly strong attack on the Church, believers, and party cadres who manifest a "conciliatory attitude toward religion" was published in *Pravda*, 28 September 1986. Politburo member Yegor Ligachev appeared to be a principal opponent of a religious revival. (See *Kommunist*, 1986, no. 15, and *Pravda*, 7 November 1986.) Among those singled out for attack has been the artist Il'ia Glazunov. (Vasilii Kisun'ko, "V poiskakh segodniashnego dnia. Polemicheskie zametki s vystavki Il'i Glazunova," *Sovetskaia kul'tura*, 10 July 1986.)

86. *Pravda*, 26 February 1986.

87. *Pamiat'* speakers have denounced Yakovlev as a Zionist agent. (*Russkaia mysl'*, 15 May 1987.) Articles criticizing *Pamiat'* have appeared in *Pravda*, *Izvestiia*, *Komsomol'skaia pravda*, *Sovetskaia kul'tura*, *Moskovskie novosti*, *Literaturnaia gazeta*, *Ogonek*, and even *Sovetskaia Rossiia*, since 1987.

88. Hans Spier, *Soviet Antisemitism Unchained: The Rise of the "Historical and Patriotic Association* Pamyat'," Research Report No. 3, Institute of Jewish Affairs (London), July 1987, pp. 3, 6.

89. *Izvestiia*, 14 August 1988.

90. See, especially, the speeches by Valentin Rasputin, Vasilii Belov, Sergei Zalygin, and Yurii Bondarev, published in *Literaturnaia gazeta*, 2 July 1986.

91. *Sovetskaia kul'tura*, 10 and 19 July 1986; *Pravda*, 21 July 1986.

92. Darrell Hammer, "Glasnost' and the Russian Idea" (unpublished manuscript).

93. The party journal *Kommunist* (1985, no. 10, pp. 45–59) published six essays extolling the Kievan epic; throughout 1985 festive celebrations were held to commemorate its anniversary. (Yaroslav Bilinsky, "Nationality Policy in Gorbachev's First Year," *Orbis*, vol. 30, no. 2 [Summer 1986], p. 341.) Gorbachev's speech on the anniversary of V-E Day saluted the "courage, tenacity, and unbending character" of "the great Russian people," who "rallied and inspired" the other peoples of the USSR during the war. (*Kommunist*, 1985, no. 8, p. 6.) Bilinsky notes that this speech is strongly reminiscent of Stalin's famous toast to the Russians in May 1945. ("Nationality Policy," p. 341.) The similarity could hardly have been accidental. A campaign to glorify the achievements of Russians in a wide variety of fields was in evidence throughout 1985. (See Vera Tolz, "Russian Nationalism in the 1980s: Echoes of Stalinist Policy," *Radio Liberty Research Bulletin*, RL 370/85 [7 November 1985], pp. 1, 3.)

94. Bilinsky, "Nationality Policy," pp. 333–40.

95. This is a point often made by critics of *Pamiat'*. See, for example, the comment by the editorial board of *Izvestiia*, 14 August 1988, and the denunciation of *Pamiat'* by General David Dragunsky in *Literaturnaia gazeta*, 17 August 1988.

96. For a perceptive analysis of the basis for these alliances, i.e., the similarity between the *ends* sought by the Russophile intelligentsia and the Church and the *means* by which Gorbachev hopes to accomplish the reconstruction of the society and economy, see Hammer, "Glasnost' and the Russian Idea."

97. Cf. Gorbachev's insistence, both in his speech to the Twenty-seventh Party Congress and in his report to the January 1987 Central Committee Plenum, that national and regional differences must not be permitted to obstruct a rational economic policy.

CHAPTER 13

Nationalism and Reform in Soviet Politics

Mark Beissinger and Lubomyr Hajda

There is a nationalities component to every facet of Soviet politics. This holds true all the more with regard to processes of political change. One can analyze reform strategies, the viability of alternative economic programs, or the controversies surrounding *glasnost'* and democratization. But without considering the ethnic dimension of these policies, it is impossible to make sense of the enormous changes that are taking place inside the Soviet Union. The intentions of the Soviet leadership to the contrary, the nationalities factor has become the issue that overshadows all others in the development of the Soviet political system.

Unfortunately, it is also the nationalities factor that was so frequently omitted in previous models of Soviet politics and in the standard projections of the Soviet future.[1] The traditional models of Soviet politics—the interest group and totalitarian approaches—raised nationality issues infrequently and contained little in the way of well-developed conceptions of ethnic politics. The ideas they did present generally lay outside the mainstream of studies of ethnic politics elsewhere in the world and were usually implied rather than stated directly. Those who subscribed to the interest group approach correctly stressed the importance of autonomous social processes. But they tended to interpret Soviet nationalities through the prism of American ethnic politics, viewing them as one among a myriad of "pressure groups" and simplistically conceiving of Soviet society as an ethnic mosaic. In some versions of the interest group approach (in particular, that influenced by convergence theory and the American "melting pot" experience) Soviet nationalities were regarded as temporal phenomena, likely to fade away as economic development proceeded. The totalitarian model, by contrast, correctly emphasized the imperial dimension of Soviet politics, but often with little sensitivity to autonomous social processes, the variations within and between nationalities, other forms of ethnic stratification around the world, or the enormous political changes that took place in the Soviet Union after Stalin's death. By and large, studies of Soviet nationalities and theories of Soviet politics remained separate entities: those who developed theories of Soviet politics rarely raised issues of ethnicity, and those who engaged in research on the nationalities seldom placed their questions within the context of existing theories of Soviet politics.

If Western experts are subject to the criticism of having paid too little attention to the nationalities factor or of being bound by ethnocentrisms, so have Soviet leaders. Indeed, their underlying assumptions shared in the inadequacies of both Western models. Like adherents of the interest group approach, Soviet leaders traditionally underrated the importance of ethnic features in society and stressed their impermanence: according to Marxist-Leninist ideology, national antagonisms would disappear with the victory of socialism, and national distinctions themselves would ultimately be transcended with the achievement of communism. Similarly, like the followers of the totalitarian model, Soviet leaders underestimated the autonomous aspects of ethnic processes and exaggerated the ability of the state to direct social development.

Mikhail Gorbachev originally placed the nationalities issue at the very bottom of his agenda. In contrast to his hard-hitting criticisms of other aspects of Soviet life, Gorbachev did not even raise the need for a reevaluation in nationalities policy until he was almost two years in office, when at the January 1987 Central Committee Plenum he criticized the quality of Soviet theoretical work in this area. At that time, he recognized that "not a single major issue can be solved . . . without taking into consideration the fact that we live in a multinational country."[2] Nevertheless, the Soviet leadership originally gave little consideration to the impact of reform on ethnic issues, and in particular to the political repercussions of *glasnost'* in a multinational context. In the aftermath of the tumultuous events of the following years, the Soviet leadership was forced to a new recognition and reassessment of what Gorbachev has called "the most fundamental and most vital question facing our society."[3] This essay explores the question why, despite the leadership's desire to the contrary, issues of nationality continually impinged upon issues of reform, eventually coming to dominate the political agenda and accelerating processes of political transformation.

Ethnic Stratification Under Stress

The primary legacy of empire in the Soviet Union is a peculiar system of ethnic stratification—one which today has come under severe stress and increasing attack. Like any multiethnic society, Soviet society is ethnically stratified. Systems of ethnic stratification, however, vary according to their complexity, the clarity of the distinctions between groups and degrees of group solidarity, and the opportunities available for social mobility.[4]

Some aspects of ethnic stratification in the USSR continue to reflect patterns established during the Tsarist period, while others have been significantly modified, both by processes of modernization and intentional policy. In particular, there was a much closer link between class and ethnicity in Tsarist Russia than during the Soviet period. For example, both the Ukrainian and Belorussian populations of Tsarist Russia were almost wholly rural, and those entering the urban world were susceptible to rapid Russification; Jews were confined geographically to the Pale of Settlement and restricted from entering certain occupations; and the landowning class in large portions of Lithuania, Belorussia, and Ukraine consisted primarily of Poles. In this respect, Tsarist Russia resembled not only other multinational empires of its time (such as the Habsburg monarchy), but also many modern states in which class and ethnic cleavages still largely coincide (as in Malaysia or South Africa). By contrast, in the Soviet period the link between class and ethnicity has been greatly eroded. Certain classes associated with particular ethnic groups, such as landowners and entrepreneurs, ceased to exist. Moreover, each nationality itself became more diversified socially with the lifting of restrictions on geographic and occupational mobility and the development of native intelligentsias, political elites, and working classes.

Viewing the Soviet Union as a whole, considerable levelling has taken place among the nationalities with regard to education, urbanization, and economic development. On the republican level, however, a certain link between class and ethnicity persists. As late as 1970 (the last year for which such data are currently available) the local Russian population in all the non-Russian republics was significantly more urbanized than the titular nationality, the differentials ranging from 27 percent in the case of Armenia to 348 percent in Moldavia. Similarly, educational levels within each republic vary sharply according to nationality; in terms of persons with a higher or secondary education, the rates for Russians residing in the non-Russian republics were from 4 percent (in Georgia) to 82 percent (in Moldavia) higher than for the titular republican nationality.[5] Interestingly, a somewhat analogous situation prevails in the Russian republic. Ukrainians, Belorussians, Latvians, Georgians, Armenians, and Uzbeks residing in the RSFSR are more urbanized than the Russian residents of the republic. Likewise, the Ukrainians and Belorussians of the RSFSR (data on other union-republic nationalities within the RSFSR are lacking) have higher levels of education than do the Russians.[6] Thus, although the correlation between class and ethnicity in the USSR may not be as strong as in many other states, a relationship between the two exists.

Whereas an ethnic division of economic labor is the predominant feature of stratification in many multinational societies, the main feature of the Soviet pattern is an ethnic division of political labor. At the all-union level, Russians predominate in party and governmental institutions. Although Russians formed less than 52 percent of the population in 1986, 85 percent of Central Committee secretaries (n=13), 83 percent of USSR ministers and state committee chairmen (n=83), and 88 percent of the top military command (n=17) were Russians. In most republics, however, members of the titular nationality predominate within local party and governmental organizations. Thus, the ethnic division of political labor in the Soviet Union is the reverse image of the ethnic division of economic labor: in class terms there has been growing ethnic equalization at the all-union level and continuing differentiation at the republican level, while in political terms there has been increasing ethnic equalization at the republican level and continuing stratification at the all-union level. Such a pattern was bound to become explosive, for it provided channels for social mobility while at the same time closing channels for political expression.

Class stratification in the Soviet Union is less complex than in most other societies. In terms of ethnic stratification, however, Soviet society is more complex even than most other multinational societies. John Armstrong's functional typology of the USSR's non-Russian nationalities well reflects the complexity of this pattern. With the Russians as a standard of reference, Armstrong distinguishes five major types of ethnic groups on the basis of their degree of social mobilization, the objectives of official policy, and their degree of assimilation: the internal proletariat, mobilized diasporas, "younger brothers," state nations, and "colonials."[7] In addition, there are significant intragroup differences which have traditionally served as a base for reinforcing intergroup patterns of stratification. For instance, Ukrainian officials have been disproportionately recruited from among the more Russified eastern provinces of Ukraine, Moldavian officials—from the left bank of the Dniester (the territory of the interwar Moldavian ASSR), and Estonian officials— from the so-called "Russian-Estonians" (Estonians born or raised in the RSFSR). In this respect, Soviet rule has differed little from imperial systems elsewhere in the world, which similarly brought about enormous restratification, both between and within ethnic groups.[8]

There have been periods in which these patterns of ethnic stratification have been challenged, most notably in the 1920s. Nevertheless, until recently they displayed a remarkable stability overall. By the 1930s traditional patterns of ethnic stratification in the political sphere began to reemerge and were harnessed by Stalin as a means for asserting control over Soviet society. Russian language and culture came to be viewed again as an adhesive binding a disparate population. Russian cadres, manning key posts within the union republics, functioned as a control mechanism over local elites. And with the decline of Marxist-Leninist ideology, Russian nationalism increasingly became the legitimizing principle of the Soviet system.

Though the importance of nationalism as a motivating factor in Soviet politics has long been recognized by Western observers, they have often failed to differentiate between varieties of nationalism. Modern nationalism, as it emerged in nineteenth-century Europe, was closely connected with the ideas of self-determination and the sovereignty of the nation-state. It was, in Anthony Smith's words, "an ideological movement for the attainment and maintenance of self-government and independence on behalf of a group, some of whose members conceive it to constitute an actual or potential 'nation' like others."[9] Within the Soviet Union, this type of modern nationalism can be found in the Baltic, the western republics, and Transcaucasia. But it traditionally has had little to do with Russian national self-identity. Russian nationalism, at least in the form in which it was synthesized with Marxist-Leninist ideology at the time of World War II and even earlier, has been an imperial rather than a modern nationalism—a nationalism that emphasized ethnic stratification and domination rather than national self-determination. Within this context, any effort to alter traditional patterns of political and economic hierarchy was likely to challenge traditional patterns of ethnic stratification as well.

Ethnicity and Stagnation

It is standard to describe the problems of the Brezhnev era as a crisis of effectiveness.[10] But their implications went far beyond simple efficiency. A decline in economic performance, a growing list of untended social ills, and a political stagnation and corruption that gripped the entire administrative hierarchy also led to the emergence or sharpening of crises of penetration, participation, distribution, and legitimacy. All of these crises had clear national dimensions that eventually came to the fore under the impact of *perestroika* and *glasnost'*.

Over the course of the Brezhnev era the mechanisms of control of the center over the periphery atrophied as a result of Brezhnev's trust-in-cadres policy. The result was a blossoming of patron-client networks in local politics and the flourishing of corruption. This was true not only in the national regions, but also in the RSFSR. However, it was the discipline problem within the national regions that presented the most direct challenge to Russian imperial nationalism. Strong patron-client ties in the union republics, usually formed along ethnic lines but sometimes co-opting local Russians as well, effectively blocked the ability of the center to penetrate local governments and to control policy processes and outcomes. While occurring to some extent in all regions, this development reached an extreme in Central Asia, where local mafia bosses emerged, at times outside the party and exercising control over it.[11] These diffuse ties were compounded by patterns of development and ethnic stratification within the region; ethnic Russians remained largely confined to urban centers, creating a social situation that was ripe for the flourishing of patronage along ethnic lines.

Political systems in Third-World countries have frequently faced this type of penetration crisis, in which strong and diffuse social forces have blocked the effective implementation of policy enunciated by the central government. On the one hand, without challenging these diffuse social forces directly, leaders face the prospect of continually finding their policy aims distorted and frustrated. On the other hand, confronting them and attempting to uproot them has often been a source of violence and instability.

A participation crisis also developed in the late Brezhnev period, with a visible national dimension, both at the elite and the mass levels. Political scientists have long noted a strong relationship between education and political participation. Within the Soviet context, however, the challenges an increasingly educated population presents for a regime that traditionally did not allow far-reaching autonomous participation in politics revolve largely around national issues. One result of Soviet nationalities policy has been the growing level of education among all nationalities and the rise of national intelligentsias. The Soviet leadership did not foresee, however, that these national intelligentsias would eventually seek to promote their native cultures and to protect them from encroachments from the dominant Russian culture. Under Brezhnev, the rapid rise in educational levels among all national groups made conditions ripe for an expansion of autonomous political participation along national lines.

At the mass level, ethno-demographic processes created a second participation crisis. Political and social equilibrium in plural societies has often been upset, sometimes with unexpected rapidity, by demographic processes. In the Soviet case, the progressive decline in the Russian share of the country's population was bound to put a strain on the existing system of ethnic stratification in the political sphere. At the same time, divergent regional trends were destabilizing in their own particular ways. In Estonia and Latvia, for example, the continuing influx of Russians and the erosion of their own numerical strength intensified the alienation of the indigenous nationalities from the system. Increasing linguistic assimilation in Ukraine, while opening doors to participation for the assimilated elements, estranged the more nationally conscious Ukrainians. And the burgeoning numbers of Central Asians and their refusal to migrate raised the specter of a large and growing proportion of the population that was clearly differentiated culturally, religiously, and racially from the rest, remaining unintegrated into the system.

A third crisis concerned resource management and distribution. There have been significant variations in the degree to which various union republics have received subsidies from the central government. In general, there has been a net flow of income to Central Asia as part of efforts to modernize the area. In a period of economic stringency, this pattern of subsidy was bound to be challenged. This challenge was further complicated by the significant new investment that local elites were demanding in the face of the growing water shortage affecting the region. In the late Brezhnev era, Central Asian elites, through their representatives in the center, were increasingly vocal in presenting their demands. Moreover, Brezhnev's consensual style of decision making and his trust-in-cadres personnel policy led to a burgeoning of localism not only in Central Asia, but throughout the Soviet Union.

Whereas nationalism is an ideological movement, localism refers to administrative action aimed at promoting the interests of one's own administrative unit, regardless of its national composition. Localism is an inherent feature of any bureaucracy, since all bureaucrats prefer more resources to carry out their programs. But nationalism intersects with localism when the interests of an administrative unit come to be identified with the interests of a particular national group that resides in it. In the Soviet case, a federal administrative structure and the concentration of national groups within their own administrative units has meant that distribution crises inevitably become nationality crises.

Finally, one can identify the outlines of a legitimacy crisis in the late Brezhnev period that had clear national ramifications. Lucian Pye has observed that crises in almost any realm of politics "can ultimately culminate in a problem of legitimacy, for in a sense all crises raise questions about legitimacy."[12] The crises of effectiveness, penetration, participation, and distribution described above deepened the malaise into which Soviet society slipped and fed the revival of old nationalisms and the rise of new ones. A major development of the time was the growth of what might be called anomic nationalism throughout the Soviet Union. In contrast to both modern and imperial nationalisms, anomic nationalism is a response to the dislocation and anomie that modernity produces. This is the negative image of nationalism in the modern world, the driving force behind fascism, Khomeiniism, and other antimodern, mobilizational movements.[13] There are various shades of anomic nationalism, most of which fall far short of this type of political extremism. Nevertheless, anomic nationalism can become radical and revolutionary, particularly if extremist elements are given the opportunity to organize openly.

Anomic nationalism in some form made its appearance among most Soviet nationalities during this period. It usually assumed the form of environmental or cultural preservation movements that aimed to maintain what was commonly seen as "the national heritage" against the encroachments of modernization. But anomic nationalism had a particular appeal within the Russian context, for it well expressed the lack of confidence that the dominant national group felt about its own future. That confidence was shaken by the dislocations of urbanization and industrialization, the irrationalities of an overbureaucratized economic system, the looming demographic threat of the Muslim peoples, an unpopular war abroad and revolt in Eastern Europe, and the prevailing corruption of Brezhnev's last days. The growth of anomic nationalism within the dominant ethnic group was a sign that the traditional imperial model was no longer working.

Perestroika as a Russian Imperial Program

The central concern of Russian imperial nationalism has traditionally been the backwardness of Russia and the need to modernize the empire in order to maintain it. As Stalin expressed it in his famous speech in February 1931 defending the breakneck pace of industrialization, the "old Russia" had been beaten repeatedly in the past "because of her backwardness . . . her military backwardness, cultural backwardness, industrial backwardness, [and] agricultural backwardness."[14] Unlike Russian anomic nationalism, Russian imperial nationalism has never been a reaction against the dislocations of modernization. Rather, it has been a modernizing ideology that aimed to "catch up and overtake" technologically superior foreign powers to enable Russia better to project its power abroad and defend its territories. In this sense, Gorbachev's original understanding of *perestroika* fell squarely into the traditional pattern of Russian imperial nationalism. Its aim was not to undermine ethnic stratification or to contain the dysfunctions of modernity, but rather to preserve the empire by furthering the modernization process.

There was an implicit imperial component to Gorbachev's early policies in almost every sphere, in part because the national dimension loomed large in the crises that the Soviet Union faced in the 1980s, in part because projecting power abroad was a major burden on the Soviet economy. Even Gorbachev's program of economic reform, involving a far-reaching decentralization of authority and an increasing role for cooperative and private enterprise, could not avoid consideration of its differential impact upon various Soviet nationalities. One reason why the authorities moved quickly to impose heavy taxes upon cooperative and private enterprise may have been that a disproportionate part of this labor is non-Russian;[15] in this situation, the high prices charged to customers and the enormous potential incomes that these entrepreneurs made provided fertile ground for national prejudices. Similarly, decollectivization within the Soviet context, if pursued with equal vigor in all republics, would be to the advantage of southern national groups and to the disadvantage of Russians. A significant increase in the effectiveness of industry could not take place without reallocating investment from one region to another, penetrating diffuse patronage networks, integrating the excess labor resources of Central Asia, and mobilizing the non-Russian, as well as the Russian, populations and intelligentsias.

The developmental crisis that Brezhnev's heirs chose to deal with first was the penetration crisis. Penetration crises generally come to a head when the "ruling elite seeks to modify the prevailing authority system" and to break through the diffuse social ties that block policy implementation.[16] Given the way in which ethnicity reinforced patron-client ties in the Soviet context, it is not surprising that the brunt of the discipline campaigns unleashed by Yurii Andropov (and later continued by Gorbachev) fell upon the union republics, particularly in Central Asia. In almost every instance, efforts to uproot patron-client networks increased national tensions, at times fueling political instability. In Kazakhstan in December 1986, local party officials, threatened with the loss of their positions and their patronage networks, played a major role in the outbreak of nationalist discontent.[17] The Gorbachev leadership's approach to resolving the penetration crisis was to assign both more Russians and more local officials with experience in Moscow to key positions within the hierarchy.

Similarly, Gorbachev's approach to the distribution crisis was also indicative that *perestroika* originally aimed not at diluting ethnic stratification, but rather strengthening it. Representation of nationalities at the center of the Soviet system has tended to become a focus for presenting material demands.[18] Significantly enough, by 1988 Gorbachev's leadership and elite had become the most Russian in the entire history of the Soviet Union. If in 1982 non-Russians constituted 38 percent of the Politburo, by 1988 that figure had dropped to 15 percent. Those particularly affected were the non-Slavs, who in 1982 made up 24 percent of the Politburo, but by 1988 were only 5 percent. Similarly, within the Central Committee, there was a decline in non-Russian representation from 33 percent in 1981 to 31 percent in 1986.[19]

The growing Russian (and Slavic) character of the Soviet leadership and elite after Brezhnev's death was a clear sign of who won in the struggles over positions and resources. In Gorbachev's early years in power investment shifted towards the machine-building industries of central Russia, Western Siberia, Ukraine, and Belorussia and away from Central Asia. The decision to abandon the Siberian river diversion project may have been sound on ecological grounds, but it left the question of development in Central Asia, with its huge pool of untapped labor resources, unresolved.

But the most remarkable developments in nationality affairs during the early Gorbachev period were in response to the Soviet Union's participation and legitimacy crises. Gorbachev's policy of *glasnost'* was an integral part of his reform package. It was an effort to overcome the legitimacy gap that had developed during the Brezhnev era and to alter the behavior of the Soviet population by mobilizing it against bureaucratic domination in economic and political affairs. But *glasnost'* was also an admission that the modernizing aims of *perestroika* would not succeed unless accompanied by a marked shift in political power, which, whether the Soviet leadership recognized it or not, included shifts in the prevailing system of ethnic stratification. Western scholars have long observed that "an expansion of political participation seems to have one effect in a multi-ethnic society and another in a homogeneous culture." In an ethnically pluralistic society, "the same political decisions that have a unifying effect under conditions of low political participation can have a disintegrating effect when there is large-scale political participation."[20]

Glasnost' and Nationalism

If *perestroika* began as a Russian imperial program, *glasnost'* by contrast injected a strong anti-imperial current into Soviet politics. *Glasnost'*, to the leadership's chagrin, inadvertently encouraged the expression of nationalistic sentiments, among both Russians and non-Russians. Moreover, it reinforced old nationalisms that had long existed (as in Armenia or Ukraine) and gave rise to new nationalisms where they were weakly developed before (as in Belorussia or Moldavia). Even small and relatively unknown groups (such as the Gagauz) began to agitate for cultural autonomy, expressing a new national awareness that previously could only simmer below the surface.

Glasnost' undermined the prevailing system of ethnic stratification in a variety of ways. First and most obviously, it provided formal communications networks among members of a national group for issues that could only be informally communicated before. It is significant, for instance, that the boldest movies of the early *glasnost'* period—*Repentance* and *Is It Easy to Be Young?*—were both filmed by non-Russian directors in the Georgian and Latvian languages respectively. *Glasnost'* broadened the range of issues open for discussion in all media and was pursued with as equal vigor in the union republics as in the center.

Second, *glasnost'* challenged traditional patterns of ethnic stratification by providing opportunities for the organization of alternative, unofficial

314 MARK BEISSINGER & LUBOMYR HAJDA

groups. One of the key developments in Soviet politics under *glasnost'* was the astounding variety of organizational life that it called into being. By 1989 there were some sixty thousand unofficial groups, most of which had emerged since 1987.²¹ In the multinational Soviet context, it was only natural that a significant number of these groups were specifically national in their aims and interests. Some, such as the anti-Semitic Russian nationalist organization *Pamiat'*, represented the extremist fringe of a broader national awakening. Others, such as the Taras Shevchenko Ukrainian Language Society or the *Tuteishyia* group in Belorussia, were efforts at language and cultural preservation. Still others constituted the embryos of alternative political parties. In spite of attempts by local authorities to prevent them from organizing, in nearly every republic popular fronts emerged, attracting hundreds of thousands of followers, including a large number of Communists. In Estonia, for instance, almost half of the 106 members of the leadership of the Estonian Popular Front were party members, while in Latvia 30 percent of the delegates to the founding congress of the Latvian Popular Front were Communists.²² Though ostensibly created to aid the party's goals of restructuring, these fronts in a number of cases succeeded in becoming the leading political force of their republics, commanding the allegiance of the overwhelming majority of the population, toppling local party secretaries, and in some cases capturing local party organizations and turning them into vehicles for the expression of nationalist demands to the center.

Third, *glasnost'* challenged imperial control by delegitimizing institutions and leaders associated with the dominant system of ethnic stratification. Exposés of massive corruption, attacks upon past leaders, and discussions of the serious social and economic problems facing the country had a demoralizing effect upon those segments of the population that were integrated into the dominant value system, at the same time emboldening those who were not by portraying an image of a weakened state. For instance, in both Kazakhstan and Armenia, mass nationalist unrest was preceded by open attacks in the central press on republican party leaders.²³ Similarly, the incessant public assaults on bureaucracy that occurred under Gorbachev frequently became the occasion for non-Russians to attack the excessive centralization of power in Moscow; so common was this phenomenon that Givi Gumbaridze, first secretary of the Georgian Communist party, saw fit to explain that "anger against bureaucratic fiat really should not be confused with anti-Russian sentiments."²⁴

Fourth, *glasnost'* undermined traditional patterns of ethnic stratification because attacks on Stalin that it unleashed could not be separated from attacks on the system of ethnic stratification that Stalin created. The Soviet empire has been Stalin's most enduring legacy and the issue which his successors have found the most difficult to confront. When Stalin was criticized for his dictatorial style of rule, for the excesses of collectivization, the terror, and his cult of personality, it was impossible to ignore the Nazi-Soviet pact that led to the incorporation of the Baltic states into the Soviet Union, the Ukrainian famine of 1932–33 and its millions of victims, or the destruction of national cultures that took place during the Stalin years. Indeed, in the wake of Gorbachev's attack on Stalin at the October 1987 Central Committee Plenum, all of these issues came to be raised in the media, as well as by unofficial groups.[25]

Finally, *glasnost'* challenged the bases of empire by fostering a high rate of political participation. As Myron Weiner has observed:

> An ethnic group that is politically passive and whose members do not participate in political life may more easily be assimilated or . . . incorporated into political life than an ethnic group that is already self-conscious of its own identity and is already politically organized to deal with the political system in which it lives. . . . [W]here ethnic minorities are already self-conscious participants in the political system, then the option of assimilation as a means of building national sentiment is generally not feasible.[26]

Not only did the scope of participation increase overall, but *glasnost'* also legitimized new forms of political participation—specifically, the demonstration. A political learning process took place within the intelligentsia and the population in this regard: one unrepressed nationalist demonstration or instance of communal violence indirectly led to another, with the Soviet media themselves acting to disseminate information. In Armenia, the first demonstrations on the Nagorno-Karabakh issue in October 1987 occurred one day after a demonstration in Erevan on ecological issues. The demonstrations by Jews and Crimean Tatars in Moscow in spring 1987 helped to spark the major outbreak of secessionist demonstrations throughout the Baltic republics in summer 1987, which in turn helped to fuel the events in Armenia in fall 1987 and winter 1988. The inability of the government to control the situation in Nagorno-Karabakh throughout 1988 and 1989 further demonstrated the weakness of the state and encouraged outbursts of nationalist protest and violence elsewhere in the country. And since all the nations of the Soviet Union are part of a single system of stratification, there has been a dialectical relationship between various nationalisms. Not only was there a "demonstration effect" to nationalist demonstrations and communal violence, but an upsurge of nationalism among non-Russians fed growing nationalism among Russians as well.

Gorbachev clearly did not comprehend the degree to which *glasnost'* would eventually become a vehicle for the expression of specifically national issues. The challenges that *glasnost'* posed to the dominant system of ethnic stratification were the unintended consequences of *glasnost'*, not their intended effects. Yet, it is probably true to say that *glasnost'* has been more effective in arousing nationalist sentiments than it has been in mobilizing a constituency for economic reform. Without institutions capable of channeling and resolving these nationalist demands, *glasnost'* became a dangerously destabilizing policy.

Democratization, Nationalism, and Political Stability

Any program of reform must be understood as a two-stage process, the first involving de-institutionalization, the second—re-institutionalization. De-institutionalization means pulling people out of established roles and patterns of behavior, in the Soviet case—hierarchical patterns of behavior. Re-institutionalization involves the creation of new institutions capable of channeling political participation. *Glasnost'*, in the sense of greater freedom of expression and choice in social organization, represents the de-institutionalizing side of Soviet reform. In addition, reform was supposed to involve the creation of new institutional mechanisms—in the workplace, the press, the courts, the party, and other political institutions—for integrating the autonomous political demands to which *glasnost'* gave rise.

During the first three years of Gorbachev's rule, the pace of de-institutionalization considerably exceeded the pace of re-institutionalization—a fact of enormous political significance. In his classic work on political stability, Samuel Huntington argued that political institutionalization must keep pace with political participation if political order is to be maintained.[27] Under Gorbachev, the rate of political participation, particularly on a national basis, considerably outstripped the pace at which that participation was institutionalized. The result was that the Soviet political system destabilized along ethnic lines.

As Gorbachev, mindful undoubtedly of the explosion of nationalist unrest that had swept the country in the previous year, observed in January 1988, the party had begun to

> . . . lag behind the processes taking place in society. We learned this in many respects last year. Wherever we lagged, many things appeared that later caused anxiety in society. We are learning lessons from this and drawing conclusions— not only at the level of the political leadership and government, but also in the republics and the provinces. . . .[28]

To use Eisenstadt's terminology, political loyalties in an age of *glasnost'* had become "free-floating."[29] The task that confronted the party was to recapture these political resources or see them captured by other groups, particularly national groups. National demands had to be institutionalized within the official political structure or demobilized.

The aim of democratization in the party and the state was to recapture political loyalties by channeling demands into the party's official institutions rather than onto the streets. Soviet political institutions were to be remade to enable them to act as forums for the expression and resolution of autonomous demands, including the resolution of interethnic conflicts. Toward this end, the Nineteenth Party Conference in June 1988 endorsed the introduction of competitive elections for seats in the all-union legislature, as well as for elections to major party posts. These changes were later codified by the constitutional amendments of December 1988, which permitted competitive elections for seats to a new Congress of People's Deputies.

The success of Gorbachev's democratization strategy as a means for quelling nationalist unrest, however, was complicated by several factors. In the first place, political loyalties in many parts of the country had already been captured by alternative groups, particularly nationally based groups.

When the first competitive elections in Soviet history were held in March 1989, party-sponsored candidates suffered astounding losses, in some cases losing even when they were the only candidates on the ballot. In the Baltic republics and Moldavia, candidates endorsed by the popular fronts achieved near complete electoral sweeps.

Moreover, party discipline itself was unravelling in the wake of electoral competition, which focused the attention of party officials and legislators on demands emanating from below. The first secretary of the Kiev oblast party committee, for instance, complained about the tendency of Communist candidates to "fight for great popularity without regard for the party's charter, party discipline, or party ethics."[30] National divisions within society were penetrating deeply into the party. After the Nineteenth Party Conference, the party in some parts of the country had, in the words of Arnolds Klautsen, first secretary of the Riga city party committee, "gone underground."[31] This paralysis of the party, particularly on nationality issues, was illustrated well in the multiple postponements of the long-promised Central Committee plenum on the nationalities question. When the plenum finally did convene in September 1989, it called for a "renewal" of the Soviet federation, but laid out no coherent vision for how that was to be achieved.[32]

Democratization also brought with it growing disagreement over the extent of the powers of republics and territories. The issues of whether a republic has the right to annul laws enacted by the USSR Supreme Soviet, annex a territory belonging to another union republic, establish its own diplomatic relations with foreign states without explicit approval from Moscow, introduce its own currency, control all land and property on its territory, and even secede from the USSR altogether—all have become the subject of a series of political and constitutional crises.[33] Thus, as political participation expanded, the basic rules of the system came under increasing challenge.

After the convocation of the Congress of People's Deputies in May 1989, the center of the policy-making process drifted away from the party and onto the floor of the legislature, providing non-Russian groups with greater opportunity than in the past to influence government decision making. At the same time, the party's claim to be the "leading and guiding force" of society increasingly came under attack, as the issue of a multiparty system began to be openly debated. Whether the Soviet Union could survive the transition to a multiparty system is an open question. Nearly all the potential political competitors to the CPSU that have emerged, with the exception of the Democratic Union, are ethnically based groups—the various popular fronts and nationalist movements that have emerged in the non-Russian republics and the RSFSR. This suggests that a transformation of the party system could have a disintegrative effect upon the political process, and that the survival of the Soviet Union in its current territorial configuration may well necessitate one-party rule. In much the same vein, Yegor Ligachev has argued that a multiparty system would be "fatal" to the Soviet Union because it would bring about "the disintegration of the USSR."[34] On the other hand, a parliamentary opposition has already emerged—the Interregional Group of Deputies; it comprises a coalition of various groups, including representatives from some non-Russian popular fronts. Were the CPSU to relinquish its monopoly over the party system, the stability of the Soviet state might well rest on the prospects for building similar types of coalitions that cut across ethnic boundaries.

Beyond Empire?

While it is true that states are extremely durable entities, and relatively few have disintegrated as a result of ethnic strife, the same cannot be said of multinational empires. The Soviet Union has always straddled the divide between state and empire. Its future as a state has now been staked on its ability to overcome its imperial legacy. As the British learned long ago, empire and *glasnost'* ultimately do not mix. And precisely because of this, the Soviet state is confronted with the uncomfortable choice of redefining the limits of *glasnost'* or redefining the basis of empire.

Gorbachev came to power with the idea of modernizing the Soviet empire in order to maintain it; within several years' time, his thinking had evolved to the position that the empire should be transcended without being dissolved, that it was necessary to move beyond empire without surrendering the *imperium*. This meant turning an odd and involuntary conglomeration of nations, united only by their common experience of Russian imperial domination, into a consensual and voluntary union. History not only gives no precedents for such a transformation; it suggests that the idea itself is utopian.

In an era of democratization, the basic national dilemma facing the Soviet Union goes far beyond the party's own temporal power; rather, it is the very survival of the Soviet Union as a political entity and its search for a non-imperial legitimating principle. Russian imperial nationalism failed in its purpose, for not only did the empire lag behind a changing world, but it also demonstrated that it could not catch up without dismantling its traditional system of ethnic stratification, that it could not restructure without democratizing. Russian imperial nationalism has exhausted itself as an ideology. And while Russian anomic nationalism could form the basis for an imperial restoration, it is not likely to provide a stable or lasting solution to the Soviet Union's ethnic and social problems. Russian anomic nationalism would retard economic growth, since it seeks to protect society against the encroachments of modernization that result from reform, such as the introduction of markets and the dislocation and differentiation that this process involves. The United Front of Russian Workers, a mass movement representing striking Russian coal miners and disgruntled Russian workers from the Baltic republics and Moldavia that was formed in Sverdlovsk in the fall of 1989, is one example of how Russian anomic nationalism combines an antimarket animus with the defense of Russian national interests in the imperial periphery. Perhaps more important, Russian anomic nationalism antagonizes other nationalities, sharpening the legitimacy crisis in the periphery at a time of enhanced ethnic assertiveness among non-Russians.[35] In a period of widespread ethnic mobilization, a Soviet state that seeks to derive its legitimacy from Russian anomic nationalism risks courting high levels of violence and even civil war; yet paradoxically, a Soviet state without Russian nationalism is a state without a social base.

Discovering a new social base that is non-imperial in character will not be easy. Notions of "ethnic confederation" or "consociationalism" have been proposed by some as one solution to this problem.[36] But in the Soviet context, such ideas are likely to prove inadequate. Lenin realized long ago that within the context of the Russian Empire an ethnic confederation could not hold together if it ventured beyond cultural autonomy. Many of the conditions that are associated with successful consociationalism are simply absent in the USSR. Although Soviet nationalities are highly concentrated geographically, they generally do not live in segmental isolation from one another. Moreover, they have a long history of a hierarchical division of political labor along ethnic lines. Perhaps most important, agreement among elites over the heads of the masses is no longer feasible in a period of expanding political participation.[37] While Gorbachev's formula of "a strong center and strong republics" would seem to rule out any embrace of the confederal principle, the radical decentralization of authority that territorial *khozraschet* implies, as well as persistent demands from the Baltic republics for the confederalization of the party, indicate that some degree of evolution in this direction has already occurred. Yet, if the experience of other countries is any guide, consociationalism could actually exacerbate rather than mollify ethnic tensions.

In groping toward a non-imperial formula for legitimacy, Soviet leaders will encounter serious obstacles in nearly every realm of policy making. Linguistic and cultural demands are relatively easy to satisfy, since they do not entail the diversion of large amounts of resources. But they aggravate a problem that, from the center's point of view, is already acute in some areas: the inadequate knowledge of the Russian language among non-Russians, particularly Balts and Central Asians. Moreover, local Russians in the non-Russian areas have tended to oppose far-reaching cultural concessions to non-Russians, fearing pressure to adapt to local cultures and erosion of the dominant pattern of ethnic stratification. Precisely this issue was at the center of a paralyzing series of strikes by Russian workers in the Baltic republics and Moldavia in late summer 1989. It may well be that in this sphere the Russians themselves pose the greatest obstacle to the Soviet state's quest for a non-imperial legitimacy.

An alteration of the division of political labor among ethnic groups by redressing the underrepresentation of nationalities in the center and by increasing local control over their titular administrative units would be difficult to control. A number of loyal non-Russian elites have expressed their impatience with the lack of representation of their nationalities within the Kremlin.[38] But in the aftermath of major crackdowns on corruption in many republics, and with mass movements controlling the allegiances of many non-Russians, trustworthy non-Russian elites are in scarce supply. Representation in the center would provide non-Russians with channels for presenting demands that in the past were ignored. In effect, such representation is already taking place outside party channels, through the vehicle of the Congress of People's Deputies and the restructured Supreme Soviet. But at a time of enormous mass mobilization, there is no predicting how such representation will affect the agenda of the state. Finally, there is no guarantee that newly placed national cadres in the localities will not be co-opted from below, as has happened already, in different ways, in Lithuania, Estonia, and Uzbekistan. The social situation that fostered the penetration of diffuse patronage networks into republican party organizations in the first place has not changed, and the power of the demonstrating and voting publics to make and unmake local leaders has already been revealed in Lithuania, Georgia, Leningrad, and elsewhere.

Defusing territorial-recidivist and secessionist demands is an aim of all states. In the Soviet context, such demands raise the unpleasant specter of a domino effect: that, if these claims were satisfied, numerous other groups, both internal and foreign, would demand territorial adjustments. Consequently, in the cases of the Crimean Tatars and the Armenians, the authorities have attempted to convert recidivist demands into linguistic-cultural and material demands. Secessionist demands in the Baltic republics present a more direct challenge to the territorial integrity of the Soviet Union. In view of the magnitude and strength of Baltic separatism and the difficulties that any government in Moscow faces in trying to contain it, it may well be that a policy of selective dismemberment makes sense—one that would allow Baltic independence but attempt to dissociate it from other cases, thereby suppressing the domino effect and preventing the secessionist fever from spreading. So far, outside the Baltic secessionist demands have been prominent only in Transcaucasia. Therefore, that the Finlandization of the Baltic would directly lead to the Austro-Hungarianization of the entire Soviet Union is not a foregone conclusion. In fact, there are good reasons— economic, historical, and social—why some nationalities might not want to secede from the Soviet state, preferring a far-reaching autonomy to independence.

Given the difficulties of finding a non-imperial legitimating formula, one that successfully integrates Russians and non-Russians in a period of heightened political participation, the most likely outcome, short of a revision of glasnost', is sustained crisis. The Gorbachev leadership has lurched from one political crisis to another, each closely related to the nationalities issue and the instability that it unleashes. More crises undoubtedly loom on the horizon. But crises need not be destructive of reform; it may even be that, in the Soviet context, crises act as a catalyst for more extensive changes that otherwise would be unacceptable. In an era of reform, the nationalities problem presents Soviet leaders with their most serious challenge, one that virtually guarantees that Soviet political evolution will be neither smooth nor simple.

Notes

1. For a critique of the traditional lack of attention to nationality issues in Sovietology, see Alexander J. Motyl, "'Sovietology in One Country' or Comparative National Studies?" *Slavic Review*, vol. 48, no. 1 (Spring 1989), pp. 83–88.

2. *Pravda*, 28 January 1987.

3. *Pravda*, 19 February 1988.

4. See Tamotsu Shibutani and Kian M. Kwan, *Ethnic Stratification: A Comparative Approach* (New York: Macmillan, 1965), pp. 48–54.

5. Calculated from *Itogi Vsesoiuznoi perepisi naseleniia 1970 goda*, vol. 4 (Moscow: Statistika, 1973), pp. 475–548.

6. Ibid., pp. 405–433.

7. John A. Armstrong, "The Ethnic Scene in the Soviet Union: The View of the Dictatorship," in Eric Goldhagen, ed., *Ethnic Minorities in the Soviet Union* (New York: Praeger, 1968), pp. 3–49.

8. See, for instance, Rene Lemarchand, "The State and Society in Africa: Ethnic Stratification and Restratification in Historical and Comparative Perspective," in Donald Rothchild and Victor A. Olorunsola, eds., *State versus Ethnic Claims: African Policy Dilemmas* (Boulder, CO: Westview, 1983), p. 54.

9. Anthony D. Smith, *Theories of Nationalism* (New York: Harper and Row, 1971), p. 171.

10. See Timothy Colton, *The Dilemma of Reform in the Soviet Union*, 2d ed. (New York: Council on Foreign Relations, 1986), pp. 39–43; Mark R. Beissinger, *Scientific Management, Socialist Discipline, and Soviet Power* (Cambridge, MA: Harvard University Press, 1988), pp. 261–84.

11. A classic case was that of Akhmadzhan Adilov, a farm boss in Uzbekistan, who imprisoned, tortured, and killed those who refused to help him run his private underground empire, including local party bosses. See *Literaturnaia gazeta*, 20 January 1988.

12. Lucian Pye, "The Legitimacy Crisis," in Leonard Binder et al., *Crises and Sequences in Political Development* (Princeton: Princeton University Press, 1971), p. 136.

13. See Smith, *Theories of Nationalism*, pp. 8–24; Elie Kedourie, *Nationalism* (London: Hutchinson and Company, 1960).

14. J. V. Stalin, *Works*, vol. 13 (Moscow: Foreign Languages Publishing House, 1955), pp. 40–41.

15. It is significant that the strongest opposition to heavy taxes on cooperatives has come from Baltic deputies within the Supreme Soviet. (See *New York Times*, 26 May 1988.) Latvia, Armenia, Estonia, Georgia, Moldavia, and Lithuania had the highest per capita ruble value of production by cooperatives among union republics in 1988. (See *Ekonomicheskaia gazeta*, 1989, no. 13 [March], p. 14.)

16. Joseph LaPalombara, "Penetration: A Crisis of Government Capacity," in Binder et al., *Crises and Sequences*, p. 206.

17. See *Komsomol'skaia pravda*, 10 January 1987.

18. See Steven Burg's essay in this volume.

19. Figures for the Politburo are based on official information on nationality for all full and candidate members. Figures for the Central Committee are based on official information on nationality for 289 of the 319 full members of the 1981 Central Committee and for 251 of the 307 full members of the 1986 Central Committee.

20. Myron Weiner, "Political Participation: Crisis of the Political Process," in Binder et al., *Crises and Sequences*, pp. 160, 182.

21. *Pravda*, 27 December 1987 and 10 February 1989.

22. *Sovetskaia Estoniia*, 14 January 1989; U.S. Foreign Broadcast Information Service, *Daily Report: Soviet Union*, 14 October 1988, p. 49.

23. For the attack on the Armenian first secretary, Karen Demirchian, see *Pravda*, 18 January 1988, and on the first secretary of Kazakhstan, Dinmukhamed Kunaev— *Pravda*, 9 February 1986.

24. *Zaria vostoka*, 9 June 1989.

25. On the Nazi-Soviet pact and its commemorations in the Baltic republics, see, for example, *Pravda*, 18 and 24 August 1989; *Izvestiia*, 23 August 1989; and all the republic-level newspapers in Estonia, Latvia, and Lithuania dated 23 August 1989. On the Ukrainian famine, see *Ogonek*, 1987, no. 51, pp. 10–11; *Pravda Ukrainy*, 8 July 1989; and the series of articles and reminiscences published in the literary-political monthly *Zhovten'* (Lviv) over the course of 1989. On collectivization and famine in Kazakhstan, see *Kazakhstanskaia pravda*, 14 and 17 January 1989.

26. Weiner, "Political Participation," p. 182.

27. Samuel P. Huntingon, *Political Order in Changing Societies* (New Haven: Yale University Press, 1968), pp. 8–92.

28. *Pravda*, 13 January 1988.

29. S. N. Eisenstadt, *The Political Systems of Empires* (New York: The Free Press, 1969), pp. 27–28.

30. *Pravda Ukrainy*, 18 May 1989.

31. *Sovetskaia Latviia*, 8 January 1989.

32. For coverage of the plenum, see *Pravda*, 20–24 September 1989.

33. On the multiple constitutional crises that occurred between the Estonian government and the government of the USSR between November 1988 and April 1989, see *Sovetskaia Estoniia*, 19 May 1989.

34. Quoted in Vladimir Kusin, "Gorbachev's Plan to Reform the Party," *Radio Free Europe Research: Background Report (Soviet Union)*, no. 131 (27 July 1989), p. 2.

35. See Dina Spechler's essay in this volume.

36. See, for instance, the discussion in *Sovetskaia Latviia*, 10 August 1989.

37. On the conditions conducive to consociationalism, see Arend Lijphart, *Democracy in Plural Societies: A Comparative Exploration* (New Haven: Yale University Press, 1977), pp. 164–76.

38. See the speech by the Azerbaidzhani first secretary, Abdul-Rakhman Vezirov, in *Materialy plenuma Tsentral'nogo Komiteta KPSS 25 aprelia 1989 goda* (Moscow: Politizdat, 1989), p. 74.

Index

Abkhazians, 240, 244–245
Afanasiev, Yurii, 12
Afghanistan, 84, 91, 157, 161
Agriculture
  in Baltic republics, 218
  in Central Asia, 256, 257, 268
  employment in, 47–49, 56, 58, 239
  in Georgia, 232
Aitmatov, Chingiz, 142, 273, 274
Ake, Claude, 24
Akhundov, Veli, 229, 230
Aliev, Geidar, 27, 230, 232, 233, 245
Andropov, Yurii, 163, 188, 223, 258,
  294–295, 303(n83), 312
Anisimov, Evgenii, 19
Aral Sea, 268
Armenia, 121, 228–249
  and Azerbaidzhani conflict, 15–16,
    37–38, 39, 87, 245–248
  See also Armenian Gregorian Church;
    Transcaucasia
Armenian Gregorian Church, 153, 241
Armstrong, John A., 15–16, 99
Arutiunian, Suren, 223
Assimilation. See Russification
Astra, Gunārs, 223
Azerbaidzhan, 174(n86), 228–249
  and Armenian conflict, 15–16, 37–38,
    39, 87, 245–248
  See also Transcaucasia

Badz'o, Yurii, 194
Bagirov, Kiamran, 233
Bailes, Kendall E., 10
Baltic republics, 204–225
  autonomy and independence, 63,
    212–213, 225, 320

dissent in, 221–224, 292
economy, 215–218
and identity, 15, 119, 204–205, 218–
  219
immigration into, 213–215
and literature, 141–142, 219–220
and nationalism, 31, 39, 205, 209–
  212, 224
politics, 206–213, 224–225, 317
religion, 220–221
and Soviet military, 83
Barker, Ernest, 6–7, 20
Bashkirs, 111, 114, 115, 118–119
Basmachi movement, 225
Belorussia, 175–199
  and assimilation, 119–120, 122,
    125(n14)
  culture in, 175–176, 183–184,
    183(table), 185, 186–193
  demographic change in, 181,
    182(tables), 183
  dissent in, 196–197, 198, 199
  politics, 178–179, 184–185, 185(table)
  religion, 15, 162, 165
Bembel, Aleh, 197
Berdnyk, Oles', 195
Biddulph, Howard, 33
Bodiul, Ivan, 176, 179
Bolshevik revolution. See Russian
  Revolution
Bolsheviks, 8, 9. See also Russian
  Revolution
Borovik, Genrikh, 11–12
Brazauskas, Algirdas, 211, 212
Breslauer, George, 33
Brezhnev, Leonid, 35, 43, 74, 176–177,
  257, 278(n6)

and religion, 148–152, 159–168,
173(nn 74, 75), 174(nn 84, 85, 87).
See also Religion, and politics
and Russian nationalism, 294–298,
303(n80), 314. *See also* Nationalism
and society, 1–4, 5–9, 11–12, 20,
22(n16), 122–123, 186–187, 306,
309–311
in Soviet West, 176–181, 184–185,
185(table), 193–199
in Transcaucasia, 229, 230–234
See also Identity, political; Ideology;
Political stability
Population. *See* Demographic change
Productivity. *See* Labor, productivity
Pugo, Boris, 208, 211
Pye, Lucian, 310

Rashidov, Sharaf, 36, 138, 257, 258
Rasulov, Dzhabar, 257
Reform, 4–6, 306
cultural, 190–193, 267, 278
economic, 26, 38, 62–64, 66–67, 269,
277, 312
political, 25, 27, 225, 258–261, 312,
315–318
religious, 165–168
See also Glasnost'; Perestroika
Religion
and language, 96–98, 159
and nationalities, 15–16, 122, 150,
152–159, 204, 220–221, 248–249,
269–273, 288
and politics, 2, 3, 148–152, 159–168,
173(nn 74, 75), 174(nn 84, 85, 87),
196, 205, 222, 223, 233–234, 241,
300(n39), 304(n85)
and Soviet military, 90
See also Armenian Gregorian Church;
Georgian Orthodox Church;
Identity, religious; Islam; Judaism;
Lithuanian Catholic Church;
Russian Orthodox Church;
Ukrainian Catholic (Uniate) Church
Resources
development of, 53, 54, 65, 214–215,
266
distribution of, 31–34, 37, 38, 39, 43,
66, 254, 277, 291, 310
water, 268, 280(n33), 296, 313

Roman Catholic Church, 155–156, 160.
See also John Paul II; Lithuanian
Catholic Church; Ukrainian
Catholic (Uniate) Church
Romania, 179–180
Rudenko, Mykola, 194, 195
Russian Empire. *See* Tsarist Empire
Russian nationalism. *See* Nationalism,
Russian
Russian Orthodox Church
and politics, 2, 150–152, 162–165,
167–168, 172(n67), 196, 272, 296,
297
and Russian nationalism, 13, 15, 286
and Russification, 96, 148–149, 190
See also Religion
Russian Revolution, 2, 11, 72–73, 255
Russians
in Baltic republics, 213–214, 215
in Central Asia, 263, 264
and nationalism, 2–3, 12–14, 17, 74,
292–294. *See also* Nationalism,
Russian
and Soviet politics, 24, 27, 34, 38–
39, 257, 261, 290, 307–308, 319
in Soviet West, 181–183
status of, 2, 8, 74, 83, 92, 307
in Transcaucasia, 235
Russification, 124(n2)
and ethnic reidentification, 114–123,
116(fig.), 117(table), 120(table),
121(table), 126(n32), 224, 248–249,
308
language and, 75–77, 76(table), 79–
81, 95–109, 111–112, 122, 183–184,
196, 218–219, 239–240, 240(table).
See also Language
military and, 73, 77–81, 83, 86, 90–
91
non-Russians and, 11, 35
and religion, 148, 149, 150, 205,
240–241
and Russian nationalists, 2–3, 12
and World War II, 110–114, 118
See also Identity; Sovietization
Russo-Japanese War of 1904–1905, 10–
11
Ryzhkov, Nikolai, 213

Sakharov, Andrei, 196
Science, 10, 185, 267

dissent in, 193–198, 207, 221–224, 241–248, 274–276, 292. *See also* Unrest

economy, 10–11, 31–32, 46–54, 59–67, 185–186, 215–218, 232, 267–269. *See also* Economy

labor in, 54–59, 213–215, 266, 267–268. *See also* Labor

as a multinational state, 1–4, 6–10, 11–20, 28–30, 32, 43–46, 59, 64–67, 83, 95–123, 175–176, 181–185, 186–190, 204–207, 218–220, 224–225, 228–229, 234–241, 247, 248–249, 253–256, 261–267, 272–273, 305–311, 318–320. *See also* Nationalities

politics, 24–28, 30–40, 176–181, 184–185, 187, 198–199, 207–213, 230–234, 256–261, 277–278. *See also* Politics

reform in, 4–6, 62–64, 66–67, 190–193, 311–318. *See also* Reform

religion, 148–168, 220–221, 233–234, 269–273. *See also* Religion

and Russian nationalism, 282–298. *See also* Nationalism

Unrest
in Baltic republics, 211, 213, 221–224, 225
in Belorussia, 193, 196–197
in Central Asia, 260, 274–276
in Moldavia, 181
in non-Russian republics, 31, 37–38, 186, 292, 297–298, 313–315
in Transcaucasia, 230–231, 242–248
in Ukraine, 177, 193–196, 197–198
See also Glasnost', unrest and; Political arrests; Political stability;

Union of Soviet Socialist Republics, dissent in

Urbanization, 47–48, 48(table), 229, 307
in Baltic republics, 205
in Central Asia, 264
and language, 96, 240
in Soviet West, 184
in Transcaucasia, 239
See also Demographic change

Urbšys, Juozas, 220

Usmankhodzhaev, Inamzhon, 36, 258, 260

USSR. *See* Union of Soviet Socialist Republics

Usubaliev, Turdakun, 257

Uzbekistan, 29, 32–33, 253–278
politics, 35–36, 258, 259–260, 278(n1), 321(n11)
See also Central Asia

Vagris, Jānis, 211, 212
Vaino, Karl, 208, 209, 210, 214
Vaivods, Julijans (Cardinal), 156, 160
Väljas, Vaino, 210–211, 218
Vezirov, Abdul-Rakhman, 233
Virgin Lands campaign, 256
Voss, Augusts, 206

Weiner, Myron, 315
World War II, 100, 110–114, 118, 151

Yakovlev, 225, 295
Yakunin, Gleb, 151, 167
Yusupov, Ismail, 257

Zahrebel'nyi, Pavlo, 14–15, 23(n35)
Zarobian, Zakov, 242
Zdebskis, Juozas, 223
Zimmerman, William, 31–32
Zinoviev, Alexander, 19